Transformation Management

Transformation and Innovation Series

Series Editors:
Ronnie Lessem, University of Buckingham, UK
Alexander Schieffer, University of St. Gallen, Switzerland

This series on business transformation and social innovation comprises a range of books informing practitioners, consultants, organization developers, and academics how businesses and other organizations can and will have to be transformed into viable 21st Century enterprises. A new kind of R&D, involving social, as well as technological innovation, needs to be supported by integrated, active and participative research in the social sciences. Focusing on new, emerging kinds of public, social and sustainable entrepreneurship originating from all corners of the world and from different cultures, books in this series will help those operating in the area of interface between business and society to mediate between the two in the way that business schools once did until, as is now argued, they lost their way and business leaders came, in many cases, to be seen as at best incompetent and at worst venal and untrustworthy.

Transformation Management

Towards the Integral Enterprise

RONNIE LESSEM AND
ALEXANDER SCHIEFFER

GOWER

Gower Applied Business Research
Our programme provides leaders, practitioners, scholars and researchers with thought provoking, cutting edge books that combine conceptual insights, interdisciplinary rigour and practical relevance in key areas of business and management.

Published by
Gower Publishing Limited
Wey Court East
Union Road
Farnham
Surrey, GU9 7PT
England

Ashgate Publishing Company
Suite 420
101 Cherry Street
Burlington,
VT 05401-4405
USA

www.gowerpublishing.com

British Library Cataloguing in Publication Data
Lessem, Ronnie.
   Integral research and innovation : transforming enterprise
   and society. -- (Transformation and innovation)
   1. Social responsibility of business. 2. Organizational
   change--Social aspects.
   I. Title II. Series III. Schieffer, Alexander.
   658.4'08-dc22

   ISBN: 978-0-566-08896-4

Library of Congress Cataloging-in-Publication Data
Lessem, Ronnie.
   Transformation management : towards the integral enterprise / by Ronnie Lessem and
   Alexander Schieffer.
      p. cm. -- (Transformation and innovation)
   Includes bibliographical references.
   ISBN 978-0-566-08896-4 (hbk) 1. Management--Social aspects. 2. Social responsibility of
   business. 3. Industrial organization--Social aspects. 4. Organizational sociology. I. Schieffer,
   Alexander. II. Title.
   HD30.19.L47 2009
   658.4'06--dc22

                                                                                    2009016211

Mixed Sources
Product group from well-managed
forests and other controlled sources
www.fsc.org Cert no. SA-COC-1565
© 1996 Forest Stewardship Council
FSC

Printed and bound in Great Britain by
MPG Books Group, UK

Contents

List of Figures

Prologue: Time for Transformation!

... if corporations run their businesses with the sole aim of gaining more market share, and earning more profits, they may well lead the world toward economic, special and environmental ruin. But if they work together ... they can bring food to the poor, peace to war-torn areas, and renewal to the natural world. It is our obligation, as business leaders, to join together to build a foundation for our world peace and prosperity.

Ryuzaburo Kaku,
Former Chairman of Canon

It is ironic – and as we feel, timely – that we should be completing this text on *Transformation Management: Towards the Integral Enterprise,* at the very time, in Autumn 2008, where economic and financial disintegration and economic unsustainability have become the order of our day. Yet all the talk in the media is about 'shoring up the system', by re-capitalizing the banks, so that they can return to their 'normal' functioning, as opposed to transforming the way we design and run our enterprises, let alone the economic basis of our societies.

Instead of thinking in terms of transformation, then, there is a lot of talk of where to 'allocate blame' for the current crisis, which, after all is not merely an economic crisis. For global warming and the accompanying energy shortages are bearing increasingly upon us. These problems, combined with the gap between the rich and the poor, get worse every day. Moreover, the proverbial and so-called 'clash of civilizations' has now reached global proportions. In summary, religious and ethnical fundamentalism (culture), environmental destruction and communal decay (nature), corruption and closed societies (politics), rampant materialism in conjunction with abject poverty (economics): for us, these are all interdependent symptoms of a deeper underlying – and untransformed – cause.

For us the underlying cause is that an increasingly one-sided form of politics and economics has eclipsed the diversity of our nature and culture. In fact, rather than economics and politics building on nature and culture, the reverse has prevailed. Specifically, the 'west' has dominated over the 'rest'. The inevitable result has been a 'clash of civilizations', rather than a dialogue. What kind of dialogue are we alluding to? We mean the dialogue between you and me, between local communities and global systems; between the north and south, east and west of our globe; between the public and the private, the civic and the environmental sector of our societies. All that.

Transformation, for us, arises, when such dialogue – you may also call it creative interaction or co-creation – between diverse cultures and natures arises. But such dialogue does not just happen by itself. At least not on the large scale, that Canon's legendary former Chairman Ryuzaburo Kaku is pressing for in the opening quote.

So in this book we offer an integral approach to design and run organizations in their respective communities and societies whereby they engage in such a dialogue and co-creation, within and without. Within then, such an organization equally embraces its ecological (nature), civic (culture), public (technology) and private (economic) each in equal proportion. Without, such an organization acts as a bridge between an individual and a society. An organization, which integrates the four inner dimensions and is thereby fully grounded in its society, can address such burning issues, that Kaku mentions: providing, as such, food for the poor, peace to war-torn-areas, renewal of the natural world, ultimately establishing, in association with others, a foundation for world peace and prosperity.

We shall demonstrate in this book, in theory and in practice, that we are not simply driven by morals (let's do something good for the planet) or aesthetics (integral is beautiful). That is well and good. But, altogether, we are driven to pursue truth, beauty, goodness and utility in addressing the deeper causes of the dysfunctioning of our enterprises, our communities, our societies and the world at large. For us then, as we shall progressively reveal, a main cause is the state of disintegration of our organizations and societies.

We have also discovered, in the course of our research, in the rare cases of the integrated organizations that we had the privilege to study, that they have been able to bring their public and private, civic and environmental functioning into dynamic balance. They were able to reach out to other organizations and societies in a co-creative way. And exactly here, in that co-creative space between nature and culture, politics and economics lies the key to transformation, evolution and social innovation.

Transformation Management, then, is the fruit of decades of probing into the inner cause, why individuals, organizations and societies are often disintegrated and unsustainable, and therefore ultimately dysfunctional. It is the fruit of decades of research and development, of educational programmes on transformation and innovation, of executive education and consulting.

With Transformation Management, we are laying a new path to integration. As you go through the book, you will discover that Transformation Management is not just a new model. It is much more. Transformation Management forms the basis for a new management curriculum, ultimately serving to fundamentally transform the prevailing management education, most especially the MBA world. The way we educate managers and organizational leaders nowadays has a lot to do with the functionality of our organizations and society. Transformation Management is hence an attempt to build a new educational – theoretical as well as practical – framework, to enable the design and management of functional, integrated and sustainable organizations. In other words, Transformation Management is also about the Transformation *of* Management.

What then are key elements of such a transformation? We shall be arguing in this book that whereas the pre-modern period, in world history, was an era of local *dependence,* of for example the peasants on the feudal lord, and the modern era has been an age of national *independence,* culminating in a post-colonial period, we are currently living in an era of *interdependence*. Ironically, and in this case negatively, such interdependence has become evident to many amongst us only through contemporary environmental, food and energy crises as well as ethnic and religious fundamentalism.

In the positive terms, with which this book is concerned, such an interdependent era is *trans*-cultural, *trans*-disciplinary, and *trans*-personal, and altogether *trans*-formational. Moreover, the *trans*-sectoral nature and scope of an 'integrated' or 'integral' enterprise is required to accommodate all of such. Only a few pioneering enterprises, ranging from a Sekem in Egypt to Grameen in Bangladesh, from Broad Air Conditioning in China to Virgin in the UK, have begun to grasp that integral truth. We shall therefore feature them extensively in this book.

For us, then, the ultimate resolution of the financial crisis, if not also the energy crisis, and indeed the crisis of our civilization, lies neither in government ownership, nor in financial regulation, nor indeed in the media indulgence in 'the blame game', but rather in a much more fundamental transformation and re-integration of enterprise and society. Building such an Integral Enterprise is indeed the core objective of Transformation Management. We shall now take you through such a step-by-step process to achieve just that.

Endorsements

In these troubled times it takes Lessem and Schieffer and just a handful of others to remind us that sustainable wealth can only be created by generating wealth for other people. Hooked as we are on own speculative self-interests we ignore the challenges of transforming our own systems. It is time to pay heed to those showing us how wealth arises from voluntary reciprocity, as opposed to unilateral manipulation of assets.

Prof Charles Hampden-Turner, School of Engineering, Cambridge University, UK

... draws from the very best examples from the past, recognises the realities of today and seeks to develop innovative solutions for the future. It is welcomed by the International Business Leaders Forum which itself is committed to leadership transformation.

Adam Leach, Chief Executive, International Business Leaders Forum, UK

... With their book, Lessem and Schieffer present everyone with the opportunity to understand and perform a transformation of their business model. 'Transformation Management' is therefore an outstanding piece in today's management literature.

Dr Ibrahim Abouleish, Founder and President of Sekem Group, Egypt, Recipient of the 'Right Livelihood Award' (Alternative Nobel Prize)

Transformation Management is one of those rare management approaches that builds on the culture of particular worlds, enabling politicians, businessmen and civic activists, to build integral institutions upon our own local soils, while taking account of the wisdom of others.

Mfuniselwa J. Benghu Esq., Member of South African Parliament, Author of *Ubuntu: The Essence of Democracy* and *Ubuntu: A Global Philosophy for Humankind*

Over the past two decades China has transformed from a command economy to a socialist market economy with many the social, economic and environmental challenges to be addressed and overcome. Looking ahead the world's economic landscape will be very different than it is now and there is an urgent need to seek innovative solutions to the world's burning issues. Transformation Management makes an important contribution to the thinking that will be a necessary foundation for new approaches to the role of business in society.

Prof Dong Keyong, Dean of the School of Public Administration, The Renmin University of China

In Loving Memory of our Fathers:
Abraham Lessem and Egon Jakob Schieffer

PART 1

Introduction:
The Fundamentals of
Transformation Management

Towards Transformation Management

Core Question:
How Do We Re-invent Management and Enterprise

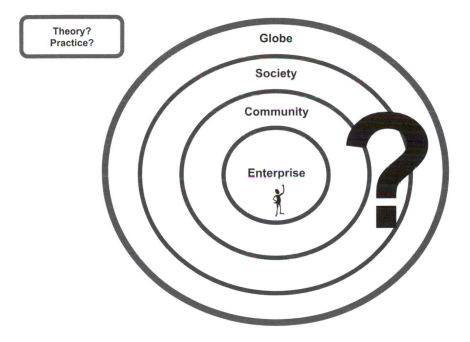

1 *Management and Transformation*

From Independent Business Towards the Integral Enterprise

1.1 Introduction: Transforming the Enterprise in Society

A NEW BUSINESS AND SOCIETAL IMPERATIVE

The time has come to fundamentally rethink the way in which organizations are run. This includes rethinking how organizations contribute to their societies. It also takes into account how individuals, like you, within such organizations engage with both these enterprises, whether public, private or civic, and also your communities. And it includes ultimately how this whole process can be further enhanced, through social – alongside technological – innovation. Why? The world's economic and socio-political landscape has changed dramatically in less than a generation. Climate change (and its concomitant economic and social consequences) calls upon us to acquire a new understanding of nature and its impact on organizations. Food insecurity, global pandemics, failures of democratic governance, transnational crime and corruption, energy and – most especially in the autumn of 2008 – financial crises, as well as 'civilizational' schisms, unprecedented inequity and grinding poverty, migration and mal-integration, and altogether intractable conflict, are increasingly interlinked and globalized in their causes and consequences.

Further, and specifically on the business front, the above-mentioned credit crunch, corporate and credit scandals, consumer activism and globalized civil society, as well as mobilization against certain corporate practices, are putting unprecedented pressures on all forms of enterprise, and obliging corporations to reorient their interaction with nature, their employees, consumers and civil society, if not to re-examine the workings of the economic and financial systems as a whole.

These challenges demand fundamentally new responses from all institutions, as well as from the educators and consultancies that serve them. To the extent that every individual, organization and community reaches its limits at one point or another, the financial system above all at this point of time, so the needs for ongoing renewal of each, that is each according to its particular nature and culture (Anglo-Saxon in the current financial case), is the overall imperative Transformation Management addresses.

FROM TECHNOLOGICAL TOWARDS SOCIAL INNOVATION

In this turbulent context then, 'business as usual' is proving increasingly problematic. As a result, managers, leaders and activists have to fundamentally review the way they design, build and run organizations. Business with its enormous societal impact, in association with public, civic and environmental enterprises, will have a critical role to play in this process. And socio-economic innovation will need to accompany the hitherto much better known technological equivalent.

Organizational and societal leaders alike are reviewing conventional management (inclusive of change management), leadership and entrepreneurship to come up with more effective and 'sustainable' – approaches to engaging with today's burning issues. We argue that this current incremental approach is no longer enough. *There is a need to fundamentally challenge our current understanding of all of such management, leadership and entrepreneurship paradigms, and to take appropriate action as a result.* Why so?

IN SEARCH OF A NEW FORM OF INTEGRAL ENTERPRISE

We need to engage in a fundamental challenge of the existing paradigm by investigating how a specific enterprise needs to be designed and run, in order to contribute to the sustainable evolution of the particular society in which it is lodged. We are therefore not *In Search of Excellence*, the famous management book of the 1980s by Peters and Waterman,[1] but in search of a new form of *Integral* Enterprise that emerges out of a particular culture and society. In doing that, we need to tap into a wide range of knowledge sources, from anthropology to economics, from ecology to political science, and shall not limit ourselves, to the conventional range of disciplines, typically consulted when it comes to the functioning of an organization. These usually are economics and management, behavioural psychology and perhaps some sociology. By reviewing the relevant knowledge base we are simultaneously also redefining the disciplines of management, on which principles modern day organizations are built and, as we shall show, not only in the private sector of society. Over the course of this book, we shall illustrate, how limited is the knowledge base, on which management is built, and how the discipline itself needs to be fundamentally challenged and renewed. Transformation Management, the approach we introduce here, makes an attempt to transcend conventional management, fundamentally, and in context.

In our transformational journey, in redefining management and enterprise we shall engage in a fourfold process which allows us to build the new enterprise upon knowledge acquired from four different sources: nature, culture, science and management itself. The knowledge of all these four sources will be integrated in the new relevant knowledge base of the organization. Furthermore, we shall disclose the core transformational principles that we identified within nature and culture. Such principles enable human enterprise to engage in continuous renewal, as nature has been able to do for billions of years, and some civilizations, like the Australian Aborigines before the Europeans intervened, for thousands. Hence, before we look at the actual functioning of the enterprise, which conventional management deals with in a rather narrow way, we shall first look into what we can learn from nature and culture.

Based on nature, culture and science, as well as management, we are ultimately engaged in renewing the very base of management itself, now significantly enriched. Nature, culture, science and (renewed) management, then all serve to contribute to a new integral design of the enterprise. We call such an *Integral Enterprise*. Figure 1.1 provides a first overview of such.

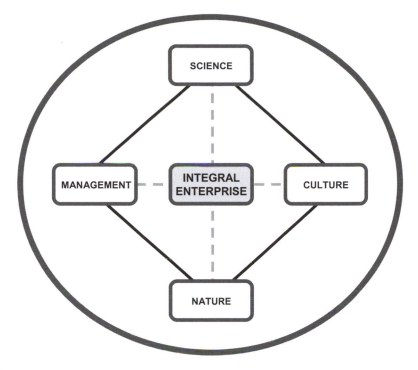

Figure 1.1   Overview framework of an Integral Enterprise

In what follows we review the core principles and recent developments in what we term Transformation Management, that ultimately gives rise to such an Integral Enterprise. We thereby also identify the necessary evolutionary steps, which lie before us, drawing on a wide variety of cultures and disciplines. We shall also particularly highlight the challenges current day enterprises are facing. We start with nature, and with transformation.

1.2 Revisiting Nature: A Transformational Perspective

THE ENTERPRISE AS A LIVING, INTERCONNECTED SYSTEM

Most people think of sustainability in terms of saving the planet. Goerner argues[2] that we need to change our societal dream from a late-modern nightmare of untrammelled greed (as recently magnified by scandalous bonuses in the financial world) to an integral prophecy of sustainable vitality achieved by following nature's own plan for healthy development. She and her colleagues show how today's shift from modern to *integral society* mirrors the last shifts from the Renaissance, Reformation, Scientific Revolution and Enlightenment already under way.

For Peter Drucker,[3] every few hundred years in Western history there occurs a sharp transformation. Within a few short decades, society – its world-view, its basic values, its social and political structures, its arts, its key institutions – rearranges itself. We are currently living through such a time. Each great change, moreover, produced a new system of society, organized around what philosopher Stephen Pepper[4] calls a new *world hypothesis,* a new vision of *'how the world works',* which is itself woven around a *root metaphor.* Medieval society, for example, built itself around the metaphor of 'God's Design', a hidden, organizing, master plan guiding all things. Its successor, modern society, saw the rise of the 'machine' metaphor, a logical system of material parts connected by mechanical cause and effect. Yet nowadays integral reformers are reweaving civilization around the image of an 'ecosystem', or *web,* symbolic of our interconnected age, in our terms, moreover, such a web being constituted of diverse natural and cultural nodes.

Interestingly enough, in a recent book by American biologist and psychologist, David Loye,[5] it has been thought, then, for over 100 years that Darwin only identified two major principles of evolution, Natural Selection and Variation. Of course he also claimed Sexual Selection was another major factor, but there is yet another major principle of evolution he identified, that has been totally ignored. In essence it was one, which today we identify in terms of 'self-organizing processes'. Expanding in subtlety and power from the animal to the human level, Darwin probed the dimensions of what today is being explored at the leading edges of science and spirituality as the great new prospect for understanding not only learning but even more so *conscious* evolution – or of how we can not only more effectively better our own lives but also the lives of all of us. It is the challenge of how each one of us, once so awakened, may serve our species and all species as evolutionary outriders for the surge into the future.

1.3 Revisiting Culture: A Transcultural Perspective

THE CHALLENGE OF MOVING BEYOND A MONOCULTURAL PERSPECTIVE

It is taken for granted, at least in most business schools, that management, as an overall concept, does not vary from country to country. For Peter Drucker and other management thinkers, management is universal. That is why management is management, all over the world, and why the Masters of Business Administration (MBA) is a standardized MBA. It has remained a largely unrecognized fact that management remains a predominantly American discipline, as is leadership and entrepreneurship.

Drucker, however, argued that the way the managerial work is done is strongly influenced by national traits, traditions and history. He regarded management as a social function, embedded in a tradition of values, customs and beliefs, and in governmental systems. Management is – and should be – culture conditioned. In turn, managers and management shape culture and society. Thus, although management is an organized body of knowledge, and as such is applicable everywhere, it is a 'culture' in itself, and is therefore not 'value-free'. That having been said, most of the examples that Drucker cites of leading management thinkers or of exemplary organizations are Anglo-Saxon: American and British. And while the word management is centuries old, its application to the governing of an institution is a particular American achievement. Drucker actually never builds upon the cultural approach that he had initially proclaimed. He, like most management, leadership and entrepreneurship theorists, remained a universalist in his monocultural approach.

Hence, most leading management thinkers leave us somewhat confused as to the extent to which they see management as universal in its nature and scope. What is clear is that their major reference points, theoretically and practically, are American. An MBA in Beijing today is pretty much the same as one in Boston. There is an understanding that cultural conditioning may affect the conduct of business, but certainly no hint that the very concept of management in itself as taught in the respective business schools may need to vary in accordance with the societal sector or the culture to which it is applied.

1.4 Revisiting Science: A Transdisciplinary Perspective

THE SOCIAL INNOVATION CHALLENGE

The trends in the fields of entrepreneurship and enterprise, which we introduce later in this chapter, have indeed transformational potential. And yet, that having been said, the 'social situation' in the world is increasingly deteriorating – while, incidentally, the 'technological situation' is thriving. In short, notwithstanding the evolution of entrepreneurship in the past decades, particularly in the arena of social entrepreneurship, there remains a sincere lack of social innovation. What we mean by such 'innovation' is that the very structure and functioning – as opposed to merely the values and practices of the micro enterprise and of the macro economy that surrounds it – needs to be transformed fundamentally. This has not yet happened.

In other words, there is no fully-fledged social equivalent to technological innovation in the corporate world. Moreover, in the academic world, so-called research methodology is completely disconnected from research and development, while the social sciences languish behind the natural sciences when it comes to innovation.

THE CHALLENGE OF BUILDING INNOVATION INTO THE ORGANIZATION

The need to be innovative is emphasized in every book on management. But beyond this the books have little to say about what management and organization needs to build upon, to direct, and to actualize such social innovation. Most attention is given to *business administration* – what a strange term to have settled upon – and the core educational platform for that is the MBA. Not enough attention is given to promoting such innovation, and no thought has been seemingly given to the evolution of socially oriented research and development to accommodate such.

Initially, there were good reasons for this mismatch. When management first became a concern in the early years of this century, the great need was to learn how to organize, structure and direct the large-scale human organization that was suddenly coming into being. Innovation was seen as a separate job, usually the job of the lone 'inventor'. Or else it was a predominately technical concern, that of 'research'. Now however, we have entered a time of change. While there are newly proliferating technological changes, the need for innovation will be equally great in the social field.

FINDING AN ORGANIZATIONAL FRAMEWORK FOR SOCIAL INNOVATION

The oldest example for institutionalizing innovation, though again not social innovation, within a business corporation, is probably the development department at Du Pont founded in the early 1920s. It is not only a research department – Du Pont has a big, separate research laboratory. The job of the former is to develop new businesses – production, finance and marketing are as much its concerns as technology, products and processes. 3M has done the same. The closest we have come to a more broadly based approach to building social innovation into the organization is the work on organizational knowledge creation. We shall see explicit thinking related to such in Chapter 10, but here we still focus on Drucker's thinking.

MOVING FROM KNOWLEDGE MANAGEMENT TO KNOWLEDGE CREATION

The productivity of every developed society, for Drucker already in the 1970s, depends increasingly on making knowledge work productive and the knowledge worker achieving. Such new knowledge work is carried out in large, complex, managed institutions. A main challenge to managing work and working is the arrival of what he terms the employee society and the emergence of knowledge work at the centre of so-called post-industrial society. However, Drucker fails to review the actual functioning of a business in that light. But how would an organization have to be designed to move from knowledge management to knowledge creation? And what has been the response to that from the management educational establishment?

MAKING THE SOCIAL SCIENCES AND HUMANITIES EXPLICIT

The problem was that Drucker and most management thinkers who followed him have never been explicit about the range of the social sciences or the humanities, upon which they have drawn. Though Drucker was implicitly transdisciplinary in his approach, drawing to some extent on psychology, sociology and political science, his primary focus was upon his own discipline, that of political economy. As such he patently failed to draw, for example, upon anthropology, philosophy, religion or indeed ecology, as has been the case for management thinkers since, at least until, very recently.

BROADENING THE BASE OF MANAGEMENT EDUCATION

For Drucker then, management is not only codified experienced but also an organized body of knowledge. However, he does not identify where that knowledge comes from, in relation to the social sciences that underlie it. He himself, as we have said, was a political economist, which invariably influenced his approach to management.

For him, our society in the twentieth century has become a society of organizations. Organizations depend on managers and once they grow beyond a certain size they need professional managers.

Drucker, though, leaves us in a state of doubt as to the primacy of business's role in society; it remains unclear to which extent its *economic* functioning is exclusive or inclusive of its broader psychological and social orientations, given that Drucker, at least in the 1970s, was by and large oblivious to environmental factors. Social problems, for Drucker, are to be seen as business opportunities. The most significant opportunities for converting social problems into business opportunities, for him, may not lie in new technologies, products or services. They may lie in solving social problems, that is, in social innovation which then directly or indirectly benefits and strengthens the company or industry. However, this agenda is still to be taken forward, as we argue, by new forms of enterprise, designed to bring forth social innovation. Drucker implicitly agrees with this argument. Though he introduced the notion of the 'Accountable Enterprise', which he considered to be a more appropriate term than the overused 'Free Enterprise', he maintained that rather than developing new laws for business in society there is a need for a new enterprise model.

Given the fragmented and unsustainable states today's social systems are in, we argue, that a new enterprise model, that transcends conventional management, needs to put a particular emphasis on 'integration' and 'integrity'. The past decade had been full of disaster stories (e.g., Enron, WorldCom) caused by the lack of personal integrity of (primarily) business enterprises.

Such brings us to review the current state of the functioning of an enterprise and the underlying management education. Moreover, in the course of ultimately transforming management, from an additionally 'transpersonal' perspective, we seek to build on our prior transformational, transcultural and transdisciplinary orientations

1.5 Revisiting Management: A Transpersonal Perspective

THE CHALLENGE OF TRANSFORMATION: MOVING BEYOND 'PROFIT WITH PRINCIPLES'

The influential work of Harvard's Ira Jackson and Jane Nelson on *Profit with Principles*[6] reflects the value based expansion of traditional business towards a more intense engagement with society. There are many other authors who argue that a new set of values would solve the problems. Consequently, for example, codes of practice (e.g., in Corporate Ethics and Corporate Governance) have emerged worldwide. However, the moral codes provided by such expanded perspectives fail to provide a new structure and functioning of enterprise and do not challenge the current economic functioning of society. Moreover, they patently fail to take account of a *particular* organization or society, be the latter Singapore, Senegal or Sri Lanka.

By ratifying such thereby generalized codes and promoting their corporate social responsiveness accordingly, many corporations feel that they have done everything to comply with international business standards. A true evolutionary impulse is missing, one which would serve to evolve, on the one hand, both the micro structure and functioning and the macro economy and environment of business, and, on the other, a particular individual, organization and society, simultaneously and interactively.

REVISING ENTREPRENEURSHIP EDUCATION

According to Professor of Management Thought Ellen O'Connor,[7] based at the University of Paris Dauphine, more and more business schools, like Harvard and Duke in America and Oxford University in the UK, have been establishing social entrepreneurship centres, which she terms HPSE (high profile social entrepreneurship). These HPSE centres reside in the elite business schools, which need to keep up with the latest trends, applied, as such, across the board, to all people and places, monolithically. They have grown out of the 'new economy' of the 1990s, when wealthy entrepreneurs, like Bill Gates and Geoff Skoll, have engaged in venture philanthropy, promoting, for example, social venture competitions at business schools. Such high-profile programmes, however, are still based on the neo-liberal paradigm, focused on the role of self-regulating markets in providing not only increased individual wealth, but also general improvements in society generally, as opposed to a society, particularly. So there is no specific innovation and overall transformation.

The retreat in many places of the 'welfare state' arguably contributes to this social entrepreneurship trend, serving to uphold the notion that social benefits, including social goals such as poverty reduction, environmental protection, health care and meaningful employment are best produced by a kind of market activity. Thereby 'social entrepreneurs' combine resources with a view to delivering goods and services, which provide social improvements and change. Ultimately, so we argue, such HPSEs do not promote transformation. They are still rooted in a primarily economic paradigm, whereby the standardized market rules. They have not reconceived of themselves in a cultural as well as natural, political as well as economic light. In short, social entrepreneurship is still too close to the notion of 'Western' economic entrepreneurship.

MOVING BEYOND A PURELY ECONOMIC ORIENTATION

At the same time, and increasingly, entrepreneurial-minded non-profit leaders are bringing the tactics of the private sector to the task of solving social problems. This approach operates within a conception of entrepreneurship that makes legitimate a representation of social problems as economic ones with business solutions. Social entrepreneurs have the same core temperaments as their industry-creating peers but instead use their talents to solve social problems. So indeed claims William Drayton, the founder of the well-known and duly admired Ashoka, the worldwide network for such social entrepreneurs (www.ashoka.org). Most authors on social entrepreneurship follow an old pattern of individual entrepreneurship, albeit now in a social context. Hence, 'social entrepreneurship' retains (unconsciously) its business and economic pre-emphasis, in theory if not also in practice, and fails to clearly differentiate the political and economic, cultural and environmental nature and scope of its new activities. That leads us to the next critique.

REDEFINING THE 'SOCIAL'

Recent attempts to either expand existing notions of entrepreneurship, as in the case of the private sector, or to introduce additional forms, all have one thing in common: They are trying to respond to a deteriorating 'social climate' and to address developmental issues in societies. In these attempts the term 'social' was used in a rather undifferentiated manner in that it includes 'all that is not economic'. Such prohibited original thinking, that not only reconceived of the economic dimension (as does Yunus's concept of a Social Business), but also the other dimensions of society.

NOT FALLING INTO THE 'LEADERSHIP TRAP'

The idea now that personalized and thereby generalized (in fact largely 'Western') leadership is an evolved form of management, as is common currency today, is for us an inversion of the truth. As such, it detracts from an authentically transpersonal – self (personal), organizational (impersonal) and societal (communal) – approach to management. Moreover, and for us, the transpersonal functions of management build on the prior transformational, transcultural and transdisciplinary approaches. In that richly trans-formative context we can see how impoverished the standard leadership and management education has become.

Rakesh Khurana from Harvard Business School criticizes strongly, in his recent award-winning book '*From Higher Aims to Hired Hands*', not only the lost societal purpose of today's American Business Schools, but also their unhealthy engagement in 'leadership'. Khurana states:

> ... *by delegitimating the old managerial order and turning executives into free agents, or individual leaders, they had cut managers off from their moorings. These moorings connected them not just to the organizations they led, and the communities in which the organizations were embedded, but also in the end to the shareholders they were purportedly serving. The resulting corporate oligarchy had no obligation other than to self-interest. Lacking the religious framework invoked by the founders of the modern university-based business school, such as Quaker based Joseph Wharton, or shared agreement about basic societal values, contemporary schools have no meaningful language for civic discourse about the ultimate purpose of these secular institutions. Thus we have been left only with empty rhetoric about leadership or excellence.*[8]

MOVING BEYOND THE INDIVIDUALIST 'WESTERN' NOTION OF LEADERSHIP

Not only does such contemporary leadership lack a social scientific and indeed professional base, but also its often sole emphasis on the 'individual' reinforces an individualist and materialistic paradigm as well as the consequent growing disconnection between organizational leaders and enterprises on the one hand, and communities and society on the other. This deficiency is what we seek to redress, through (the) Transformation (of) Management.

REVISING THE FUNCTIONING OF THE ENTERPRISE

Peter Drucker, an Austrian émigré to the USA during the Nazi period, has, more than anyone else, 'invented' the theory and practice of management in the latter part of the twentieth century. Legendary are his classic texts on *Management*[9] and *The Practice of Management*.[10] For Drucker, with the emergence of the large-scale organization, management represented *the* keynote social innovation in the twentieth century.

Yet, while the evolution of enterprise has been seemingly going on, the specific structure and functioning of business as a whole has remained largely untouched. That is why we have written this book, to remedy that very situation. Indeed marketing remains marketing, even if the emphasis shifts towards service; and finance remains finance, even though there is talk (as opposed to much action) of natural and social as well as financial capital. This leads us to a critical review of the discipline of management, which has taken over from entrepreneurship, at least in large-scale enterprise. In the process we again reveal the limitations of a primarily monocultural and unidisciplinary, as opposed to transcultural and transdisciplinary approach, to management.

RENEWING MANAGEMENT AS A DISCIPLINE

While its roots go back 200 years, management as a distinct function is particular to the twentieth century, when major social tasks have to be performed by organized institutions – business enterprises, school systems, research laboratories, governments.

However, ever since Drucker put management on the map in the 1950s to 1970s, there has been no enduring social innovation in the way we manage, and indeed no overall structure or process for facilitating such. Why has the need for such a renewal of the discipline of management, though, become all-important?

REVISING THE EXISTING MANAGEMENT EDUCATION

It is surprising to see, that, despite the fundamental flaws of our present day economic system and the enormous difficulties we have in designing truly sustainable organizations, the underlying management education (primarily the MBA) and the theory and practice related to the basic functioning of an organization have by and large not changed over the course of the past 50 years. In addition, this perspective on management education is primarily an Anglo-Saxon Western one. Such stasis has resulted in a major imbalance.

There is, however, *increasing awareness, that there is indeed a lack of transformative knowledge built into our management educational systems*. We jump from tool to technique, from instrument to initiative. Looking closely, we can see how lost we are in our efforts. While there are millions of workshops on change management, there is hardly one (if any) integral educational programme on overall transformation, which serves to fundamentally review the structure and functioning of the business-in-society. We need to build up a more coherent understanding of such and learn how we can build Transformation Management as well as social innovation into our educational as well as our consultancy processes so that we can make these accessible and appropriate. In the process it is also important that we move beyond a monosectoral perspective.

MOVING BEYOND A MONOSECTORAL PERSPECTIVE

Management, by now, has become an all-pervasive discipline. Originally, it was targeted for a new emerging breed of business administrator, better known as 'manager'. However, the discipline of management has since been introduced to organizations from all sectors of society. In fact, the way it has been introduced is extremely clumsy, if not altogether damaging to the overall integrity of the not-for-profit organization. Indeed, by implanting such alien, private sector-related concepts and techniques, born and bred in business schools or consultancies, a monosectoral perspective has been reinforced.

1.6 Towards New Forms of Enterprise in Society

1.6.1 NEWLY EMERGING FORMS OF ENTREPRENEURSHIP

Expansion of the traditional notion of private enterprise

The role of business-in-society over the past two decades has come a long way from promoting general philanthropy, corporate social responsibility (CSR) and corporate social investment. We have seen a gradual expansion of the traditional notion of private enterprise, whereby an increasing number of organizations are putting more and more emphasis on societal engagement. Corporations are reaching out towards culture, education, environment and other fields. Cross-sector partnerships are encouraged, and the term public-private-civic partnership is by now part of a common part of business vocabulary. Business is then reaching out to society at large, as well as vice versa, acknowledging that such engagement is vital in order to ensure its own survival and growth.

A prominent case in point, with which we are directly involved, is the International Business Leaders Forum (IBLF), initially established in 1990 in the UK by the Prince of Wales to promote responsible business practice in developing and transition economies. Working closely with more than 100 large multinational corporations, IBLF is exploring new approaches to developing the role of 'business in society', in transsectoral partnership with public, civic and multilateral enterprises. In a recent repositioning, IBLF now argues that business needs to move to 'the heart of sustainable development', to the benefit of both itself and also the communities within which it operates. The growing gap between the rich and the poor and the advent of climate change and peak oil and indeed food prices, makes business leaders realise that something more than CSR is required.

A prominent representative of such is Unilever's current Group CEO, Patrick Cescau, who said in a recent speech on *Beyond Corporate Social Responsibility*[11] that social innovation, as well as sustainable development need to become joint drivers of business growth. For us such social innovation needs to be seen in the same guise, in a social context, as research and development – both academic and corporate – in a technological one. While, then, the private sector is looking for new and more meaningful ways of societal engagement, the civic sector has developed its own approach: the 'social enterprise'.

Entrepreneurship in the civic sector: the rise of social enterprise

In the United States today non-profit organizations are the fastest growing category of enterprises. In policy-making and in discussions on how to balance the role of government, business and civil society, social and civic entrepreneurs get central attention. 'Social entrepreneurship' is seen to be engaging in many different initiatives, in the health sector, in the environment, among NGOs, in the informal sector in the third world, and in other cultural and social domains. Such new initiatives, over simplistically from our point of view, are viewed as a form of R&D in the welfare system, innovating new solutions to intractable social problems. They help communities to build up social capital.[12] One new form of such is the so-called social business.

Entrepreneurship between the private and the civic sector: emerging 'social business'

Nobel Laureate Muhammad Yunus (by way of his own example through the Grameen enterprises in Bangladesh) has promoted a new form of 'social' business as a 'hybrid' between conventional private and social enterprise. For him, both concepts fall short. The private entrepreneur, for Yunus, is deemed to be dedicated to one mission only – the maximization of profit. Yet the reality is very different. People are not one-dimensional. They are multidimensional. They have the potential to self-actualize, to realise heightened levels of consciousness. Mainstream free-market theory, for Yunus, suffers from a 'conceptualisation failure', a failure to capture the essence of what it is to be human. It actually ignores higher levels of 'world-centric' consciousness.[13]

Yunus goes on and argues that in the conventional theory of business we have created a one-dimensional human being to play the role of business entrepreneur, the so-called economic entrepreneur. We have insulated him or her from the rest of life, the religious, emotional, political and social, which characterize the 'social' entrepreneur. However, that puts also the latter into a box. This is where Yunus's concept of 'social business' comes in. Entrepreneurs establish a 'social business' not to achieve limited personal gain but to pursue social goals. A social business respects the multifaceted motivations of the entrepreneur, including his or her 'business' orientation, which, of course, includes the generation of profits to secure the economic sustainability of the business. Hence, such an enterprise is simultaneously social *and* economic. We now turn from the social business to the environmentally oriented enterprise.

The emerging eco-enterprise

Conventional wisdom has involved comparing and contrasting 'transactional management' and 'transformational leadership'. For us this has meant merely putting old wine in new bottles, as the basic form of the enterprise remained unchanged. There is a fundamentally new form increasingly visible, which so far has been subsumed under the social enterprise: the eco-enterprise. With eco-enterprise we mean enterprises, which have a strong environmental orientation, and are deeply rooted in nature and nature's principles. For Catherine Campbell, a South African social psychologist currently based at the London School of Economics:

> ... *growing ourselves and our communities in harmony with the land is seldom recognized as an entrepreneurial activity. Although a majority of the world's population lives on the land, only a tiny fraction of people in the industrialized world do, and most theories of entrepreneurship emanate from the latter. We have discredited our enterprising physical selves and commoditised the business of living. In fact, we exist today because our foremothers foraged and gathered and, later, accomplished the transition to gardening and agriculture.*[14]

According to Campbell, modern notions of entrepreneurial behaviour are in many ways idealizations of the mythical hunter. But our species did not survive by hunting alone. Close study of a subsistence relationship with 'Mother Earth' reveals the quintessential entrepreneurial responsibility for our individual and collective process of self-creation and self-nurturing. Unlike industrial production or knowledge work, work that occurs with and for the land is axiomatically concerned with space and place. Such 'grounded' entrepreneurial activity becomes a mutually beneficial interaction between and among individuals, and between people and nature, as they collectively create meaning for themselves and their community. Indeed, Catherine Campbell is calling for a transformation in our understanding of enterprise, one that is grounded in nature, if not also in culture, rather than in economics.

'Bioregionalism', for example, is a result of such eco-entrepreneurial efforts. It dramatically reframes the entrepreneurial process, shifting the emphasis from a human to an eco-systemic orientation, whereby we become more rooted in place and space. Modern-day permaculture is another influential attempt to move towards more localized energy-efficient and productive living arrangements. Permaculture claims, that this is not a choice, but an inevitable direction for humanity. Rebuilding local agriculture and food production then, localizing energy production, rethinking healthcare, rediscovering local building, in the context of zero energy building, rethinking how we manage waste, all build resilience and offer, according to Rob Hopkins, one of the key proponents of permaculture, the potential of an extraordinary renaissance.[15] We now turn from the economic, social and environmental to the public sector.

Emerging public enterprise in a redefined 'public space'

Recently upcoming discourses from Scandinavian academics Daniel Hjorth and Bjorne Bjerke make the case for the emergence of a public form of entrepreneurship via a redefinition of 'public space'. Starting from a conviction that entrepreneurship belongs primarily to society rather than the economy, and that we need to understand life rather than simply business to fully appreciate the entrepreneurial processes, Hjorth and Bjerke suggest locating entrepreneurship in the public domain.[16] According to them, it would be appropriate to conceive of today's society as consisting of three sectors:

1. one common sector (the traditional public sector financed by taxes);
2. one business sector driven by market forces; and
3. a newly called public sector, where community goals are achieved by creating through engaging in social processes, including 'public businesses'.

Hjorth and Bjerke use the concept 'public' to think their way back from 'social and society'. They do this as a reaction against how managerial economic rationality has come to define and refer to the 'social' while being called upon to provide expert knowledge in the recent urge for 'reinventing government'. Such a perspective on public enterprise can be contrasted with the neo-liberal attempt to limit citizenship to the role of consumer choices in a market. Rather, a different view of citizenship is developed, that involves a creative 'making use' of the public space between state institutions and civic society. In this new discourse on social entrepreneurship the public citizen is reviewed as an enterprising self. Public entrepreneurs, for Hjorth and Bjerke then, serve to create new forms of 'sociality' in the face of withering state institutions.

1.6.2 ENTERPRISE IN SOCIETY: A STATE OF FERTILE CHAOS

In introducing the changing face of enterprise in today's society we have focused on three core trends. We have first described the ongoing expansion of business's engagement in society and its reaching out to society's other sectors while exploring new concepts of doing so. Second, we have reviewed how social enterprises have established themselves as a counterbalance to the shortcomings of the private and public sectors. Third, we have indicated that there are now a variety of emerging entrepreneurial forces, such as the 'social business' (positioning itself simultaneously in the business and in the social world), the eco-enterprise, as well as attempts at a redefinition of public enterprise. Figure 1.2 serves to illustrate such core trends.

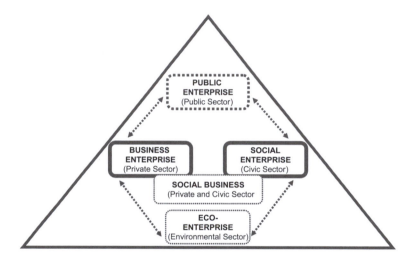

Figure 1.2   Types of enterprises in the societal arena of PPC partnerships

Note: (Established Types = Full Line/Emerging Types = Dotted Line)

Further building upon these trends is the emerging notion of cross-sector partnerships, most commonly termed public-private-civic (PPC) partnerships. There are also significant attempts to consolidate educationally upon such partnerships. This is, for example, illustrated by the 'Partnering Initiative', an educational joint venture of IBLF and Cambridge (UK) University (www.thepartneringinitiative.org).

We regard these developments as 'fertile chaos', serving to acknowledge a need for transformation. More specificly, they acknowledge a need for new forms of transsectoral entrepreneurship and transformed enterprises, including new ways of partnering between different types of enterprise.

1.7 Conclusion: Transformation (of) Management

DIFFERENTIATION, TRANSFORMATION, INTEGRATION

We have tried to demonstrate the need for fundamental evolution of the way in which we conceptualize and run enterprises in our society. We thereby have argued that current day management theory and practice is not building on the range of knowledge sources that are vital for the sustainable functioning of an organization. As such, nature's lessons (as embodied, for example, in ecology and biology) are as much neglected as is knowledge rooted in culture, or to be more specific, in the cultural diversity humankind represents. As a result, management has not only become an overly narrow discipline serving to define the relevant knowledge base of an organization in a rather limiting way, it has also not recognized the enterprise as a knowledge creating entity, which, as such, becomes a social innovator.

The conception of today's enterprise is still too much rooted in a mechanistic and individualized world-view, strongly influenced by Western thinking. As such it fails to take into account the natural and cultural context, is still lodged within the prevailing economic system and has not built in the notion of social – as opposed to technological – innovation.

Hence, most organizational responses to the core social issues they are facing tend to be segmented, fragmented and lack integration. We have illustrated that fundamentally revised forms of 'enterprise in society' have been recently emerging, though still in embryonic form, including a new cross-sectoral orientation, which could provide some elements of an integrated and holistic response to global and local challenges.

We have also identified the fact that there is no purposeful, social equivalent to technological innovation, built into academic research in the social sciences, consultancy based process interventions or indeed corporate R&D. Such a differentiated 'social – as opposed to technological – research look' at the situation we are collectively facing is crucial in order to set the scene for the necessary evolutionary steps.

The gravity and complexity of such challenges makes it evident that we are not talking of minor modifications or changes, but of fundamental transformation. Such a transformational process is aiming at providing answers to the identified challenges in a newly integrated format. Ultimately, we have set out in this chapter to review and renew the way we run organizations today. In order to fully accomplish such, as this book as a whole will reveal, we offer four fundamentally transformed perspectives.

FOUR FUNDAMENTALLY TRANSFORMED PERSPECTIVES

To be clear, we don't want to throw the baby out with the bathwater. Management, leadership and entrepreneurship have had their place. But, as we see it, *leadership and entrepreneurship represent the originally dynamic thesis, management the stabilizing antithesis, and Transformation Management is the dynamic-stabilizing synthesis.*

Transformation Management provides the following four fundamentally transformed perspectives on the way in which we will need to run organizations, duly and newly embedded in societies (see following Tables).

1. From a Transactional (Competitive) Perspective
to a Transformational (Co-Creative) Perspective

Revisiting Nature

Linking Competition and Co-creation

Via Activating Transformational Flows
- The Organization as a Living System
- Turning from Competitive Strategy to Strategic Renewal
- Building upon Self-Organizing Processes

2. From a Monocultural (Western)
to a Transcultural (Worldly) Perspective

Revisiting Culture

Linking Local and Global Knowledge

Via Promoting Interaction between Transcultural Forces
- Building upon cultural Diversity
- Enterprise as a cultural Entity
- Acknowledging the cultural Contexts
- Evolving transcultural Products, Processes and Enterprise

3. From a Unidisciplinary (Economic Pre-Emphasis)
to a Transdisciplinary (all Social Sciences) Perspective

Revisiting Science

Expanding the Knowledge Base and Enabling Social Innovation

Via Probing into Transdisciplinary Fields
- Making the Social Sciences and Humanities Explicit
- Simultaneously focusing on technological and social Innovation
- Broadening the Base of Management Education
- Institutionalizing social Innovation in the Organization

4. From a Depersonalized (Organizational)
to a Transpersonal (Self/Organization/Society) Perspective

Revisiting Management

Transforming the Functioning of Enterprise and Management Education

Via Building up Transpersonal Functions
- Beyond the individualist 'Western' Notion of Leadership
- Linking the Personal (Self), with the Impersonal (Organization) and the Communal (Society)
- Grounding the Transpersonal Functions in particular indigenous Soils while also Drawing upon Exogenous Knowledge

These four fundamentally new perspectives pave the way for the Integral Enterprise.

The Integral Enterprise: *From a Monosectoral (Private Sector Predominant) to a Transsectoral (All Sectors) Perspective*	
Towards the Integral Enterprise	**Transformation Management: Applying the Four New Perspectives** • Integrating Nature, Culture, Science and (New) Management • New emerging Forms of Enterprise and Entrepreneurship in all Sectors of Society (from extended Private Enterprise, to Civic and Social Enterprise, from Social Business to Eco-Enterprise) • New Forms of Public-Private-Civic Integration; New Enterprise Concept equally relevant for Business and Organizations for other Sectors of Society

Our critique of conventional management, entrepreneurship and leadership as well as the corresponding educational frameworks prepares the ground for an evolutionary step in our perception of how we run organizations in society. We are aware of the numerous contributions from modern 'Western' management, leadership and entrepreneurship literature that are pointing towards such evolutionary change. However, until today, we are lacking a new worldly framework, which allows and enables organizations to make this evolutionary leap. The prerequisites to such a new discipline are enormous. In a nutshell, such a new discipline needs to satisfy the following demands:

- enabling the building of a sustainable, resilient enterprise;
- making the enterprise relevant to a particular society by bringing it closer in touch with its specific origins and destination;
- providing an integrated perspective on the organization-in-society which is not only valid for private enterprise, but also for organizations from other sectors of society;
- providing an integrated perspective for the three interdependent levels of self, organization and society;
- providing a new synthesis for management, entrepreneurship and leadership and through that a platform for transformed educational frameworks in such fields;
- providing a process for continuous renewal and ongoing innovation for the organization, while ultimately being open to;
- engaging with diverse ideological platforms ranging from capitalism and democratic socialism to contemporary environmentalism.

Transformation Management sets out to respond to these demands. As a new discipline it promotes the design and ongoing renewal of an enterprise in a particular cultural and societal context. It further integrates, as illustrated, four flows, forces, fields and functions respectively, from nature, to culture, to science to (renewed) management. Indeed, each of these represents one of the four fundamentals of Transformation Management. As such, the Integral Enterprise is comprised simultaneously of a transformational perspective (rooted in nature), a transcultural perspective (lodged in a fundamentally new understanding of culture), a transdisciplinary perspective (lodged in the social sciences and humanities), as well as a transpersonal perspective (redefining the functioning of the enterprise). Figure 1.3 provides a refined overview on the core constituencies of the Integral Enterprise.

In the following chapter we establish the overall framework for Transformation Management, building upon each of the fundamentals, and the overall Integral Enterprise.

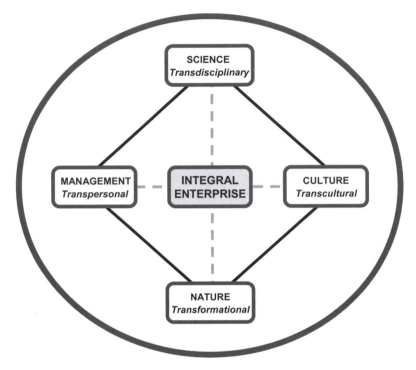

Figure 1.3   Refined overview framework of an Integral Enterprise

References

1. Peters, T. and Waterman, R. H. (2004). *In Search of Excellence*. London: Profile Books.
2. Goerner, S. et al. (2008). *The New Science of Sustainability. Building a Foundation for Great Change*. Chapel Hill: Triangle Center for Complex Systems.
3. Drucker, P. (2008). *Management*. New York: Harper Collins.
4. Pepper, S. (1957). *World Hypotheses*. Los Angeles: University of California Press.
5. Loye, D. (2007). *Darwin on Love*. Carmel: Benjamin Franklin Press.
6. Jackson, I. and Nelson, J. (2005). *Profits with Principles*. New York: Doubleday.
7. O'Connor, E. (2006). *High Profile Social Entrepreneurship*. In: Steyaert, C. and Hjorth, D. (2006). *Entrepreneurship and Social Change*. Northants: Edward Elgar.
8. Khurana, R. (2007). *From Higher Aims to Hired Hands*. Oxford: Princeton University.
9. Drucker, P. (2008). *Management*. New York: Harper Collins.
10. Drucker, P. (2006). *The Practice of Management*. New York: Harper Collins.

11. Cescau, P. (2007). *Beyond Corporate Social Responsibility: Social Innovation and Sustainable Development as Drivers of Business Growth*. Speech given at INSEAD Fontainebleau Campus on 25 May 2007.
12. Leadbetter, C. (2002). *Up the Down Escalator*. London: Viking.
13. Yunus, M. (2006). *Creating a World Without Poverty*. New York: Public Affairs.
14. Campbell, C., in Steyaert, C. and Hjorth, D. (2006). *Entrepreneurship and Social Change*. Northants: Edward Elgar.
15. Hopkins, R. (2008). *The Transition Handbook. From Oil Dependency to Local Resilience*. Devon: Green Books.
16. Steyaert, C. and Hjorth, D. (2006). *Entrepreneurship and Social Change*. Northants: Edward Elgar.

2 *The Four Fundamentals of Transformation Management*

From an Independent to an Interdependent Fourfold Perspective

2.1 Introduction: The Four Fundamentals

In Chapter 1 we introduced the emerging trends in, and shortcomings of, the fields of enterprise and entrepreneurship, management and leadership. Our critical review of these is based on many years of social research, management education and process consultancy in both Transformation Management and also social innovation all over the world. During this time we have identified four fundamentals of transformation, which, if applied, we believe to be key to a sustainable Integral Enterprise.

	The Four Fundamentals of Transformation
1.	Transforming Competitive Strategy into Strategic Renewal *via Transformational Flows*
2.	Transforming Organizational Development into Cultural Dynamics *via Transcultural Forces*
3.	Transforming R&D into Social Innovation *via Transdisciplinary Fields*
4.	Transforming the Functions of Management *via Transpersonal Functions*

These four fundamentals represent what is missing in an ahistorical (decontextualized), monocultural (Western), monofunctional (business) and unidisciplinary (economic) enterprise, management and leadership. Moreover, even when such crosscultural and transsectoral management is taken into account, no coherent model for the sustainable enterprise in a particular society has been developed so far. In this chapter we shall introduce such a coherent framework, which will be further substantiated, theoretically and practically, in the course of this book. In the following we shall briefly introduce the four fundamentals. We illustrate how they are interconnected and together constitute the core pillars of Transformation Management.

FIRST FUNDAMENTAL: ACTIVATING TRANSFORMATIONAL FLOWS

This first fundamental involves releasing the full potential of an enterprise through engaging in transformational processes in relation to a specific self, organization and community.

The transformational flows introduce the dynamic and ultimately transformational Strategic Renewal, which is our equivalent of conventional strategy.

Based on a fourfold transformational process, which we have coined the GENE (an acronym which stands for grounding, emerging, navigating and effecting), we illustrate how the GENE-ius of a social organism can be released.

In this initial case, by drawing on ecology, biology and other natural sciences, as well as on the humanities, we root our approach deeply in nature and culture. Hence, the origination of a new form of enterprise involves us tapping into our collective origins by combining nature's and humanity's wisdom. Thereby, we build on natural as well as cultural vitality, and on the way living systems develop forms, that enable continuous adaptation and renewal, and ultimately transformation.

SECOND FUNDAMENTAL: PROMOTING INTERACTION BETWEEN TRANSCULTURAL FORCES

This second fundamental involves learning to manage organizations in fundamentally different worlds. Engaging with cultural diversity is the key!

Culture is not just a mere ingredient of management and organizational theory, a subset of organizational behaviour, corporate culture or indeed managing across cultures. It is much more than all of that. For us it constitutes the cultural force that builds on the natural flow of Transformation Management. That is probably the single most revolutionary aspect of our work. We shall demonstrate in this book, how culture, and an understanding of one's cultural and societal context, as well as that of the 'other', which you individually and collectively engage, provides the basis for a sustainable and thereby integrated organization. The design for such integration is embodied in our Four World model, spanning the globe from the south to the east to the north, to the west. The Four World model represents the transcultural, as opposed to the conventionally monocultural, forces. These forces are embodied in humanism (south) and holism (east), rationalism (north) and pragmatism (west). They are deeply rooted in nature and culture and provide the basis for an integrated global perspective as well as for a differentiated societal one.

The transcultural perspective is formed out of the differentiation and integration of the cultural particularities of the south, east, north and west of the globe, and the diverse cultural morphologies of each world region. Interestingly enough, this archetypal Four World perspective can be translated into an integrated perspective of each social organism: from society, to the organization, to the self. We demonstrate this in detail later in this chapter.

THIRD FUNDAMENTAL: PROBING INTO TRANSDISCIPLINARY FIELDS

This fundamental and now integral field involves broadening the knowledge base of the organization to accommodate local as well as global knowledge, the humanities as well as the broad range of social sciences.

Conventional management and leadership theory is, so our argument goes, too narrowly defined, in that it is usually universally and all too often economically, and partly psychologically and behaviourally, framed. Thereby it does not build on the local knowledge base of the society in which an enterprise is lodged. To draw on such requires you to be exposed, at least to some degree, to anthropology and sociology, ecology and systems theory, depth psychology and spirituality, geography and history, as well as, of course, to politics and economics. Overall, such a transdisciplinary perspective enables you to include and activate the local knowledge base of the society/culture in which a particular organization is rooted. Such a local knowledge base is then brought into meaningful interaction with the global knowledge base. The various disciplines serve to broaden the primarily economically based 'Western' conventional perspective to incorporate, for example, more 'northern' systems perspectives, more 'eastern' spirituality, and more 'southern' anthropological sources. Further, by probing into a broader base of transdisciplinary fields, the organization is enabled to engage in transformative research, designed to lead to social innovation.

FOURTH FUNDAMENTAL: BUILDING UP TRANSPERSONAL FUNCTIONS

This fourth fundamental involves embodying Transformation Management in the conventional business functions while also aligning self, organization, society and, ultimately, the globe.

The differentiated and integrated approach of Transformation Management, evolved out of its transcultural (rather than Western), transdisciplinary (beyond economics) and transformational (as opposed to transactional) perspectives, allows us to see the functioning of the enterprise in a new light. Specifically we witness the development of an originally personalized and trait based approach to leadership, followed by a depersonalized and segmented functional perspective (marketing and operations, human resource and finance) of the organization towards a transpersonal one. This transpersonal orientation interconnects self, organization and society, as well as ultimately the globe.

Through such evolved functions the enterprise is newly integrated in society. Such integration enables an organization to serve profoundly a society's needs, increasing the relevance of the organization to the particular community in which it operates. We now turn to the new integral form of the enterprise, which is the culmination of Transformation Management.

INTEGRAL ENTERPRISE: FROM CORPORATE SOCIAL RESPONSIBILITY TO SOCIETY BUILDING

The new integral form involves the enterprise as 'society builder', encompassing public and private, civic and animate (environmental) sectors, rather than being a merely private 'profit maximizer'.

The transformed enterprise is characterized by an inclusively natural (animate), cultural (civic), social (public) and economic (private) form. For us, what is key is the reintegration of the enterprise in a particular society, whereby it assumes a private-public-civic-animate (environmental) form. Such a new form enables the enterprise to simultaneously evolve its community, consciousness, knowledge and sustainability. Such a fully integrated enterprise is aligned with the natural, cultural, technological and economic context it is embedded in and it becomes an intrinsic society builder. This is the ultimate aim of Transformation Management. In fact, it is such a 'trans-FORM-ation', which lies at the core of our work. We shall now give a detailed overview on each fundamental, starting with the transformational flows.

2.2 Transformational Flows: Nature and Community

FOUR WORLDS IN NATURE AND CULTURE: LIVING FRAMEWORKS FOR TRANSFORMATION

The situation we find ourselves in today is, in our 'Four World' terms, as follows: the pragmatic west has lost touch with its roots in the natural south; the rational north has become disconnected from the consciousness raising east; the east itself has spun out of control trying to accommodate an overpowering west; and the south remains impoverished. On an organizational level, we can equally see a dominance of the financial and operational dimension, while the human and environmental dimensions have been neglected.

Hence, there is a need to understand the inner dynamics of transformation to enable us to bring the Four Worlds into a state of creative interaction, promoting a new dynamic balance between all four elements. This is equally relevant for all levels: self, organization and society. Again, as a first step, let us go back to the original journey of humankind.

The journey of humankind, as we shall see later, provides a living framework of transformation. For what has occurred is that the journey through the Four Worlds settled into the creation of four fundamental cultural forms or morphologies that are distinct from each other and yet part of one story. Each part of the world has developed a particular strength, each one building on the other. The full integration of all four elements is crucial for the full integration of an individual and social organism as illustrated by Figure 2.1.

The fourfold cultural transformation process that we identified deeply resonates with transformation processes that we found in nature. Indeed, culture builds directly on nature. While life emerges out of its environment, the environment needs to be continually transformed by life, so that it remains life-supportive. In essence, first, the individual unit of survival is simultaneously a unit of transformation, and second, the transformation process is the engagement of the individual unit with other units thereby creating new, intelligent forms without losing the essence of the original. Through this process nature ensures ongoing adaptation: life is preserved and sustained. This is illustrated in Figure 2.2

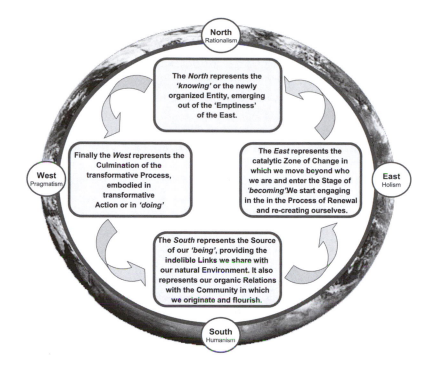

Figure 2.1   Four Worlds as a living framework for transformation

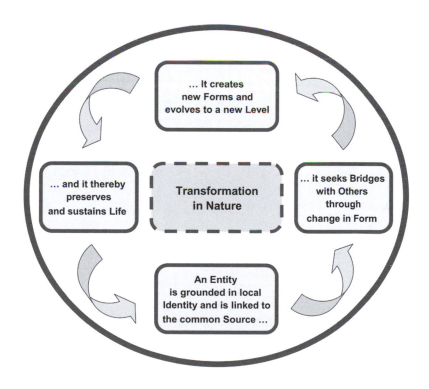

Figure 2.2   Transformation in nature

A GENERIC VERSION OF THE FLOWS OF NATURE AND CULTURE: THE GENE

In our own research we have evolved such a flow, which we have called the GENE, an acronym that stands for grounding, emerging, navigating and effecting. It is in that context that we are talking about releasing the transformative GENE-ius of the self, the organization and the society.

The GENE is our fourfold transformational rhythm. It represents the implicit pattern that underlies all natural and cultural processes. The GENE drives the process towards wholeness and integration in each system. It is this rhythm of renewal that continuously determines and guides the journey – the journey towards releasing the GENE-ius of people, organizations and societies.

The GENE is equally rooted in nature and culture (just compare the inner rhythms of Figures 2.2 and 2.3). Culturally, the GENE emerges through the meeting of different worlds. Yet such a creative interaction between horizons is very much the exception rather than the rule. That having been said, ironically, the key to any cultural renaissance, whether in Europe, in the arts and sciences in the fifteenth and sixteenth centuries, or in Japan, in technology and management, in the twentieth century, lies in the creative interaction between different cultures: here between north and south in the one case, East and West, in the other.

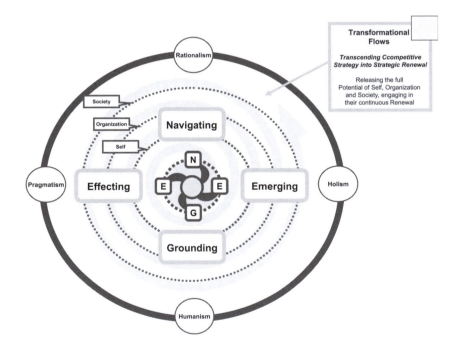

Figure 2.3   The first fundamental – activating transformational flows

Nature and culture, hence, hold the key for the flow rhythm. The GENE is a distillation of nature's and culture's transformative wisdom. The direction that a particular entity takes is in this cycle continuously reconnected to its own ground. From there it connects with others and gradually, by completing the cycle, evolves new forms of adaptation. Thus, the full GENE-ius of an organism is released. For organizations, which follow such a transformative cycle, transformation ultimately becomes a Four World process of grounding (humanistic), emerging (holistic), navigating (rational) and effecting (pragmatic). Such increases the resilience of an organization significantly, as the organization continuously renews its strategic orientation. It is doing so, by touching base with its societal and cultural grounds on an ongoing basis through continuously reengaging with the GENE-Flow. This 'touching base' enables the organization to reconnect with the societal and cultural reality, and to respond accordingly to it.

BEYOND INDIVIDUAL LEADERSHIP: SELF, ORGANIZATION AND SOCIETY

The flow is equally relevant for all living organisms: the self, the organization and the society. These three levels (ultimately culminating in a global perspective) are deeply interlinked and interdependent. Each level holds an integrated fourfold. The compartmentalization of the three fields is an artificial distinction that has led to isolating perspectives and a disintegration of these three dimensions. Overcoming these artificial distinctions we also move beyond the current overemphasis on individual leadership to a more systemic perspective. Figure 2.3 illustrates how the GENE-spiral continuously propels itself through the interdependent levels of self, organization and society, thereby serving to align them.

We have actually identified for each level a particular variation of the GENE-theme. As we can see, in the Table below, the flow of transformation in the case of you the self moves from the formative to the transformative; for the organization, from pioneering to integration; for society, from the magical to the integral. All of the three specific rhythms are closely aligned with the generic rhythm of the GENE.

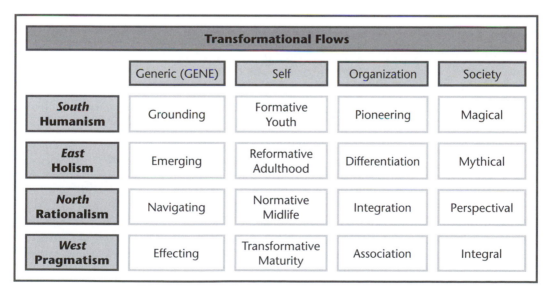

Transformational Flows			
	Generic (GENE)	Self	Organization	Society
South Humanism	Grounding	Formative Youth	Pioneering	Magical
East Holism	Emerging	Reformative Adulthood	Differentiation	Mythical
North Rationalism	Navigating	Normative Midlife	Integration	Perspectival
West Pragmatism	Effecting	Transformative Maturity	Association	Integral

WORKING TOWARD INTEGRATION OF SELF, ORGANIZATION AND SOCIETY

Each of the three levels of self, organization and society has its particular fourfold cycle. As all levels represent living organisms, which build on each other, you can notice a deep resonance between the three rhythms. For example, the individual 'reformative' referring to the inner development of a person resonates with the civic dimension of an organization where it engages in developing its employees as well as engaging with society. This, in turn, resonates with the cultural context in which both, individual and organization, are embedded. Continuously applying the transformative flow to the three levels enables them to develop shared perspectives, each contributing to the larger entity of which they form a part. We now turn from the transformative to the transcultural.

2.3 Transcultural Forces: Culture and Spirituality

NATURAL FLOWS TO CULTURAL FORCES

To understand how transformation works we need to start with a deep understanding of our own indigenous, cultural forces, be they English or Eritrean, American or Argentinean. This is the particular transformational equivalent to an exploration of an organization's role in its environment. At monocultural Harvard Business School, for example, this is called 'Managing in the Business Environment' (MBE). From our transcultural perspective that includes an understanding of how the principles of transformation are manifested in different cultural environments. So how does transformation take place in culture? We start with the story of mankind's journey around the world.

FROM SOUTH TO EAST TO NORTH TO WEST

Once upon a time man started his journey around the globe in Africa. It is in Africa, in the south of our planet, where the cradle of (wo)mankind can be found. The human journey continued in the east, before (wo)man moved to the north, then, finally to the west.

Using molecular techniques to measure degrees of biological relatedness in DNA, scientists have identified that just about 100,000 years ago the ancestors of all of humanity arose along the Great Rift Valley of Africa, in the communal 'south' of the Four Worlds. They moved out from there, northeast across the Sahara, southwest into what is now South Africa, northward across the Arabian Peninsula and east to India. From there they fanned out to Europe and Russia, from New Guinea to Australia, into Siberia and across the Bering land bridge to the Americas.[1]

Revisiting the human journey provides us with the framework to challenge the fragmented worldview that has pervaded for so long in that it treats human cultures as disjointed and fragmented. This is made all the more seemingly real by treating culture as an artefact, a set of practices that codes a certain kind of behaviour. *Our approach to culture is entirely different on two counts: one, we see culture in the larger movement of humankind's journey through the Four Worlds, and two, we perceive culture as a natural extension of nature.*

So as we can see, in terms of mankind's journey, the European 'north', and even more so, the American 'West' came very late in the day.

Figure 2.4   (Wo)Mankind's journey from south, to east, to north, to west

This movement from south to east, to north to west can, interestingly enough, also be found in the generic evolution of individual societies. The following Table illustrates this evolution and underlines how the integration of the Four Worlds (on a global level, but also within each society) helps to bring about an integrated perspective on society:

The Four World Perspective Translated into the Evolution of Human Communities and Societies	
South **Nature and** **Community**	Nature represents the first Step in Human Evolution (small Groups of Hunters and Gatherers/hardly any Language Skills) Nature can be described as the *Life Giving System*
East **Culture and** **Spirituality**	First cultural Expressions (starting with early burial Rites) emerge (Wo)Man looking for Meaning/Rising Consciousness/Wo(Man) defines himself in Relation to Nature and 'more than Nature' (gods) Culture is about the Development of *Meaning Giving Systems*: Rites, Cults, Religions, etc.
North **Science and** **Technology**	At a next Step man organized himself. The societal North represents the *Order Giving System* and is about Science, Technology and institutionalized Power, Hierarchies, Developments of Structures, Roles and Functions as well as the Formation of Communities, States, etc.
West **Economics and** **Management**	At a final Step, (Wo)Man engaged in Trade and established *Exchange Systems*

Back to the global cultural morphologies, what then are the particular cultural capacities of each world region?

DIFFERENT CULTURAL CHARACTERISTICS (MORPHOLOGIES) BUILD ON EACH OTHER

Figure 2.5 illustrates the cultural strengths of each of the Four Worlds. We argue that while each world has developed over time a particular set of strengths, it also, to be fully functional, needs to embody the other three worlds; in fact, it needs to continuously reach out to the other worlds, in order to be in an integrated state of dynamic balance.

The four morphologies are not only a geographic orientation. Much more than that, they constitute an archetypal representation of the inner fourfold of living organizations, such as individual people, organizations and societies. As such, we associate the 'inner' south with humanism and nature, the east with holism and culture, the north with rationalism and science, and the west with pragmatism and enterprise.

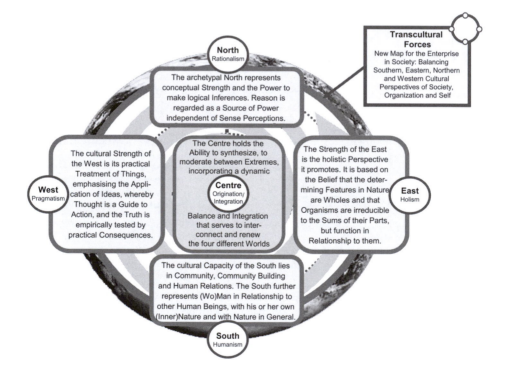

Figure 2.5   The second fundamental – activating transcultural forces

It is, however, fascinating to see, how this pattern still resonates, to some degree at least, on a global geographic level, while we acknowledge that historical and actual patterns of migration as well as modern communications lead to many hybrid combinations.

The Four Worlds are rooted in an ancient archetype of wholeness and integration, which can be found in endless variations in all cultures, from the mandala to the medicine wheel. In this archetypal picture it is the south, which is most closely related to physical nature and to his or her fellow (wo)man, represented by humanism. The archetypal east is home to the evolutionary dimension of the person (holism), while the archetypal north represents such a person's rational dimension. And it is the archetypal west that holds the pragmatic dimension, which, as in the other cases, is only of full value, if it embodies and thereby stays connected to the other three dimensions.

While we are not saying, that for example humanism is only rooted in the South (hence in Africa), or holism is only rooted in the East (hence in countries like India, Japan or China), we argue, that each world region has evolved over time one inner dimension that seems to be stronger developed than the others. The East has arguably the longest and deepest tradition in the area of holism, spirituality and non-material aspects, while, for example, the West, has developed an enormous capacity for the pragmatic and material expression. Moreover, each world, when isolated and conflict ridden, has its downside – tribalism and nepotism in the South, fundamentalism in the East, totalitarianism in the North, materialism in the West. Of course, you find all aspects in every society, in every organization, in every individual. And we argue that it is ultimately about integrating these four positive dimensions within the fields of the self, the organization and the society, albeit retaining your particular, for example 'Western', pre-emphasis. The pragmatic West needs not only the rational Northern dimension, but also the holistic Eastern dimension and the humanistic (people, community and nature orientated dimension) of the South. Each dimension needs the other in order to be truly meaningful and effective. In fact, when one dimension is isolated from the worldly others it becomes distorted.

If you regard this as too farfetched then examine carefully the current state of our globalized world where a one-sided domination of a) economic principles is b) all developed in a heavily dominant west. It is this fragmented and one-sided perspective that, in our view, is one of the core reasons for many of the problems that the world community currently faces.

BASED ON THE ULTURAL MORPHOLOGIES, DIFFERENT CULTURAL FORCES CAN BE IDENTIFIED

Based on the four morphologies, different cultures have developed particular cultural orientations. We draw on the innermost forces within a particular self, organization or society that often provide the context for the transformational journey. The organizations referred to in each world (for example, Visa in the West) will be elaborated upon in Chapters 12 to 15.

Examples for expressions of such local cultural forces are African 'Ubuntu' (South), Japanese 'Kyosei' (east), the Nordic 'Naringsliv' (North) and the Anglo-Saxon 'Individuation' (West), among others. From our experience, each society, each organization, each individual resonates most with one cultural force, while the others are less present. Figure 2.6 above provides examples of cultural forces in the Four World regions, including corporate cases that have consciously built on such cultural forces.

It became obvious to us in our work around the world, how these cultural forces are – as a dominant cultural expression – an integral part of the identity of a person, an organization and a society. Transformational processes, hence, always have strong cultural forces lodged in a particular local identity and need to be built on them. From such a strong 'home base' an organism can productively engage with the larger entity

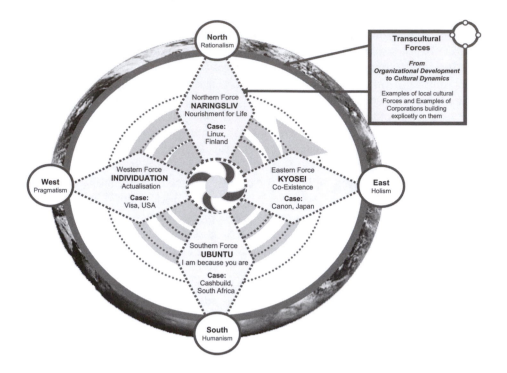

Figure 2.6   The second fundamental – examples of transcultural forces

and contribute in a coherent way to it; the self can contribute to the organization, the organization to community and society, the society to the global perspective. *That's why we call one of the core rhythms of a healthy transformation process: 'From Local Identity to Global Integrity'.*

Ultimately, the Four World model provides a new map for the enterprise. With this approach we illustrate how each world region has developed its particular cultural strengths and set of local capacities, that, if successfully activated, form the basis for local transformation processes and social innovation. This particular strength can then contribute to global solutions, if brought in balanced interaction with other cultural capacities. The Four Worlds form a framework for such creative interaction, allowing each society, each organization and each individual to identify its particular strengths and the strengths of 'the others'. It is remarkable to see, how the Four Worlds – as an 'archetypal' representation – equally resonates on the level of the global cultural landscape, as well as on a societal, organizational and individual level.

CREATIVELY ENGAGING WITH DIVERSITY, ON ALL LEVELS

The Four World approach focuses on the 'creative activation' of the diverse elements of each social system while working towards more integrated perspectives.

Creative interaction between the parts of a whole is only possible if there is a rich understanding and appreciation of cultural, sectoral, societal, organizational and individual diversity. Reactivating these cultural forces is one of the core aspects of this approach. It is lodged in the insight, that *in order to fully activate and harness the specific strengths of an organization, it is important that it remains truly lodged in the societal and cultural grounds on which it is built.* Transformation processes start with the development of a local identity (of self, organization and society), whether this is rooted, for example, in the Ubuntu philosophy of interdependence in Southern Africa or in Japan's concept of Kaizen promoting continuous improvement in Japan.

If we do not understand who we are and where we come from we cannot possibly know where we wish to go and determine how to get there. We cannot transform consciously and achieve our full individual or organizational potential. Only when there is an understanding of our local identity can we contribute to the global integrity of the system we live and work in: the community, the organization, the society, and ultimately the world. Only then can we meaningfully and productively link the local and the global, and one culture with another. Such transformation processes then also serve to overcome fragmentation on an individual, organizational, communal, and societal level. We now turn from transcultural forces to the transdisciplinary fields that underlie Transformation Management.

2.4 Transdisciplinary Fields: Science and Technology

BEYOND ENTERPRISE, MANAGEMENT AND LEADERSHIP

The underlying disciplines that conventional programmes on business studies, business administration or indeed management and leadership in general draw upon, specifically in the social sciences, are economics and statistics, behavioural and social psychology, as well as a small dose of systems theory and sociology. In other words, the conventional management wisdom on strategy and organization, marketing and operations, human resources and finance, are lodged in such underlying disciplinary fields. As such anthropology and ecology, depth psychology and political theory, are completely ignored.

Not only that, but this narrow base is effectively drawn from the 'West', essentially from America. The rest of the world – that is our other three worlds – hardly gets a look in. Moreover, and particularly damaging for our purposes, the whole of the humanities is left out of account. Given the fact that Transformation Management draws upon local identity with a view to developing global integrity, this means that enterprise, management and leadership, by comparison, are fundamentally flawed. For local identity, as we have said, draws pre-eminently on nature and culture. That means that not only anthropology and ecology, but also philosophy and theology, geography and history, as well as the humanities in general – art and architecture, music and dance, literature and theatre – are all important. This will be addressed in our forthcoming book on *Integral Economics*.

FROM MONODISCIPLINARY TO TRANSDISCIPLINARY PERSPECTIVES

In other words, and to retrace steps, approaches to enterprise and entrepreneurship, developed out of economics arose predominantly from what we term the 'Northwest' – in this case that means predominantly Britain and America as well as France and Austria to a smaller extent. Interestingly enough even Germany, the birthplace of Karl Marx, and the centre, together with France, of European philosophy, hardly got a look in, never mind

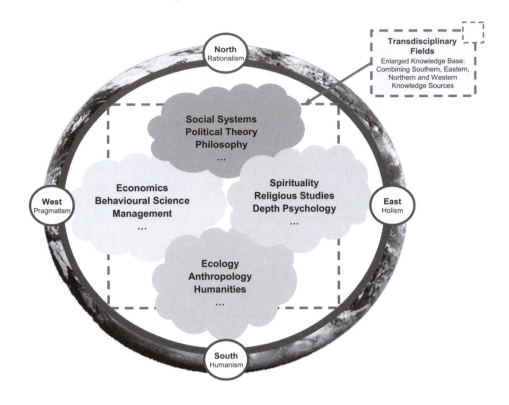

Figure 2.7   The third fundamental – transdisciplinary fields (overview)

Italy, Spain or Russia. It is actually only very recently, as we saw in the last chapter, that sociologists, psychologists and even philosophers have begun to engage with now 'social' entrepreneurship.

The field of management, interestingly enough, and the leadership studies that followed in its footsteps, are totally Western (American) in their origins. The only significant exceptions to such are discrete elements of Japanese management (related to the management of people and operations). In fact, with the consolidation of the America-style business schools all over the world, and the recent onset of Reagonomics, the underlying economic, monodisciplinary orientation has become even more pervasive.

As a counter to such, in the new millennium, we witness two significant trends towards the transdisciplinary orientation we adopt. The first is the diversification from business to social and even eco-enterprise, which draws upon psychology, sociology, political science and even ecology as underlying disciplines. The second is the comparatively recent advent of 'crosscultural management' and indeed of 'corporate culture', which has something of an anthropological tone to it, also extending its reach into literature and theatre, in terms of storytelling. Yet, at the present time, these remain like drops in the economic and behavioural ocean, which is precisely why overall social, as opposed to technological, innovation, is inhibited.

TECHNOLOGICAL TO SOCIAL INNOVATION

Interdisciplinary development in the natural sciences, in biochemistry, in neurobiology, in medical electronics, and so forth, have led to a proliferation of innovation, facilitated by the application of scientific method. In the social sciences and humanities, hitherto, such innovation has been inhibited for two major reasons. First the different social disciplines, such as economics and anthropology, political science and psychology, have remained largely segregated from one another, and secondly so-called 'scientific method', in the social sciences, has remained academically esoteric rather than practically useful. We shall demonstrate in Part 4 of this book, how a transdisciplinary perspective enables the organization to build an enlarged and relevant knowledge base. Further, by applying research to such an enlarged knowledge base in a transformative way, the enterprise can become a social innovator.

We now turn from social disciplines to business functions.

2.5 Transpersonal Functions: Economics and Management

In order to fully 'function', individuals, organizations and society each need to differentiate and integrate their life sustaining activities. However, the functions of the three levels are often disconnected. One of the reasons lies in the enormous specialization of society as a whole; the larger picture (the connecting patterns) is not any more visible. By overcoming that 'disconnection' (fragmentation) we move from a narrow understanding of Business Administration to a transpersonal and transsectoral perspective.

UNDERSTANDING THE SHARED FUNCTIONING OF SELF, ORGANIZATION AND SOCIETY

Each living human organism (self, organization and society) needs to integrate various functions in order to stay alive. These functions – today – are merely outer expressions of the deeper original meaning they once had. Engaging in transformation we need to deeper understand the southern, eastern, northern and western oriented functions, in order to enable them to build on each other and to then mutually reinforce each other. The four functions of each level resonate deeply with the cultural morphologies, as can be seen in the following table.

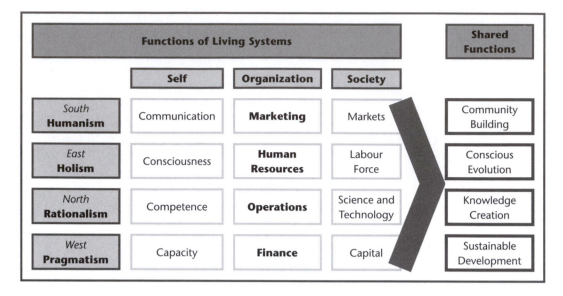

By reconnecting the main shared functions of self, organization and society, organizations play a particular important role. They are the bridge between self and society. They provide the context for further evolution, which can reach out into society and have a transformative impact there. Business, as a major force in modern society, has a particular role to play in providing a context for individual transformation and in developing new, evolved forms of communities, organizations and ultimately societies.

There are four core functions to be identified within the self, the organization and the society: community building arising out of marketing, communications and markets (South); conscious evolution emerging out of human resources, consciousness and labour (East); knowledge creation as a transformation of operations, competence and science/technology (North); and sustainable development emerging out of finance, capability and capital (West). These four evolved functions relate strongly back to the four archetypal expressions of the four directions: community building and humanism (Southern); conscious evolution and holism (Eastern); knowledge creation and rationalism (Northern); and sustainable development and pragmatism (Western).

FUNCTIONAL GROUNDING TO EFFECT

In fact, we have found it quite extraordinary, in our review of the emerging literature on leadership and entrepreneurship, that the conventional functions – marketing, human resources, operations, finance – have been left totally out of account. It is, for us, as if the body as well as, in the best cases, the spirit and soul of enterprise have been considered, but not the mind.

We shall now demonstrate how the core functions can be further evolved in order to release their GENE-ius. We build here on existing trends that can be found in all those functions. However, so far, there has not been any consistent framework and curriculum to provide a learning and development context for an integral evolution of all functions across all fields.

THE SOUTHERN FUNCTION: FROM MARKETING TO COMMUNITY BUILDING

The Southern 'functional transformation', to begin with, is about the evolution of marketing into community building. The fulfilment of individual and communal need, inherent within a 'Southern' humanistic approach has been overtaken by the 'Western' exploitation of the consumer, thereby aggressively satisfying wants. Such an evolution of marketing is a process whereby the fulfilment of authentic communal needs, through mutual exchange, takes the place of the exploitation of inauthentic individual wants.

THE EASTERN FUNCTION: FROM HUMAN RESOURCES TO CONSCIOUS EVOLUTION

The Eastern 'functional transformation' is about the evolution of human resources into conscious evolution. As Personnel Management evolved from the management of people to Human Resource Management (HRM), so people became an economic resource like any other. From a holistic perspective, the 're-sourcing' of the human involves a developmental approach to enhancing the levels of consciousness of not only individuals but also of organizations and whole societies.

THE NORTHERN FUNCTION: FROM OPERATIONS TO KNOWLEDGE CREATION

The Northern 'functional transformation' is about the evolution of operations into knowledge creation. With the advent of the Japanese manufacturing revolution in the last twenty years, the development of the knowledge worker and the knowledge creating enterprise has transcended land, labour and capital. The management of ideas has overtaken the management of employees. From such an evolved perspective management and worker are replaced by knowledge work.

THE WESTERN FUNCTION: FROM FINANCE TO SUSTAINABLE DEVELOPMENT

The Western 'functional transformation' is about the evolution of finance into sustainable development. The notion of reciprocity and exchange, inherent within economic relationships and double entry book keeping, can be connected to inclusive life principles rather than exclusive financial relationships. The role of money in society thereby evolves from a transactional to a nurturing relationship, ultimately giving rise to complementary currencies and other means of sustainable development.

We now turn finally to the new transsectoral form of the Integral Enterprise.

2.6 Developing a New Form of Public-Private-Civic Enterprise

ARRIVING AT A NEW FORM: THE INTEGRATED PUBLIC-PRIVATE-CIVIC-ANIMATE ENTERPRISE

An enterprise, which has successfully transformed its core functions, has the potential to reach a new form. Or, in other words, it has been 'trans-Form-ed' into a sustainable and Integral Enterprise.

The transformed enterprise is characterized by a simultaneously natural, cultural, technological and economic form. For us, it is the reintegration of the enterprise in society, whereby it newly assumes a public-private-civic-animate (environmental) form; that is the key to transformation.

Moreover, such a 'formal' transformation in the nature and scope of the micro enterprise, cannot effectively take place without a parallel transformation of the macro economy. Although, the full subject of such would be the making of another book (see our forthcoming book *Integral Economics* to be published in the Spring of 2010 by Gower Publishing),[2] the fault line in so much of the current work on transformative leadership or on organizational transformation, as well as on the newly emerging field of social entrepreneurship is the total lack of any consideration whatsoever of the macro economy, in one society or another.

HOW THE FOUR WORLD PERSPECTIVE LEADS TO A NEWLY INTEGRATED PERSPECTIVE ON SOCIETY

The diversity built into the Transformation Management model, represented in the different cultural strengths of the Four Worlds, is reflected at a societal level by the different ideologies, that is capitalism, socialism, what we term 'culturalism' and environmentalism. At an organizational level it is reflected in the private, public, civic and animate sectors. It is through this orientation to the fourfold of the public-private-civic-animate that the organization also contributes to build up of a capitalism-socialism-culturalism-enviromentalism at a society. The integrated fourfold, that results, is the core expression of the identity of the organization, and also of the society.

CONTRIBUTING TO A NEW FORM OF A SUSTAINABLE ECONOMY AND SOCIETY

Ultimately then as we have seen, on a macro level, we are reaching for a newly sustainable form of economy and society. Such an integrated form extends beyond narrow perspectives of capitalism or socialism, including also culturalism (whereby an economy and society builds purposefully on its culture) and environmentalism.

It is here, on a societal level where nature and culture find their rightful place next to science and technology as well as economics and management.

Having reached a new form on a micro and macro level, the GENE-ius of the self, organization and society has been further realized. It is a big step towards freedom, in a sense of freeing our full potential.

2.7 Conclusion: Towards the Integral Enterprise

Engaging deeply in a transformation process for us results in a totally new way of understanding and acting upon our organizations and their interaction within society.

Transformation Management provides the overall architecture. In a step-by-step process we have introduced the four fundamentals in a first overview. All of them will be laid out in full detail in the chapters to come. Figure 2.8 provides a full visual overview on the core model of Transformation Management.

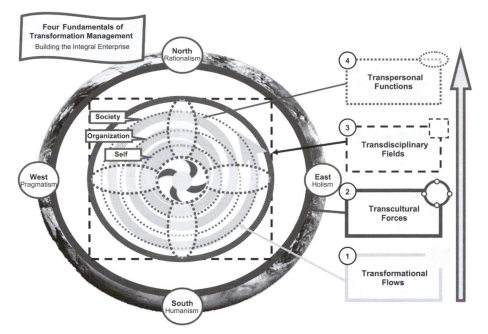

Figure 2.8   The Transformation Management model

The following Tables summarizes the four fundamentals of Transformation Management.

The First Fundamental of Transformation Management	
From Competitive Strategy to Strategic Renewal *via Transformational Flows underlying Nature and Community*	• Transformational Flows are rooted in Nature and Community and engage the Enterprise in its continuous Renewal • The natural transformational Flows transcend the previously mechanical transactional Way of being of the Enterprise • They engage the Organization in a circular fourfold Process of Grounding, Emergence, Navigation and ultimately transformative Effect • They are simultaneously applied to the three Levels of Self, Organization and Society • The transformational Flows continuously stimulate the Enterprise to ground itself in its particular social and cultural Context. Thereby, the Enterprise not only connects with the particular burning Issues of its Context, it also gets in touch with its cultural Grounds and Capacities • Within the Organization, the transformational Flows institutionalize Strategic Renewal, which substitutes for the conventional notion of Competitive Strategy

The Second Fundamental of Transformation Management

From Organizational Development to Cultural Dynamics
via Transcultural Forces underlying Culture and Spirituality

- The transcultural Perspective positions the Enterprise within a Four World Framework, enabling it to build on its particular Set of cultural Capacities
- Thereby a monocultural Perspective is overcome and the Enterprise learns to manage in diverse Worlds
- Further, by creatively activating the particular Strength of the southern, eastern, northern and western Perspective, the transcultural Forces stimulate Innovation in the Organization
- Within the Organization, the transcultural Forces are embodied in a field of Cultural Dynamics, transcending conventional Organizational Development

The Third Fundamental of Transformation Management

From R&D to Social Innovation
via Transdisciplinary Fields underlying Science and Technology

- The transdisciplinary Fields access the local Knowledge Grounds of a particular Enterprise, linking it to global Knowledge Grounds. Further they combine the social Sciences with the Humanities
- Thereby the entire Knowledge Pool, relevant for the Development of the Enterprise is accessed and the previously unidisciplinary Perspective on Management, with its previous Pre-emphasis on Economics, is overcome
- The Expansion of the Enterprise's Knowledge Base and the creative Interaction of different Disciplines strengthen the Enterprise's Capacity to engage in Social Innovation
- Within the Organization, the transdisciplinary Fields are embodied in a revised R&D activity, focusing on bringing about Social Innovation

The Fourth Fundamental of Transformation Management

Transforming the Management Functions
via Transpersonal Functions underlying Economics and Management

- Based on transformational Flows, transcultural Forces and transdisciplinary Fields, the Enterprise is now ready to evolve its own Design towards a higher Level of Integration and Sustainability
- Within the Organization, the four core Functions of the Enterprise (Marketing, Human Resources, Operations and Finance) are gradually transformed into Community Building, Conscious Evolution, Knowledge Creation and Sustainable Development
- In the same Process, the Organization aligns the three Levels of Self, Organization, Society

The Integral Enterprise *Applying the Four Fundamentals of Transformation Management*	
From CSR to Society Building *Arriving at the new Transsectoral Form of the Integral Enterprise*	• Applying the previous Fundamentals has 'trans-FORM-ed' the Organization, which has acquired the Design or new Form of a sustainable and integral Enterprise • By building progressively on Nature and Community, Culture and Spirituality, Science and Technology and Economics and Management underlying the four Fundamentals, the organization has integrated its animate (ecological), civic, public and private forms. It thereby became fully re-integrated in Society • This is the precondition for becoming – on a sustainable basis – an active 'Society Builder'. At this stage, the enterprise has transcended also its conventional approach to CSR (usually an add on in most organizations) into 'Society Building' • It is here, at this final stage, that the Enterprise actively stimulates Transformation of the Macro Level in which it is operating, serving to promote a mix of socialism, capitalism, culturalism and environmentalism

We now turn to the second part of this book and to the first fundamental of Transformation Management. We are starting out in the south, with nature and community and the underlying transformational flows.

References

1. Suzuki, D. (1997). *Sacred Balance*. Vancouver: Greystone Books.
2. Lessem, R. and Schieffer, A. (2010). *Integral Economics*. Farnham: Gower Publishing.

2 *The First Fundamental of Transformation Management*

> **Transforming**
> **Competitive Strategy**
> *into Strategic Renewal*

Core Theme within Transformation Management:
Grounding of the Enterprise
in Nature and Community
by Activating the Underlying Transformational Flows

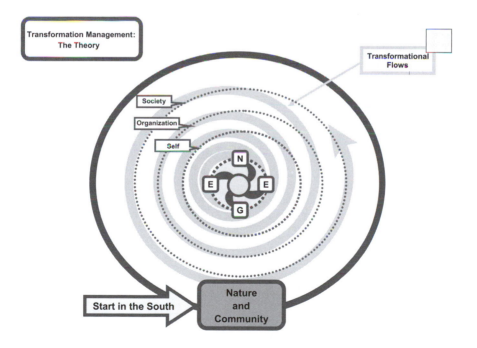

**Transforming
Competitive Strategy
*into Strategic Renewal***

Core Outcome for the Integral Enterprise:
1. **Building a Resilient Organization**
2. **Releasing Natural GENE-ius**
3. **Institutionalizing Strategic Renewal**

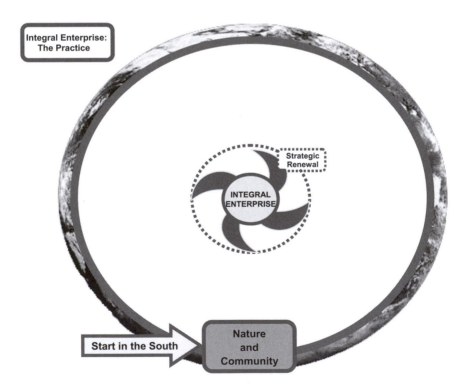

3 *Nature and Transformation*

Releasing GENE-ius

3.1 Introduction: Starting with Nature

We start our transformational journey by learning from nature's transformational principles. Thereby we locate our individual, organizational and societal being in nature. As such our starting point, as per conventional business administration, is not reflected in 'strategic doing', but in 'being vital'. Such natural vitality is not located in market driven GM or GE in the American 'west', but in organizations such as Sekem in Egypt or Broad Air Conditioning in China (see Chapter 16), both strongly rooted in nature. In other words, our 'reason for being' is not a market mechanism but a natural organism, imbued with a flow quality, a continuing interchange between diverse elements. What do we mean by such interchange?

For us, overall, the core stimulus for transformation lies in the 'trans', that is in the creative interaction between one enterprise and another, between one world and another, or between individual, organization, community and society. It is the local in interaction with the global, the indigenous merging with the exogenous, the static engaging with the dynamic, the north with the south, the east with the west. As the stimulus for transformation and thereby also for innovation lies in the trans, we need to understand how to purposefully orchestrate interaction, in both micro and macro terms, between different elements of one living system or between living systems.

Enabling nature – and thereby the existence or 'being' of a living system – to become the starting point of our transformational journey towards the ultimately integrated enterprise, brings us to our first fundamental transformation. It takes us from doing business to being 'life-like', and, as such, from economic strategy to strategic renewal. We thereby follow four core modes of human existence: being, becoming, knowing and doing. These modes are, among others, adapted from the British psychologist John Heron's work on Personhood.[1] As by now you are familiar with the overall structure and process of Transformation Management, we introduce these four modes in a Four World format.

Interestingly enough, the southern ground is exactly in tune with the mode of 'being', the eastern emergent realm with the mode of 'becoming', the northern rational world with the mode of 'knowing', and the western pragmatic world with the mode of 'doing'. These core human modes have been translated on an *organizational* level into the four core conventional functions of an enterprise: from marketing, representing the 'southern' being of the enterprise (its field of existence, its customer base, its markets); to human resources, representing the 'eastern' becoming of the organization (where its personnel is developed); onto operations, embodying the 'northern' knowing of the enterprise (its processes); to, finally, finance, representing the 'western' doing of the organization (where ultimately the transaction takes place). Again, all these functions are vital for an organization to survive and develop, becoming thereby embedded in society.

The vital functioning on a *societal* level is for us, at least from an economic perspective, constituted of markets ('southern' being), labour force ('eastern' becoming), technology ('northern' knowing) and capital ('western' doing). In a more general sense we see these in terms of nature (south), culture (east), politics, science and technology (north) and economics and management (west). Each living system – from self to organization, from community to society, and ultimately from society to world – need not only to attend to itself, but also contribute to the vital functions of the larger living system in which it is embedded. Indeed, it needs to do so, as we shall demonstrate, to ensure its own survival and development. In short, the vitality of one living system is dependent on the vitality of others.

The strategy or intentional direction of a living system needs, therefore, to integrate the vital and interdependent manifestations of self, organization and society, the enterprise thereby being the bridge between individual and community. In this new 'natural' light, the conventional wisdom on organizational strategy needs fundamental transformation, and this is what this and the following two chapters are about.

The first fundamental of Transformation Management offers such a transformed perspective on competitive strategy, which we call *strategic renewal*. Strategy, in this new guise, is a prerequisite for the organization (as well as for self and society) to become sustainable.

In this light, the transformational flows enhance the 'being' of self, organization and society. The transcultural forces, our second fundamental, enhance the 'becoming' of self, organization and society. The transdisciplinary fields, the third fundamental, serve to redefine the knowledge base of the integrated enterprise, and thereby to promote the vital mode of 'knowing', that is of self (knowing), organization (operations) and society (knowledge). Fourth, for us, the transpersonal functions promote the 'doing' (or functioning) of self, organization and society. The transsectoral form of the resulting Integral Enterprise serves to promote the dynamic balance and integration of all four vital modes, from being, becoming, knowing and doing, thereby aligning self, organization and society.

This is the 'omega point', that is the final form of Trans*form*ation Management; as such, it is simultaneously and interactively embodied in nature and community, culture and spirituality, science and technology as well as economics and management. In our own 'theory of the firm', the public and the private, is now integrated with the civic and the animate (environmental).

The transformation of the conventional perspective on strategy is, hence, key. Strategic Renewal then is at the very centre of the process. From here, from the centre, the process of transformation starts, and it is the integrative power of a strategy transformed into strategic renewal that enables us, from thereon, to gradually build the Integral Enterprise.

Altogether, then, this requires us to adopt a fundamentally new perspective on the enterprise and its interaction with self and society (including community). We shall introduce such a new perspective, based on nature's principles, within this chapter. We are starting by retracing steps and acknowledging the conventional understanding of strategy, and thereafter establishing the underlying, natural principles of transformation. Afterwards we return to strategy in the following chapter.

3.2 Origins of Strategy

TRACING THE ROOTS OF STRATEGY

The term *strategy* has its roots in the Greek word 'strategia', meaning 'office or command of a general'. It links the word for army or expedition (*stratos*) with the word for leader (*agos*). The 'army' represents a highly structured governing or political body, which in our approach is represented by the archetypal north. Agos is the etymological root for 'acting', which, in our Four World terms, is represented by the west. Hence, one could argue, that strategy is basically a northwestern term.

FROM A NORTHWESTERN STATIC PERSPECTIVE ON STRATEGY TO AN UNDERSTANDING OF THE ORGANIZATION AS A LIVING SYSTEM

Traditionally managed firms saw themselves as finely calibrated machines: efficient, logically organized, numbers-driven, separate from nature and society, which are treated as externalities, focused on the bottom line, and driven by a small team of executives who set the strategy for the entire organization. Their cultures, management and accounting systems place a high value on nonliving, capital assets.

Contemporary knowledge on the functioning of living systems, in particular of organizations, however, emerges increasingly from disciplines such as ecology, biology, (individual and organizational) psychology, cultural and environmental studies. Together, they have gone far beyond the conventional 'machine metaphor' of an organization.

The emergent private (business), as well as public and civic, and, in particular, the 'animate' enterprise sees itself increasingly as an organic, living system, a community of people with diverse skills, closely integrated with nature and society, focused on serving life. As such living assets are the means whereby nonliving assets are created.

That corresponds with the transformational topography we introduce in Chapter 6. In it we find nature, together with culture at the core of a social system (see Figure 6.1). In that chapter we will demonstrate, that if a social system fails to integrate this deepest layer, it is not sustainable.

Therefore, as a next step, we shall engage with nature, and thereby evolve the multifaceted flow of organically based strategic renewal that transcends mechanically based, competitive strategy.

3.3 Strategy to Ecology

THE ECOLOGY OF TRANSFORMATION

'To shake a tree is to shake the earth', is an ancient East African saying, vividly evoking an image of nature as an interconnected whole where dividing lines and boundaries are amorphous and permeable. So, for that matter, where does a leaf begin? And where does it end? Likewise, what are the boundary edges of a lake or a sea? When systems are seen from the ecological perspective, clear-cut demarcations and boundaries just stop making sense. If a leaf, for instance, ended at what we traditionally perceive to be its contour, it would die instantaneously. And so would the entire ecosystem. The so-called edges of leaves are, in fact, highly amorphous linkages with the environment and the sun. What every schoolchild learns to define as photosynthesis is basically a scientific description of the leaf's relationship with the sun.

And ours too, for every time we breathe in a lung full of oxygen that keeps us alive, we are breathing in the relationship of leaf and sun. Where do we end then? Certainly not at the contours of our body. Our skins too are highly porous linkages to the outside, without which we would not survive. What digests the meal you have just had is not 'your' digestive system, but a highly sophisticated alliance between your body and millions of microbes that live in your intestines.

Nothing in nature can be demarcated into individual entities. So for instance soil sustains life on earth and nutrients are recycled back into the soil with the help of certain bacteria. But where does the soil itself come from? In the old biology, it was taken as a given, something that exists as the environment. What we now know is that the soil is continually being created by the plant and animal life that lives off the soil. We know that carbon dioxide is pumped down by life on the surface after dissolution in water near the rock surface. The water may have come from rainwater or fed by nearby spring and rivers. This solution now causes rocks to weather. The microorganisms aid this process and more soil gets created. Without life there would be no soil, but only regolith, the rock rubble of dead planets.

What the new ecology teaches us is that *the very emergence and the maintenance of life is itself an ongoing transformative process.* Moreover, this is achieved by life being in a state of continual change itself, not opposing the forces of the environment, but flowing with them. *Life and the environment are partners in co-creation.* To take another example of this co-creative aspect, aquatic blades of grass reduce stream velocity, thereby forcing the waters to drop their silt load and the decaying plant material they carry along. Both these effects increase channel deposition, which creates more soil and nutrients for plant roots. Plants grow stronger, denser. This reduces velocity further, creating more deposition. Deposition displaces water. The stream overflows and spreads out, greatly expanding its surface area as it flows over. The water's energy drops drastically. Nourishing water and silt are spread over a broad channel, nourishing more lush growth. This growth creates greater accumulations of spongy, absorbent, plant material, spreading the slowing water even wider.

The interaction between natural energy and life's energy is the chief principle of co-creation. The interaction is often so subtle, so insignificant that we don't even see it. Each small shift in equilibrium creates another small shift. Each new equilibrium covers the tracks of the previous change. *The power lies in the accumulative consistency with which these changes shift equilibrium in life's favour. Life creates conditions for more life, which in turn create conditions for more life. These loops create change, not stability. By shaping the development of its environment, life allows itself to be shaped by the environment. Co-creation provides us with a very viable, long-lasting, sensible and sustainable model of transformation.* It is equally applicable to organizations and societies.

While life emerges out of its local environment, the environment needs to be continually transformed by global life so that it remains life-supportive. This is the essence of the process of transformation in which first, the individual unit of survival is simultaneously a unit of transformation, and second, the transformation process is the engagement of the individual unit with other units thereby creating new, intelligent forms without losing the essence of the original.

THE FOUR WORLDS OF TRANSFORMATION IN NATURE

The purpose of transformation through a co-creative process is to sustain a future in which resources become available to as wide a base as possible, and diverse units of local life work with a common global principle to sustain life as a whole. We begin, as such in the south, then move east, then to north and end up in the west. In doing so we traverse the journey of humankind, which by now you will have seen is our overarching transformative principle.

How does this principle work its way? To answer that, we apply the Four World rhythm. In doing so, we describe *four sub-processes that are crucial for transformation in natural systems*: from the formative to the reformative, on to the normative and, ultimately, the transformative.

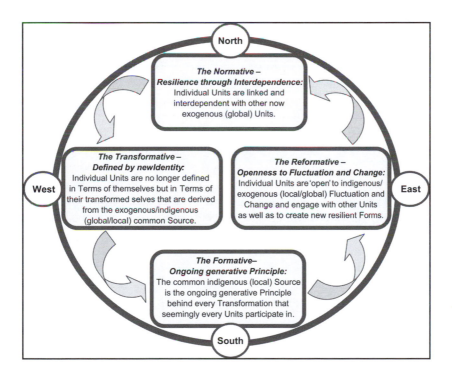

Figure 3.1   Crucial sub-processes for transformation in natural systems

Together these four processes provide the basis for an ongoing transformation process. Clearly, if we are looking for a model of transformation, we need look no further than the system of our natural environment that has successfully survived and flourished for millennia. As we saw earlier, nature engages in a continuous transformative process that seeks to sustain life. Interestingly enough Peter Senge, in his latest book on *The Necessary Revolution,* strongly reinforces this natural orientation:

> *We need to ask, what would a way of thinking, a way of living, and ultimately an economic system look like that worked based on the principles of the larger natural world And how do we create such a way of living in our organizations and societies, step by step.*[2]

We now explain how, for us, the natural process works.

STARTING IN THE FORMATIVE SOUTH: THE ONGOING GENERATIVE PRINCIPLE

The rule of the common source is the same one that enables the transformation of a chrysalis into a butterfly. The caterpillar's organs and tissues dissolve into an amorphous soup-like state only to reconstitute into the structure of a butterfly's body that bears absolutely no resemblance to the caterpillar at all. The chemical complexity of turning into a butterfly is incredible and science still has no explanation for why this metamorphosis has evolved. But there is a clear picture emerging of how the process works. The two hormones that regulate the process ensure that the cells moving from larva to butterfly know how they are going to change. Some cells know when to die, others digest themselves, some turn into eyes, some into wings. The whole process of transformation requires a very delicate and precise rhythm between creation and destruction. The transformation of a chrysalis into a butterfly is linked to its source in the rhythm of the cosmos. In the same way, the prolactin that generates milk in a mother's breast is unchanged from the prolactin that sends salmon upstream to breed, enabling them to cross from saltwater to fresh. The insulin in a cow is the same as the insulin in an amoeba; both serve to metabolise carbohydrates.

How does each cell 'know' how to remain linked to the generative principle of the common source? The answer is simple: the universality of a cell or for that matter, any other unit, is contingent upon it being fully itself. What that means is that in the act of truly being yourself, you are at once universal.

Therefore, the role of organizations and societies is to participate in continuously creating and sustaining a common future in which resources and benefits transcend the Four Worlds of the organization or society and encompass as wide an area as possible. The only way this can be done is when the society is simultaneously rooted in itself while engaging with other societies and the larger environment to bifurcate into other forms. So on the one hand business would naturally depend on society and its external environment for its growth and for resources, but on the other hand, it would participate in transforming its environment so that it is sustainable and conducive to doing business. This it can do only by engaging with other units of transformation.

Life is innately intelligent. White cells make intelligent decisions by being able to differentiate between invading enemy bacteria and harmless pollen. As we saw in the previous section, cells participate in the welfare of the whole without the slightest hesitation; if necessary they die to protect the body. Cells keep in touch with every other cell, adapting from moment to moment. They recognize each other as equally important and stay engaged in a continuous interplay of co-dependence.

MOVING TO THE REFORMATIVE EAST: OPENNESS TO FLUCTUATION AND CHANGE

Another example of nature's ongoing transformative process is building resilience through diversity. David Suzuki, the renowned Canadian ecologist writing in *Sacred Balance*[3] refers to the quaking aspen, the white-barked trees as an example of how nature operates as a system. Shoots may grow up from a root more than fifty feet away. So the aspen is really a super organism, a system that is made up of a network of interconnections. But for the system to remain healthy and thrive and grow, it has to have a diverse landscape. So some parts may grow in moist soil, and through their common underground roots, share the water with other portions, perhaps growing in mineral-rich soil higher up.

What Suzuki is saying is that if at each level of complexity – cell, organism and ecosystem – new kinds of structures and functions emerge, the totality of all life on the planet can be taken as a single entity too. But this totality of life, the convergence of all living and non-living matter into a single system is necessarily dependent on all the divergences that make the system possible. As Nobel laureate Roger Sperry[4] points out, new properties that arise from complexes cannot be predicted from the known properties of their individual parts. These emergent properties only exist within the whole. No single species is indispensable, but the sum-total of all life maintains the fecundity of the earth.

How does life then achieve its extraordinary resilience? The answer is *genetic polymorphism*. When a species such as the Siberian tiger is reduced to a few survivors, its long-term future is under threat because the range of its genetic variability has been radically diminished and therefore has fewer options to adapt to changes in the environment. Suzuki goes on to emphasize how a diverse mixture of gene variants is a fundamental characteristic of a vibrant, healthy species, a reflection of its successful evolutionary history and continued potential to adapt to unpredictable change. Population geneticists believe that *the most successful species are found in places that are connected 'by bridges' to the outside.* Thus each isolated community can evolve a set of genes adapted to its local habitat, while the migrants become a means of introducing 'new blood' – different genes with a new potential to respond to change.

This is precisely the grave danger that monoculture, in nature and in culture, presents to the world. Diminishing varieties of crops and widespread use of a single, selected strain of crop automatically makes a species vulnerable. In 1970, approximately 80 per cent of the 26.8 million hectares planted in corn in the USA carried a special genetic factor that was carefully positioned by the seed companies for higher productivity and profit. But that very trait rendered the species vulnerable to a specific parasite. Within three months, virtually all fields were affected and wiped out. *Monoculture, physically and also for us in terms of humanity, is the enemy of life's evolutionary strategy.*

Suzuki goes on to talk about the assortment of climatic and geo-physical conditions on the earth 'from the searing heat of deserts to the frigid cold of permafrost above the Arctic circle, from steamy equatorial river systems to dry grasslands, from the depths of the oceans to the soaring heights of rarefied mountain kilometres above sea level and to the inter-tidal junction between air, land, and sea'. Life flourishes in all these conditions.

Even where species diversity is limited, the genetic variation within a species in one watershed will differ from that within the same species in another. *Every ecosystem is special because it is simultaneously local and global.*

THE NORMATIVE NORTH: RESILIENCE THROUGH INTERDEPENDENCE

Elisabet Sahtouris,[5] contemporary biologist and thinker, writes about the enormous crisis we face because the most central and important aspect of globalization, its economy, is currently being organized in a manner that violates the fundamental principles by which healthy living systems are organized. She writes about natural principles that operate in our bodies and in our families. We intuitively and collectively grasp such principles without any problem. So not many people starve three of their children to over-feed the fourth, or beautify one corner of the garden by destroying the rest of it. But strangely we begin to lose sight of those principles at the level of our local communities, towns or nations.

And globalization of humanity definitely does not conform to the principles of living systems in that it flouts a critical principle of cooperation. A relatively small part of humanity is involved in decisions and has the power to serve its own interests, often at the expense of other parts. From a living systems perspective, if we treat globalization as a process that is happening to a natural living system we call humanity, then we can see how economies that violate the fundamental principles by which living systems are organized, threaten the demise of human civilization. Biological research of the last few decades, on the evolution of nucleated cells, multi-cellular organisms and mature ecosystems as cooperative enterprises, is updating our ingrained view of antagonistic competition as the sole driving force of evolution. As George Soros says, 'there is something wrong with making the survival of the fittest a guiding principle of civilised society. This social Darwinism is based on an outmoded theory of evolution'.[6]

Once the polymorphic process has taken place, life settles into its new form, assured in its resilience.

HEADING TO THE TRANSFORMATIVE WEST: TRANSFORMED INTO A NEW IDENTITY

Each species formed this way becomes part of the transformed ecosystem that thrives because of the simultaneity of individual and universal forces embodied in it. At each level of complexity – cell, organism and ecosystem – new kinds of structures and functions emerge. The totality of life on our planet can be taken to be a single, resilient entity that has remained sustainable for so long because it is inherently transformative. Suzuki refers to the single envelope of atmosphere that encircles the earth, while water flows around the continents, creating great islands. The entire conglomerate of living things makes a wonderfully complex, interconnected community held together by the matrix of air and water. The entire layer of protoplasm (the living material within cells) on the globe is intermeshed into a living, breathing entity, which has survived through an immensity of time and space. All the living things, in their transformation, persist on their own, healing, replacing, adapting and reproducing in order to continue.

Ecosystems are highly resilient systems because their identities are not derived out of themselves but out of its relationships with its environment. So a corn stalk may be autonomous but its autonomy is derived from the fact that it is interdependent with its environment. That is the reason why the ecosystem is described as an autopoietic (from the Greek, meaning 'self-production') structure, based on the work of Maturana and Varela in the seventies.[7] The Chilean scientists compared autopoietic systems to allopoietic systems. So a car is the latter, as it contains the same molecules from showroom to junkyard. Its identity is given by the manufacturer and nothing changes. By contrast, autopoietic structures in life change molecules all the time and yet, somehow remain the same. So what exactly is this self-contained identity? That is precisely the relationality with the environment.

So on the one hand, transformation is effectively realized in the individual species and sub-parts that thrive through their separate identities. But paradoxically enough, what makes them and the whole ecosystem sustainable is the fact that they are inextricably part of a pattern of relationships. The overall process of transformation can be summarized in Figure 3.2.

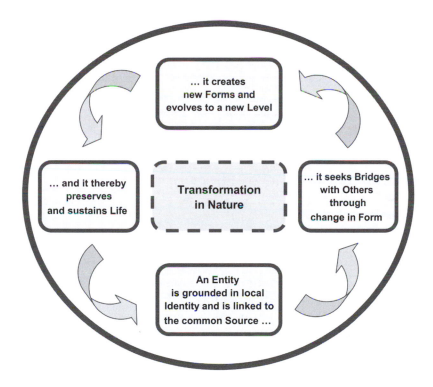

Figure 3.2   Transformation in nature

As mentioned earlier, perhaps the most beautiful illustration of the transformational process in nature is that of the caterpillar turning into a butterfly. The caterpillar's original form (its 'local identity') has to be de-formed and reformed in the chrysalis stage, before, through a course designed or normed by nature, it is ultimately transformed in a butterfly (Figure 3.3).

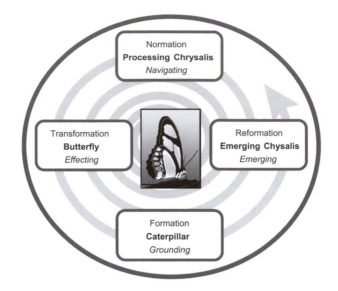

Figure 3.3   Transformation in nature – from caterpillar to butterfly

We now turn from such a transformational flow, rooted in nature, to our own interpretation of such, embedded in our GENE. To illustrate the proximity of both rhythms, formative to transformative and our GENE, we will incorporate the GENE (grounding, emerging, navigating, effecting) terminology to be shown later in Figure 3.4.

3.4 The GENE: Grounding to Effect

3.4.1 OVERVIEW OF THE GENE

Through our own ongoing research and development over the past decade, we have evolved a transformational pattern, which we have called the GENE of transformation. This flow embodies the above-mentioned premises and is applied in various forms, always connecting local and individual identity with what we term 'global integrity' as an integrative process. It is in that context that we talk about releasing the transformative GENE-ius of the self, the organization and the society. The GENE is the nucleus of transformational processes based on the Four World approach. Its four core stages are southern grounding, eastern emergence, northern navigation and western effecting.

From GENE to GENE-I-U-S

The GENE is set in motion by an inner spark, an initiation of an individual or a community, who either experience an internal impulse for growth, change or transformation which is calling for internal integration, or an outer impulse for such, which is caused by addressing an outer issue. In any case, it is this initial tension between the I (Individual) and the Other – which we call here the 'U' (You) – that initiates the transformation process, and which, by working its way through the four stages helps to release the full GENE-I-U-S of the living system, whereby the 'S' synthesizes or synergizes the I and the U.

After the stage of grounding, something has to give, create the impetus for transformation and that impulse has to come from the outside. This is the dynamic process that follows the static grounding stage. As such there is dissolution of the old, for without an opening out to change through the influence of an external agency, there is simply no transformational flow. The axis needs to spin out of its original moorings in order for the transformation to emerge as a process.

After the first two G-E stages of grounding and emerging, the process now has to evolve to a stage where it forms itself as a navigating entity. Without this process of explicit articulation the transformation process remains incomplete. Finally, the fourth strand is about the process effecting itself through an integration of the previous three stages, manifesting concretely in the physical world. Like a hologram, it embodies the three other stages within itself. Moreover, the four stages are each alternatively static and dynamic, one following the other in a rhythmic orientation. We now follow each in turn.

3.4.2 THE TRANSFORMATIONAL GENE

Southern grounding: promoting identity

The ultimate goal of transformation is to evolve local identity – for your self, organization and society – towards global integrity. Along the way, you reach into the grounds of your being, and that of your organization or society.

For example, Wasfi Atoum, a public relations manager for a large Jordanian industrial company, was deeply affected in his childhood and youth by the injustices perpetrated in his local town by narrowly based tribalism. When he joined our Masters Programme on Transformation Management, he set out to turn his role and his company from ones built around strong personalities and clannish groups, towards a veritable knowledge creating organization (including self and community), albeit building upon the Islamic values that were such a strong part of their shared heritage.

There are a number of dimensions to how we understand such value grounds:

- Value provides the ground and the purpose, the *raison d'être* for everything that is produced or offered, building on everyday social reality.
- Value gives a sense of purpose to structures, systems and processes.
- Value is the creation of meaning in an institution for those within and without.
- Value builds and preserves the organizational and community culture through consensus.
- At their best, value based organizations are visionary work places, characterized by a powerful contribution to society.

In fact, all the cases we are citing in this book are strongly value-laden organizations – whether it is the value of life itself at Grameen, mother earth at Sekem, alleviating global imbalances at Canon, or freedom of expression at Linux.

Local identity is rooted or grounded in the being or 'life-world' of a local people. Such an indigenous world is lodged in nature and culture, formatively and experientially. We refer to this grounded world as southern though it is to be found all over the world, because of its deep roots in mankind's place of origin, where nature and culture continue to exercise a major influence. Such represents the very grounds of our being.

Eastern emergence: towards a non-entity

Well-grounded, traditional leaders, enterprises and communities, while strongly rooted in cultural meaning, have a static quality to them. When confronted with modernizing forces, they tend to become either corrupted or subordinated. Rather than drawing upon the GENE they invariably get caught up in the 'wild west'. As we loosen our socialized grip on our longstanding value grounds, or indigenous source, we need to open up to what is emerging around us, and thereby undo the past, with a view to creating a future out of it. A good model to follow, metaphorically, is that of the caterpillar, which, in emerging from an initial egg into a beautiful butterfly, dissolves into a pupa along the way. Further, 'emergence' can be described as follows:

- Emergence stimulates the transformative journey, in which structures and systems develop and evolve cross-catalytically. It involves processes of destruction and creation, and an intermittent and discontinuous, but *flowing wholeness,* lodged within an interconnected, unbounded field.
- The emergent, *far-from-equilibrium* developments give rise to a new *dynamic balance,* weaving together, past and future, indigenous and exogenous, one world and another; destroying static concepts of structures and systems, leading to a new order.
- Such emergent processes are therefore *destabilizing;* they creatively 'undo' the rigid structures of the 'west' and orderly systems of the 'north', so that the momentum built reworks the prior aims and concepts established.
- What emerges is not merely what happens between structures and systems; on the contrary, processes work around and through structures, making them *porous and permeable,* continually open to new possibilities.
- Without such conscious evolution, the organization remains disconnected and abstract; processes *undo* predetermined notions of order and procedure.
- At their best, process-driven, emergent leaders, organizations, and societies, are dynamic, highly *innovative* work places; at their worst totally unpredictable, and lurching from one state to another.

Becoming what we term a local-global 'non-entity' is a necessary aspect of transformation whereby you enter into that no-man's land between the familiar (self) and the other, the indigenous and the exogenous. In that emergent world of loss of identity, of letting go of the old with a view to becoming the new, the power of imagination becomes all-important. Such an aesthetic sensitivity in the process of knowledge creation is necessary to make the strange global 'other' familiar and the familiar local 'self' strange. This is the time for the local to interact with the global. This is the time where different horizons are fused, expressed, for example, when Japanese spirit met up with global technique, and up sprang Toyota.

This is the point where the indigenous meets up with the exogenous, the tacit with the explicit, and the subject with the object, with a view to dissolving the old subject-object divide and creating a new union in between them. This is the chrysalis stage, where the old caterpillar has dissolved and the new butterfly is waiting to be born. We identify such a perspective with the 'east' because of its deep, philosophical and aesthetic engagement with so-called non-being and non-duality. It also reminds us of the Japanese principle of no-thing (*mu*), out of which, for Sony's co-founder, the late Akio Morita, everything can emerge.

Northern navigation: building an entity

Northern consolidation, combination, or conceptualization involves the establishment of new sets of propositions, evoked out of the prior 'eastern' world of the imagination:

- Profound theories lead you to conceive of your organization or community as a *complex system or network* rather than a simple structure, with interconnected patterns and relationships.
- Systems enhance the notion of order by connecting individual points into linear and *cross-linear relationships;* such systematic linkages serve to enhance predictability, order and control.
- Without such systems, structures remain disconnected and lacking in coherence; *systems give direction* to both structure and imagination.
- Such systems and frameworks use *rational analysis* in which the particular follows logically from the general; problems are tackled through attempts at realizing consensus.
- At their best, systematically undertaken *strategic projects are ethical*, serving to 'do right', with a collective benefit to all; at their worst they are alienating and bureaucratic.

As we re-emerge (east) out of our value grounds (south) in order to conceptualize ourselves anew, different kinds of institutional frameworks are designed. However, they are yet to be internalized.

The purposeful navigation of the newborn self, organization or society that we are seeking to establish, represents the *knowing* consolidation of the prior process of becoming. As such the fully-fledged new concept, as an organization or system, product or entity, is established out of the prior fusion of horizons. In fact, the success of the 'northwest' in business, in Europe and America, is born out of just such a 'global' fusion. This has recently been the case for Japan, as a fusion of eastern and western horizons, and perhaps also now may become so for China.

In all these cases, there is a genuine combination between being and becoming of different cultures and societies, though it is only in the case of Japanese business, that this has been made explicit. In fact, the Japanese 'knowledge creating company' (see Chapter 14) – explicitly builds in such an 'east-west' linkage. Conversely, in many a developing society, one local identity dominates or distorts the other, rather than serving to establish a genuinely transnational entity. We finally turn west.

Western effect: achieving integrity

In order to realize 'western' efficiency and effectiveness certain steps are necessary:

- Structure building requires us to perceive any strategy as an *assembly of parts*, like in a machine. It further requires making use of inductive logic, to building up your strategy.
- The structural world is highly differential – categories are created instinctively inside the structure giving a preliminary *sense of order* to the strategic activity.
- Clearly laid-out categories, including a *clear set of aims*, making focus easy, coupled with an easy internalization of knowledge.
- Structures are built on *convergent logic*: for every problem, there is one solution; every cause one effect; there is one way to do a particular thing well, thereby adding value.
- At their best, clearly structured activities lend themselves to effective *problem solving*, with clearly defined sections to each, neatly delegated functions, supervision and monitoring of all required tasks; at their worst the bottom line dominates over all else.

Such 'western' excellence or effectiveness involves purposefully incorporating all three other worlds into your own. Ideally, this would mean standing at the centre of all Four Worlds. Such a practical and empirically based realization of worldliness makes for 'global integrity'. In addition, we need to recognize that:

- Each world is incomplete and imbalanced in itself and needs the other three to become fully operational.
- Each of the Four Worlds has its underdeveloped or dysfunctional manifestation, and its developed, or functional, one.
- Global Integrity in one world is potentially a condition reached when one world is able to engage with the other three worlds and with its own depths.

Understanding the conceptual framework of the GENE is an important first step in transforming the conventional approach to organizational strategy into self, organizational and communal renewal. Equally important is to understand how the GENE can be institutionalized in the enterprise in order to engage the organization in flows of continuous renewal. For that, we first describe two practical applications of the GENE before we turn to the transformational ecosystem.

3.4.3 THE TRANSFORMATIONAL GENE IN PRACTICE

Applying the GENE to bring about strategic renewal

In our work with clients or in educational programmes such as our Masters Programme participants continuously apply the GENE in order to bring about transformation in the organizations or communities in which they are lodged. Figure 3.4 gives an overview on the kind of questions that need to be reflected on each stage of the GENE.

We now guide you, by way of short examples, through the GENE-cycle of two transformation agents, both bringing about strategic renewal in their organizations. The first is Wasfi Atoom from Jordan.

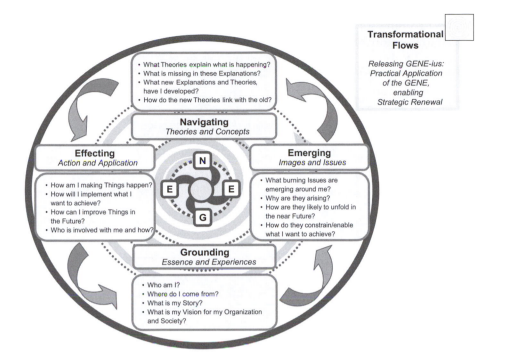

Figure 3.4   Applying the GENE

Case: Wasfi Atoom and the King Abdullah II Design and Development Bureau

GROUNDING OF THE PERSON IN LOCAL JORDANIAN SOILS

Wasfi Atoom through his journey of personal development prior to the Masters' Programme was challenged with traditional values in his tribal society that led to a misconception of Islamic principles. This was later the barrier in front of his efforts to study in western countries. Despite many attempts to create a new reality during his childhood toward liberalization, and despite the fact that the challenge was greater than him, including the fact that the head of the tribe was his father, he achieved some success through establishing, for example, a youth club among other changes. Subsequent to many other challenges in his life, when he approached his 38th year, and having become involved in management in KADDB (King Abdullah II Design and Development Bureau), he started his transformational journey with the University of Buckingham and TRANS4M in which he overcame many challenges to create a new reality. Doing this journey he was engaged in linking culture, religion, tribe, heritage, nature, people and himself, into a local identity aiming towards a global integrity.

EMERGING RESEARCH QUESTION AND BURNING ISSUE

Based on his Arabian Islamic background, Wasfi discovered that the core issue to be resolved lies in Islam or more accurately, the tone and the need to reform the Islamic thought process and interpretation of Qu'ran. Therefore he built this imaginal or ideal perspective upon the contemporary Islamic philosopher Iqbal: 'have a heart like Jesus, thoughts like Socrates, and a hand like the hand of a Caesar, but all in one human being'.

Wasfi relates this philosophy to the Qu'ranic verses that serve to enhance equity among people and to introduce how much the Qu'ran respects human relations: which is contrary to much of the extremist Islamic ideologies presently espoused.

NAVIGATION – FINDING A SUITABLE KNOWLEDGE BASE
Wasfi has built his theoretical guidance on the Four Worlds' transformational approach to exogenous ideas, which starts from the knowledge creating society, in which he developed a knowledge spiral that describes the interaction between indigenous and exogenous knowledge in four modes which come together as a new business wisdom: 'think local – act global'. This approach is contrary to the conventional mantra which considered 'best practice' and which involves a process of 'thinking global, acting global'.

EFFECT – ORGANIZATIONAL RENEWAL AT KADBB
After Emergence and Navigation Wasfi integrated the indigenous Islamic knowledge with the exogenous to produce one model based on the core values in Islam alongside the Four Worlds exogenous approach, involving faith, mysticism, diversity, integrity and he implemented such to transcend the traditional thoughts on science and modern technology, to create a new reality built on rapid local and global changes to serve the future generations. The implementation of this model is being carried out in his organization KADDB and through its Joint Ventures (JVs). The result is reflected in greatly enhanced creativity in the organization and encouragement to act, now, at the national level. KADDB has also taken its part in establishing a Jordanian knowledge creating society through building enabling entities to give innovators in Jordan opportunity to utilize their ideas to serve their community and society. An example is that of the N–CAIR innovation centre.

Case: Yehya Khaled Shehadeh and the Royal Society for the Conservation of Nature

GROUNDING
Yehya's transformation project has evolved out of the great challenge, which Yehya is facing as the recently appointed Acting Director General of the Royal Society for the Conservation of Nature (RSCN). RSCN is a non-government organization dedicated to biodiversity conservation and to integrating the conservation programme with economic development while seeking more public support for RSCN's mission. Now Yehya occupies the most senior management position in this large and well-respected institution. He is required to maintain RSCN's effectiveness and prove that the existing institutional capacity can successfully accommodate the change of leadership.

EMERGING RESEARCH QUESTION
In preparing himself for this challenge, Yehya examined some of the key experiences in his private and working life that have helped to shape his current perspectives on institutional management. Yehya remembered his childhood, growing up as a Palestinian refugee, with all the feelings of repression by politically motivated forces and the need to escape his 'destiny' through education; and he examined his earlier experiences of working for RSCN and how, as a newly appointed field researcher, he saw for the first time the potential conflicts between protecting nature and maintaining the livelihoods of poor Bedouin herders. He also reflected on his participation in the RSCN's major capacity

building programme that had been based largely on western approaches and saw a need to begin integrating some of the values of his home culture; the same culture that was sustaining the Bedouin herders and the Palestinian community to which he belongs. And finally he contemplated the issue of poverty and repression in a global context, noting its enormous impact on ecosystem integrity and how this can only be dealt with by involving civil society to a greater extent in the work of conservation organizations. Out of this process of reflection and contemplation, Yehya's desire to improve and sustain the institutional development of RSCN was always in his mind with an emerging view as to how this would be achieved in this journey.

NAVIGATION – BUILDING A RELEVANT KNOWLEDGE AND THEORY BASE

To help Yehya to find the right approach to implementing these objectives, he looked at the basic definitions of civil societies and studied how civil society based organizations had developed in Islamic and Arabic cultures; and he related their development to institutional development theories from the east and the west. It became clear that his traditional Arabic tribal systems have been highly modified and subsumed under European occupations and American influences and that, even today, both civil and government institutions in the Arab world often have a modernist, largely western face, hiding a disrupted sub-culture based on the old patriarchal, nepotistic tribal systems. However, during the study, he rediscovered the Islamic concept of 'Taqwa', a value system based on individual responsibility, and he recognized its potential as a force for supporting the development of RSCN. Yehya concluded that 'Taqwa' could be merged into Lessem and Schieffer's 'Four Folding Institution' model to create a 'Five Folding Institution' model, with 'Taqwa' (the sense of responsibility) at its core, representing a merging of western and Islamic thinking appropriate to the current institutional stage of RSCN and to the Jordanian society at large.

EFFECT – RENEWAL WITHIN RSCN

Working with the RSCN's senior and middle managers, workshops and meetings were held to explain and discuss all aspects of the 'Five Folding Institution' as a basis for RSCN's transformation programme. By introducing the project theories to the team, they were able to see the obvious applications to their own work situation, and they were able to see the benefits of 'management by values' approach to the long-term success of RSCN.

Through the process, the team participated actively in developing innovative ways to express RSCN's core values. They also contributed to translating these values into the yearly staff appraisal. Yehya stressed, that despite the short life of the project, its impact is already clear in the following initiatives:

- RSCN staff have shared the 'Taqwa' concept and are looking into ways of incorporating it in their management approaches.
- RSCN has launched its first advocacy committee to gain more public support for its activities. So far it has run two campaigns against government proposals to use natural resources in unsustainable ways and has managed to mobilize public opinion against these two proposals.
- RSCN has been furthering its cooperation with the private sector, using their experience to develop and update its financial policies and procedures. The new systems will provide professional operational performance services to RSCN.

- RSCN has been a key player in promoting the Fair Trade movement in Jordan as a means of providing a more equitable sharing of benefits for small producers, in the context of environmental safeguards. In this way, it is reaching out to a wider cross section of civil society.

In October 2006, months after having completed his Masters Programme on Transformation Management with us, Yehya wrote the following note to the Masters group:

> *I am pleased to inform you that RSCN has won the prestigious 2006 Green Apple Environment Award in recognition of its environmental good practice in conducting the 'Save Jordan's Trees' Advocacy Campaign. I want to remind you that this campaign and the establishment of the advocacy committee was a main component of one of my projects for the transformation programme. I also would like to inform you that the award will be presented to the RSCN at London at the House of Commons on Monday 20 November 2006. The annual Green Apple Environment Awards reward and promote environmental best practice around the world. Congratulations to all of us!*

With Wasfi and Yehya we presented two successful cases of GENE application that led to Strategic Renewal within their respective organizations. However, it is important to create the necessary supporting conditions within the organization in order for transformation to happen. That brings us to the transformational ecosystem.

3.5 Institutionalizing Strategic Renewal through the Transformational Ecosystem

The GENE, as the life flow for ongoing renewal or re-gene-ration of a living system can equally be regarded as a process of organizational knowledge creation. Indeed the four process steps of the GENE (grounding, emerging, navigating, effecting) resonate remarkably with the knowledge creating spiral of Japan's 'eastern' organizational sociologists Nonaka and Takeuchi (socializing, externalizing, combining, externalizing). This spiral is introduced in their renowned work on *The Knowledge Creating Company*,[8] promoting the 'hypertext organization' as a new organizational model.

We are linking our work with that of Nonaka and Takeuchi, when we introduce the transformational ecosystem. In our work with organizational transformation we have learned that most strategic initiatives fall short because of the lack of such ecosystems. We then experimented within organizations by identifying 'embodiments' (individuals or groups) for the various elements of the GENE, who then would – each in their own capacity – co-creatively support the transformational process. The four types we identified are the steward (supporting the grounding phase), the catalyst (emerging), the educator (navigating) and the facilitator (enabling the ultimate realization of the project). We established such a cast of characters as an 'ecosystem', set in the context of our educational and developmental activities, enabling a strategic initiative to flourish.

How then does such an ecosystem work? Knowledge creation, in this ecosystemic sense, is an ongoing process of transformation, brought forward by an individual or a group within the organization. If a senior member of the organization then decides to support such, s/he becomes the steward of this initiative. An ecosystem is formed to enable the initiative to go the full transformational circle. In each of the four cases from grounding to effecting it can be an individual or a group within the organization. Further, not in all cases does each role need to be related to a particular person, as the initiating individual or group may already sufficiently embody one or two of the qualities required by each character within the ecosystem. Figure 3.5 illustrates the transformational ecosystem.

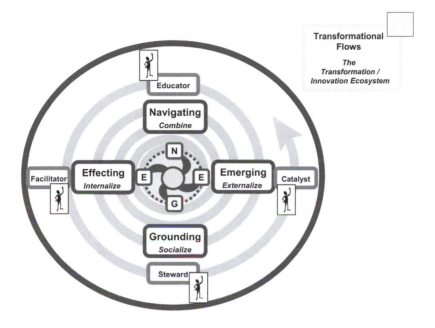

Figure 3.5   Transformation/innovation ecosystem

In the following we briefly outline the nature and scope of each character.

3.5.1 THE SOUTHERN STEWARD

Grounding is first promoted by 'southern' stewardship, normally involving a senior politician, community leader or business executive:

* whose role it is to ensure that the transformation will be rooted in the culture and nature of the individual, organization and society;
* thereby being well socialized or grounded within each, nature and culture of a particular context. Furthermore, they need to be both politically and communally acceptable and also inspirational to those affected by the proposed strategic project at hand.

Role of the Steward
• Is actively engaged in thinking about the Future, while being simultaneously rooted in his or her cultural Past, with a View to transforming his or her Enterprise-in-Society • Leans towards social Innovation • Normally has a strong Involvement with Community based or political Enterprises • Is a leading edge Practitioner in his/her field, and will ideally have a Track Record in organizational and Community Development • An All Rounder as opposed to a narrowly based Specialist

3.5.2 THE EASTERN CATALYST

Emergence is, second, the realm of 'eastern' catalysation, the role, for example, of a developmental consultant:

• whose task it is to subsequently enable the initiating individual or group to access its own imaginal realm through culture (art, religion, etc.);
• thereby helping the individual or the group to externalize knowledge, that is to make implicit knowledge within their organization explicit.

Role of the Catalyst
• Instead of well laid Course Curricula and ready-to-work Action Plans, s/he focuses on emerging, ever changing, intertwined Agendas of individual and strategic Issues, located within a Field of Possibilities • Uses Instability and Crisis to provoke continual individual Questioning and self, organizational and societal Learning and Knowledge Creation, through which Futures are discovered/created • Fosters creative Interaction with other Actors in the wider Environment, open to a Multiplicity of Worlds amongst Participants, participating Organizations and Societies • Seizes on small Differences in individual and cultural Requirements and Perceptions, and amplifies Feedback, building these into significant Differentiators for People, Organizations and Societies • Has usually had Exposure to behavioural or Life Sciences as well as to organizational, Business or Community Development

3.5.3 THE NORTHERN EDUCATOR OR RESEARCHER

Navigating knowledge through the enterprise is the role of the 'northern' educator or subject expert:

• whose role it is to enable the individual or group to actualize their strategic initiative within their organization, by adding propositional or conceptual weight to their original idea, that is;

- combining together their own newly developed insights with generally recognized theories in a relevant area, thereby linking local (indigenous) with global (exogenous) knowledge.

Role of the Educator/Researcher

- Academics, Researchers or Consultants skilled at adapting Theory to Practice and particularly knowledgeable about the Fundamentals of Transformation Management
- Having experience of undertaking Action Research where they are required to respond to the individual and corporate Needs of their Clients
- With conceptual Knowledge and actual Experience of, respectively, Community Building, Conscious Evolution, Knowledge Creation and Sustainable Development, as well as the public-private-civic-animate Form in which such Functions are contained

---

3.5.4 THE WESTERN FACILITATOR

Producing a full effect is promoted by the 'western' facilitator:

- to enable the learners to work fully through the GENE with a view to realizing a transformational effect within the organization – that is the practical application of the strategic initiative;
- thereby drawing upon experience (south), imagination (east), concepts (north) and their application (west).

Role of the Facilitator

- Normally has a behavioural Science Background with a developmental Orientation
- Is in tune with the overall Purpose and Design of Transformation Management
- Manages and develops Relationships within the Knowledge creating Community
- Monitors and evaluates the Progress of Individuals and the Group
- Supports the transformational Process set in the Context of the Transformational Flow, promoting simultaneously self, organizational, communal and societal Transformation

---

3.6 Conclusion: Towards Strategic Renewal

In conclusion then, we essentially describe *transformation as a co-creative process, which seems to be the very spring-source of life's successful record of evolution.* Based on this important principle of co-creation, life has successfully lasted for millennia. The principle is a simple one: life evolves by creating conditions in which it can thrive and evolve. The crux, however, is the very process of creating the right conditions: this is what the GENE model and the corresponding transformational ecosystem is all about.

We have criticized that conventional discourse on transformation, which all too often ignores nature and culture, treating them as external to human activities. Nature is perceived as an environment that is the subject of control, as a natural consequence of what is ubiquitously termed progress. Culture is perceived as the sphere and context for human behaviour in societies that shapes values, ethics and practices. However both are seen to be extrinsic to human activities of management, politics and most other endeavours, so that such nature and culture are not specifically contextualized by managers. For us, by way of contrast, *nature and culture are the primary source of our transformational flow.*

The GENE model works when individuals, organizations and societies embark on the journey from their grounding in their local identity to effecting global integrity. For us this is the path of strategic transformation.

The GENE distils the local-global dialectic that shapes natural and cultural processes of evolution, following the four steps of grounding, emerging, navigating and effecting. The GENE deeply resonates, as we have shown with the Four World rhythm, whereby each individual, organization and society needs to have its Four Worlds:

Grounding	Grounded in Identity	→	South
Emerging:	Emerging as a Non-Entity	→	East
Navigating:	Navigating a new Entity	→	North
Effecting:	Effecting Integrity	→	West

In summary, the GENE is the most all-encompassing transformative rhythm we have identified. It is the inner *gene*rator of transformation, directly derived out of nature and culture: it represents life itself. That's why we call it also life flow. The GENE is the guiding rhythm of all other transformational rhythms to follows while we work ourselves through the four fundamentals of transformation.

As we shall further see in Chapter 5, the GENE can be applied – each time with specific variations – at all social systems: self, organization, community and society. In formal business and management educational terms its equivalent is strategy, to which we now turn in more detail.

References

1. Heron, J. (1992). *Feeling and Personhood*. London: Sage.
2. Senge, P. et al. (2008). *The Necessary Revolution*. New York: Nicholas Brealey.
3. Suzuki, D. (1997). *Sacred Balance*. Vancouver: Greystone Books.
4. Sperry, R. (1982). *Science and Moral Priority*. New York: Columbia University Press.
5. Sahtouris, E. (1996). *Earthdance: Living Systems in Evolution*. Alameda: Metalog Books.
6. Soros, G. (2000). *Open Society*. New York: Little Brown.
7. Maturana, H. and Varela, F. (1991). *Autopoiesis and Cognition: The Realisation of the Living*. Boston: Kluwer.
8. Nonaka, I. and Takeuchi, H. (1995). *The Knowledge Creating Company*. Oxford: Oxford University Press.

4 *Strategic Renewal*

From Economic to Ecological

4.1 Introduction: A Conventional Understanding of Business and Strategy

4.1.1 WHAT IS A BUSINESS?

We continue the task of transforming strategy, taking on from where the previous chapter left off, by now reviewing the conventional understanding of business and strategy in the literature. To do so, we turn to two icons, both inevitably American, of twentieth-century management theory: Peter Drucker (Austro-American) and Michael Porter (Anglo-American). While Drucker, in the latter part of the last century, was instrumental in putting management as a discipline on the landscape, and thereby defining business, its purpose and functioning, it was Michael Porter, even more recently, who particularly advanced the understanding of corporate strategy.

The purpose of a business

Profit and profitability, for Drucker,[1] are crucial – for every society even more than for the individual business. Yet profitability is not the purpose for but a limiting factor on enterprise. Profit is not the rationale of business decisions but the test of their validity. There is only one valid definition of business purpose: to create a customer. It is the customer who determines what a business is. To supply the wants and needs of a customer, according to Drucker, society entrusts wealth-producing resources to the business enterprise. For us indeed, in focusing on the individual customer, Drucker is unconsciously adopting a 'western' thereby individualistic orientation.

Two entrepreneurial functions: marketing and innovation

Because its purpose is to create a customer, the business enterprise has two – and only these two – basic functions: marketing and innovation. They produce the results, and all the rest are costs. A business is set apart from all other human organizations because it markets a product or service. A business enterprise, moreover, can exist only in an economy, which considers change natural and acceptable. And business, for Drucker, is the natural organ of growth, expansion and change. The second function of a business, therefore, is innovation. It is not enough for the business to provide just any goods and services; it must provide better and more economic ones.

Non-technological innovations are supposedly as important, for Drucker, as technological ones. Innovation for him can be defined as the task of giving human and material resources new and greater wealth-producing capacity. This is especially important for developing countries. They can import technology, but they have to produce their own social adaptations to make imported technology work. Managers then must convert society's needs into opportunities for profitable business. Unfortunately Drucker, while pursuing such a social line, never really applies it in practice, by articulating exactly what he means by social innovation; perhaps because he never consciously roots his own thinking on business and management in the social sciences as a whole, if not also the humanities.

Business mission, strategy and innovation

For Drucker moreover, not intuition, but a clear, simple and penetrating theory of the business characterizes the truly successful entrepreneur. It demands asking 'what is my business and what should it be?' Only a clear definition of the mission and purpose of the business provides the basis for priorities, strategies, plans and work assignments. It is the starting point for the design of managerial jobs – structure follows strategy. And strategy requires 'knowing what our business is and should be'. Deciding what is our business strategy is a genuine decision, which must be based on divergent views. Each alternative rests on different assumptions about the reality of the business and its environment. It always involves a high-risk decision.

Who is the customer is, for Drucker, the first and crucial question in defining business purpose, underlined by the question of what is value to the customer? The customer never buys a product. They buy the satisfaction of a want. That is where marketing comes in. Sooner or later even the most successful answer to the question 'what is our business?' becomes obsolete. 'What will our business be?' aims at adaptation to anticipated changes. It aims at modifying, extending, developing the existing business. But there is also the need to ask the question 'what should our business be?' What opportunities are opening up for a different business? That is where innovation comes in. However, and as we have already indicated, Drucker never fully developed such a notion of innovation, from a social as well as a technological and economic perspective. The next, seminal influence on strategy, some 20 years later, has been Harvard's Michael Porter. Actually, Porter, to whom we now turn, has focused most recently on society as a whole, which represents for us his most seminal work, adopting an approach which is somewhat more ecosystemic than Drucker's.

4.1.2 COMPETITIVE STRATEGY

Four elements and states of competitive advantage

In 1990 Michael Porter published his masterly work on *The Competitive Advantage of Nations*.[2] A team of researchers, under his direction, analyzed the performance of leading economies around the globe, to uncover the sources of their competitive advantages in particular industries. In Ricardo's 'theory of comparative advantage' one nation was more competitive than another if its factor costs, in a particular field of agriculture or industry, were comparatively lower. In Porter's new 'theory of competitive advantage' there are four inputs or elements to consider rather than just one, and similarly four outputs, or states of economic development:

1. factor conditions;
2. demand conditions;
3. industry clusters and supporting industries; and
4. company structure and strategy.

First element: factor conditions

Porter has argued that factor conditions is only one of four interacting elements that have to be systemically taken into account in assessing competitive advantage. The other three are demand conditions in each industry; the structure, strategy and rivalry of firms within it; and the status of the 'industry cluster', that is the supporting and related industries.

Factor conditions include human, physical, financial and knowledge resources. The stock of factors at any particular time, both physical and human, is less important than the rate at which they are created, upgraded and made more specialized in specific industries. On the one hand factors may be basic – natural resources, unskilled and semi-skilled labour, as well as debt capital; or, on the other hand, factors may be advanced – information infrastructure, skilled personnel, as well as sophisticated financial instruments. On the other hand, factor conditions may be generalized, facilities or skills applying to a wide range of industries, or specialized – applying to particular industries or industry clusters.

Advanced and specialized factors, needless to say, make the more vital contribution to competitive advantage. Further, what Porter calls 'selective disadvantage', refers to a lack of basic resources, which provides a spur to competitive achievement. Japan is a good example for such a selective disadvantage.

Second element: demand conditions

Demand conditions emerge from a nation's political, social and cultural values. National passions, Porter argues, translate into internationally competitive industries with striking regularity, be they represented, for example, in British gardening tools or in Italian fashions. To the extent that a nation's buyers are sophisticated and demanding so its firms will gain competitive advantage. Moreover, to the extent that these domestic buyers' needs anticipate similar needs in other parts of the world, so international competitive advantage will be realized. So, for example, the Japanese domestic demand for small and compact electronic products has foreshadowed parallel requirements in the rest of the industrialized world.

In the final analysis, for Porter, it is demand quality that counts more than quantity, in stimulating the achievement of ultimate competitive advantage. Such 'quality' incorporates exacting standards from individual and commercial buyers, as well as from regulatory bodies. Moreover, the more advanced and specialized the nation's factor endowment the more able it is to respond to such qualitative requirements.

Third element: industry clusters and related and supporting industries

Competitive advantage, Porter found, arises out of close working relationships between suppliers, producers and distribution chains in a particular industry. The emerging value chain constitutes an interdependent system with many linkages that has to be managed. As a result physical proximity, whereby economic motivations and local pride are intermixed is a significant influence on competitive advantage.

In fact, mutually enriching industry clusters of related as well as supporting industries, proved to be a critical feature of competitive advantage. Diversification, moreover, within such a cluster, was liable to be much more successful than diversification without. Finally, Porter found that the Italians and the Japanese are much better at such clustered diversification and development than the British and Americans.

Fourth element: firm structure, strategy and rivalry

Porter found two critical aspects to company strategy and structure in attaining competitive advantage. On the strategic side intense domestic rivalry, encouraging not only a diversity of species but also the survival of the fittest was his Darwinian conclusion. Coupled with this he uncovered the need for invention and entrepreneurship, stimulating and stimulated by new business formation.

On the structural side Porter's conclusions were more unusual. He found that compatibility between national family, social and educational structures and forms of business organization were all important. For example, whereas German regimentation and technical orientation is reinforced socially and commercially, Italian improvisation and family orientation is successfully reinforced in both instances.

Competitive advantage through successful combination of the four elements

Competitive advantage arises, in the final analysis, when the system of interrelated elements combines together to work as a dynamic whole. According to Porter factor creation, for example, is most strongly influenced by domestic rivalry, and the rate at which factors are created and upgraded is shaped by the presence of related and supporting industries. Once a cluster forms the whole group of industries becomes mutually supporting. Moreover, aggressive rivalry in one industry tends to spread through the cluster to others. Finally, the more exposed firms are to international competition the more pronounced the clustering, in face of such globally based competition. Nations gain an important competitive advantage, then, when government policy is supportive of intra-cluster exchange.

While Peter Drucker and Michael Porter provide the necessary backdrop to the traditional understanding of business and strategy, we now review how the field of enterprise and strategy has further, and even more recently, evolved, under the emergent influence of nature and ecology on strategy and management. These latter approaches have more resonance with our own approach to transform competitive strategy into strategic renewal.

4.2 The Nature of Strategy

4.2.1 STRATEGIC ORIENTATIONS OF THE ENTERPRISE BASED ON DIFFERENT PERSPECTIVES ON NATURE

The conventional economic orientation, as adopted by Drucker and Porter, has been replaced here by our natural orientation. For us, it is nature and then culture, where our Transformation Management starts, and politic and economics is where it ends. We align, moreover, such a natural orientation to strategy with our Four Worlds.

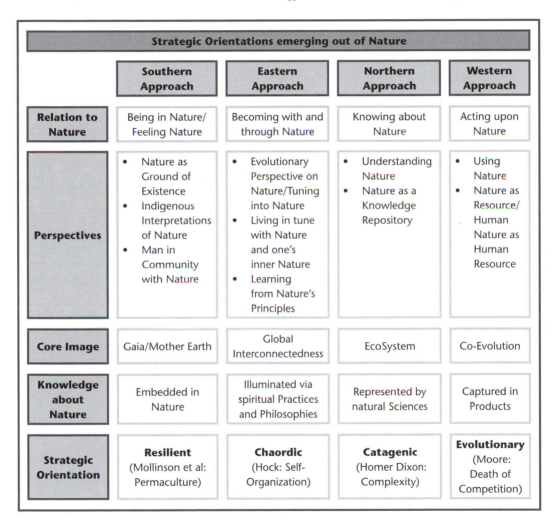

Strategic Orientations emerging out of Nature			
	Southern Approach	**Eastern Approach**	**Northern Approach**	**Western Approach**
Relation to Nature	Being in Nature/ Feeling Nature	Becoming with and through Nature	Knowing about Nature	Acting upon Nature
Perspectives	• Nature as Ground of Existence • Indigenous Interpretations of Nature • Man in Community with Nature	• Evolutionary Perspective on Nature/Tuning into Nature • Living in tune with Nature and one's inner Nature • Learning from Nature's Principles	• Understanding Nature • Nature as a Knowledge Repository	• Using Nature • Nature as Resource/ Human Nature as Human Resource
Core Image	Gaia/Mother Earth	Global Interconnectedness	EcoSystem	Co-Evolution
Knowledge about Nature	Embedded in Nature	Illuminated via spiritual Practices and Philosophies	Represented by natural Sciences	Captured in Products
Strategic Orientation	**Resilient** (Mollinson et al: Permaculture)	**Chaordic** (Hock: Self-Organization)	**Catagenic** (Homer Dixon: Complexity)	**Evolutionary** (Moore: Death of Competition)

We start then in the 'south', drawing our strategic inspiration partly also from the Australian aborigines.

4.2.2 RESILIENT STRATEGY: A SOUTHERN PERSPECTIVE

The Transition Movement: promoting more ustainable living arrangements

Resilience, for Irish permaculturalist Rob Hopkins[3] the co-founder of the Transition Movement in the UK, refers to the ability of a system – from individual people to whole economies – to hold together and maintain its ability to function in the face of change and shocks from the outside. Further, for Hopkins, the move towards more localized energy-efficient and productive living arrangements is not a choice; it is an inevitable direction for humanity. As such, we need new stories that paint new possibilities, that reposition where we see ourselves in relation to the world around us, that entice us to see the changes ahead with anticipation of the possibilities they hold, and that will, ultimately, give us the strength to emerge at the other end into a new, but more nourishing world.

However, unless we can create this sense of anticipation, elation and a collective call to adventure on a wider scale, any government response will be doomed to failure. Rebuilding local agriculture and food production then, localizing energy production, rethinking healthcare, rediscovering local building materials in the context of zero energy building, rethinking how we manage waste, all build resilience and offer the potential of an extraordinary renaissance – economic, cultural and spiritual. We now turn specifically to resilience thinking.

Living in a complex world

For ecologists Walker and Salt,[4] moreover, optimization does not match the way our societies value things. It promotes the simplification of values to a few quantifiable and marketable ones, and demotes the importance of unquantifiable and unmarketable values, such as the life support, regenerative and cleansing services that nature provides, collectively known as 'ecosystem services'. It also discounts the values placed on beauty or on the existence of species for their own sakes. *The more you optimize elements of a complex system of human and nature for some specific goal, the more you diminish that system's resilience.* A drive for an efficient optimal state outcome has the effect of making the total system more vulnerable to shocks and disturbances. *The key to sustainability lies in enhancing the resilience of social-ecological systems, not in optimizing isolated components of the system. Resilience thinking presents an approach to managing natural resources that embraces human and natural systems continually adapting through cycles of change.*

The first step involves considering a systems perspective of how the world works:

- We are all part of linked socio-ecological systems.
- These are complex adaptive systems.
- Resilience is the key to sustainability within these.

The second step is to develop an understanding of two central themes that underpin resilience thinking:

- *Thresholds*: Socio-ecological systems can exist in more than one kind of stable state; if a system changes too much it crosses a threshold and behaves differently.

- *Adaptive Cycles:* The system moves through four phases – rapid growth, conservation, release and reorganization.

We now turn from such resilience thinking to permaculture.

From resilience to permaculture

For Australian co-founders of *permaculture,* Mollinson and Holmgren,[5] substantively based on the practices of the Aborigines, there were 12 guiding principles of permaculture:

1. *Observe and Interact:* A post-peak oil world will depend on detailed observation and good design rather than energy-intensive solutions.
2. *Catch and Store Energy:* Energy passes through natural systems, stored in such (e.g. water), so we need to make best use of these; move 'capital' from the bank to the resources we have around us.
3. *Obtain a Yield:* Any intervention we make in a system ought to be productive; for example, productive trees in public places or edible roof gardens.
4. *Apply Self-Regulation and Accept Feedback:* A well-designed permacultural system is able to self regulate, requiring minimum intervention, like a woodland ecosystem requiring no weeding and fertilizer.
5. *Use and Value Renewable Resources:* Where nature can perform particular functions, like aerating soil (worms) or building soil (trees), we should utilize these rather than thinking we can replace them.
6. *Produce no Waste:* The concept of waste is reflective of poor design; every output from one system should become the input to another; we need to think cyclically rather than in linear systems.
7. *Design from Patterns to Details:* We need to see our work in the wider context of watershed, regional or global economy, to keep clear sense of the wider canvas on which we paint and the forces affecting us.
8. *Integrate rather than Segregate:* Permaculture is the science of maximizing beneficial relationships, weaving holistically between the different elements of the place.
9. *Use Small and Slow Solutions:* The smaller and more intensive solutions are, the more resilient they will be.
10. *Use and Value Diversity:* A diversity of small businesses, local currencies, food and energy sources is far more resilient than centralized systems, globalization's version of monoculture.
11. *Use Edges and Value the Marginal:* The 'edge', where two ecosystems meet, is more productive than either on their own.
12. *Creatively Use and Respond to Change:* Natural systems are constantly in flux, evolving and growing.

We now turn from permaculture, lodged in physical nature, to self-organization, linking physical and human nature as well as culture.

4.2.3 CHAORDIC STRATEGY: AN EASTERN PERSPECTIVE

Self-organization

For Dee Hock, the founder of Visa, and at the same time a student of 'eastern' philosophies of interconnectedness, it is of paramount importance that new concepts of organization and strategy, as an amalgam of chaos and order, are developed. Such concepts need to be aligned with life's principles, derived from nature. For him:

> ... *life is not a right. Life is a gift, which comes bearing a gift, which is the art of living. And community is the marketplace where we give our gifts and receive the gifts of others. When our individual and collective consciousness becomes receptive to new concepts of organization which that way of thinking suggests, societal organizations may yet come into harmony with the human spirit and the biosphere.*[6]

Hock, whose passion was to engage in the evolution of organizational concepts in tune with the principles of nature explains why, for him, current day management got it all wrong:

> *Just as the machine metaphor was the father of today's organizational concepts, the industrial age was the mother. Together, they dominated the evolution of all institutions. The unique processes of the age of handcrafting were abandoned in favour of mechanistic, command-and-control organizations. To produce huge quantities of uniform goods, services, knowledge and people, those organizations amassed resources, centralized authority, routinized practices, and enforced conformity. This created a class of managers, expert at reducing variability and diversity to uniform, repetitive, assembly-line processes endlessly repeated with ever-increasing efficiency. Thus the industrial age became the age of managers. ... People are not 'things' to be manipulated, labelled, boxed, bought and sold. Above all, they are not 'human resources'. We are entire human beings, containing the whole of the evolving universe.*

Living communities

For management consultant and student of systems thinking Joseph Bragdon, corporations are to be seen as living communities – systems that, like bees and flowers, thrive on an intricate web of living relationships. Take away these relationships and the firm, like an isolated bee, will die. Nonliving assets are easy to manipulate and control, because they are guided by rational, mechanistic laws. Living systems, however, are continually in flux – networking, learning, adapting and changing in response to the ebb and flow of life around and within them. Hence, we can understand living assets only by taking a non-linear, systems approach. This requires the freedom to self-organize in pursuit of natural interests; and it requires environments that are safe for and supportive of their enterprises.

The traditional model of the firm sees only chaos in the living systems of society and nature: raw energy, social conflict and other 'uneconomic' behaviours. The mental model of the corporation that emerged in the nineteenth century looked to impose order on that chaos by centralizing authority and scientifically managing by objectives. They sought to overcome chaos by seeking to control it. As such, even concepts like the 'triple bottom line' are still framed within the main objectives of optimizing profits and sales. The life affirming perspective inspires loyalty, learning and innovation. Product design, in this latter case, involving life cycle assessment (LCA) ensures that customers get the benefits of energy efficiency, reliability and durability, and that at the end of a product's service life it can be reclaimed or recycled to add value for someone else.

Case of living system: Toyota, Japan, the world's greatest manufacturing company

The auto industry is an excellent setting in which to demonstrate the conceptual understanding of an organization as a living system because it has been a bastion of traditional command-and-control management. The industry is well known for periods of overproduction followed by massive layoffs, and North America's two largest automakers, GM and Ford, have been cited for numerous human rights violations. Whereas GM and Ford operated under quantitative targets imposed by management, Toyota decided to let the flow of work in its plants relate to the qualitative means of employees and their working environment – their process knowledge, the infrastructure for learning and communicating, and their responsiveness to customers. To improve the rate of flow, employees were given incentives to connect, self-organize and exchange knowledge so they could learn as they worked to devise a better system. When orders are slow, rather than laying off production workers, Toyota finds other work for them.

The company's vision of 'Greener Cars, Greener Factories, Greener Planet' resonates with the 'biophilic' impulses of stakeholders. In the words of Toyota's President Fujio Cho: '*We need to strive for zero omissions at all stages of the automobile ... we are determined to lead the world in firmly establishing the use of environmental technology.*' Toyota allocates costs to one of three basic purposes, in accordance with living systems principles: volume costs (to operate the business) contribute to metabolic sustenance; structure costs (to maintain the business) support natural refurbishment of the living system; newness costs are an investment in adaptation. Viewing costs, revenues and profitability in the context of these purposes recognizes that a business, like any life system, must maintain continuing and effective relationships with the world around it. For other automakers, accounting systems are based on quantitative targets, rather than on nurturance of relationships. Toyota's profits per vehicle are at the upper end of the auto industry scale, in spite of having some of the world's best paid and cared for employees. Toyota's skill in networking and managing by means – from the way it organizes its production and accounts to the way it connects with its stakeholders – is a prime example of an effective industrial ecology.[7]

We now turn from south and east to north, and from a resilient and a chaordic to a so-called catagenic approach to strategy.

4.2.4 CATAGENIC STRATEGY: A NORTHERN PERSPECTIVE

Why nature counts

The twenty-first century, for student of complexity Thomas Homer Dixon[8] at the Trudeau Center for Peace and Conflict Studies in Toronto, will be the Age of Nature. We will learn, probably the hard way that nature matters. We are not separate from it, we are dependent on it, and when there is trouble in nature there is trouble in society.

The anthropologist Gregory Bateson cited by Homer Dixon said that *the source of all our problems today comes from the gap between how we think and how nature works*. We face a mounting range of insoluble problems because the DNA of our dominant institutions is based on machine age thinking, like 'all systems must have someone in control', and change only happens when a powerful leader drives change. Yet, we all know that in healthy living systems control is distributed and change occurs continually. But we are so habituated to the 'someone must be in control' mindset that we fail to imagine real alternatives. Meanwhile, for Homer Dixon, we are faced by five major stresses, as well as two multipliers.

Stresses and multipliers

Five major stresses, so-called tectonic stresses are accumulating deep underneath the surface of our societies. Homer Dixon distinguishes between:

1. *Population Stress:* arising out of the differences in growth rates between rich and poor societies, and the spiralling growth of mega-cities in poor countries.
2. *Energy Stress:* above all from oil scarcity.
3. *Environmental Stress:* from increasing damage to land, water, forests, fisheries.
4. *Climate Stress:* from changes in the make-up of our atmosphere.
5. *Economic Stress:* from global financial instabilities and growing income gaps.

In addition to these five stresses are two multipliers, which combine with the stresses to make breakdown more likely, widespread and severe. The first is increasing speed and connectivity of activities, technologies and societies. The second is the escalating power of small groups to destroy things and people.

The catagenic principle: renewal through breakdown

Today most experts who take our global problems seriously advocate what Homer Dixon terms a 'management' response. While this may be better than denying our problems exist, it often does not help very much. For any management policies that really address the underlying causes of our hardest problems usually require big changes in the existing political and economic order. After all, that very order is the reason why our problems are so bad. Surprisingly too, there is no term in English for the commonplace occurrence of *renewal through breakdown*. So Dixon calls it *catagenesis*, from the Greek for 'down', that is cata, and that for 'birth', which is genesis. *Whether the breakdown in question is psychological, technological, economic, political or ecological – or some combination of these – catagenesis involves the reinvention of our future.*

Breakdown is greatly disruptive to parts of the system, but it need not be catastrophic overall. Further, it can produce exactly the conditions required for a burst of creativity, reorganization and renewal. A long view of human history reveals not regular change but spasmodic, catastrophic disruptions followed by long periods of reinvention and development. Breakdown is something that human social systems must go through to adapt successfully to changing conditions. In our communities, towns and cities, we can use small-scale experiments to see what kinds of technologies, organizations and procedures work best under different breakdown scenarios.

In countries that are already very rich, we especially need to figure out if there are feasible alternatives to our hidebound commitment to economic growth, because it is becoming increasingly clear that endless material growth is incompatible with the long-term viability of the Earth's environment. Thinking about alternatives to the growth imperative means thinking about alternatives to conventional economics. At the heart of this view is the assumption that the economy is separate from nature and operates much like a machine. The machine's behaviour is linear, predictable and reversible, so that it can be managed by a planet-wise class of technocrats – including central bankers and government officials – trained in the arcane science of economics. An alternative theory would recognize that the economy is intimately interconnected with nature and its energy flows. The larger economic-ecological system often does not act like a machine at all. Instead its behaviour is marked by threshold effects, and often neither predictable nor controllable. An alternative view would also recognize that there is no substitute for such precious things as biodiversity and benign climate. It would help people to understand that conventional economics is not gospel truth but rather a potent ideology – a blend of scientific finding, analytical gymnastics, value judgements and self-congratulation. Advance planning means that we need to develop a wide range of scenarios and experiment with technologies, organizations and ideas.

Scientists moreover have found that complex systems that are highly adaptive – like markets and even the immune system of mammals – tend to share certain characteristics. First of all, the individual elements that make up the systems are extraordinarily diverse. Second, the power to make decisions is not centralized in one place. These powers are distributed and then linked together in a loose network that allows them to exchange information on what works and what doesn't. Third and finally, highly adaptive systems are unstable enough to create unexpected innovations but orderly enough to learn from their successes and failures. We're all familiar with just such a system – the Internet, and its subsystem, the World Wide Web. So far, though, we've barely tapped their potential as powerful instruments for problem solving, adaptation and social inclusion. The advent of 'open source' though, through Linux and Wikipedia, may mean that the situation is changing.

So far, though, open-source approaches have been applied to solving technical problems like the creation of complex software or databases. Now we urgently need research, Homer Dixon claims, to see if we can use this kind of problem-solving approach to address the social, political and environmental issues discussed here. Such open-source communities would be better able, then, to act with common purpose in a moment of contingency, and seize the opportunity for catagenesis. We now turn, finally, from catagenic to evolutionary.

4.2.5 EVOLUTIONARY STRATEGY: A WESTERN PERSPECTIVE

Death of competition

James Moore is a respected American business consultant, drawing upon conventional Darwinian evolutionary biology. Yet his orientation towards *The Death of Competition*[9] is startling. For Moore, the presumption that there are distinct, immutable businesses within which players scramble for supremacy is a tired idea whose time is past. The new business paradigm, for James Moore as for his compatriot Peter Senge, requires thinking in whole systems.

> *With nature and not machines as their inspiration, today's innovators are showing how to create a different future by learning to see the larger systems of which they are a part and to foster collaboration across every possible boundary. These core capabilities – seeing systems, collaborating across boundaries, and creative problem solving, form the underpinnings for the shift in thinking we now require.*[10]

Starting with understanding the big picture rather than specific products and services, business evolution for Moore therefore becomes a more important concept than simply competition or cooperation. In that sense *an enterprise would have to undergo a mindshift from one of competing to co-evolving with the institutions and individuals to which it relates*.

As leaders then evolve into gardeners so they develop, according to Moore, an eco-community supported by a foundation of interacting organizations and individuals. This emerging community produces goods and services of value to customers, who are themselves members of the ecosystem; member organisms also include suppliers, lead contractors and, indeed, competitors. In the fields of automobiles, electronics and telecommunications this has now become almost second nature to the Fords and the Mazdas, the Intels and the Toshibas, the Siemens, the Alcatels and the Vodafones.

Over time, they co-evolve their capabilities and roles, and tend to align themselves with the directions set by one or more of the companies. The function of an ecosystem leader, which for example Intel plays in the world of semiconductors, is valued by the community. For it enables members to move toward shared visions so as to align their investments, and to find mutually supportive roles. Organizations compete to unite disparate contributors to create powerful total solutions, and then to establish thriving business ecosystems dedicated to providing these solutions to customers. These solutions depend not only on the core product or service, but on a variety of complementary offers that enhance the customer experience. Ultimately, as Moore affirms, returns from the 'core business' are also invested in leadership and support for the ecosystem itself, for 'alliance community development' activities.

The major factor today limiting the spread of realized innovation, for Moore, is not a lack of good ideas, technology or capital. It is rather the inability to command cooperation across broad, diverse communities of players who must become intimate parts of a far-reaching process of co-evolution. In the classical paradigm of industry based competition, products and even product leadership have become comparatively easy to dislodge. Newcomers simply clone the required technologies or programmes, make the requisite investments in technologies and people, and have a go at it. By contrast, the environment-shaping leader of a business ecosystem like a Microsoft or a Benneton, set the stage for a co-evolving system, which becomes difficult to dislodge.

For as such a leading evolutionary strategist:

- finds ways to better embed contributions into the products and processes of adjacent institutions, as well as to shape architectural standards and customer preference;
- ties together stronghold sub-ecosystems and/or uses them to create new positions in adjacent territories;

- finds some aspect of value creation where the niche is becoming important and no player has made a strong stand.

How then, in such an evolutionary context, do businesses evolve over time? Again, we identified a fourfold process, in line with our GENE, cycling from pioneering to renewal.

From pioneering to renewal

1. Pioneering
Entrepreneurs firstly struggle to form embryonic ecosystems that, while hardly mature, are at least complete enough to fulfil the needs of initial customers. Doing something of dramatic value, compared to what is already available to customers, is the *sine qua non* of the early days of a business ecosystem. The first sewage systems built in London in the nineteenth century, seemingly offered such dramatic value, in terms of service and hygiene, and the water utilities have endeavoured to retain that value as they have expanded.

The pioneering goals then are primarily to do with learning, that is learning what value proposition works and discovering how to provide it, through a combination of:

- first, intense customer interaction to find out how customers think and to get clues of how they want to use the product;
- second, finding sponsor/patron customers committed to helping the core offer evolve fruitfully, as early adopters perceiving the dramatic potential of the innovation at an early stage.

2. Expansion
At a second stage of an emerging business ecosystem, the *successful formula is more broadly applied and made more reliable and replicable*. Additional waves of customers and other stakeholders are recruited. The overall focus is upon identifying and rounding up the most desirable potential allies available, that is the best customers, strongest suppliers and most important channels of distribution.

Ecological communities mature in at least two ways: first they expand in biomass, grasslands get denser, trees grow taller, populations of animals multiply. Second they mature through increased genetic diversity, adding species, elaborating synergistic relationships, becoming ever more artful in turning resources into community life. The diversity of members in a business ecosystem makes it more robust and resilient, providing variety to its offerings, and a host of creative ideas to help spawn further evolution. Expansion, hence, requires a compelling vision of value, and the ability to scale up the ecosystem to provide such.

3. Authority
To stay successful, a lead institution must maintain and fortify its ability to shape the future direction and investments of the ecosystem's key customers and suppliers, thereby maintaining the authority and the uniqueness of its contribution to the community, while also encouraging community-wide innovation and co-evolution.

Intel's systems business, for example, and its relationship to the microprocessor business had traditionally been seen in industry, not in ecosystem, terms. The Intel products group in the early 1990s saw the potential to drive new ideas and innovation into the business system in a new way. Intel used to design circuits. Now, according to Moore, they worry more about the nature of industrial democracy and the design of the interactions among companies, organizations and individuals who shape markets. Intel's architecture labs are now promoting an open framework for investment, a framework that invites others to bring their innovation to the personal computer platform. The framework is particularly valuable in making a place for smaller, highly creative companies; to help coordinate the investments of others, rather than make these themselves. In Moore's terms, as 'chip heads willing to learn', managers starting out with a semi-conductor industry orientation became ambassadors to a larger, more diverse community of companies. Investor relations personnel at Intel got Wall Street to recognize that the company is not simply a capital intensive producer of a commodity but an important member of the fabric of information industries.

Moore argues, that regardless of whether stage three enterprises lead or follow, the opportunity environments in which they operate are populated by centres of *intense co-evolution*. Such organizations do not necessarily need to be the shapers of the business ecosystem they join. This is especially the case if they trust and respect its leadership, but they must find a valued contribution to make. Most of all, they need to make a contribution enduringly critical to the ecosystem, and embed it in the fabric of the community. This brings us to the ultimate stage of either renewal, or alternatively death.

4. Renewal or Death

Longevity or sustainable development finally, for Moore, comes from finding ways to inject new ideas into the existing ecosystem, thereby establishing a system of symbiotic relationships of lasting value relative to what else is available. Few institutions around the world have reached such an ultimate stage of development.

In most stage four ecosystems, individuals are competent and dedicated in their specific contributions. It is the ecosystem as a whole, which is under-performing, and not the individual species. Leadership and strategy in the age of business ecosystems must therefore bring several elements together for organizational reform and corporate renewal to have a chance:

* survey the opportunity landscape and understand the current power players and their interests and assets;
* develop valid information about the performance of the whole business ecosystem, and what it means for this ecosystem to succeed. How can this be measured? What factors are required for success? How might these factors be influenced to improve performance?
* organize things to affect the aspects of the business ecosystem that require transformation, taking responsibility for the most important co-evolving factors and actors.

We are now ready to conclude, and we draw on the latest work of Peter Senge to help us in that respect.

4.3 Conclusion: The Necessary Revolution

In this chapter, we started out from a conventional understanding of business and strategy, at least as conceived by two of its leading management thinkers. From there we explored, based on different strategic orientations on nature embedded in the Four Worlds, the nature of strategy. We thereby identified different evolved forms of conventional strategy.

From a 'southern' perspective we rediscovered the principles of living systems, expressed, in this case, in permaculture in aboriginal Australia, and in the Transition Movement, originally coming, via Rob Hopkins, from Ireland. We termed this approach towards strategy 'resilient strategy'. From an 'eastern' perspective, we came up with the term, via Dee Hock, of a chaordic strategy, which promotes the renewal of the enterprise through self-organization. A 'northern' orientation towards strategy is Thomas Homer Dixon's catagenic approach, which promotes the reinvention of our self, organization and society, out of breakdown, through generating the conditions for a burst of creativity, reorganization and renewal. From a 'western' perspective, finally, we introduced James Moore's evolutionary approach to strategy, which explicitly transcends competition and substitutes it with co-creation.

Certainly, there are further approaches to transcend the conventional approach to strategy, imbuing it with natural vitality. We do not promote, as such, any particular approach, whether southern, eastern, northern or western. We favour instead a balanced integration of the strategic principles identified. Concertedly, they enable the enterprise to evolve towards a resilient, chaordic, catagenic and evolutionary approach to strategy – instead called, so we suggest, strategic renewal (see Figure 4.1).

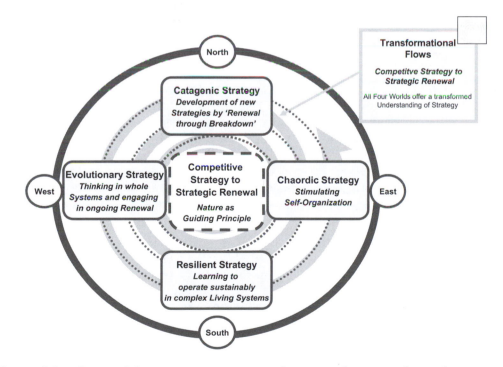

Figure 4.1   Competitive strategy to strategic renewal – new orientations to strategy

The integration of all four principles, again, represents a cyclical GENE-like rhythm, which can be viewed as follows:

From Competitive Strategy to Strategic Renewal *Integrating Strategic Orientations from the South, East, North and West*		
Resilient Strategy	Strategy grounded in an Understanding of the Principles of Nature and of living Systems and an Awareness of how to operate in such	→ **Southern Grounding**
Chaordic Strategy	Creating Space for new strategic Orientations to emerge, following Principles of Self-Organization	→ **Eastern Emergence**
Catagenic Strategy	Development of new strategic Concepts by consciously engaging in the Breakdown of an old System, thereby creating Space for Reconceptualization and Renewal, enabling Self, Organization or Society to navigate in a fundamentally changed Environment	→ **Northern Navigation**
Evolutionary Strategy	Thinking in whole Systems (and thereby also integrating southern, eastern and northern Approaches to Strategy) the evolutionary Orientation leads us to engage in an ongoing, cyclical Process of Renewal (from Pioneering to Renewal)	→ **Western Effecting**

All in all, such a fundamentally transformed orientation towards strategy is necessary to bring about, what Peter Senge called *The Necessary Revolution*. We conclude this chapter, in anticipation of the one that follows, by extending the nature-laden transformation of organizational strategy to self and society. We do that with the significant help of Peter Senge and his American, environmentally oriented colleagues Bryan Smith and Nina Kruschwitz, Joe Laur and Sara Schley, whose work came to light as we were completing our own.

For Senge, the 'infant global society' we have birthed has entered its first life or death crisis. To help us resolve this environmental crisis we need to draw on the wisdom of long-lived cultures, like the Australian aborigines, who believe that other plant and animal species have much to teach us. *Such a regenerative society is about life flourishing, not just about human life.*

We are, individually speaking, a young species, who very recently, in a virtual second of life's day on earth, expanded to fill the world. As such, we are uncertain of our niche. Like teenagers, we are about to discover that we are not the centre of the universe – not even the centre of life on this planet. We are but one of millions, and our merit depends not on our ego but on our contribution.

Ultimately, for Senge, living systems control themselves based on webs of relationships rather than through hierarchically controlled organizations. Building enterprises based on cultures of relationship – that are organizations that not only work like nature but are more harmonious with nature – may be the defining institutional feature of a regenerative society.

To focus more specifically on such a transformational flow, applied to self, organization and society, we turn to Chapter 5.

References

1. Drucker, P. (1977). *Management: Tasks, Responsibilities, Practices*. London: Pan.
2. Porter, M. (1990). *The Competitive Advantage of Nations*. New York: Macmillan.
3. Hopkins, R. (2008). *Transition Handbook: From Oil Dependency to Local Resilience*. Devon: Green Books.
4. Walker, B. and Salt, D. (2006). *Sustaining Ecosystems and People in a Changing World*. New York: Island Press.
5. Holmgren, D. (2002). *Permaculture*. Victoria, Australia: Holmgren Design Services.
6. Hock, D. (2006). *One from Many*. San Francisco: Berrett-Koehler.
7. Bragdon, J. (2006). *Profit for Life – How Capitalism Excels*. Boston: SOL.
8. Homer Dixon, T. (2007). *The Upside of Down: Catastrophe, Creativity and The Renewal of Civilisation*. London: Souvenir Press.
9. Moore, J. (1997). *The Death of Competition*. New York: Wiley.
10. Senge, P. et al. (2008). *The Necessary Revolution*. New York: Nicholas Brealey.

5 *Self, Organizational and Societal Renewal*

The Journey of Transformation

5.1 Introduction: Engaging in Transformational Cycles of Ongoing Renewal

THE TRIPLE BOTTOM LINE OF SELF, ORGANIZATION AND SOCIETY

Based on the transformational flow that we have introduced in the previous chapters, we shall now demonstrate its relevance for self, organizational and societal transformation, initially, in this chapter, in theory and subsequently in practice. Indeed, a cyclical rhythm from formation to transformation can be identified in all living systems. Moreover, such rhythms draw upon diverse disciplines: from ecology to psychology, from sociology to history, serving as a bridge between nature's transformational flows on the one hand, and transcultural forces and transdisciplinary fields on the other. Whereas most transformationally oriented thinkers, like Senge, Moore, Homer Dixon and Hopkins tend to focus on either organizational or else self-transformation, we focus on all, interdependently, together.

In our approach to Transformation Management, self, organization and society then constitute the theatre of action bearing upon transformation. In other words, what is distinctive about Transformation Management is that it applies, simultaneously and interdependently, to individual, institutional and communal 'levels', at one and the same time. In fact, *one of the distinctive features of our work is this 'triple bottom line', or grounding, whereby transformation is rooted neither in a person, an institution, or community, one in isolation of the other, but in all of them together.*

In most literature on management, leadership and learning transformational processes are applied solely to the development of the individual, rather than to the institution, as has been the case in the previous chapter, and the community in which the individual is lodged. Through illustrative case stories we demonstrate how these three levels are interlinked, drawing now on human, alongside physical, nature. That is also why we have chosen a spiral to help you visualize the transformational flows. The transformation of living systems, then, is an ongoing spiralling process, serving to continuously renew an interweaving self, organization and society. Let us briefly retrace steps.

DYNAMIC APPROACHES TOWARDS LIVING SYSTEMS

The shift to a dynamic and developmental approach towards living systems, as we have seen for example in James Moore's approach to a co-creative, evolutionary strategy, reflects a shift in the development of modes of scientific thought in general over the past three millennia. In biology for example, the first scientific step was that of classification. Botany and biology spent 2,500 years giving taxonomic attention to plants and animals. The next step, after classification, was so-called 'ontogeny'. Attention turned to the origins, development and direction of a phenomenon. In the last 150 years, therefore, nearly every social and natural science has been transformed from a structure and system oriented perception of the phenomena under investigation to a process and value oriented one. This occurred in astronomy with Laplace, in logic with Hegel, in history and political economy with Marx, in biology with Darwin, and in psychology with Piaget and with Jung. Interestingly enough, it has not yet applied in our field, in that neither leadership nor management, generally speaking, carry that developmental impulse. That is why we have established Transformation Management as a new discipline.

For the renowned French Swiss psychologist Jean Piaget,[1] primary attention is paid to the progressively individuated self in an ever-expanding life field. A stage transition has occurred when enough accommodation has been undertaken to require and make possible a transformation in the operational pattern of the individual or collective whole. This leads to what the organizational psychologist, Elliot Jaques, has called 'requisite organization',[2] that is a matching of individual and organizational cognitive capacities, or to what the Swiss psychologist Carl-Gustav Jung has termed 'self-regulation'.[3]

SELF-REGULATION

For Jung, all the essential functions of the physical body and of the human psyche operate in accordance with the *principle of dynamic opposition*. In other words they are arranged in opposing systems, which, in health are kept in balance through a process of positive and negative feedback. Thus hunger is balanced against satiation, sleep against wakefulness, and vice versa. Jung was convinced that the human psyche, like the body, was a self-regulating system. The same, of course, could be said for an entire organization and for society.

We strive to perpetually maintain a balance between opposing propensities, while, at the same time, seeking our own individuation. A dynamic polarity exists then between surface personality and deep self, between masculine and feminine consciousness, between extroverted and introverted attitudes, between modernity and tradition. Thus the greatest and most important problems of life and work are all fundamentally insoluble. They must be because they express the necessary polarity inherent in every self-regulating system. They can never be solved, but only outgrown. Jung saw the whole life cycle as a continuing process of metamorphosis. What matters is not so much what we are, or what we have been, but what we are in the process of becoming. That is the very essence of the individuation, or indeed transformation process. Development of the personality and organization is not a simple, linear progression but a spiral with progressive ascents and regressive descents. Probably the best contemporary exponent of such individually oriented adult development is the American developmental psychologist, Daniel

Levinson, and his work on the *Seasons of Man's Life*.[4] This leads us to a closer examination of life cycles of living systems, from self, to organization, to society.

5.2 Life Cycles of Living Systems

5.2.1 THE CYCLE OF YOUR INDIVIDUAL LIFE: FROM TEENS TO MATURITY

For Levinson the components of your life are not a random set of items, like pebbles washed up at the shore. Rather, like threads in a tapestry, they are woven into an encompassing design. Recurring themes in various sectors of your life and work help to unify the overall patterns of the tapestry. Individual's lives differ widely in the nature and patterning of these themes. *Your life structure consists of a series of alternating stable and changing periods.* We can refer to these as *structure building periods and transitional, structure-changing periods*. Together they make up transformation. The primary task of every stable period is to build a life structure. You must make certain key choices, form a structure around them, and pursue values and goals within that structure. A transitional period terminates the existing life structure, and creates the possibility for a new one. The primary tasks of every transitional period are to question and reappraise the existing structure, to explore various possibilities for change in self and society, and to move towards commitment to the crucial choices that form the basis for a new life structure in the ensuing stable period. We are now introducing the four life stages, as per Levinson, in greater detail.

The first formative life stage: childhood and youth

Forming a Dream
Levinson identifies four 'exploratory tasks', which engage us, in the course of a 'healthy' childhood and youth. Sadly enough, should the early stage of our lives be 'unhealthy', socially and psychologically, we will carry such an unfulfilled load into the future. For some that may provide an extra spur to development, for others an extra burden. The first such task is that of 'forming a dream'. The vicissitudes and fate of the dream have fundamental qualities for development. In its primordial form, the dream is a vague sense of self-in-world. It is associated with a sense of identity, the 'I am' feeling, the experience that 'I exist', that self and society are, ultimately, properly matched. At the start it is poorly articulated and only tenuously connected to reality, although it may contain concrete images such as winning the Nobel Prize or setting up of an enterprise. It may take a dramatic form as in the myth of the hero, the great artist, or indeed a Nelson Mandela performing magnificent feats and receiving special honours. It may take the mundane forms of the excellent craftsman, the husband-father in a certain kind of family, the high performing manager, or the greatly respected member of your community.

Forming Mentor Relationships
A mentor may act as a teacher to advance the youthful skills and intellectual development. Serving as a sponsor, he or she may use his or her influence to facilitate your entry and advancement into organization and society. Such a mentor may be a host and guide, welcoming the initiate to a new occupational and social world and acquainting the novice with its values, customs, resources and cast of characters. Through his or her own

virtues, achievements and way of living the mentor may be an exemplar that the young person can admire and seek to emulate.

The mentor has another function, one that has most relevance also at a societal level, and this is developmentally the most crucial one: to support and facilitate the realization of an individual, organizational or societal dream. He or she fosters development by believing in the other, by sharing in the other's dream and giving it his or her blessing. We now turn from mentorship to forming an occupation.

Forming an Occupation

Young people who make a strong occupational commitment in the early twenties, without sufficient exploration of external options and inner preferences, often come to regret it later. Interestingly enough, and in our 'fourfold' context, such exploration should involve natural, cultural and political, as well as economic pursuits. On the other hand, those who don't make a commitment until the thirties, or who never make one, are deprived of the satisfaction of engaging in enduring work that is suitable for the self and valuable for society.

Forming Love Relationships

One of your first developmental tasks, as a young person, is to form the capability of having adult, peer relationships with a 'loved one'. Interestingly enough, at a societal level, we in the 'west' and the 'north' increasingly hear the call, especially from the 'south' and 'east', that we should love and respect them. It is not enough, for example, to offer aid or debt forgiveness, but justice in trade involves resolving the need for reconciliation for the injustices of the past, those of a social as well as an economic nature. Your formative development, according to Levinson, prepares you partially, but never sufficiently to undertake this work of love and reconciliation. In the light of the formative difficulties we experience, it is small wonder that relating to the other should be a lifelong task.

The second reformative life stage: adulthood

Reformative Orientation

Unlike the conventional wisdom on life stages, from psychotherapists like Jung and Levinson, who come from Europe and America, and who claim that the major 'reformation' starts at midlife, we claim that, for those of us coming from societies in transition it is different. Levinson does give us a prospective bridge across this developed-developing society divide, though, in terms of what he describes as an 'early adult transition'. For us, such a reformative stage, and particularly for those of us based in societies in transition, can extend from young adulthood to early midlife, say, as an individual, from the late teens to the early forties. Thereafter, the 'normative' can emerge, in later midlife, out of the reformation.

Early Adult Transition

The first task for the young adult, for Levinson, is to move out of the pre-adult world, to question the nature of the world and your place in it, to modify or terminate relationships with important persons. The second task is to make a preliminary step into the adult world, to explore its possibilities; to imagine yourself as a participant in it; to consolidate an initial adult identity; to make and test some preliminary choices for adult living.

In a society in transition, such an individual, developmental agenda is set within the context of a similar process going on in the society as a whole. The great danger that such transitional societies, and the managers and organizations within them, face, is that they are led, prematurely, to conform to an external norm, rather than evolving their own one, through a process of thorough reformation.

First Adult Structure

As a young person, for Levinson, you have two primary yet antithetical tasks. First, you need to explore the possibilities for adult living, to keep your options open, to avoid strong commitments and maximize your alternatives. This task is reflected in a sense of adventure and wonderment. The second task is to create a stable life structure, to become more responsible and 'make something of my life'. If the first predominates life has an extremely transient, rootless quality. If the second predominates, there is a danger of committing yourself prematurely to a structure.

Age 30 Transition

According to Levinson, in the late twenties the provisional quality of the twenties begins to end and life becomes more serious, more for real. A voice from within the self says 'if I am to change my life – if there are things in it I want to modify or exclude, or things missing I want to add, I must now make a start, for soon it will be too late'. In most cases then, the life structure of the late twenties is incomplete or fragmented. The 'Age 30 Transition' therefore provides an opportunity to work on the flaws in the life structure formed during the previous period, and to create the basis for a more satisfactory one. For some the transition proceeds smoothly; for most it takes a more stressful form.

Settling Down to a Point

As a young adult the 'settling down' phase is your main vehicle for realizing youthful ambitions and goals. In this period a person, institution or society has two major tasks. First you need to establish a niche in the world, to anchor yourself more firmly, and to develop competence in a chosen field. You thereby seek to become a valued member of a valued world. Second you have to work to 'make it'. Whereas the first task contributes to the stability and order of a defined structure, the second involves a progression within that structure. However, at this reformative stage, there will still be a lack of overall resolution.

The third normative life stage: midlife

Tasks of Renewal

To the extent that an individual has consciously engaged with reformation, it will create a firmer basis for life and work in the ensuing phase. To the extent that adult reformation fails, there will be inner contradictions that are reflected in the flaws of a next stage.

Midlife Transition

Developmentally, this is the period when the creative tension between self, organization and society comes to a head. *The midlife transition is a time of severe crisis.* The butterfly is struggling to emerge from the chrysalis. You question nearly every aspect of your life and feel that you cannot go on as before. The neglected parts of your self urgently seek expression. Internal voices or competencies that have been muted for years now clamour to be heard. 'I cannot live with myself any more'. Oftentimes, a successful business entrepreneur or executive, like Microsoft's Bill Gates or financier-philanthropist George Soros, will create a foundation to serve such a hitherto neglected purpose or part of the world that calls their attention.

Balancing and Integrating

The rapidly lengthening life span in modern society has stimulated widespread concern with the era of late adulthood. We are beginning to seek ways of improving the quality of life for the elderly, and of managing the economic burdens involved. Much less attention has been given to a problem of equal or greater significance, specifically the rapidly growing percentage of the population in middle adulthood. Unless the quality of life in this generation can be improved, Levinson asserts, the middle age will be under strain and society will continue to be short of creative leadership. While occupational roles have become more specialized we need more people who can contribute as leaders, managers, mentors, sources of traditional wisdom as well as vision and imagination. Moreover, as corporations approach such midlife, they need to fuse together their economic and political, natural and cultural concerns. This represents a return to the relationship orientation at the formative stage of development, but at a whole new level. Yet at this stage your newly formed self-concept, business or social concept, is inclusive but still divisive. In a few cases this division yields to the call of radical actualization. Levinson calls this 'Legacy Stage'. For us this is the ultimately transformative stage.

The fourth transformative life stage: maturity

Imagery of the legacy tends to flourish during the midlife transition, as part of the work of the young/old polarity. Your legacy, as an individual or institution, is what you pass onto future generations. For us lodged between self, organization and society our legacy could include: creative products; enterprises or influences on others. People differ enormously in their views about what constitutes a legacy, but, for whole societies, their cultures are manifestations of such. Although the real value of your legacy is impossible to measure, in your individual or organizational mind it defines to a large degree the ultimate value of your lives – and claims to immortality. We now move to the organizational life cycle, drawing on Bernard Lievegoed.

5.2.2 THE ORGANIZATIONAL LIFE CYCLE: FROM PIONEERING TO IMPLEMENTATION

Bernard Lievegoed was one of the major 'path breakers' in organizational development. His book on *The Developing Organisation*,[5] published in 1969, which proved to be ahead of his time, provides insights on how the phases in the development of a human being informed the development of organizations. As we can see, there are some connections between Moore's ecologically oriented, and Lievegoed's socially centred approach.

Lievegoed described three phases typical in the development of organizations. Though his main focus was on business enterprises, the generic phases have relevance beyond the economic realm. The first phase is the pioneer phase.

First pioneering phase

'In its pure form, a pioneer enterprise is an enterprise that is still being run by its founder. It comes into being as a result of a creative act by a human being.'[6] For Lievegoed, the characteristics of so-called pioneer enterprises are:

- Leadership is autocratic.
- Communication is direct.
- The style of organization is person oriented.
- The working style is improvisational.
- The work force: 'one big family'.
- The pioneer's market: known customers.

Lievegoed illustrates vividly what may happen, when a pioneer organization becomes 'over-ripe' and has reached the threshold of a new development. Such a stage is reached when the original strength of the pioneer organization, its closeness, has become its weakness. Often, at this moment, the founding pioneer and his/her leadership and management style are increasingly questioned by employees and demands are made to a) respond in a different way to external challenges (new technologies, altered economic situation, etc.) and b) to organize the operations in a more systematic, differentiated way.

Second phase of differentiation

For Lievegoed, the 'historical answer to the problems of the over-ripe pioneer enterprise came in the form of scientific management',[7] or, in other words, of classical management. When organizations, in the 2nd half of the nineteenth century were for the first time confronted with the challenge of industrial production on a large scale, large-scale enterprises emerged and called for a reorientation and reorganization of management. It was primarily two people who laid the foundation for such a new kind of scientific management: the engineers Frederick Taylor (1856 to 1915) from the US and Henry Fayol (1841 to 1925) in France. 'Scientific management is based on a logical ordering of functions, tasks, things and processes. It assumes that the productivity of an organization increases the more the people concerned succeed in behaving according to the formal organizational plan. The norms for human behaviour in the work situation comply first and foremost with the demands made by the technical process.'[8] The core principles of the phase of differentiation were:

- Principle of mechanization.
- Principle of standardization.
- Principle of specialization.
- Principle of coordination.

The differentiation of the 2nd phase is an essential prerequisite for an organization if it is to function on a long-term basis on a larger-scale and with greater complexity. However, increasing differentiation and systemization of an organization can lead to rigidity, coordination problems, vertical communication problems, decrease of motivation and thereby individual productivity and many more. For Lievegoed 'in order to escape from the dilemma of the over-ripe second phase … the time seems to have arrived for a complete revision of the model'.[9] At this stage the organization, if it continues to develop (most in fact do not) enters the phase of integration.

Third phase of integration

In this phase, for Lievegoed, it is crucial that the organization develops a social subsystem and integrates it with the already existing economic and technical subsystems. For Lievegoed this is a gradual process, but a necessary one. It is characterized by the following assumptions:

- Interlinked, smaller, relatively independent units are set up.
- Self-planning, self-organization and self-control ensue.
- The system rests on the conviction that every person can and wants to develop.
- Personal fulfilment can be achieved in the work situation.

The Austrian management consultant, Fritz Glasl, a close collaborator of Lievegoed, has taken Lievegoed's three phase model of organizational development on to a fourth stage, reflecting the challenges of our times. This phase is called the associative phase.

Fourth phase of association

Glasl claims that organizations have arrived indeed at a new threshold, which requires another evolutionary step. He argues that 'it is not only important to structure and manage one's own organization well, but we have to recognise that our own organization can only be successful if it sees itself as:

- a whole interdependent network of relationships between different organizations and stakeholders.
- this does not mean that 'my' organization becomes subordinate and disappears, but that it is important how this entity related to others in an ongoing network of cooperative relationships.
- these are the 'shared destiny relationships' because an enterprise has to enter into a relationship with a variety of organizations in its environment; a relationship which is characterized by an attitude of responsibility, or a certain permanence, and which is based on continuous development.'[10]

In many ways, our own integrated approach, as we shall see, takes on from where Glasl and Lievegoed leave off. We now turn from organization to society.

5.2.3 THE CYCLE OF SOCIETAL TRANSFORMATION: FROM MAGICAL TO INTEGRAL

Jean Gebser was a Professor of the Study of Comparative Civilisations at the University of Salzburg in the middle of the last century. What was becoming increasingly evident for Gebser was that the individual was being driven into isolation while the collective was degenerating into mere aggregation. These two conditions, isolation and aggregation, were, for him, clear indications that individualism and collectivism were becoming deficient and a new form was required.

However, before we can describe the new, Gebser maintains, we must know the old, or, as per the title of Gebser's book, we must know the *Ever-Present Origin*.[11] Looking back on human endeavour, Gebser distinguishes three structures of societal consciousness – *magical, mythical* and *mental* – and a fourth one to come – *integral*, altogether preceded by an original *archaic* structure. A true process, of development, always occurs in quanta, which is in leaps, or in mutations. As can be seen below, we have linked Gebser's structures of consciousness with (the) Transformation (of) Management to which you have been exposed here.

Stage 0: origin or archaic structure (community)

Taken together, micro- and macrocosmic harmony is nothing less than the perfect identity of man and the universe, in their original form.

Stage 1: magical structure (enterprise)

The man of magic has been released from his identity with the whole. The more man became conscious of himself the more he began to be an individual. Man now stands up to nature. He tries to exercise her, to guide her, striving to be independent of her; then he begins to be conscious of his own will. Here is man the maker, fighter, and indeed entrepreneur.

Stage 2: the mythical structure (leadership)

Just as the archaic structure was an expression of original community, and the magic structure an expression of enterprise, so the mythical structure, thirdly, is an expression of self. While the magic structure leads to a liberating struggle against nature through a disengaged awareness of the external world, the mythical structure, in turn, leads to the emergent awareness of the internal world of the soul. To look into the mirror of the soul is to become conscious; to apprehend the soul, through myth, is to become conscious of self. Everyone who is intent on surviving – with worth and dignity – must sooner or later pass through the agonies of emergent consciousness.

Stage 3: the mental structure (management)

Events of 500 BC in Greece had to be repeated, according to Gebser, around 1250 AD by European man. Then, however, his basis was considerably broadened because of three major achievements: the Greek theory of knowledge, the Hebrew doctrine of salvation and Roman legal and political theory. From the standpoint of the perspectival European world this mental structure is 'rational', from the root ratio meaning to calculate, to think, to understand. Indeed the name for the Indian lawgiver Manu, the Cretan King Minos and the Egyptian King Menes are all most likely derived from the root man, the 'measurer'.

Stage 4: the integral structure (integration)

By integration Gebser means a fully completed and realized wholeness – the re-establishment of the inviolate and pristine state of origin by incorporating the wealth of all subsequent achievement. The concretion of everything that has unfolded in time and coalesced in a spatial array is the integral attempt to reconstitute the 'magnitude' of man from his constituent parts, so that he can consciously integrate himself with the whole. While Levinson (American), Lievegoed (Dutch) and Gebser (Austrian) all adopt somewhat different, transformational orientations, they all build upon an original 'vitality' in the living systems, and its progressive – spiralling – unfolding.

We must then achieve the new integral structure without forfeiting the efficient forms of the previous structures. The new consciousness structure, moreover, has nothing to do with might, rule and overpowering. It cannot be striven for, only elicited or awakened. What is needed therefore is care, a great deal of patience, and the laying aside of many preconceived opinions. There is a need for a certain detachment toward oneself and the world in order to prepare from the leap into the new mutation.

5.2.4 THE GENE AS THE OVERALL TRANSFORMATIONAL RHYTHM

On all levels, the fourfold rhythm of the GENE can be recognized as the guiding rhythm for transformation. Based on the GENE, we are articulating for each level dynamic transformational fourfolds. The reader may be surprised how established theories and concepts on transformational processes provide evidence for the cyclical rhythm the GENE is intimating.

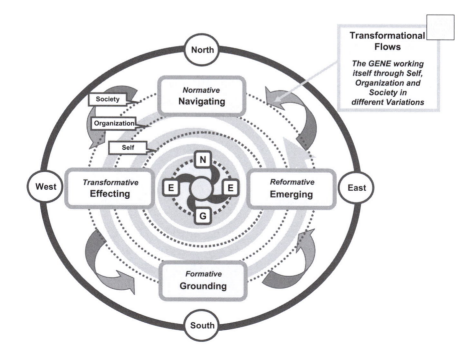

Figure 5.1   Releasing the GENE-ius of self, organization and society

In summary, we have been introducing the following rhythms:

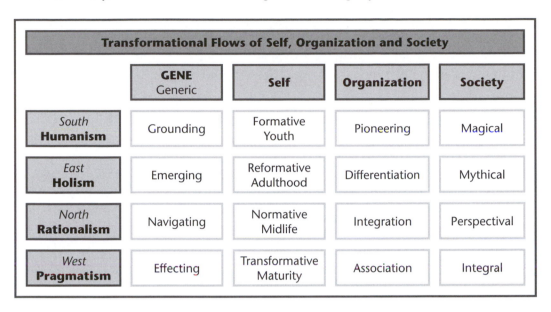

Transformational Flows of Self, Organization and Society				
	GENE Generic	**Self**	**Organization**	**Society**
South **Humanism**	Grounding	Formative Youth	Pioneering	Magical
East **Holism**	Emerging	Reformative Adulthood	Differentiation	Mythical
North **Rationalism**	Navigating	Normative Midlife	Integration	Perspectival
West **Pragmatism**	Effecting	Transformative Maturity	Association	Integral

We now turn from theory to practice, for individual, organization and society in turn. In doing so, we cite three evocative, individual, organizational and societal case stories.

Individually we introduce South Africa's Nelson Mandela; organizationally we focus on Bangladesh's Muhammad Yunus and Grameen Bank; and in the societal case will be illustrated by the story of Sultan Qaboos and the Sultanate of Oman. In all three cases, self (Mandela, Yunus, Qaboos), organization (ANC, Grameen Bank, Government of Oman) and society (South Africa, Bangladesh, Oman) are deeply interconnected. However, for the purpose of illustration, we shall focus in each case on one level in particular. In each one, we shall follow a fourfold rhythm, as suggested by Levinson for the self (Mandela), by Lievegoed and Glasl for the organization (Grameen), and by Gebser for society (Oman). We start with Nelson Mandela's life stages, as expressed in his own worlds, and as depicted from *The Long Walk to Freedom*.[12]

5.3 The Transformation Journey of Self, Organization and Society

5.3.1 TRANSFORMATION OF THE SELF IN PRACTICE: THE CYCLE OF LIFE OF NELSON MANDELA

The first formative stage: Mandela's childhood and youth

The Formative Stage
'Apart from life, a strong constitution and an abiding connection to the Thembu royal house, the only thing my father bestowed upon me at birth was a name, Rohnlahla. In Xhosa it literally means "pulling the branch of a tree", but is colloquially interpreted as a "troublemaker". I was born on 18 July 1918 at Myezo in Qunu, a tiny village on the banks

of the Mbashe River in the district of Umtata, the capital of the Transkei. It was a place apart from the world of great events, where life was lived as it had been for hundreds of years. My father, Gadla Henry Mphakanyiswa, was a chief by blood and by custom. I am a member of the Madiba clan, named after a Thembu chief who ruled the Transkei in the 18th century. My father was an acknowledged custodian of Xhosa history, and it was partly for that reason that he was valued as an advisor to the king'.

Forming a Dream

'In my final year at the Wesleyan College we were informed that the great Xhosa poet, Krune Mqhayi, was going to visit the school. Mqhayi was actually an imbongi, a praise singer, a kind of oral historian who marks contemporary events and history with poetry that is of special meaning to his people. The assegai stands for what is glorious and true in African history; it is a symbol of the African as warrior and the African as artist. For too long we have succumbed to the false gods of the white man. But we shall emerge and cast off the foreign nation'.

Forming Mentor Relationships

Mandela had several mentors over the course of his adult life starting out with his first law firm in Johannesburg:

> I was taken on by Lazar Sidelsky, a partner at Wilkin, Sidelsky and Eidelman. Taking on a young African articled clerk was virtually unheard of in those days. No matter how small the job Mr Sidelsky would explain to me what it was for and why I was doing it.

For Mandela, his kindred spirits, Walter Sisulu, Oliver Tambo and others also played a mentor role:

> I cannot pinpoint a moment when I became politicised, when I knew I would spend the rest of my life on the liberation struggle. To be an African in South Africa, then if not now, means that one is politicized from the moment of one's birth, whether one acknowledges it or not. As a black person, your life is circumscribed by racist laws and regulations that cripple your growth, dim your potential and stunt your life. This was the reality, and I could deal with it in a number of ways, and the new friends and colleagues that I was meeting would influence that choice … Walter Sisulu's house in Orlando African township was a Mecca for activists and ANC members.

Forming an Occupation

In a transitional society like South Africa, such an occupation, or vocation, may be societally, as well as, or indeed instead of, organizationally based. For Mandela:

> In fact I was far more certain, in those days, what I was against than what I was for. I acquired the complete works of Marx and Engels, Lenin and Stalin, Mao and others, and probed the philosophy of dialectical and historical materialism. First and foremost, though, I was an African nationalist fighting for our emancipation from minority rule and the right to control our own destiny, in the wake of apartheid.

The second reformative stage: Mandela's adulthood

Early Adult Transition

For Mandela, from an early stage, he questioned not only the political state of South Africa, but was also critical to local traditions:

> The regent was anxious for me to attend Fort Hare, until 1960 the only residential centre of higher education for blacks. Fort Hare was characterised by a level of sophistication, both intellectual and social, that was new and strange to me. By Western standards, its worldliness might not seem much, but to a country boy like myself it was a revelation. With the prospect of securing a BA there, I would finally be able to restore to my mother the wealth and the prestige she had lost after my father's death. That was my dream and it seemed within reach. In fact it was the very education that the regent had afforded me that had caused me to reject tradition. I was not prepared to have anyone, even the regent, select a bride for me. Justice and I agreed that the only choice remaining was to run away, and the only place to run to was Johannesburg, where I wanted to study law.

We can see, illustrated by Mandela's case that, in a society in transition, the individual, developmental agenda is set within the context, of a similar process going on in the society as a whole. Mandela's adulthood, from its very beginning, was oriented towards a new South Africa. Referring to the ANC's Freedom Charter, Mandela stated:

> The charter was in fact a revolutionary document because the changes it envisioned could not be achieved without radically altering the economic and political structure of South Africa. It was not meant to be capitalist nor socialist but a melding together of the people's demands to end the oppression. In South Africa, merely to achieve fairness, one had to destroy apartheid itself, the very embodiment of injustice.

Settling Down to a Point

For the young adult, the settling down to a point is, as per Levinson, the main vehicle for realizing youthful ambitions and goals. In Mandela's case his 'settling down' was the development of a fearless and uncompromising commitment to his life's goal. Such got particularly articulated in the notorious Treason Trial at Rivonia:

> I was made, by the law, a criminal, not because of what I had done, but because of what I had stood for, because of what I thought, because of my conscience. Can it be any wonder to anybody that such conditions make a man an outlaw of society? But there comes a time, as it came in my life, when a man is denied the right to live a normal life, when he can only live the life of an outlaw because the government has decreed to use the law to impose a state of outlawry upon him. More powerful, then, than my fear of the dreadful conditions to which I might be subjected in prison is my hatred for the dreadful conditions to which my people are subjected outside prison throughout this country. … Whatever sentence Your Worship sees fit to impose upon me for the crime for which I have been convicted before this court, may it rest assured that when my sentence has been completed I will still be moved, as men are always moved, by their conscience; I will still be moved by my dislike for racial discrimination against my people, so that when I come out from serving my sentence I will take up again, as best as

I can, the struggle for the removal of those injustices until they are finally abolished once and for all.

The third normative stage: Mandela's midlife

Every developmental transition, for Levinson, presents the opportunity and the necessity of moving forward toward a new integration of four key polarities. This is most particularly the case, for him, at midlife. For us set in the context of Apartheid South Africa, such renewal, or re-formation, was a necessarily ongoing concern already in Mandela's adulthood, so that midlife, and ultimately maturity, are concerned with integration. However, in Mandela's case, his 27 years in prison, after the age of 40, served to prolong his midlife phase, delaying the onset of his legacy.

Mandela's normative stage is perhaps best represented by his famous statement in the so-called Rivonia Trial, where he faced up the ultimate exigencies of life and death:

During my lifetime I have dedicated myself to this struggle of the African people. I have fought against white domination; I have fought against black domination. I have cherished the ideal of a democratic and free society in which all persons live together in harmony and with equal opportunities. It is an ideal, which I hope to live for and achieve. But if needs be, it is an ideal for which I am prepared to die.

The fourth transformative stage: maturity and legacy stage

Perhaps, Nelson Mandela's statement, on the day of his inauguration as president of South Africa, provides a flavour of this final stage. For Mandela:

On the day of the inauguration I was overwhelmed with a sense of history. In the first decade of the 20th century, a few years after the bitter Anglo-Boer war and before my own birth, the white skinned peoples of South Africa patched up their differences and erected a system of racial discrimination against the dark skinned peoples of their own land. The structure they created formed the basis of one of the harshest, most inhumane, societies the world has ever known. Now in the last decade of the 20th century, and my own eighth decade as a man, that system has been overturned forever and replaced by one that recognised the rights and freedoms of all people regardless of the colour of their skin.

We now turn from Mandela, as an individual, to the organization, Grameen.

5.3.2 TRANSFORMATION OF THE ORGANIZATION IN PRACTICE: THE CASE OF GRAMEEN

Orientation to Grameen

The Grameen Bank based in Bangladesh has come a long way in 30 years, when it was founded by Bangladeshi Professor of Economics, and by now Nobel Peace Laureate Muhammad Yunus. From $27 lent to 52 people in 1976 to $2.3 billion lent to 2.3 million families in 1998. Grameen programmes now stretch around the world, from Ecuador to Eritrea, from the Norwegian Arctic Circle to Papua New Guinea, from Chicago's inner city ghettos to remote mountain communities in Nepal – by the new millennium 58 countries had become Grameen clones.

The entire meaning of what Grameen has preached is that the poor are bankable. That one can lend to them on a commercial basis and make a profit. Those banks should and can serve the disinherited of the earth, not only out of altruism but also out of self-interest. Treating the poor as untouchables and outcasts, for the bank's founder Muhammad Yunus, is immoral and indefensible, and also financially stupid. His message is always the same: poverty can be eradicated in our lifetime. We only need the political will. Such a statement needs to be repeated over and over again because we can only build what we are able to imagine. Only if we conceptualize a world without poverty, so Yunus, are we able to build it.

Grameen is in fact the soundest financial institution in Bangladesh today. Unlike other banking establishments, the object of the financial exercise is not, primarily, to earn a good commercial return but, rather as an instrument of cultural production, to enhance people's liberty, their equality and their fraternity. For Yunus, the objective is to enable people to make the most of their lives, so that they become authors of their own destiny. We are now retracing the organizational life cycle of Grameen, building on Yunus's book *Banker of the Poor*.[13]

Pioneering phase

One of the origin's of Grammen is the story of Sufia Begum. For Yunus, her story made him sit up. He couldn't believe that a woman, crafting bamboo chairs, could suffer a life of bonded labour – bonded to her money lender – because she was unable to find the 20 cents a day to fund her business. So he drove to the local branch of the Janata Bank, a government institution and one of the biggest in the country, to negotiate a loan on Sufia's behalf. He failed, utterly, to secure any kind of loan without collateral. So he ended up advancing the money himself, but that was no kind of long-term solution. Meanwhile Muhammad was in the process of discovering, as he put it, '*the world's basic banking principle – the more you have the more you get; if you don't have it, you don't get it*'.

Perhaps unwittingly banks had designated a class of people as 'not creditworthy', meaning 'we can't touch you'. Out of desperation, Yunus was led to question the most basic banking premise, that of collateral. Having complained for so long, moreover, that banks discriminate against women, he wanted most of his prospective borrowers to be such. And it was from that vantage point that Grameen was started.

Because they knew nothing about how to run a bank for the poor, Yunus and his economic students, as would-be bankers, had to learn from scratch. In January 1977, when they started, Yunus looked at how others ran their loan operations, and learnt from their mistakes. In Bangladesh, conventional banks and credit co-operatives always demanded lump sum payments. This was a major psychological hurdle for borrowers. Grameen therefore did exactly the opposite, making the payments so small that the borrower would not even notice it. They decided to make it a daily payment. The monitoring would also therefore be easier. Moreover, it would enhance the self-discipline of the borrower, and give them the confidence they could manage it. For ease in accounting the loans had to be paid off in one year.

In 1978 Yunus, now in his late thirties, took a two-year leave of absence from his university. He wanted, by this stage, to gain official recognition as a bank from the central authorities in Bangladesh. They wanted him to prove that his banking approach was generalizable. So he picked the most difficult region in the country as a proving ground.

Tangail District was in the midst of a war situation. Armed guerillas in an underground Marxist dissident movement called the 'People's Army' were terrorising the countryside. The villages he passed through seemed so Godforsaken, and the poor so frail and emaciated that Yunus felt he had come to the right place. This is where the challenge lay.

The ex 'People's Army' turned out to be excellent Grameen staff. They had wanted to liberate the country with guns and revolution, and now they were walking around the same villages and roads extending micro-loans to the destitute. They just needed something to believe in, some cause to fight for. Yunus channelled their energies towards something far more constructive than terrorism. What is business, Yunus maintains, if not using your courage and despair to make things happen. The Gono Bahini (People's Army) in Tangail had a lot of fighting spirit waiting to be channelled in the right direction. Why not give them a chance to do something constructive for society?

Grameen looked at conventional banks and turned everything upside-down. Conventional banks ask their clients to come to their office. An office is a terrifying place for the poor and illiterate. So they decided to go to the clients. The entire Grameen system is based on such.

In a commercial bank, bankers are only answerable to their shareholders, to maximise the bank's profits, subject to limits set by governments and regulators. Grameen too is answerable to shareholders. *With the exception of the 8 per cent of stock owned by government, its shareholders are its borrowers.* The bank seeks a high return for its shareholders, but this may be in the form of improved housing and standard of living. Paying such a dividend in kind, instead of in cash, that is changing their day-to-day lives, is what is most important. In Grameen then, *people's needs and lives is not a sideline, it is what comes first and foremost. All the rest is merely a means to advance its goals of transforming the lives of our borrowers and their dependants.*

Success, therefore, is not measured by bad debt figures or repayment rates – though such records need to be kept – but whether the miserable lives of our borrowers have become less miserable, less difficult. Yunus would like, ultimately, all his borrowers to rise above the poverty line. Special housing loans, for example, have provided leak-proof homes for 425,000 families; while another 150,000 homes have been built from Grameen-funded enterprises. Grameen, as such, is promoting social as well as economic change. It wants women, hitherto adjudged second-class citizens, to make decisions about their fate and their families.

Phase of differentiation

Securing Group Support

Meanwhile, on the Grameen project, they adapted and changed as they went along, significantly discovering that the formation of a group was crucial to the success of their operations. Individually a poor person feels exposed to all kinds of hazards. Group membership gave a feeling of protection. Individually, a person tends to be erratic, uncertain in his or her behaviour. But group membership provided support and pressure, making the borrower more reliable. A sense of intra-group and inter-group competition, moreover, helped everyone to be an achiever.

Moreover, it reduced the supervisory load of the bank worker as it increased the self-reliance of the group. Because the group approved the loan request of each member, it felt morally responsible for the loan. So if any member of the group ever got into trouble, the group usually came forward to help out. Each prospective borrower had to go through a lot of training so that they fully understood what Grameen was about. Each of the five, within a group, knew that if they failed they would let the whole group down, because the group would have to find another suitable member.

For Yunus then, set within his own storied world:

... when the borrower finally receives her loan, she is literally trembling, shaking. The money is burning in her fingers. Tears roll down her eyes because she has never received so much money in her life. She carries it as she would a delicate bird, until someone tells her to put it away in a safe place. She cannot believe such a treasure has been put in her hands. All of her life she has been told that she was no good, that, being a woman, she only brought misery to her family, because they now had to pay for a dowry, which they could not afford. But today, for the first time, an institution had trusted her with all this money. She is stunned. She promises herself she will never let down this institution, which has trusted her, so much. She will struggle to make sure every penny is paid back. And she does it.

At first Grameen extends loans to only two group members. If these two repay regularly for the next six weeks, two more members can become borrowers. The chairman of the group is the last borrower of the five. When the first-time borrower pays back her first instalment there is enormous excitement because she has proved to herself she can earn the money to pay the second instalment, and then the third. It is an exciting experience for her. It is the excitement of discovering the worth of her own ability, and this thrilling experience seizes her; it is palpable and contagious to anyone who meets or talks to her. She discovers something inside of her that she never knew she had. The Grameen loan is not simply cash. It becomes a kind of ticket to self-discovery. The borrower begins to explore her potential. As Yunus puts it, for every one of Grameen's two million borrowers there is a thrilling story of self-discovery.

Promoting Centres of Excellence

If one group member defaults, no other can get a loan. In practice, if one member is in difficulty, the others work out a practical solution that assures repayment. The organization of up to eight groups in a 'centre' is another way Grameen found to develop leadership skills and develop self-help techniques. Centres meet in the village with a bank worker at a regularly scheduled times, usually early in the morning so as not to conflict with work arrangements. At these weekly meetings members make repayments, make deposits to savings accounts and discuss new loan requests. If a member is in trouble the bank worker can help to find a solution. Each group elects a chair and a secretary. Each centre elects a chief and a deputy-chief that serve for one year, and cannot be re-elected.

Developing Trusting Relationships

There is no legal instrument between the lender and the borrower. Grameen feels its relationship is with people, not with papers. It builds up the human link based on trust. Grameen succeeds or fails depending on how strong its relationship is with its borrowers. It places trust in people and they, in turn, place their trust in Grameen. The meaning of the word 'credit' is trust. And yet over the years that commercial banking has been institutionalized, for Yunus, it has built its entire edifice on the basis of mistrust. Today banks tend to assume that every borrower is going to run away with the money, so they tie him or her up with all kinds of legal papers. If one of the Grameen bank workers is robbed – a very rare incident – usually all of the borrowers in that village will find out who did it and hunt them down. More often than not they force the thief to return the money. Grameen then assumes that every borrower is basically honest. That not only saves having to fill endless documents but, in 99 per cent of cases, the trust turns out to be vindicated.

Low Key – Small Way

A guiding principle to Grameen's work, then, is to start in a low-key and in a small way. Why hurry? If poor people have survived without Grameen for all these centuries, they can survive without it for many years to come. Grameen's objective is to develop a system that works, not to rush out a service at breakneck speed. Grameen is a self-help organization. It wants to liberate the genius of individuals to create a better life for themselves. In its Tangail expansion, moreover, it developed a procedure it would use over and over again.

The manager, usually accompanied by an associate manager (a trainee who would soon be given the responsibility of setting up a new branch – many of who were ex students of Yunus) arrives in a village where Grameen has decided to set up a branch. It is most important that these two have no office, no place to stay and no one to get in touch with. They arrive without knowing anyone, and without an introduction. The first assignment is to understand and document everything about the area. The reason Grameen does this is to make its bankers as different as possible from government officials who arrive in a village creating an aura of tremendous importance around them. So manager and associate have to pay for a room, and they are not permitted to stay in fancy surroundings.

They can find shelter in some abandoned house or council office. At first nobody believes they are bank officials. After a few days the villagers learn that both of these strangers who have moved into the village have masters degrees. They are highly educated university graduates. Local schoolteachers are usually the first to recognize their educational status. The manager and his associate walk for miles every day to talk to villagers and answer their questions. They explain the procedures for forming a group. In order to make certain that we favour the most disadvantaged, it is Grameen's policy to accept only women's groups which are located the farthest away from the location of the branch.

When a young manager gets the opportunity to set up a branch, it is his or her first chance in life to make a reputation for themselves. There is a sense of adventure. Their training has prepared them to climb a difficult mountain. Now they want to conquer the highest peak. To give Grameen maximum exposure, the manager invites the village leaders, religious leaders, teachers and government officials, to a 'projection meeting' at which some high ranking Grameen official explains everything in detail, giving the villagers either the option to accept Grameen with all its rules and procedures or, within a specified time frame, to tell it to leave the village. So far, no village has ever asked it to leave, but giving people the option makes it clear there is no compulsion. In 1982, Grameen launched its expansion programme to cover five widely separated districts: Dhaka in the centre of the country, Chittagong in the southeast, Rangpur in the northeast, Patuakhali in the south, and Tangail in the north.

What is amazing, for Yunus, is how smoothly and 'biologically' micro-credit works: just as investment capital of much larger amounts creates dividends, so does its smallest and least significant form. It is the natural wellspring of creative and economic life, so that people can add investment capital to their human capital to improve their lives and the world around them. Some of the west's greatest geo-strategists see the world locked into future cultural struggles, such as Christianity versus Islam. At Grameen they do not look at the world that way. They make loans to Muslim, Hindu, Christian and Buddhist women alike; all religious and cultural groups are represented on the board of directors. There is no reason for religious and cultural wars if the poorest can, through their own self-help, their own micro capital, develop and become independent, active, thinking and creative human beings. Micro credit, for Yunus, may not be a cure-all, but it is a force for change, not only economic and personal, but also social and political.

Phase of integration

On 2 October 1983, Grameen became a corporate entity, the 'Grameen Bank'. Until then staff had been recruited on a temporary basis, and they had worried that sooner or later the project might terminate, and they would be out of a job. As soon as Grameen became an independent bank they automatically became permanent staff. They were jubilant. Yunus held the opening ceremony in a big open field in the village of Jamarki in Tangail. Selected groups of borrowers from several branches were invited to participate, and staff were invited from all nearby branches. They filled the field. Other guests came from Dakha, including Finance Minister Munith.

It was a wonderful day, full of bright sunshine. It began with recitations from the holy Koran, as is customary on such occasions. Speeches from the women borrowers were quite emotional. For all of the people who had laboured long and hard to get to this point, it was a dream come true. Muhammad stared at all the women seated in their colourful red, green, ochre and pink sarees, hundreds of barefoot borrowers who had travelled from near and far to join the celebration. They had voted with their feet. There was no doubt about their commitment to break away from poverty, which brings to light another 'liberation story', that of Jorimon:

> Jorimon was one of the members who was there that day. She was born around 1952, suffered a terrible skin rash that almost killed her at the age of 6 and which still scars her today; as a child she also suffered terribly from ringworm. At the age of 10, she was married off to a poorhouse worker twelve years her elder. She had two sons and a daughter. During the famine of 1974 she and her children spent the year in near starvation. Her husband used to beat her up on the slightest pretext and he was always threatening to divorce her. In spite of working non-stop she and her husband knew nothing but suffering, hunger and sorrow.

> On December 29th, 1979, she and four other women joined the Grameen bank project and in January, her group received its first loan for 600 taka. With the paddy-husking business that she started Jorimon was able to repay her first loan by January, 1981. During this first year she and her family never went hungry thanks to the earnings generated by the Grameen loan. She also had enough money to buy clothes for her family, and had some profit left over. At

first her husband was very worried about her joining the group, but once it worked out without problems, he accepted. She went on to buy a cow and to build a house with her profits.

In her words 'previously we went hungry for days on end; I worked like a slave in other people's houses; I walked from village to village with a heavy load of firewood on my head, trying to get some money in return. We had no home of our own. People used to ignore us all the time. No one looked at us with grace or favour ... But today God has shown us the path to happiness through a bank loan'.

Phase of association

Replicating the Grameen Programme

In replicating Grameen, Yunus maintains, one must remember right from the beginning that, if the recovery rate is not near 100 per cent, no matter how good it looks, it is not Grameen. All the strength of Grameen comes from this near-perfect recovery performance. It is not merely the money, which is reflected through this recovery rate, it is the discipline, which speaks loud and clear through it. Replications of Grameen, he advocates, should also not compromise on the target population. He advises replicators to start with the bottom 25 per cent of the population, and to focus on the poorest women. The International Dialogue Programme, held four times a year in Bangladesh, is a good introduction for would-be replicators. Today Grameen-type credit programmes are being replicated in 58 countries: 22 in Africa, 16 in Asia, 15 in the Americas, 5 in Europe. As in Bangladesh, Grameen discovered that the rate of interest is not as important as the fact that credit is available to the poor. The poor can pay 20 per cent to 30 per cent without a problem. The liberating force of credit is so great that the borrowers are able to dream up innumerable new activities.

The Grameen Trust – The People's Fund

Many replication programmes of Grameen now exist, as we have seen, around the world, and these need staff training. Such training is provided through the Grameen Trust via what is called the International Dialogue Programme. It requires chief executives of replicating organisations to spend 12 days in Grameen, mostly in its branches, so as to immerse themselves in the day-to-day functioning of the organisation, to absorb the realities of poverty and to understand the role of credit in the individual borrower's life. But, as already intimated, there is now much more to Grameen than providing its borrowers with access to micro credit.

Providing for Housing

Now that the commercial side of the Grameen Bank had proved itself and is actively changing people's lives, Yunus wanted to build on this success and expand into other areas, public and private, civic and animate, so as to improve the quality of life of Grameen's borrowers, as well as that of the community in general. Specifically, he was looking towards market oriented ways of improving the social infrastructure, which the government was not providing, or was providing inadequately.

Grameen has expanded the types of loans it makes available to borrowers to finance such quality of life items as water wells, flush toilets and housing. It is also creating self-financing enterprises that will cover its borrowers' health, retirement and education, as well as meet the needs of the community at large. To date 13 years since it opened up its housing loan facilities, it has extended a total of £150 million in loans to build 450,000 houses with near perfect repayment in weekly instalments. At the same time, similar housing loan schemes opened up by the conventional commercial banks collapsed.

Health and Retirement

Survival for Yunus is not only financial, but also emotional and psychological. Doing nothing all day is cruel, undignified and unhealthy, not only for the people concerned, but for the community at large. What better way to achieve human dignity than by doing something creative, of the person's own choosing, that makes him or her feel useful. Of course, many old people are too infirm to work, but old age should not be a reason to have your emotional and psychological rights taken away from people. On the contrary, senior citizens should enjoy inalienable human rights like everyone else, the same opportunity to lead creative and productive lives.

Around the world, national health programmes are in crisis. Whether it is the 'free market' system of the United States, or the 'nationalized' systems of England, France or Germany the poor are not adequately protected. In Bangladesh, where the government spends generously, the quality of services – for Yunus – are appalling. That is because doctors who become government employees often neglect their duties in favour of private practice. Grameen is trying to make health care available to all its borrowers, and to other villagers, on a self-financing, cost-recovery basis, asking people to pay $3 per family per year, as a health premium. So social infrastructure is indeed part of poverty alleviation. But good infrastructure, by itself, will not create wealth. It creates a required enabling environment in the war against poverty.

Clothing the Nation

Today in Bangladesh there are one million handloom weavers desperately looking for a product for their market. In 1993, Grameen created an independent, non-stock, not-for-profit company to do just that. It was called Grameen Udddog (Initiatives). The objective of the company was to link up the traditional handloom weavers with the export oriented garment industry. The weavers produced the cloth Grameen asked for, and, for Yunus, it was beautiful. They themselves took great pride in the export market. The name given to the fabric was 'Grameen Check'. In three years total sales per annum have gone up to $15 million, and it is expanding. Today 8,000 weavers are involved with Grameen, and their Check is sold all over Europe. In the meanwhile, domestically, Grameen Check has become a household name. Every young person wants to wear it. It has become a matter of pride and a social statement: we are proud of our heritage. To cope with this newly emerging domestic market, another company has been created, Grameen Shamogree (Products), which is focusing on a wide variety of Bangladeshi handicrafts.

Fish Farming – Feeding the Poor

Fish farming was Grameen's next port of call. As it had no background in such, it enrolled staff on crash courses on how to farm fish. Grameen sent staff to China to learn about pond management and hatchery operations. Practical skills were developed through learning by doing. Eventually the large initial capital investment and the training of staff began to pay off. Grameen organised the poor around the ponds to become partners in business. They gave their labour, guarded the ponds against poaching and Grameen provided all the inputs, technology and management. Technology is an essential prerequisite for raising productivity, but unless Grameen directs who it is who will receive the increased production, it will end up – Yunus believes – in the hands of the rich.

GrameenPhone – Technology for the Poor

The government of Bangladesh issued three cellular licences in 1996 to Grameen. On Independence Day, in March 1997, a service was launched, which promised to bring IT to all the people of Bangladesh, even the poorest. Grameen formed two independent companies, one for profit (GrameenPhone), and the other not for profit (Grameen Telecom). The former is a consortium made up of four partners: Telenor of Norway (51 per cent), Grameen Telecom (35 per cent), Marubeni of Japan (9.5 per cent) and Gonophone Development Company (4.5 per cent). GrameenPhone was the recipient of the licence. It will serve all urban areas by building a nationwide network. Grameen Telecom will buy bulk airtime from GrameenPhone and retail it from Grameen borrowers in all the villages of Bangladesh. One Grameen borrower in each of the 68,000 villages will become 'the telephone lady'. She will sell the service of the telephone to the villages and earn money. New information technology will become the source of her income generating activity. Thus the village will be connected to the world through a poor woman who uses the most modern communication system available to earn a better living for herself.

Grameen also hopes to make the Internet available in rural areas throughout GrameenPhone network. Grameen Cybernet, an Internet service provider will create international jobs for the children of Grameen borrowers. These boys and girls will be able to serve companies around the world in various capacities from their own village homes or offer community office spaces. By bringing internet facilities into distant rural areas many labour intensive enterprises can be located in those otherwise isolated regions, such as data entry services, data management businesses, global answering services, typing and transcription services, accounting services and so on. Finally, a non-profit Internet service provider, Grameen Communications, will make the Internet available to educational and research institutions in Bangladesh. There is no reason to suppose that in the future the Grameen telephone lady will limit herself to renting out her phone; as technology and energy sources evolve, Yunus can imagine her providing her fellow villages with a capacity to send and receive faxes and e-mail, becoming a door-to-door communication centre.

We now turn from Grameen, as an organization, to Oman, in this case in brief outline, as a whole society.

5.3.3 TRANSFORMATION OF THE SOCIETY IN PRACTICE: THE CASE OF THE SULTANATE OF OMAN

From archaic community ...

The development of Oman in the past 40 years deserves a detailed examination. Oman's Sultan Qaboos, who took over power in 1970, led the country step by step from massive underdevelopment in all sectors to a modern nation. 'Today Oman is recognized as one of the most impressive examples of socio-economic recovery in modern times.'[14]

Compared to other Arabic nations, it is striking to witness the progressive introduction of democratic institutions, which make the whole country a classic example of 'Good

National Governance' in the Middle East and beyond. Despite the intense relationship of the Sultan to European culture (parts of Qaboos's earlier education took place in England and Germany and he remains a strong supporter of European classical music) Oman until today has been remarkably true to its Arabic-Muslim roots. The governance institutions of the country, which had been introduced by the Sultan, are not copies of western institutional models, but relate directly to Oman's cultural traditions. This includes for example the 'Maglis Al Shura' and the 'Maglis Al Dawlah', both mainly democratically elected organs of local government, whose main duty is the evaluation of the performance of the national government.[15] Every year for a period of three to six weeks, Qaboos himself tours the country, accompanied by a number of his ministers, virtually as a 'mobile government'. Qaboos made it a task for himself to personally meet as many local representatives as possible to gain an accurate picture of the needs of his countrymen and women. In the words of Qaboos: 'To fail to give one's people a voice in their destiny, to regard them as automatons only to be directed and not consulted, is a sure way to disaster. This has never been the Omani way, and I have every intention of ensuring that this popular form of participation is further developed to the benefit of my people and country.'[16]

... to integral society

Many sources underline the enormous impact that such sensible incorporation of local culture has also had on the corporate sector. This is confirmed by for example, McBrierty und Al Zubair: 'The institutions that underpin the developing 'knowledge economy' within Oman have capitalised on a deep-rooted Omani entrepreneurial spirit and its long tradition as a trading nation. Objectively, the basis for this transformation ... is to be found in the initiatives taken by the Sultan.'[17] Altogether, McBrierty and Al Zubair conclude with reference to Islam, that the urban design and the build environment in Oman is inspired from the Islamic notion of harmony and balance between the financial capital, social capital and natural capital. All species and human are viewed as communities and they are governed by the same laws of succession and survival. The world of ideas (reformed by Islam) shape and form the material world; one follows the other like a shadow. The 'ever present origin', as per Gebser's theory on societal evolution, becomes indeed tangible in the Omani case.

5.4 Conclusion: Self, Organizational and Societal Transformation

The whole process of individual, organizational and societal development, ultimately, is dynamically connected, each successive spiral stage linked to and adding to the previous ones. Each stage marks the rise of a new set of capacities. These add to and re-contextualise previous patterns of strength without negating or supplanting them. Certain life issues recur, though each successive stage addresses these at a new level of complexity.

Each stage represents a widening of vision and valuing, correlated with a parallel increase in the depth of person-hood, institution-hood and society-hood. This all makes for qualitative increases. Transitions from one spiral stage to the other are protracted, painful, dislocating or aborted. Arrest can and does occur at each stage.

In our transformation work and programmes we do not see an individual or organization as a passive receptacle for whom and which training or consultancy must be brought in order to stimulate learning or change. Rather as an agent of transformation you recognize the agenda upon which you or your institution as well as your society is already embarked. Part of your maturity is the realization that you can facilitate or thwart its development, but cannot yourself invent it. Such an approach suggests a kind of lifelong capacity to nourish and to keep buoyant your personal or your organizational 'life-project'.

We now turn from the transformational to the transcultural.

References

1. Piaget, J. (1975). *The Child's Conception of the World*. Lanham: Littlefield Adams.
2. Jaques, E. (1991). *Executive Leadership*. Oxford: Blackwell.
3. Stevens, A. (1994). *On Jung*. Harmondsworth: Penguin.
4. Levinson, D.J. (1979). *The Seasons of a Man's Life*. New York: Knopf.
5. Lievegoed, B. (1969). *The Developing Organisation*. London: Tavistock Publications.
6. Lievegoed, B. (1991). *Managing the Developing Organisation*. Oxford: Basil Blackwell.
7. Lievegoed, B. (1991). *Managing the Developing Organisation*. Oxford: Basil Blackwell.
8. Lievegoed, B. (1991). *Managing the Developing Organisation*. Oxford: Basil Blackwell.
9. Lievegoed, B. (1991). *Managing the Developing Organisation*. Oxford: Basil Blackwell.
10. Glasl, F. (1997). *The Enterprise of the Future*. Stroud: Hawthorn Press.
11. Gebser, J. (1985). *The Ever-Present Origin*. Ohio: Ohio University.
12. Mandela, N. (1994). *The Long Walk to Freedom*. Grand Rapids: Abacus.
13. Yunus, M. (1999). *Banker to the Poor*. New York: Public Affairs.
14. McBrierty, V. and Al Zubair, M. (2004). *Oman: Ancient Civilization and Modern Nation*. Dublin: Trinity Press.
15. McBrierty, V. and Al Zubair, M. (2004). *Oman: Ancient Civilization and Modern Nation*. Dublin: Trinity Press.
16. Plekhanov, S. (2004). *The Reformer on the Throne*. London: Trident Press.
17. McBrierty, V. and Al Zubair, M. (2004). *Oman: Ancient Civilization and Modern Nation*. Dublin: Trinity Press.

The Second Fundamental of Transformation Management

**Transforming
Organizational Development
*into Cultural Dynamics***

Core Theme within Transformation Management:
**Enabling the Creative Emergence of Enterprise
Through Culture and Spirituality
by Promoting Interaction Between Transcultural Forces**

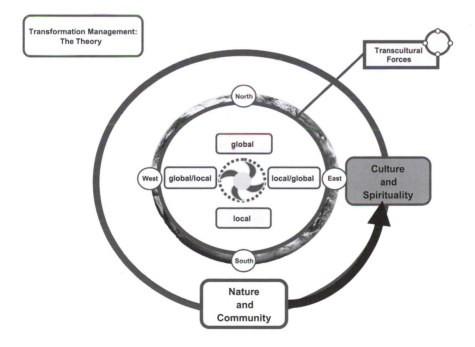

Transforming
Organizational Development
into Cultural Dynamics

Core Outcome for the Integral Enterprise:
1. **Building a Developing Organization**
2. **Realizing Natural GENE-ius**
3. **Implementing Cultural Dynamics**

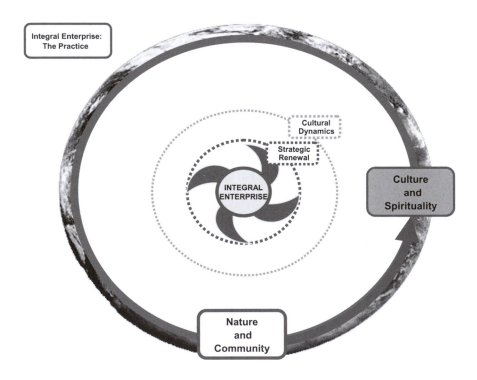

CHAPTER 6 *Culture and Transformation*

Corporate Culture to Transformational Topography

6.1 Introduction: From Clash of Civilizations to Co-Creation of Cultures

CULTURE: A WESTERN BLINDSPOT

We now turn from nature to culture. In the previous chapters on transformational flows, we built on the affinity with nature which is becoming ever more important today, as we face up to a potential environmental cataclysm. As such we developed a perspective on strategy, which was more natural and organic than economic and mechanistic in orientation. In the next three chapters on the cultural forces, we seek to transcend that western blindspot, one in which a *Clash of Civilizations*,[1] as Harvard's political scientist Samuel Huntington argues, gains significant precedence over any more productive interaction between such cultural horizons. Again, following our strategic re-orientation towards transformational flows, we move from competition (clash) to co-creation (complementarity).

Interestingly enough, in the evolution of management and organization theory, it is sociology and more especially behavioural psychology, alongside political economy, which has ruled the social science roost, rather than anthropology. Anthropology, then, has been restricted to the analysis of so-called 'primitive' societies; and even with the advent of corporate culture, over and above organizational behaviour, it was psychology and sociology, rather than anthropology again, that took pride of place. So within the two major generalist fields of business administration – that is strategy and organizational development – it is respectively economics and behavioural science, rather than ecology and anthropology, which have taken the lead. No wonder there is a pervasive lack of natural and cultural contextualization.

FROM AN ANALYTICAL TO A DEVELOPMENTAL PERSPECTIVE ON CULTURE

In fact, while Charles Handy from the UK, the pre-eminent authority on *Understanding Organisations*[2] was a classics scholar, the leading expert on *Culture and Organisation*,[3] Geert Hofstede from the Netherlands, has – like his countryman Fons Trompenaars in *Riding the Waves of Culture*[4] – drawn upon sociology rather than anthropology as their source material. The well known 'map' of culture and organization that Hofstede developed (see following Table) illustrates that he, like Trompenaars, have used their cultural insights to inform management attitudes and behaviours. They did, however, not use it, as we are doing here, to evolve the structure and functioning of enterprises in particular cultures.

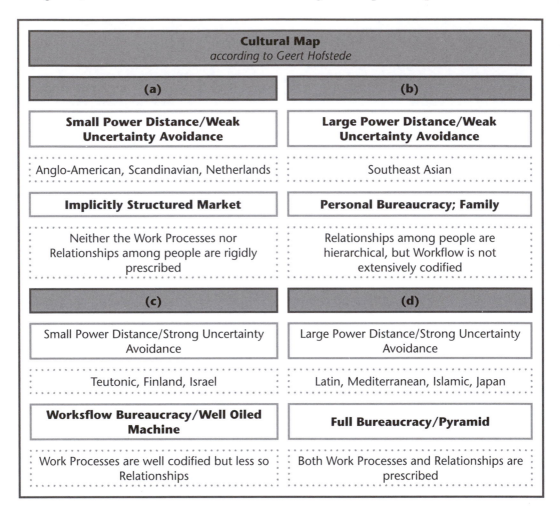

In other words, both Hofstede's and Trompenaars's approaches to cross-cultural management are analytic as opposed to developmental, focused on organizations rather than, in addition, on societies. In our transcultural orientation, we thereby part company from them. We therefore turn now from cross-cultural management to culture and transformation.

6.2 Towards a Transcultural Orientation

Transcultural forces are the second fundamental of Transformation Management. Now that nature is being increasingly taken into organizational and societal consideration, it is culture, in this deep sense, which is still, and continuingly, ignored. Culture, in our context, refers to the inclinations and institutions, ideologies and images of each society, organization or individual. We argue that there is no transformation without engaging with the deepest images, the surface inclinations, and that which lies in between of ourselves, our organizations and societies. These deepest layers, as we shall demonstrate, influence our in between philosophical systems and frameworks; as a result, they also influence the way we do research and generate new knowledge.

Such knowledge, usually arising out of a particular 'northwestern' culture, is then framed in scientific disciplines, specifically the natural and social sciences. And these disciplines are instrumental in the ways we design, organize and run organizations and institutions. The disciplines of economics and management, for example, underlie how we design, organize and run business enterprise. And the way we define our organizations, if not also our societies, is then a crucial determinant of behaviour. If we want to fundamentally transform these upper layers, we need to engage with the deepest most influential layer: incorporating art, religion and indeed culture itself.

SCRATCHING THE SURFACE: THE SHORTCOMINGS OF CONVENTIONAL CROSS-CULTURAL TRAINING

Of course, culture has to some extent been recognized within the context of 'enterprise in society', the broad assimilation of Hofstede's and Trompenaars's work being a good indicator of that. Not only is the term 'corporate culture' part of common business vocabulary, but management education has also been enlarged by cross-cultural training. However, most cultural and cross-cultural training is focused purely on the surface layer of behaviour. Its main orientation is towards training managers to understand other cultures with the purpose of being able to successfully manoeuvre people and things in a different cultural context. Such cross-cultural training does not lead to understanding how institutions are constructed, based on different cultural orientations, nor does it serve to provide in-depth understanding in the core philosophies of another culture. If philosophy is introduced, it happens mostly in a superficial way; for example, a quotation of Confucius is used in isolation to demonstrate a particular behavioural trait commonly found in China. The shortcomings of such an approach are that it a) leads to cultural stereotyping and b) overlooks the potential that lies in a meaningful transcultural interaction.

We shall demonstrate that engagement between the cultural depth of your own organization and society with that of another culture is crucial to Transformation Management. African Muslim Scholar Ali Mazrui, based in America but originally from Kenya, coined the phrase 'creative synthesis'. For him, any civilization could only come into existence because it has embodied, at least at one stage in time, the capacity to engage openly and creatively with other civilizations. There is an enormous co-creative potential in what we term indigenous-exogenous transcultural interaction, and we shall illustrate this aspect in detail, during the course of this book. But let us first continue our argument, why there is a need to engage with culture on a deeper level.

THE CASE OF LOCAL IDENTITY

The other core argument for starting with culture is identity. The Brazilian Paolo Freire, one of the pre-eminent educators of the twentieth century, recognized clearly the importance of a 'local identity':

Before I could become a citizen of the world I was and am first a citizen of Recife. The more rooted I am in my location the more I extend myself to other places so as to become a citizen of the world. No one becomes local from a universal location. The existential road is the reverse. I am a citizen of Recife. I am first from Recife, from Pernanbuco, and a Northeastern. Afterward I became a Brazilian, a Latin American and a world citizen.[5]

Hence, in order to make a meaningful contribution to the larger entity it is part of, a social system needs to first become authentically local.

That means that it is crucial for any enterprise, aiming to make a significant and sustainable contribution in a community or society, to engage deeply with the social and cultural context of that society. Similarly, on an individual level, we first need to know ourselves, before we can truly contribute to others. This seems to be common sense; however, it is easily overlooked. Further, such a perspective is challenged, as people perceive the world as increasingly monocultural.

BUT ARE WE NOT LIVING IN A GLOBAL VILLAGE?

In a time in which we live in a global village, of World Wide Webs and of ever faster and larger communication systems, we tend to submit too quickly to the illusion, that the local has become irrelevant, and all that counts is the global perspective. Alternatively, as multinational enterprises, *we tend to first 'think global' with a view to only thereafter 'acting local'. Conversely, we maintain that 'feeling local' is the place to start, 'acting global' is the place to end, and 'becoming transcultural' is what lies in between.*

In our work on different continents, we are often confronted with the argument of 'irrelevance of culture'. The core arguments are 'basically all humans are the same' and 'the core human values are universal'. The other perspective is that culture does not play an important enough role any more, as migration (as one of the core social problems of the twenty-first century), but also global communication technologies and networks, as well as globalized entertainment, have transformed the world into a monocultural community.

On the surface, we can empathize with such arguments. However, they contain a variety of problems:

- *Misunderstanding of the Other:* Often, we witness an unwillingness to acknowledge cultural diversity, seeing it rather as an obstacle, which is to be overcome quickly. This inhibits a thorough understanding of the differences between cultures and individuals.
- *Misunderstanding of the Essence of Self:* We lose the opportunity to see ourselves in a new light by purposefully engaging with, rather then denying, diversity. Such an attitude prevents us from learning new things, rooted in different cultural capacities. Moreover, and as we argue in our work on *Integral Research and Innovation,*[6] it also prevents us from engaging in social innovation, geared to the needs and aptitudes, and indeed overall understanding, of a particular society.
- *No Meaningful Interaction between the Other and the Self:* Ultimately, we may lose the creative spark that can be found in meaningful interaction between different cultural perspectives.

Furthermore, Huntington's 'clash of cultures' remains one of the core perceived reasons for many global conflicts. Thereby resisting the prevailing trend towards (by the way: western) monoculturalism, many countries retreat into their own parochial culture. In many such cases, whole societies turn to fundamentalism, parochialism or traditionalism, overemphasizing a narrow and inward looking perspective on their culture. This isolating and insulating behaviour inhibits such a culture from meaningfully engaging with other countries and thereby inhibits its ability to co-evolve, or, in our transformational terms, to 'emerge' from their prior grounds. Yet there is a need for each social system to first recognize its own local soil, before it can meaningfully engage with the outside world.

THE LOCAL AND THE GLOBAL BELONG TOGETHER

If we fail to develop 'local identity', evolution is inhibited; so argues, as intimated earlier, the prominent Kenyan-American scholar Ali Mazrui.[7]

Mazrui's introduces Africa as a case of a missing 'local identity'. He argues that it is the compact between Africa and the twentieth century, which is all wrong. This involves turning Africa's back on previous centuries – an attempt to 'modernize' without consulting cultural continuities, an attempt to start the process of 'dis-Africanizing' Africa.

For Mazrui, if the Jews of the Diaspora had scrambled to change their culture as fast as Africans in their homelands seemed to be doing until recently, the miracle of Jewish identity could not have lasted the two or three additional millennia in the wilderness. Many Africans even today seem to be undergoing faster cultural change in a single generation than the Jews, in Mazrui's opinion, underwent in the first 1,000 years of dispersal.

Africa, for him then, is at war. It is a war of cultures. It is a war between indigenous Africa and the forces of western civilization. It takes the form of inefficiency, mismanagement, corruption and decay of infrastructure. The crisis of efficiency on the continent is symptomatic of the failure of transplanted organs in the state and the economy. Indigenous African culture is putting up a fight. It is as if the indigenous ancestors have been roused from the dead, disapproving of what seems like an informal pact between the rulers of independent Africa (the inheritors of the colonial order) and the west – a pact which continues to allow the west to dominate Africa. It is as if the ancestors are angry at the failure of Africans to consult them and to pay attention to Africa's past. It is as if the apparent breakdown and decay in Africa today is a result of the curse of the ancestors. Or is it not a curse but a warning, a sign from the ancestors calling on Africans to rethink their recent past, their present and their future and calling on them to turn again to their traditions and reshape their society anew, to create a modern future Africa that incorporates the best of its own culture.

European colonial rule in Africa, in fact, was more effective in destroying indigenous African structures, embodied in its institutions, than destroying African culture, embodied in its art forms and religions. The shallowness of imported economic structures, as we have indicated, was due to the promotion of western tastes without developing the ability and inclination to co-create between different cultures. The shallowness of imported political institutions was partly due to the moral contradictions of western political tutelage. For transferred institutions simply did not take root; they remained, however, torn between privatization and miniaturization, anarchy and tyranny. But in the final analysis, the shallowness of imported institutions was due to the culture gap between new structures and ancient values, between alien institutions and ancestral traditions. There may therefore be a case for re-establishing contacts with familiar landmarks of yesteryear and then restarting the journey of modernization under indigenous impetus, first restoring its indigenous local identity.

Two broad principles, Mazrui suggests, should influence and inform social reform in Africa in the coming decades. One is the imperative of looking inwards towards ancestry (our grounding); the other is the imperative of looking outward towards the wider humanity (our emerging). African ancestors, on the one hand, need to be consulted with respect to African usage, custom and tradition. But since, on the other hand, the world is becoming a global village, the compact has to include sensitivity to the wider world of the human race as a whole. Before a seed germinates it has to decay. A new Africa may be germinating in the decay of the present one – and the ancestors are presiding over the process.

Mazrui's illustration is not only an argument for a healthy interaction between the local and the global – whereby the local needs to be restored before it can reach out to the global; it is also an argument for the capacity of culture to provide a meaningful transcultural link between the past and the future, between tradition and modernity.

CULTURE IS THE NECESSARY LINK BETWEEN TRADITION AND MODERNITY

For many people, the engagement with culture is primarily a backwards-looking activity. Understanding another culture means knowing about its history, having seen its major (mainly historic) monuments and artefacts, knowing its traditions. But *when we understand culture as the meaning giving system of a society then it becomes a current, ever evolving force, which can best be experienced in active engagement with today's human beings as well as with local nature, not with yesterday's historical beings.* Such an engagement, however, would then include tapping into the deeper layer of oneself and the other. In such a meaningful interaction, philosophies, arts, history and social psychology of a country become important, but not as a backwards-oriented knowledge archive. Much more, they become a means for mutual understanding and ongoing renewal.

The culture of a particular community or society also incorporates its seminal stories, revealed in history, mythology, religion and in the arts. Such a pool of stories is a continuously unfolding phenomenon, forming an important ingredient of the local identity of a social system. If the main story is broken, be it because a society or an organization have failed – be it through decline, oppression, war or, in the case of an organization, bankruptcy – there is a strong need for 'restoring' the story. Such can be equally seen on the level of the individual: the story we tell others about ourselves is of great importance to us, and we spend a great deal of time in making sense of our individual storylines. It is in such stories, that the core contribution that a particular social system has to offer as well as its specific cultural force, can be found. That is another core argument for the significance of engaging with culture.

CULTURE HOLDS THE 'MESSAGE' THAT EACH CULTURAL GROUP HAS TO OFFER TO CIVILIZATION

W.E.B Du Bois, the original pan-Africanist and Harvard educated sociologist in nineteenth century America, was deeply committed to 'taking culture seriously'. Indeed he was concerned to define the scale of values in the concept of race from vertical and hierarchical to horizontal and egalitarian, thereby making it more appropriate to a pluralist democracy of diverse races and ethnic groups each of which had a 'message' to offer civilization. In many ways, therefore, our own work relates strongly to Du Bois's research, albeit that our work is applied specifically to social and economic transformation and innovation.

The unique 'messages', for Du Bois, are manifested in cultural achievements. His was an effort to make room for the 'space of values' for a positive appreciation of the cultural achievements of people of African descent specifically, and of other groups generally.[8]

That having been said, the raging conflicts and genocidal wars in the former Soviet Union and former Yugoslavia, as well as in South Africa, India, Sri Lanka, Rwanda and Burundi, justify the re-examination by contemporary scholars of the prophetic voice of Du Bois. His prophecy that 'the problem of the 20th century is the problem of the colour line, the relation of the lighter to the darker races', has by and large been fulfilled. What is therefore required is that the darker races get their act together to give their complete message to the world.

For Du Bois, the history of the world is the history not of nations but of races, and he who would ignore or seek to override the race idea in human history ignores or overrides the central thought of all history. What then is race? It is a vast family of human beings, generally of common blood and language, always of common history, traditions and impulses, who are both voluntarily and involuntarily striving together for the accomplishment of certain ideals of life. Du Bois then saw racial differentiation, in the twentieth century, as crucial to the development of mankind's potential. In his mind, the function of each race was to 'develop for civilization its particular ideal, which shall help to guide the world nearer and nearer to the perfection of life'. His perspective is hence clearly opposite to that of Harvard political scientist Samuel Huntington who has focused, as we saw, exclusively on the 'clash of civilizations'.

In conclusion, Du Bois was particularly concerned with what he described as 'the levelling of cultural patterns' resulting from the operation of monopoly capitalism. This process was seen as destructive to global civilization because of its corrosive effect on the very source of cultural innovation, that is cultural differences. Thus he argued:

If the levelling of cultural patterns is going to continue to be the attitude of the modern world, then we face a serious difficulty in so-called race problems. They will become less and less matters of race, so far as we regard race as biological difference. But what is even more important, they will become less and less matters of conflicting cultures.

It is surprising to see, that many African researchers or researchers on Africa, as Mazrui and Du Bois, emphasize the importance of acknowledging cultural diversity and the specific contribution each culture has to offer, and indeed are seeing it even as a source for innovation. We shall now turn to the counterargument of Amartya Sen, Nobel Laureate for Economics and others, who sees culture as a rather limiting dimension.

CAN THE CULTURAL PERSPECTIVE BE LIMITING?

We now take a leaf out of Amartya Sen's book on *The Argumentative Indian*. Here the Indian Nobel Laureate for Economics argues strongly for reasoning and against the danger of cultural stereotyping.[9]

For Sen, people's choices may be constrained by the recognition that they are, say, Jewish or Muslim, but there is still a decision to be made by them regarding what importance they give to that particular identity over others that they may also have – related, for example, to their political beliefs, sense of nationality, humanitarian commitment or professional attachment. Identity is thus quintessentially a plural concept, with varying relevance of different identities in distinct contexts.

Indeed Sen cites Samuel Huntington who has partitioned the world into such categories as 'western civilization', 'Islamic civilization', 'Buddhist civilization' and 'Hindu civilization'. There is, as a result, a tendency to see people mainly – or even entirely – in terms of their religion, even though that attribution of a singular identity can miss out on much that is important. This segregation has already done significant damage to the understanding of other parts of the global history of ideas, ignoring the flowering of science, maths and literature pursued by Muslim intellectuals, particularly between the eighth and thirteenth centuries.

Sen argues, that it is, for example, not assumed that, say, Isaac Newton's scientific work must be understood in primarily Christian terms, although he did have Christian beliefs, nor presumed that his contributions to worldly knowledge must somehow be interpreted in the light of his deep interest in mysticism (important as mystical speculations were to him). In contrast, when it comes to non-western cultures, religious reductionism tended to exert a gripping influence. For example, there is a widespread tendency to presume that none of the general intellectual works of Buddhist scholars or Tantric practitioners in India and China could be 'properly understood' except in the special light of their religious beliefs and practices.

Hence, the possibility of reasoning, for Sen, it is a strong source of hope and confidence in a world darkened by horrible deeds. We can reason about the right way of perceiving and treating other cultures, other claims, and examine different grounds for respect and tolerance. We can also reason about our own mistakes and try not to repeat them. Similarly, for example, environmental deterioration frequently arises not from any desire to damage the world but from thoughtlessness and lack of reasoned action – separate or joint – and this can end up producing dreadful results. To prevent catastrophes caused by human negligence or obtuseness or callous obduracy, we need practical reason as well as sympathy and commitment.

What about the sceptical view, Sen inquires, that the scope of reasoning is limited by cultural differences? There is first the view that reliance on reasoning and rationality is a particularly 'western' way of approaching social issues. Members of non-western civilizations do not, the argument runs, share some of the values, including liberty and tolerance, that are central to western society and are the foundations of the idea of justice as developed by western philosophers from Immanuel Kant to John Rawls. Sen calls this argument the claim of 'cultural boundary'.

The second difficulty concerns the possibility that people reared in different cultures may systematically lack basic sympathy and respect for one another. They may not even be able to understand one another, and could not possibly reason together. This could be called the claim of 'cultural disharmony'. Since atrocities and genocide are typically imposed by members of one community on another, the significance of understanding between communities cannot be overstated. And yet, such understanding may be difficult to achieve if cultures are fundamentally different from one another and prone to conflict.

Can Hutus and Tutsies, Hindus and Muslims, Israeli Jews and Arabs, overcome their 'cultural animosities?' As such we hear of the 'clash of civilizations', and Huntington goes on to assert the need for the 'renewal of western identity', while others assert the 'irresistible victory of Asian values'.

The cultural anthropologist Clifford Geertz, as cited by Sen, contrasts the theories of two leading anthropologists: Marshall Sahlins, he writes:

> *is a thoroughgoing advocate of the view that there are distinct cultures, 'each with a total cultural system of human action'. The other anthropologist, Gananath Obeyesekere is a thoroughgoing advocate of the view that 'people's actions and beliefs have particular, practical functions in their lives, and these should be understood along psychological lines'.*

Neither approach rules out communication between cultures, even though this may be an arduous task if we follow Sahlin's interpretation. But we have to ask what kind of reasoning the members of each culture can use to arrive at better understanding, sympathy and respect.

The central issue here, for Sen, is not how dissimilar distinct societies may be from one another, but what ability and opportunity the members of one society have – or can develop – to appreciate and understand how others function. If the reasoning and values that can help in the cultivation of imagination, respect and sympathy needed for better understanding and appreciation of other societies are fundamentally 'western' there would be grounds for pessimism. But are they?

THE FORCE OF WESTERN DOMINANCE

It is in fact very difficult to investigate such questions without seeing the dominance of contemporary western culture over our perceptions and readings. The force of such dominance is well illustrated by the recent millennial celebrations. The entire globe was transfixed by the end of the Gregorian millennium as if that were the only authentic calendar in the world, although China, India, Iran and Egypt, among others, all have their own calendars that are considerably older than the Gregorian one.

Western dominance, for Sen, is similar in other arenas. Consider, for example, the idea of 'individual liberty', which is often seen as an integral part of 'western liberalism'. Modern Europe and America, including the European Enlightenment, have certainly had a decisive part to play in the evolution of the concept of liberty and the many forms it has taken. These ideas have been disseminated within and without the west in similar guise to industrial organization and modern technology. But is the historical view correct?

Is it indeed true, as claimed for example by Samuel Huntington, that 'the west was the west long before it was modern'. The evidence for such claims is far from clear. When civilizations are categorized today, individual liberty is often seen as a part of the ancient heritage of the western world, not to be found elsewhere. For example, freedom and tolerance get support from Aristotle – even though only for free men, not women and slaves. However, we can find championing of tolerance and freedom in non-western authors as well, a good example being India.

Different cultures are thus interpreted in ways that reinforce the political conviction that western civilization is somehow the main, perhaps the only, source of rational and liberal ideas, where analytical scrutiny, open debate, political tolerance can prevail.

The west is seen as having exclusive access to the values that lie at the foundation of rationality and reasoning, science and evidence, liberty and tolerance, and of course rights and justice. Once established, this view of the west, seen in confrontation with the rest, tends to vindicate itself. Since each civilization contains diverse elements, a non-western civilization can then be characterized by referring to those tendencies, which are most distant from the identified 'western' traditions and values. These selected elements are then taken to be more 'authentic' or more 'indigenous' than the elements to be found in the west. For example, Indian religious literature such as the Bhagavad Gita or the Tantric texts, which are defined as differing from secular writings seen as 'western', elicits much greater interest in the west than do other Indian writings. There is a similar neglect of Indian non-religious subjects, ranging from mathematics, epistemology and natural science to economics and linguistics.

Take, for example, the case of 'Asian values', often contrasted with 'western values'. Since many different value systems and styles of reasoning have flourished in Asia, it is possible to characterize such Asian values in many different ways, each with plentiful citations. By selective citations of Confucius, and such selective quotes from many other Asian authors, the view that Asian values emphasize discipline and order – rather than liberty and autonomy, as in the west – has been given apparent plausibility. There is in effect an interesting dialectic here. By concentrating on the authoritarian parts of Asia's multitude of traditions, many western writers have been able to construct a seemingly neat picture of an Asian contrast with 'western liberalism'. In response, rather than dispute such, some Asians have responded with pride: 'Yes we are very different, and a good thing too'. We may therefore be left wondering whether Buddha, Laozi, Ashoka or Ghandi were actually Asian.

We agree with Sen that our interpretations of culture and cultural diversity have often been influenced, if not distorted by the dominating cultural power. We also acknowledge the danger of getting stuck in cultural stereotypes, which often are the basis for exclusion and conflict. And we are aware of the destructive power that culture holds if it is used as an expression of superiority over others. However, in understanding culture as the prevailing meaning giving system within a social system and, as illustrated above, as an important source of local identity, we simply don't know of a way of getting away from culture, when it comes to transformation. As such, we see the engagement with culture as the starting point, but not as the end point. Further, in the process of evolving from local identity to global integrity, we transcend the 'cultural boundaries' and 'cultural disharmony' to which Sen alludes.

In summary, both perspectives are equally important: the local (indigenous) perspective, which is strongly connected with the particular local culture and the global perspective, which is oriented towards the common patterns, values and interests, we share as humanity. The local perspective, however, so our argument goes, comes first. It is in the local cultural soil that social systems develop their initial sense of identity, of belonging to a particular community. Again, in Freire's terms 'Before I could become a citizen of the world, I was and am first a citizen of Recife ...'.[10] From that local (inner) perspective we can grow and reach out to a more universal (outer) perspective, which ultimately transcends the local. We, hence, continue on our journey by looking first inwardly, through what we term our 'transformational topography'.

6.3 No Fundamental Transformation without Engaging with Culture

6.3.1 UNDERSTANDING THE DEPTH OF CULTURE: THE TRANSFORMATIONAL TOPOGRAPHY

From images to inclinations

The transformational topography illustrates why there is no transformation without a thorough engagement with the cultural depth of a society, an enterprise or an individual. By introducing the four-layered transformational topography, our primary concern is with the process whereby in-depth images and ideas are progressively transformed into surface inclinations and attributes (see Figure 6.1). As such, once again, we revisit mankind's journey.[11] We start with the historical depths, in what we term the core, the deepest layer; we continue journeying through bedrock (second layer), towards a subsoil (third layer), till we reach, most recently, topsoil (fourth layer). As such, we lodge the behaviour of organizations – a topsoil notion – in an integral transformational topography. In fact, and as a societal example, the secret of the European Renaissance of the fourteenth to sixteenth century, is that it managed to reach down to the core, and up successively from there.

As mentioned, we have identified four vertical layers in our 'transformational topography'. In contrast organizational behaviour involves only one topographical layer (the topsoil), which is, furthermore, originated from primarily one 'western' world.

In playful terms, we recognize these as the 'Four Is': images, ideologies, institutions and inclinations. We start with the intra-cultural depths and ascend towards the surface. *For thoroughgoing innovation to occur, all four levels need to become interconnected and dynamically interactive.* We begin with images, or indeed imagination, the source of creativity and innovation, at the deepest level of the individual and society.

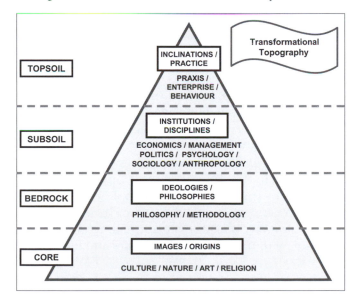

Figure 6.1   Transformational topography

Cultural images at the core

At the core of a particular society are its cultural images. They are key sources of creativity and innovation. They are the source of transformation, drawn from nature, the humanities or indeed from the depths of religion; that includes language in its original context, informing our imagination. We shall later in this chapter introduce a number of significant cultural images from all over the world. To that extent a Picasso or Goya painting is, on the one hand, innately Spanish, and, on the other hand, it speaks to the world, and many a European design innovation has followed in their suit. Similarly, at least for German sociologist Max Weber, Protestantism lay at the root of the flowering of capitalism in the modern era. The image of salvation through wealth creation originally infused the hero-archetype in the Anglo-Saxon world, so clearly embodied in a Richard Branson type of merchant adventurer. Such an image can be clearly differentiated from that of 'Kyosei', the Japanese philosophy on 'co-existence', which duly inspired a Ryuzaburo Kaku, Chairman of Canon in his role as the Japanese sage-leader. As such the Japanese penchant for miniaturization is as clearly embodied in a Bonzai tree as German precision in a Bach fugue.

Ideological inclinations at the bedrock

At the bedrock of a society are its ideological orientations, primarily represented by it philosophies and policies. Here we deal with the holistic philosophies and policies that lie well below the everyday surface. They indeed stimulate insight. In that capacity, and in recent years for example in China, Confucianism has served less distinctively as a religion and more as a secular ideology. All too often, though, such a cultural bedrock is globally imported from elsewhere – as was the case for both Russia and China in relation to communism – without being aligned with the local cultural core. This will serve to distort whatever processes of renewal take place, unless the potential for disintegration is consciously addressed. However, such an ideological imprint will fall upon stony ground if it is not embedded in the individual as well as organizational consciousness.

Institutional frameworks at the subsoil

At the subsoil of a society are its institutional frameworks, represented by its dominant systems and models. Built up from our collective intelligence, institutions become the object of concern, including comparative legal systems, political and economic structures, and predominating forms of public, private or civic enterprise. For example, these may be it a British democracy or a Botswana 'legotla', an American corporation or a Japanese 'kereitsu'. Included in this 'subsoil' layer of depersonalized systems are also the 'management models' that we study at a business school. To that extent, American models inevitably predominate. Whereas it is individuals who characteristically get things going, with their personal and formative and idiosyncratic inclinations, institutions keep things going over the long haul, with their standardizing rules and procedures.

Personal inclinations at the topsoil

At the topsoil of a society are its personal inclinations: it is only here that we engage with attitudes and behaviours. They are the ultimate fruits of our endeavours. In this way you discover how to exchange business cards in Japan, whether or not to shake hands with Arab women, how formal or informal you should be with the French, what your attitude is to time in Harare or Hamburg. In fact, everyday conversations on dealing with different cultures tend to be conducted in these sorts of instinctive 'topsoil' terms, thereby focused on individual traits and identities. Overall then, the extent to which each of these cultural layers is well or ill functioning will be dependent upon the degree of differentiation and integration.

6.3.2 DIFFERENTIATION AND INTEGRATION WITHIN A CULTURE

Each of the cultural layers is susceptible to functionality or dysfunctionality, depending upon both the degree of differentiation and integration (functionality), as opposed to repression and disintegration (dysfunctionality). In fact, the phenomenon of global terrorism is, for us, an extreme manifestation of dysfunction in the world at large.

As such it reflects a global as well as a local imbalance. Indeed, it is the ultimate and most horrendous expression of a lack of global integrity, and, as a direct result, a surfeit of local identity. Specifically, dysfunctionality is the expression of destabilizing imbalance and distortion within and between the worlds, in the same way, as functionality is a manifestation of dynamic balance and proportion. Whereas vertical disintegration often arises out of an ill functioning combination of tradition and modernity, horizontal disintegration arises out of a malfunctioning dominance of one world over another. This is astutely illustrated by Hisham Sharabi in his book on *Neopatriarchy*,[12] where he describes the deformation brought about in the Arab world by the poorly differentiated and integrated combination of tradition and modernity.

In particular, a culture acquires global integrity when each of the layers are dynamically integrated. In other words, if there is local resonance between individual inclinations, institutional configurations, ideological orientations and imaginative creations we have what we term vertical integrity. *This, for example, has until recently been the case for the great Japanese manufacturing enterprises like Canon, where the bedrock philosophy of Kyosei, or co-existence, has been reflected both in the kereitsu style of institutionalization and in the ringi style of consensus management. Conversely, in a place like Zimbabwe, where the African artistic and musical core has little if any resonance with European style education (bedrock) on the one hand, or factory and farm management (subsoil) on the other, integrity breaks down, so that one imbalanced personality, like Mugabe has become, serving to magnify the resulting distortions, is able to steal the whole show.*

Global horizontal integrity emerges when there is purposeful co-creation between cultures at each horizontal level of the transformational topography. In summary, the greater the degree of differentiation and integration the more functional the individual, organization and society. The Four World approach that circumscribes our transcultural forces a) allows for such differentiation and integration on a cultural level, within a particular culture and between various cultures and b) has been equally resonant and relevant on the levels of society, organization and the self. We shall now turn to the Four World perspective, which has been generically introduced already in Chapter 2.

6.4 The Four Worlds as a Model for Transcultural Differentiation

6.4.1 THE FOUR WORLD MODEL: A GENERIC PERSPECTIVE

The Four World perspective that we have developed, originally illustrated in Chapter 2, is to be seen as an archetypal framework and process, which allows understanding of and engaging in meaningful interaction between the various elements of one particular culture. It also allows equally important, meaningful interaction in between various cultures. Such interaction holds the key for ongoing renewal and transformation. The Four World approach highlights the specific contributions of each world, which are illustrated in Figure 6.2.

The Four World approach strongly acknowledges the local identity of each world, indeed builds on it, before it moves towards integration.

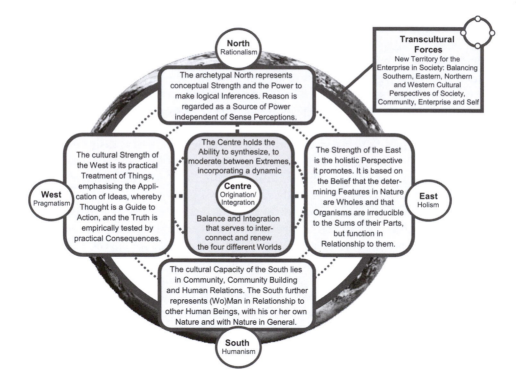

Figure 6.2   The contributions of the Four Worlds and the centre

6.4.2 LOCAL-GLOBAL ROOTS OF THE FOUR WORLD MODEL

The Four World perspective is the most generic framework we came across, allowing us to differentiate and integrate social systems on all levels, within a particular cultural context. As a social design it resonates deeply with cultural images from all over the world.

In our work on *Integral Research and Innovation*[13] we have introduced a variety of fourfold designs from all over the world. Each of them has represented, and in some cases still do, an important guiding image, lodged in the core of a particular culture. Such images range from ancient medicine wheels of Native American origin, to the Buddhist wheel of life, from the Tibetan Mandala to the Christian Cross. They include furthermore such natural phenomena as the four seasons to the four elements, and vary in their respectively cyclical, spiralling, linear and pointed formats.

Often these images don't provide any more meaning. They may still be used and 'around', but they have lost their capacity for guidance and renewal. Often they hint towards a cultural force which can be found in a specific culture, and which played a vital transformational role within this culture.

Ultimately, so we argue, there is a need for renewing these guiding images, and for thereafter transforming them from vision into action. Our integral design that we are offering here for all levels of social systems, is a step in this direction. Ultimately, we are often surprised, that the Four World archetype, wherever we introduce it, in a research or in a practitioner's context, is hardly ever questioned. There seems to be a deep transcultural resonance with this type of integral social design.

6.4.3 APPLICATION OF THE FOUR WORLDS TO ALL SOCIAL SYSTEMS

Though rooted in culture, the approach also transcends cultures, as it represents an archetypal perspective on the inner diversity of each social system. Hence, it serves as a framework for differentiation and integration of the core aspects of each social system, from self to organization, from society to the globe.

6.5 Conclusion: Cultural Differentiation and Integration

We started this chapter with a critique of the conventional approach towards organizational behaviour and culture as well as transcultural management. The prevailing approach to culture is, from our perspective, analytical and static. Cultural insights are primarily used to inform management attitudes and behaviour. They are, however, not used to evolve the structure and functioning of enterprises within their particular cultural context. We illustrated how the basic texts that inform the conventional management curricula on organizational behaviour and culture draw primarily on sociology and (mainly behavioural) psychology. Anthropology, cultural studies and in-depth psychology are left out in the cold. Our approach to culture, however, not only also draws strongly on the latter disciplines, but it involves, furthermore, organizational and societal transformation.

We illustrated in this chapter that culture is indeed a major transformational force. However, if it is not recognized as such, organizations and societies easily become stuck. On a global level, we witness such stuckness in terms of 'clashes of civilizations', which are deeply rooted in opposing cultural positions.

Our argument for revisiting the significance of culture in an organizational and societal context is not only based on many years – in the case of Ronnie Lessem, decades – of transcultural education and practice, but also on major thinkers, such as the renowned philosophers and educationalists Ali Mazrui, W.E.B. Du Bois and Paolo Freire.

Of course, dealing with culture is difficult terrain, and many like to avoid it nowadays, arguing either that the world has become a 'global village', which makes different cultural perspectives irrelevant, or, in an attempt to overcome the all too obvious cultural differences and conflicts, the argument for a 'shared humanity' (ultimately, we are all the same) is made.

We have argued, however, that such an attitude towards culture is ultimately not only inauthentic but also deprives organizations and societies of an opportunity to evolve. We acknowledge the danger of getting stuck in cultural stereotypes, which often are the basis for exclusion and conflict. And we are aware of the destructive power that culture holds if it is used as an expression of superiority over others. However, in understanding culture as the prevailing meaning giving system within a social system and, as demonstrated in this chapter, as an important source of local identity, we maintain that it is essential to take account of culture, when it comes to transformation. In short, we see such engagement with culture as the starting point, but not as the end point.

As such, we have introduced two major concepts to get in touch with the cultural depths of one's own culture and society and to purposefully enable creative interaction between different cultures: the transformational topography and the Four World model. Both models will be further evolved in the course of this book, and both have manifold ways of being applied. The topography as well as the Four Worlds enable academics and practitioners alike to differentiate between various societal layers (topography) and cultural capacities (Four Worlds). Such differentiation is the necessary prerequisite for meaningful dialogue and interaction within and between cultures. That is equally relevant for an organization, in understanding its various layers and capacities, as for a community or a society as a whole.

Both models, which have been developed in our Geneva-based Laboratory for Integral Innovation (TRANS4M), illustrate the need for an enterprise to transcend its conventional approach to organizational development, and replace it progressively by a deep understanding of, and engagement with, cultural dynamics.

A final world on the cultural image of the Four Worlds: in the eyes of many practitioners we work with, they provide a compelling, integrated perspective on a social system (not just on its culture). However, to some degree, cultural images have a kind of static element to them. As we have demonstrated in our transformational flows, we are all too aware that social organisms are continuously evolving, and there is no such thing as 'static balance' in them. The integral design is, at its best, a guiding star helping to understand and differentiate between the core elements of a social system. The main task however for any conscious social organism is for you to be able to understand, and to actively engage in and with continuously transformative processes. In that way it involves understanding how the entire organism can work towards states of 'dynamic balance'. In that way you are able to understand the transformative dynamics embedded within culture in more depth, is the focus of the forthcoming chapter on cultural dynamics.

References

1. Huntington, S. (2002). *Clash of Civilisations*. New York: Free Press.
2. Handy, C. (1993). *Understanding Organisations*. Harmondsworth: Penguin.
3. Hofstede, G. (1992). *Culture and Organisations*. Maidenhead: McGraw Hill.
4. Trompenaars, F. et al. (1997). *Riding the Waves of Culture*. New York: Nicholas Brealey.
5. Freire, P. (1998). *Pedagogy from the Heart*. New York: Continuum International.

6. Lessem, R. and Schieffer, A. (Forthcoming: 2010). *Integral Research and Innovation: Transforming Enterprise and Society*. Farnham: Gower.
7. Mazrui, A. (1986). *The Africans – A Triple Heritage*. New York: Guild Publishing.
8. Bell, B. et al. (eds) (1996). *W.E.B. Du Bois on Race and Culture*. London: Routledge.
9. Sen, A. (2005). *The Argumentative Indian*. Harmondsworth: Penguin.
10. Freire, P. (1997). *Pedagogy from the Heart*. New York: Continuum.
11. Lessem, R. and Palsule, S. (1997). *Managing in Four Worlds*. Oxford: Blackwell.
12. Sharabi, H. (1988). *Neopatriarchy*. Oxford: University Press.
13. Lessem, R. and Schieffer, A. (Forthcoming: 2010). *Integral Research and Innovation: Transforming Enterprise and Society*. Farnham: Gower.

CHAPTER 7 *Cultural Dynamics*

Beyond Organizational Development

7.1 Introduction: Organizational Culture to Cultural Dynamics

In the previous chapter we articulated the role of culture as a primary source for transformation. We made the case, based on the Four World approach for the different contributions that each 'world' culture has to make, from southern humanism to western pragmatism. We demonstrated how this is equally true at the level of society and community, organization and self.

We also introduced our so-called transformational topography, arguing how important it was to engage with culture at the deepest layer, or 'core', of a social system in order to effect true transformation.

We now explore the specific potential to meaningfully engage with the transformational capacity embedded in nature as well as, now, culture. We shall further illustrate how the combination of the two can become a key source of knowledge creation and innovation.

We differentiate, as such, between a process of engagement within a particular culture and that between diverse cultures. While the first addresses the recognition and activation of the cultural force within a culture, and thereby relates to the local identity of a social system, the latter demonstrates the relevance of meaningful co-creation between the local and the global.

7.2 Local Cultural Forces

7.2.1 RECOGNIZING LOCAL CULTURAL FORCES

Where does the transformation of a social system begin? Is there a place where it takes root, ignited by a spark that sets it into motion? That spark, as we have said, is lodged within local soil, nurtured and nourished by centuries of knowledge and practice. We refer to this as a local cultural force that is often critical to initiate a transformation process. It provides the indigenous cultural force of origination for prospective social innovation, which is promoted through subsequent co-creation.

We perceive these cultural forces, moreover, as archetypally resonating within human beings in general. However, each world region, each organization, each individual resonates most with one particular such force, while the others are less present.

Transformation Management encourages individuals, organizations and societies to reconnect with the innermost cultural forces rooted within their given context, rather than tapping primarily upon external transformative ones.

We now traverse the globe and take four examples of indigenous cultural forces, from African Ubuntu to Japanese Kyosei, from Nordic Naringsliv to Anglo-Saxon Individuation. Figure 7.1 provides an overview of this journey. We shall start, as will be the case throughout this book, in the south.

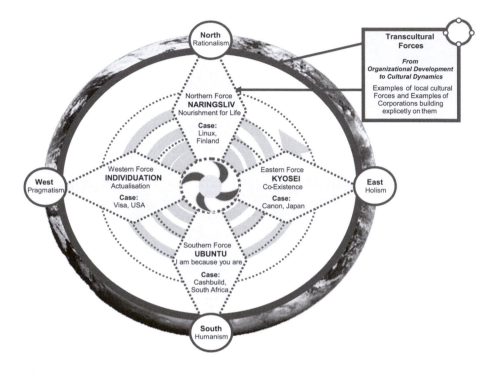

Figure 7.1 Examples of cultural forces

7.2.2 STARTING IN THE SOUTH: NTU AND UBUNTU (SOUTHERN AFRICA)

Ntu, the dynamic and rhythmic Force: Ntu – Hantu – Kintu – Kuntu

We start in southern Africa where much of our work is based, with dynamic 'Ntu' and stabilizing 'Ubuntu', the one more closely connected with nature.

For the German anthropologist and African devotee, Janheinz Jahn, in his seminal book entitled *Muntu: African Culture and the Western World*,[1] he describes *Ntu* as being a universal force among the Bantu peoples throughout sub-Saharan Africa. It is the point from which creation flows. From *Ntu* comes *Muntu* a force endowed with intelligence, human and more-than-human. *Kintu* embraces those things, which cannot act for themselves, involving plants, animals, minerals and such objectives. Space and time constitutes *Hantu*. It is the force that localizes spatially and temporally every motion, for everything is in motion. *Kuntu* is a modal force like beauty or laughter. A key component of *Kuntu* is rhythm. In every expression of African culture meaning and rhythm are intertwined. Rhythm, for Senegal's former philosopher-poet-president Leopold Senghor, is the architecture of being, the inner dynamic that gives it form, the pure expression of life force. Rhythm is the vibratory force that grips us at the root of our being. It is expressed through lines, surfaces, colours and volumes in architecture, art, sculpture and painting, through accents in poetry and music, through movements in dance. Rhythm turns all these concrete things toward the light of *Ntu*.

Ubuntu, the stabilizing force: I am because you are

The attitude of seeing people not as themselves but as agents for some particular function either to one's advantage or disadvantage is, for the late Steve Biko,[2] foreign to the African. 'We are not', he says, 'a suspicious race. We believe in the inherent goodness of man. We enjoy man for himself. We regard our living together not as an unfortunate mishap warranting endless competition amongst us but as a deliberate act of God to make us a community of brothers and sisters jointly involved in the quest for a composite answer to the varied problems of life. Hence in all we do we always place man first and therefore all our action is usually joint and community oriented. Nothing then dramatises the eagerness of African to communicate with each other more than their love for song and rhythm. Music in the African culture features in all emotional states. When we go to work we share the burdens and pleasures of the work we are doing through music. In other words, for Africans, music and rhythm are not luxuries but part and parcel of our way of communicating. Any suffering we experienced was made more real by song and rhythm. The major thing to note about our songs, moreover, is that all African songs are group songs.'

Most Ubuntu thinkers therefore formulate their views in terms of 'a person is a person through other persons', or, 'I am because you are'. In this way human dignity gains a central place and seems to be related to both morality and nationality.

For Zimbabwe's expert on African management, Lovemore Mbigi,[3] Ubuntu is rooted in four principles: morality, which involves trust and credibility; interdependence, which concerns the sharing and caring aspect of relationships, that is cooperation and participation; spirit of man, which refers to human dignity and mutual respect, implying that activities should be person-driven and humanness should be central; and lastly totality, which pertains to the continuous improvement of everything in the organization by every member of it.

In fact, it is such Ubuntu, in the field of leadership and management, which is now reaching out to the world. We shall demonstrate how Ubuntu can be a force for transformation within an organization with the South African corporation Cashbuild (see Chapter 12). As we move from the 'south' to the 'east' the cultural forces change.

7.2.3 MOVING EAST: KYOSEI (JAPAN), TAOISM AND CONFUCIANISM (CHINA)

Kyosei: living and working together for the common good

We have identified Kyosei as a transformational force coming from Japan. A concise definition of the term would be 'living and working together for the common good'. As such it is both dynamic and stabilizing in its overall effect.

Kyosei is still very much alive in current Japanese culture, as can be seen in the case of Canon (which we describe in depth in Chapter 13). The company states that 'The Corporate Philosophy of Canon is Kyosei' and translates the term into 'All people, regardless of race, religion or culture, harmoniously living and working together into the future' and the company adds reflectively: 'Unfortunately, the presence of imbalance in our world – in areas such as trade, income levels and the environment – hinders the achievement of Kyosei.'

Lin Yutang and the art of (Chinese) living

The dynamic natural and cultural force underlying such Kyosei, originally coming from neighbouring China, is nature bound Taoism, converted in Japan into Shintoism. The stabilizing one is that of Confucianism, which prevails throughout the Far East. It is indigenous Confucianism, moreover, which is forging links with the exogenous 'west', and vice versa. The term 'Confucian dynamism', for example, something of a misnomer in our terms, has seemingly served to characterize the recent economic and technological development of the Asian tigers. We would argue, conversely, that such 'eastern' dynamism comes from Taoism, which has been left behind, so that 'western' capitalism – Canon as we shall see somewhat excepted – is required to take its place.

For the twentieth-century Chinese writer and philosopher Lin Yutang,[4] Confucianism is essentially decorous, reasonable, and correct; in our terms, it represents a stabilizing force. The slightly rebellious and dynamic in spirit look to Taoism. Confucianism, through its doctrine of propriety and social status, stands for culture and constraint, while Taoism, with its emphasis on going back to nature, does not believe in human restraint and culture. Confucianism is essentially an urban philosophy, Taoism is rural – unsurprisingly, then, that in China it is the rural areas, which are being left economically behind, because Taoism has not been renewed. Confucianism is fundamentally realism and has little room for fancy and imagination. Taoism stands for the world of wonder and mystery that Confucianism fails to provide. There is a classicism (Confucius) and a romanticism (Laotse) in a nation. The latter stands for the return to nature, the rural ideal of life.

Fung Yu-Lan's philosophical writing

Fung Yu-Lan,[5] a contemporary Chinese philosopher, has also highlighted the seminal part played by Laotse and Confucius, albeit set alongside several other Chinese philosophical streams. For the Taoists, when the development of anything brings it to one extreme, a reversal of the other extreme takes place. So, one can argue, Chinese communism gave rise to capitalism, and western capitalism is giving rise to environmentalism. Everything involves its own negation. This was one of the main theses of Laotse's philosophy, undoubtedly inspired by the movements of the sun and moon and the movements of the four seasons, to which farmers must pay particular heed. 'When the cold goes the warmth comes, and when the warmth comes the cold goes.' And again 'When the sun has reached its meridian it declines, and when the moon has become full it wanes.'

This has also provided the basis for the golden mean, favoured by Confucianists and Taoists alike. Taoism and Confucianism differ, however, because they are the rationalization of different aspects of the lives of the farmers. The Taoists maintained that the highest achievement in the spiritual cultivation of the sage lies in the identification of himself with the whole of nature, that is the universe. A great deal of Confucianism is the rational justification or theoretical expression of the social system associated with rural life. Because of the latter predominating over the former Confucianism naturally became the orthodox philosophy and remained so until the invasion of industrialization from modern Europe and America changed the economic basis of Chinese life. Confucianism, then, emphasizes the social responsibilities of man, while Taoism recognizes what is natural and spontaneous to him. These two trends of philosophical thought historically complemented each other, exercising a sort of balance of power, a balance between the static and the dynamic, in the same way as the 'north' encompasses alternating institutional forces. However, today in China, if not in the Far East in general, such a balance has been lost, which is why western capitalism is required to balance out 'state order', or indeed Confucian values.

7.2.4 HEADING NORTH: NARINGSLIV (SWEDEN/SCANDINAVIA)

Naringsliv: a new guiding image?

The Nordic notion of Naringsliv is most prolifically represented, today, in Sweden and in Finland. It is in fact commonly used in Sweden as the term for business and commerce, and can be found, for example, in the name of the Confederation of Swedish Enterprise, *Svenskt Näringsliv*, or in *E24 Näringsliv*, a Swedish online business newspaper, based in Stockholm. Translated, it stands for 'nourishment for life'.

The 'Närings Liv Project' – initiated some years ago by the US-American Institute of Noetic Sciences – was one of a number of initiatives intending to tap into the ancient wisdom underlying the notion of Naringsliv. They stressed the potential of Naringsliv serving as a new guiding image, most especially relating to business's role in society:[6]

> *During times of fundamental social transformation, the emergence of a new guiding image can lead societal evolution by providing a direction for creative innovation and change. A compelling core image can act almost like a magnet, creating a powerful pull toward the future. The Swedish core image of business as närings liv, nourishment for life, may have the potential to lead and empower individuals and organizations who are exploring new ways to design their lives and work ... The metaphor of business as nourishment for life is evocative in several respects. It is simple and elegant. Since most of us already have an intuitive hunch about what provides nourishment in our own lives, it is an effective guide for reflection and decision-making. It can also serve as a bridge to our common future, connecting our concerns and commitments with those of others in practical and relevant ways.*

In our own terms, and from a northern perspective, such Naringsliv combines the natural dynamic of life itself, with the balancing force of business in the environment.

Hierarchical system and information network

Like indigenous Ubuntu and Kyosei, Naringsliv has gained reputation in other parts of the world. Narinsgliv, actually, is an amalgam of the notion of hierarchy and network, both of which are built into nature as well as culture, and are analogous to Confucianism (culturally hierarchical) and Taoism (nature's network) in the east. Similarly, in southern terms, Ubuntu embodies a relational hierarchy of responsibility between self and other, whereas Ntu embodied a dynamic, networked quality.

The hierarchical-totalist tradition, for Swedish philosophers Bard and Soderquest,[7] is characterized by the construction of the great system: a desire to find a single theory to encompass and explain the whole of existence and history. Confucius, Socrates, Plato and Aristotle are central figures within that tradition which has dominated western thought. Their ideas have been nurtured and developed by system builders ranging from Descartes and Hegel to Kant and Marx. The totalistic question is a question in search of an answer. The truth is the goal. What unites all totalists is the idea of some sort of Utopia. The idea is connected to that of an objective truth, against which the state of things can be evaluated. I think therefore I am, and because it is I who thinks it is also I who decide. Because it is I who decide I shall force reality to bend to my will. Totalist thought is in all its forms hierarchical. When humans are the measure of all things they assume an objectively unique status.

But now there is a spanner in the works. What is happening with the breakthrough of the informationalist paradigm is that this carefully constructed, universally recognized philosophical platform is under attack from several directions at once. The 'netocratic' worldview, which is based upon European thought, is certainly not new; it can be traced back to ancient Greece. However, hitherto it has not been able to form a powerful alternative to the totalistic thought that has dominated philosophy up to now. Bard has called this alternative the mobilistic tradition. It has its origins with the Greek philosopher Heraclites. Freethinkers like Lucretius and Nietzsche took this 'mobilistic' philosophy seriously. Nietzsche rejected all talk about existence having an innermost core or objective purpose. There is, he claimed, merely an endless mass of conflicting forces that are constantly jousting with one another. It is pointless to talk of a fixed state of being: it is a question of a constant state of becoming. Existence is not something: it is becoming something, in the constantly shifting interplay of conflicting forces.

We now turn to the Finnish variation on this Nordic theme, where the emphasis shifts from network and hierarchy to development and the welfare state. Interestingly enough, the Finnish people, from our experience, are extremely close to nature – from which their developmental impulse might arise – which is not surprising given the innumerable forests and lakes in the country. They are also especially proud of their culture, which is again not surprising, given the fact that they had to protect themselves for centuries against the neighbouring and invasive Russian bear!

The developmental and welfare state

The Euro-American apostle of the 'network society', Manuel Castells, and his Finnish counterpart, Peter Himanenen,[8] have argued that the performance of Finnish business in recent years has been, and still is, supported and stimulated by the policies of the Finnish state, in its double role as a development and welfare state. On the dynamic, developmental side, the state has reformed the regulatory environment by deregulation, liberalization and privatization to unleash the entrepreneurial and networking capacity of business. It also actively supported innovation, both directly through funding, and through a strengthened university system, geared towards engineering and information technology. The quality and innovativeness of the universities allowed a hacker culture to blossom and become an important source of innovation. The state also contributed a stable system of industrial relations, creating the conditions under which social partners representing capital and labour could agree in a strategy of competitiveness that would integrate workers' concerns and rights.

The effects of the stabilizing welfare state produced the citizen/workers that are well educated and well protected. They are covered by a comprehensive health care system, and have access to affordable housing, efficient public transportation, childcare, and a wide range of urban amenities. They are supported by public programmes when unemployment or illness strikes, so they are not at risk when the country engages in a major economic or social overhaul. This means that resistance to change is much lower. The state is supported in its action by a triple source of legitimacy: it is a democratic state, a redistributive state, and it embodies a national project of an independent and self-assertive Finnish nation. Though not explicitly coined Naringsliv, the Finnish approach can be regarded as another expression of this northern cultural force, even if the nourishment of life is not in the foreground.

In the west it is the individual more than the nation that counts, which leads us to individuation.

7.2.5 ENDING IN THE WEST: INDIVIDUATION (USA/WESTERN EUROPE)

Structure changing (dynamic) and structure building (stabilizing)

We understand 'individuation' here as a process whereby components of an individual, an organization or a society are integrated into a more indivisible whole. The term has been used by psychologists, sociologists, philosophers and theologians and has been variously defined by different scholars, including Sigmund Freud, Carl Jung, Erik Erikson, Friedrich Nietzsche, Henry Bergson, David Bohm and Manuel De Landa. It usually refers to the individual and his or her development, but we maintain that it is ultimately also of relevance for organizations and societies in the sense that the latter two need to provide the context and soil for progressive individuation. The typically western conqueror of nature, continually extending the 'western' frontier, can be seen, pre-eminently, in this individuating guise.

For American psychotherapist Daniel Levinson[9] the process of individuation, as we have seen in Chapter 5, involves events-activities-outcomes being woven into an encompassing design. Recurring themes in various sectors of your life and work – and by extension for us within organization and society – help to unify the overall patterns of the tapestry. Such a life course is potentially transformative, if not de-formative or indeed con-formative, and thereby alternates between structure building and structure changing. An individual, organizational or societal life structure, therefore, consists of a series of alternating stable (structure building) and transitional (structure changing) periods.

The primary task of every stable period is to build a life structure, which provides for individual and institutional integrity. You or your institution must make certain key choices, form a structure around them, and pursue values and goals within that structure. A dynamic, structure changing period terminates the existing life structure, and creates the possibility for a new one, indeed a new expression of individuality. The primary tasks of every such transitional period are to question and reappraise the existing structure, to explore various possibilities for change in individual or collective self and world, and to move towards commitment to the crucial choices that form the basis for a new life structure in the ensuing stable period. The task of a dynamic transition, then, is to terminate a time in your, your organization's, or your whole society's life-balance. This involves accepting the losses such a termination entails with a view to realizing its anticipated benefits, as well as reviewing and evaluating the past. You thereby decide which aspects of the past to keep and which to reject, and consider your wishes and possibilities for the future. You are suspended between the past and the future, struggling to overcome the gaps that separate them. Much of the past must be given up, separated from, cast out of life; and there is much that can be used as a basis for the future. Changes must be made in self and world.

Youthful identity to mature integrity

The first task for the dynamically youthful individual, entering adult life, or analogously the organization or young society, is to move out of the young world, to question the nature of the world and your (or its) place in it, to modify or terminate relationships with persons and institutions. The second task is to make a preliminary step into the formative young adult world, to explore its possibilities, to imagine yourself, or itself, as a participant in it, to consolidate an initial adult identity, to make and test some preliminary choices for adult living. Whereas the first task involves a process of structure changing, the second is a process of structure building.

Only those of us in maturity who have in some way taken care of things and people – and who have faced the triumphs and disappointments that come with being originators of products and ideas – develop what Levinson terms ultimate 'self integrity'. Such integrity, he maintains, is the individual or organizational self's accrued assurance of its investment in order and meaning, as part of a world order and grounded in spiritual depth. It is an acceptance of our own personal or collective cycle as something that had to be. Such a mature person, organization or society would know that all human integrity is at stake in the one style of integrity in which we personally or collectively partake. Our own life or culture is wrapped up in everyone else's. The absence of integrity and the danger in this stage is a sense of despair. The lack or loss of integrity is signified by the fear of individual, institutional or societal death, as if your lives or cultures were to take no account of anyone or anything of significance. The integrity of old age thus contributes to the possibility of exploration in the youthful stage.

7.2.6 IGNORING THE CULTURAL FORCE: THE DANGER OF OSSIFICATION

We explored in some depth what is the core of a society or an organization, or a person, their indigenous cultural soil that makes each unique. We examined, first at a societal level, typical forces, both dynamic and stabilizing in the four respective worlds of south, east, north and west. For us, each of these forces provides their societies, as well as the respective enterprises and individuals, with transformative potential. Such potential is constituted of both dynamic cultural forces, closely aligned with natural processes, and stabilizing ones, closely aligned with societal structures.

These cultural forces, altogether, constitute the local soil (nature and culture) and the core of our particular kind of contextualized transformation process. Each such force holds two concurrent forces: one dynamic and outer-directed, that allows a society or an organization or an individual to reach out transculturally beyond their boundaries and build bridges with other sources of knowledge; and the other stabilizing and inner-directed, providing the community, institution or person with their soul. Like twin helixes of the DNA, they constitute an essential transformational 'undertone'.

That reminds us of the renowned social philosopher Robert Pirsig who wrote the seminal work on *Zen and the Art of Motorcycle Maintenance*.[10] Pirsig identified two kinds of 'quality', that is 'dynamic' and 'static'.[11] Whereas the former promotes continual renewal and change, the latter is a force for continuity. Both are required: the inner-directed force is what preserves and nourishes the lifeline of societies and the outer-directed force is what opens the space for transformation. For example, the caterpillar-turning-into-a-chrysalis represents the dynamic quality, and the resultant butterfly the ultimately static one. What Pirsig fails to identify, though, is that each society, or indigenous community, has a different dynamic and static indigenous potential built into it. Unfortunately, most societies fail to exercise such vital forces in balanced combination, for both intrinsic and also extrinsic reasons. There are two reasons for this.

Many societies get intrinsically caught up in a static survival mode that is overly bound by tradition. From an ecological perspective, they become vulnerable to ossification. Extrinsically, and often in parallel, they are overtaken by the pursuit of the 'modern', because that is what is expected of them. In the one case they are unduly constrained by their heritage, and in the other they lose touch with it, in both cases, therefore, by-passing their potentially unique contribution to the world. In fact, and all too often, a society, or indeed an individual or organization, is caught in between these two 'inauthentic' states, as they might be called, displaying signs of a kind of societal 'schizophrenia'.

In such a case, one 'lesser developed' indigenous and often rural society will be dominated by another exogenously 'more developed' and often urban one. It will exist, thereby, in a no man's land between tradition and modernity, the indigenous and the exogenous, rural and urban, self and other. Holding on to some of its traditions, literally, for dear life, such a society may discard other traditions in the course of copying the simultaneously admired and despised dominant power. We see this, for example, continually in our work in the Middle East, where America, typically, will be despised as a political and economic 'bully boy', and yet simultaneously admired for its populist cultural offerings, its elitist 'ivy league' education, and its glitzy technology. In the terms used by management philosopher Robert Fritz,[12] the resulting indigenous behaviour is typically 'reactive' (doing as you are told by the other) or 'responsive' (following the admired crowd) rather than 'creative', that is building upon your own nature and culture while simultaneously co-creating, transculturally, with others. For it is only in this co-creative case that you (individually, organizationally, societally) are being yourself; becoming all that you could be (by proactively reaching out to others); coming to know your way ahead, and ultimately actualizing your self in a mutually enriching relationship with such others.

7.3 Relevance of Cultural Forces for Society, Organization and Self

7.3.1 IDENTIFICATION OF THE CULTURAL FORCE OF THE SOCIETY

We chose four examples of how the natural and cultural force can be identified and leveraged to provide the inner spark for a society to transform from the local to the global. There are *similar forces in each society that need to be uncovered and legitimized so that they can provide the energy needed for transformation. Often these forces are hidden and covered up by layers of practices, beliefs and subjugation. Without a proper definition of such vital forces, societies become vulnerable to fundamentalism on the one hand, and globalization on the other.*

Countries such as India provide a fascinating example of a struggle that is currently ensuing between its succumbing to unbridled western capitalism on the one hand, and the country attempting, on the other hand, to uncover and popularize practices that emerge from its cultural forces. So on the one hand the ubiquitous call centre and the rise of the middle class spending power is redefining the urban Indian landscape. Developed economies are flocking to India in search of the ultimate capitalist dream of an uncharted consumer territory inhabited by millions of newly affluent customers. However, in the midst of this, and due to the rising levels of stress and social destabilization caused by changing mores and lifestyles, a new movement is emerging that seeks to legitimize, popularize and 'sell' practices such as Yoga and Pranayama as viable options to the Coke-and-Burger phenomenon.

Practitioners such as Swami Ramdev are creating mass movements in India and raising awareness and interest in the cultural and spiritual forces that have shaped Indian thought and society for thousands of years. What is emerging is a contemporary awakening of the same force that has been around in Indian civilization for millennia. The notion that the Self is simultaneously individual and universal is at the very core of all things in Indian belief systems. There is fundamentally no duality between the two but the duality is a result of ignorance and of practices that continue to reinforce the notion that we are separated from the universe. So what creates the illusion of duality is the fabricated notion of the individual self. The duality is an abstraction, a play of thought and emotion and its need to create the self and the other. The journey of life is then interpreted as the self's search for the Brahman in which all things become one.

Business leaders such as Narayan Murthy of Infosys Technology are demonstrating that being world class can go hand-in-hand with a profound adherence to human values and to the force of Indian culture of seeking *advaita* or non-duality. The President of India, Abdul Kalam, has emerged as a leading spokesperson for this profound cultural force. A common boat-owner's son and a Muslim, Kalam became the nation's leading scientist and rocket engineer and continues to inspire a new generation of Indians to embrace modernity without losing touch with the vital spark.

7.3.2 IDENTIFICATION OF THE VITAL FORCE OF THE ORGANIZATION

Such cultural forces, moreover, are not restricted to societies but also prevail at the level of organizations and individuals. In fact, in our work with organizations going through transformational processes, we find that one of the critical factors that decides whether the transformation is successful or not, is how authentic, recognizable and vibrant is the transformational flow and transcultural force of the organization. It manifests itself through the stories that are told about the past and present leaders, about crises and resolutions, and of lives lived and not lived. These 'mythical' dimensions to organizations provide it with both inner and outer directed cultural roots that underpin their evolution and development. Without the myth, all logos are rendered meaningless and purposeless. Great leaders awaken the stories and myths that lie dormant for years and transform their organizations. Others like Narayan Murthy of Infosys imbue their new organizations with new myths and forces. In fact, in the overall context of such organizational myth, the ritual provides the stabilizing force, the unfolding story the dynamic one.

So an IKEA continues to be a highly successful business venture without compromising on its stabilizing force as an egalitarian and family oriented approach to quality, dynamically combining flexibility and innovative design for all. On the other hand, a Barclays Bank forsakes its origins with the Quakers and is rendered without identity or purpose as it struggles to compete with new players on the scene. *All too often, organizations forget their source of co-creation that lies in their stories in between themselves and their customers and communities.*

What we identify here as the cultural force of an organization is, in conventional terms, often described as the capacity of the organization or its top management to identify, articulate and communicate its core vision and purpose of existence. Apple provides an impressive example for that.

Case: the vital force of Apple, USA

Steve Jobs's question to John Sculley when he wanted to bring Sculley from PepsiCo to join him at Apple, was 'Do you want to sell coloured water for the rest of your life or do you want to take a chance at changing the world?' This question lies at the core of Apple's continuing success. Thanks to Steve Jobs, Apple reinvents itself again and again, defining and redefining the rules of the computing and now, music and mobile phone industry, while continuing to remain close to the vital force of the company that wanted to change the world. Moreover, as we probably all know, Steve Jobs individually, and Apple organizationally, had a new lease of 'midlife', when Jobs returned to the Apple fold after a prolonged leave of absence and the company has generally flourished since.

In the civic sector, organizations like the South African university CIDA, at a critical stage of its development, was trying to reconnect to its cultural force by integrating African cultural concepts in the curriculum. This can be seen as an attempt to vitalize the organization by building on the cultural forces of Southern Africa.

Case: cultural forces and contextualized education at CIDA in South Africa

At the South African business oriented university CIDA City Campus, the original impulse behind its foundation was exogenous, as CIDA's foundations were primarily rooted in consciousness based education (CBE), an educational framework developed by the eastern philosopher and spiritual leader Maharishi Mahesh Yogi. However, though CIDA made headlines as a role model for tertiary education in developing countries, this approach turned out to be futile for the organization's evolution. The main reason was that it was not including Africa's cultural background. More recently, in the process of its organizational and academic renewal, CIDA is aiming to re-root itself in the Pan-African philosophy of Ubuntu. As an even more precise articulation of these efforts, the concept of *Umsamo*, origined in Africa's Zulu culture, was promoted by former CIDA academic, philosopher and linguist, Vilaphi Mkhizi, as an indigenous metaphor for business, constituted of three pillars. First there are the responsibilities of *Umnumzane*, the male head of the household, differing from *Umama*, the second female head. The third pillar is *Iziko* representing the centre of the Zulu traditional hut, where the fire is usually made for cooking. It is around this that the whole family gathers. This approach is currently further evolved in a cultural foundation for CIDA's approach to business education. Business rooted in Umsamo would then have a combined masculine, feminine and collective connotation.

Another example is the by now world renowned Egyptian enterprise, Sekem, which has identified its vital force in the 'vitality of the sun',[13] linking it back to the vital force within Ancient Egypt, while at the same time engaging progressively with its more contemporary Muslim heritage. As a probably more negative case in point we could look at an erstwhile international organization like the UN, which is floundering because it has no vitality. When the very vitality of an organization is found lacking, there is simply no way in which it can transform itself.

7.3.3 IDENTIFICATION OF THE VITAL FORCE IN THE INDIVIDUAL

Individuals too need to rediscover and recreate themselves. They do so by renewing, in both an inner and outer directed sense, their original story that makes them who they are. This core identity or the so-called 'soul force' often takes years to unravel and becomes the storyline of an individual's struggle. To engage in discovering it is a process of self-discovery, of removing the shrouds that render the spark invisible and inaccessible. Often the very agency that stands in the way of discovering the spark is one-self. In that it means the habits, thought processes, emotions and behaviours that individuals accumulate that prevent us from seeing the obvious. Joseph Campbell referred to this search for oneself as *The Hero's Journey*,[14] in which the archetypal individual hero has to battle with the monsters on his search for the Holy Grail; the monsters, however, turn out to be none other than the illusions of his own self. Often this is referred as self-transcendence, arising, for us, out of the transformational and the transcultural, linking 'self with other' and inner depths with outer reality.

Psychologist James Hillman attempts to revise the developmental model of human nature by exploring the significance of one of its 'seed images', the *acorn*. Through an exploration of the mythological, morphological and etymological meanings of the oak's fallen little nugget he perceives the acorn as a metaphor of the soul. In the ancient Mediterranean, Northern Germany and Celtic Europe, the oak was a magical ancestor tree, and everything associated with it, the squirrels, the birds, the bees that live in it, and its acorns were equally magical. The oak symbolized wholeness and the knowledge of one's destiny. He goes on to add that in parts of ancient Greece, people use to approach the oak as an oracle and ask it questions about fate and future.

Interestingly enough, the word acorn is etymologically also related to words like act, agent, agenda and age. In that it is similar to that mysterious part of us that propels us to fulfil our life's destiny. In our Four Worlds approach we have identified the four seasons of life – youth, adulthood, midlife and maturity – as the four dynamic stages on which the vital spark performs its transformative drama. Each stage of life is a vital part of the whole process (see Chapter 5). In Greek, the word for acorn is also connected to '*ballos*' and '*bal*', meaning 'to throw' or 'cast'. Finally, the word 'acorn' derives most closely from the old High German word '*akern*', meaning fruit or produce. The acorn is both the end and the beginning.

Like an acorn, Hillman believes we are all born in our fullness, with the full knowledge of our fate packed somewhere inside us. He uses other metaphors and terms such as Plato's concept of the daimon, that invisible soul-companion born into the world right along side us, caring for us, with the full knowledge of who we are before birth, during childhood and right on up to our eventual release from this life. Hillman writes that children are the best evidence for his theory because they often demonstrate the full-grown daimon even within the context of their fragile bodies and immature minds.

I want us to envision that what children go through has to do with finding a place in the world for their specific calling. They are trying to live two lives at once, the one they were born with and the one of the place and among the people they were born into. The entire image of a destiny is packed into a tiny acorn, the seed of a huge oak on small shoulders. And its call rings loud and persistent and is as demanding as any scolding voice from the surroundings. The call shows in the tantrums and obstinacies, in the shyness and retreats, that seem to set the child against our world but that may be protections of the world it comes with and comes from.[15]

Having demonstrated the relevance of local cultural forces on the levels of self, organization and society, we are now ready to look at the dynamics of the interaction of local with global forces.

7.4 From Local Cultural Forces to Transcultural Dynamics

7.4.1 FROM THE INNER, CULTURAL FORCE TO THE INTERACTION WITH OUTER, GLOBAL FORCES

The local indigenous cultural force has the potential to act as a transformative spark within a social system. A social system with a strong inner vitality is likely to have a strong sense for its own local identity. Such a social entity, be it an organization or a society, can then engage on an equal level with cultural forces from outside: so-called exogenous forces. The act of co-creation between indigenous and exogenous, just like the bridge between your inner and outer self, we identify as transcultural.

7.4.2 A LOCAL-GLOBAL DIALECTIC

Indeed, so our argument goes, the indigenous or 'local' force needs to engage with the exogenous or 'global' to develop the transformative and transcultural momentum. This local-global dialectic becomes one of the core recurring rhythms through this book. It is all too often that transformation remains stuck at the local and parochial level, unable to develop the transcultural traction that can sustain the energy and momentum that is so critical to the full development of its process. The end result of any transformation process can only be the result of this local-global equation. The local and the global, the indigenous and the exogenous, interwoven, are akin to the twin strands of the DNA helix structure of the society or organization or the individual. We now explore the interchange between the two, that is between one indigenous culture and another (by definition) exogenous one, in the course of knowledge creation and social innovation. Africa's problem of how to creatively engage in knowledge creation and social innovation serves as the example.

7.4.3 INDIGENOUS KNOWLEDGE SYSTEMS

For Paulin Hountondji, based at Benin's University of Cotinou, the problem today is that Africa has to a large extent internalized the discourse of its former masters in its culture; that includes their denigrating views on African ways of life and thought.[16] At the same time he warns against the opposite danger, that of adopting its indigenous heritage without any critical approach, without any attempt to update and renew the intellectual legacy, in a way that allows a higher degree of rationality, and a steadier march towards efficiency and self-reliance.

Hountondji further explains that, in the process of scientific investigation as conventionally understood today, the decisive stage is neither the collection of data, nor the application of theoretical findings to practical issues. Rather it is what comes between them – the interpretation of raw information, the theoretical processing of the data collected, and the production of those particular utterances, which we call scientific statements. For example, students will, on the one hand, conduct market research using standardized analytical techniques, and, on the other hand, will apply ready made, usually US-American management concepts, such as Tom Peters's 'Seven S' – style, skills, staff, shared values, strategy, structure, systems. What they do not do is to come up with their own theories.

The one essential shortcoming of scientific activity in the former colonies, therefore, as is the case for conventional management education and research today, was and is the lack of the indigenous-exogenous transcultural stage, paving the emergent way to overall transformation. The developing country misses the central operation of creative theory building, having only the first and the third stages of the process:

- the data collection, the feverish gathering of all supposedly useful information; and
- a partial application of the research outcomes to some local issues.

The medium stage then takes place exogenously in the so-called 'mother country', that is invariably in America, Europe or perhaps today Japan. Thus science in the former colonies, like management in transitional societies today, continues to be characterized by a theoretical vacuum – the lack of those imaginatively intellectual and originally experimental procedures that depends on infrastructure that existed only in the (previously) ruling countries. This vacuum was and remains substantially the same as the industrial vacuum, both characterized by a lack of knowledge creating, economic activity.

7.4.4 IMPOVERISHED SCIENCE

Unfortunately, modern science in the overseas territories was introduced by the coloniser – as is often still the case today – in the form of an impoverished 'empirical' science.

Science was deprived of an inner qualitative element that would subsequently give rise to the theory-building activity. The theoretical emptiness of disintegrated scientific activity in the 'third world' derived from the very nature of peripheral capitalism.

We continue this legacy of the same untransformed management thought and practice by conveying knowledge to MBA or Business Studies students from developing countries, attending our educational programmes in the 'west' today. If we are lucky, there may be some local case studies offering scope for indigenous internalization. However, typically, there will be *no opportunity for communally contextualized learning*. When it comes to research, local researchers tend to address issues that are primarily of interest to the western public, specializing in the study of their own economic and social environment, usually adopting a purely empiricist orientation. In order to give a proper account of the peculiarities of indigenous, local culture, we first need to be aware of what is universal about them. We need, therefore, to take that minimum intuitive distance that allows you to put things into perspective. For this to occur an interpretive, as opposed to purely positivist, approach is usually required.

What is to be avoided by societies in transition today, whether in China, Africa or the Middle East, is to just apply traditional knowledge in agriculture or medicine, or indeed in 'indigenous' business practice, while continuing to import scientific and managerial methods from the west. Typically such western methods are poorly understood and mastered by the local users. *What is required, instead, is to help the people and their elite to create new knowledge*. In the process, people would be exposed both to exogenous knowledge and to indigenous learning environments.

For Hountondji, peripheral countries need to invent ways in which knowledge can be better shared in all its phases. They need to develop an ambitious strategy of communal knowledge creation that will allow them to freely and critically take up anything that can be useful for them in the intellectual heritage now available in the world.

Hountondji concludes that ' ... the integration of the third world into the world process of knowledge production entails, among other palpable effects, a marginalization of old elements of knowledge and know-how, along with their steady withering and impoverishment, and in worst cases, their sheer disappearing and vanishing out of people's conscious memory. In sum, the logic of extroversion, which commands the so-called modern-day scientific activity in the third world and singularly in Africa, has a binding corollary, a logic of marginalization. Shall we keep passing now and then from within the dominant system to the counter-systems, and then back again, never wondering if the two systems are compatible. Should we not explore the possibility of harmonizing them in a more viable composite, bringing them into a logical union, and thus finding out if they can in theory and practice yield coherent concepts and technical procedures that might at the very least prove minimally meaningful.'[17]

7.5 Conclusion: Towards Transcultural Learning and Co-Creation

We began this chapter by asking how transcultural forces build upon prior transformational flows, to establish the foundations for Transformation Management. The cultural force that we described, underlying a society, community, organization or individual – linking body and spirit, heart and mind – lies in a dual inner-directed and outer-directed movement.

The inner-directed movement is that of reaching into the depth of the local identity, and of celebrating the uniqueness that is implicit in every identity. But this inner movement is incomplete on its own. In order for it to fulfil its transformational and transcultural potential, it depends upon the outer-directed movement that reaches out and enters into contact with the other. Without the outer-directed force, societies and organizations either ossify or lose their vitality in succumbing to being taken over by exogenous forces. *Each individual and community, organization and society has a unique core to which it must remain faithful, as well as help to evolve.*

We illustrated in this chapter with a number of examples, what we mean by local cultural forces. We took you on a tour around the world, introducing you to:

* African Ubuntu and Ntu, as an example of a southern transcultural force;
* Japanese Kyosei (Taoism and Confucianism) as an example of an eastern one;
* Scandinavian Naringsliv (network and hierarchy), illustrating a northern one; and
* Individuation (individuality and integrity), as a western force.

Such transcultural forces, straddling the dynamic and the static within and the self and the other without, promote the capacity of a social system to transform, to create knowledge and to be innovative. Often, they provide the initial spark for a system to engage consciously in a transformation process.

The indigenous cultural force within a society or an enterprise is, on its own, not yet fertile. It needs the productive interaction with outer exogenous forces. Such an interaction is then productive if it is a meeting 'between equals', where neither force is dominating the other.

The example of Africa and its struggle to creatively engage in knowledge creation and innovation, serves as a powerful illustration of the danger that lies in failing to first identify and activate one's own local vital force and second to bring that local force in creative interaction with global forces. It reminds us again of African Muslim scholar Ali Mazrui who defined a civilization as a 'creative synthesis' of different cultures. Indeed, in this very synthesis we see a key to the evolution of a society. Similarly, Mazrui's insight can be applied to the level of the self, where the creative interaction between the self and the other serves as the evolutionary catalyst; and, of course, the same is true for an organization, whose evolution is dependent on creative interaction between various organizations. Brought to an inner-societal level, we are aware that the evolution of many societies is stuck, because the various sectors (private, public, civic, environmental) don't engage in co-creation in order to address the burning issues of a society, but often in isolation, and often in opposition to each other.

The (re)discovery of the local cultural force is instrumental for the development of a local identity. From there it is a fine line to walk to avoid an overemphasis of the local, which often leads to parochial thinking, or even fundamentalism and isolation. The challenge for self, organization or society is – once conscious of its own local identity – to reach out to the 'other' and to transcend this very identity towards contributing to the larger entity. We coined this challenging journey 'from local identity to global integrity', and it is this journey, which we shall look at closer in the following chapter.

References

1. Jahn, J. (1991). *Muntu: African Culture and the Western World*. New York: Grove Press.
2. Biko, S. (2004). *On Biko*. Johannesburg: Picador.
3. Mbigi, L. (2005). *The Spirit of African Leadership*. Johannesburg: Knowledge Resources.
4. Yutang, L. (1998). *My Country, My People*. Beijing: Foreign Languages Press.
5. Fung, Yu-Lan (1998). *Selected Philosophical Writings*. Beijing: Foreign Languages Press.
6. The Narings Liv Project at the Institute of Noetic Sciences, Sausalito, CA, USA.
7. Bard, A. and Soderquest, J. (2002). *Netocracy*. New York: Reuters.
8. Castells, M. and Himanenen, P. (2002). *The Information Society and the Welfare State*. Oxford: Oxford University Press.
9. Levinson, D. (1979). *The Seasons of Man's Life*. New York: Knopf.
10. Pirsig, R. (1974). *Zen and the Art of Motorcycle Maintenance*. New York: Black Swan.
11. Pirsig, R. (1991). *Lila: An Inquiry into Morals*. New York: Bantam.
12. Fritz, R. (1996). *The Path of Least Resistance*. New York: Ballantyne.
13. Abouleish, I. (2005). *Sekem: A Sustainable Community in the Egyptian Desert*. Edinburgh: Floris Books.
14. Campbell, J. (2003). *The Hero's Journey: Joseph Campbell on his Life and Work*. Novato, CA: New World Library.
15. Hillman, J. (2000). *The Soul's Code*. New York: Bantam.
16. Hountondji, P. (1994). *Endogenous Knowledge*. Senegal: Codesira.
17. Hountondji, P. (2002). Ex: Hoppers, C. (ed.). *Indigenous Knowledge Systems*. Cape Town: New Africa Books.

8 *Transcultural Learning and Co-creation*

From Local Identity to Global Integrity

8.1 Introduction: Why Transcultural?

8.1.1 THE LOCAL NEEDS THE GLOBAL TO EVOLVE

We have by now identified the transformational flows, inherent within nature, and the transcultural forces, that serve to enhance such. What is specifically required to combine the two is a transcultural combination of indigenous and exogenous knowledge, which, for us, promotes individual, organizational and societal learning and co-creation.

All societies are fundamentally repositories of knowledge, grounded in nature and emerging through culture, that have thereby evolved the processes to create, share and apply it. Over centuries they have developed rich, indigenous knowledge grounds that are a vital life force to the well-being of people and communities in that society. Indigenous knowledge could include specialized farming techniques that evolved over generations in Vietnam, or the mathematical developments in ancient India and Arabia. Whatever its form, knowledge is embedded in the very cultural soil of each society. That is a key fact that we may refer to as the static or stabilizing dimension of the particular society-knowledge matrix. The second and the dynamic one is that indigenous knowledge needs the exogenous knowledge contained in other worlds, and the soils of other cultures, to evolve and transculturally develop.

But let us first understand what we mean by different types of knowledge, particularly indigenous knowledge.

8.1.2 FROM INDIGENOUS TO EXOGENOUS KNOWLEDGE

The two Japanese organizational sociologists Ikujiro Nonaka and Hirotaka Takeuchi, from whom we shall hear much more in Chapter 14, have emphasized the difference between 'eastern' and 'western' approaches to knowledge, that is, in their case, the 'indigenous' east (Japan) and 'exogenous' west (USA):

> ... a 'western' or 'northern' approach thereby emphasises the absolute, depersonalised, and non-human nature of knowledge. As such, it is typically expressed in propositions and formal logic; 'easterners' consider knowledge to be a dynamic human process of justifying personal belief with a view to finding the truth. Any organization that dynamically deals with a changing

environment ought not only to process information efficiently but also to creatively transform information into knowledge, in support of a profound purpose.[1]

Supplementing Nonaka's 'east-west' orientation to such knowledge creation, we introduce at this point, in tune with our Four Worlds, a 'north-south' differentiation between indigenous and exogenous knowledge. The Brazilian Juan Flavier characterizes such an interchange as the ' ... information base for a society, which facilitates communication and decision-making. Indigenous information systems are dynamic, and are continually influenced by internal creativity and experimentation as well as by contact with external systems'.[2] In other words, and in our terms, the internal and indigenous is continually interacting with the external and exogenous.

Another definition of such interaction is from the Philippines, describing indigenous knowledge as 'the knowledge that people in a given community have developed over time and continue to develop. It is based on experience, often tested over centuries of use, adapted to local culture and environment, dynamic and changing'.[3] Finally the World Bank defines such IK, in itself, as ' ... traditional or local knowledge, referring to the large body of knowledge and skills that has been developed outside the formal educational system. IK is embedded in culture and is unique to a given location or society. IK is an important part of the lives of the poor. It is the basis for decision-making of communities in food security, human and animal health, education and natural resource management'.[4]

To understand such a process of what we term 'transcultural' learning and knowledge creation more deeply, we build knowledge-wise on the work of Japan's researchers Nonaka and Takeuchi[5] and learning-wise on British psychologist and research philosopher John Heron.[6] We start with transcultural co-creation.

8.2 Transcultural Co-Creation

BUILDING ON THE WISDOM OF THE KNOWLEDGE CREATING COMPANY

Indigenous knowledge needs to go through a transcultural, local-global developmental cycle to become fully actualized. This is what we refer to as the transformation of local identity into global integrity. But that, as discussed, is only one half of the story. The other half is that global integrity needs healthy local identities. For a northern and western society to become fully global and evolve into its worldly integrity, it must engage with and develop through cultures and knowledge systems, which are not its own, in the southern and eastern quadrants of the Four Worlds. Nonaka and Takeuchi, in their famous work on *The Knowledge Creating Company*,[7] though only partially aware of the transcultural nature and scope of their endeavours, developed a knowledge creation spiral with four iterative steps: socialize, externalize, combine, internalize. Each step represents a particular form of knowledge:

- *Socialize*: Tacit Knowledge (south/humanistic/indigenous).
- *Externalize*: Tacit-explicit Knowledge (east/holistic/indigenous-exogenous).
- *Combine*: Explicit Knowledge (north/rational/exogenous).
- *Internalize*: Explicit-tacit Knowledge (west/pragmatic/exogenous-indigenous).

This definition of the knowledge creating process is among the best we have come across, and it is easily applicable not just for organizational knowledge creation, but equally for the co-creation within and between societies (see Figure 8.1). We shall now introduce the four steps of local-global co-creation in more detail.

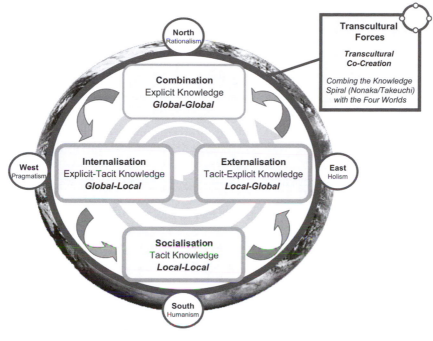

Figure 8.1 Transcultural co-creation

STARTING THE KNOWLEDGE CYCLE: SOCIALIZED IN THE INDIGENOUS

In relation to the knowledge creating process, now applied to a whole society, as opposed to a particular organization, we start with socialization. For this purpose, a consultant, educator or technology transfer agent needs to identify with a specific community. In essence, to become authentic, 'going native' or 'being local' it obviously helps to speak the local language and to be tuned in or to 'have a feeling for' local customs and traditions. But what is all-important for knowledge creating purposes, whether among the indigenous peoples themselves, or together with outsiders, is the evolution to the next stage, what Nonaka terms externalization.

EXTERNALIZING KNOWLEDGE: LINKING THE INDIGENOUS AND THE EXOGENOUS REALM

This is the crucial point when recognition of what is indigenous and local, whether a product or a process, an artefact or a religious belief, can be connected to a wider non-local context. This was what in fact happened when total quality, or 'kaizen', emerged in Japan. This was a fusion of 'eastern spirit' (wa, zen) and 'western technique' (group dynamics, statistical quality control). Such fusion or co-creation often happens 'intuitively', and the underlying processes are difficult to articulate. Gifted artists, whether architects, painters or musicians, are much more adept at the fusion between the indigenous and the exogenous, than scientists or managers. American blues singers, blending south and west, and Cubist painters, fusing together modernism and primitivism, are just two such cases in point. Moreover, in an African context, religion has proved to be much more fertile ground for such interaction than business, with the fusing together of indigenous religion and exogenous Christianity becoming almost commonplace.

Take, in contrast, the case of the Jordanian company Middle Eastern Complex (MEC), a business with which we are familiar. MEC assembles household goods in the Middle East. Its engineers work with German and Italian, Japanese and Korean, as well as now Chinese companies, and import their technologies, without consciously fusing together indigenous Arab and exogenous European or American knowledge. The co-owner and Vice-President of MEC, Darwish Al-Khalili, has now taken on the task to fuse more consciously these diverse cultural horizons, in order to develop products, which more authentically represent and address indigenous Arab culture, as well as exogenous technology, thereby building also more purposefully on a particular local set of cultural capacities.

COMBINING KNOWLEDGE: MOVING TO THE EXOGENOUS REALM

To the extent that such a communal knowledge-creating spiral is followed through, so such – often intuitive – fusion of local and global knowledge would need to be worked out on a local, indigenous basis. So for example, human relations management would need to be aligned in the Arab world with Islamic principles. Out of such a new concept of a duly local-global approach to people management, in such a case, would arise. Unfortunately, this is all too seldom done. More likely, on a typical MBA programme, in Turkey or in Thailand, in Brussels or Beijing, exogenous concepts, usually American, are taught, in a value free educational setting, as if the student was American!

In an actual business setting, moreover, such an exogenous technology, imported from a developed country, would mainly be installed by engineers, who in turn have been exposed to the exogenous principles and practices involved. Such engineers would be typically educated in the 'west', or at least in 'western' guise, and therefore be unable to explicitly link their own heritage and indigenous wisdom with what has been internalized from abroad. At least not in any explicit sense. Conversely, in the Japanese case alluded to above, the fusion of Zen Buddhism and American style continuous improvement has led to a new exogenous quality standard, that is kaizen. Why has this not been more generally the case?

INTERNALIZING KNOWLEDGE: FROM NEW EXOGENOUS TO THE FAMILIAR INDIGENOUS KNOWLEDGE

Conventional business wisdom – generally considered as 'best practice' – involves a process of 'thinking global, acting global', whereby a particular product or process, or style of management, is adapted to local people and circumstances. Indeed, more often than not, the so-called progressive international companies hand the local implementation of their global plans to 'the locals'. While that may be preferable to the expatriates holding onto the reigns, it does not lead to local knowledge creation. For that only comes about when the complete transformational cycle, including the transcultural local/global phase, takes place. If the full cycle is completed, we also turn the conventional management wisdom of 'think global, act local' on its head, at least partly. Transcultural and ultimately transformational knowledge creation, actually, starts out with feeling local, then intuit local-global, and only then moves towards 'think global', before it, ultimately ends with acting global-local (see Figure 8.2). We now turn from transcultural co-creation to transcultural learning.

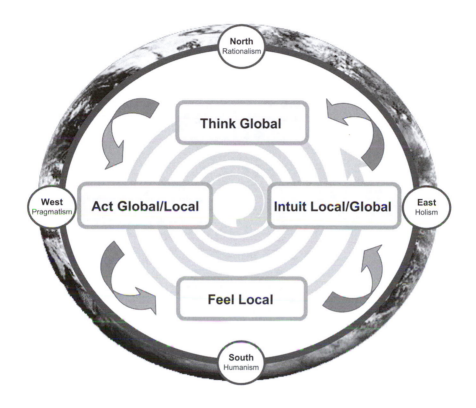

Figure 8.2   Transforming the conventional wisdom of 'think global, act local'

8.3 Transcultural Learning

BUILDING ON HERON'S MODES OF LEARNING AND CONSCIOUSNESS

John Heron applies to the individual and to groups what Nonaka and Takeuchi apply to the organization, and we to a particular society. For him, learning is not simply the assimilating of academic theory, nor is it the mere application of theory in practice, but it is again fourfold, that is experiential, imaginal, conceptual and practical.[8] In transcultural (Four Worlds) and transformational (GENE) terms developed here, the experiential is indigenous (local grounding), the imaginal indigenous-exogenous (local-global emergence), the conceptual is exogenous (global navigation) and the practical is exogenous-indigenous (global-local effect).

Heron depicted his four such modes of learning and consciousness in the form of a pyramid. Such a learning and knowledge pyramid ends at the top with the practical mode, underlining that practice has only substance if it includes the three modes coming before. In other words the west (practical) needs to build accumulatively on the south (experiential), east (imaginal) and north (conceptual) that has come before. Figure 8.3 highlights these four modes, as well as the main characteristics of each mode:

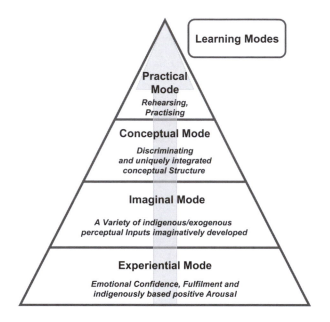

Figure 8.3   Learning modes and forms of consciousness (adapted from John Heron, 1992)

We have illustrated the close correspondence of Heron's four modes with our Four Worlds (see Figure 8.4). But there is more to it than that. Now comes the key that opens up a new current 'Four Worlds door', whereby the 'south' leads and the 'west' follows. To take an example, the now renowned 'Shona' indigenous wooden sculptures in Zimbabwe had been produced by local craftsmen for centuries. In the 1950s these were discovered by an exogenous New Zealander, by the name of McEwan, who became curator of the country's national art gallery. Being very knowledgeable about art, globally, he realized that if such local wooden sculptures could be evolved, through the use of Zimbabwean soapstone, they could become more resonant with 'modern art', globally. Combining forces with a local farmer, who offered up his land for the purpose, skilled craftsmen-artists were brought together into an artists' commune. Over the next two decades such newly evolved Shona sculpture became so well known around the world, that in the 1980s five of the world's top sculptors were reckoned to be Zimbabwean.

Compare then such a fusion of cultures with the tragic cultural fission that has taken place between west and south in Zimbabwe today. In fact, there is nothing as indigenously precious as 'land', and if such land is expropriated by exogenous people, without a subsequent process of reconciliation and renewal, all hell breaks loose. In this case, such hell is personified by the behaviour of Robert Mugabe.

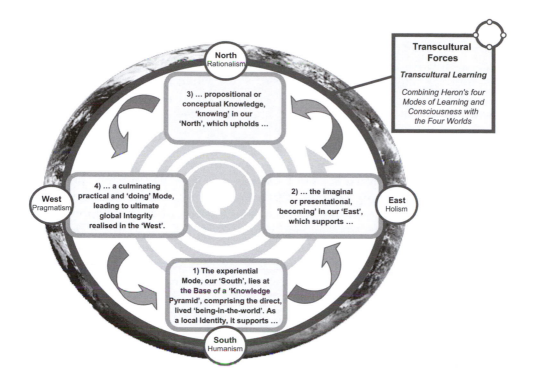

Figure 8.4   Transcultural learning

In our terms, mankind's origins in the African south reflect the historical base of the knowledge spiral (Nonaka) or modes of learning (Heron). The western frontier serves to actualize the being-becoming-knowing-doing quest. Such 'western doing' is then grounded in and empowered by all the prior forms – southern, eastern and northern. To borrow terminology used by the world famous physicist David Bohm,[9] each successive world is 'enfolded' within the others. *So south is enfolded in the east; then the south and east are enfolded in the north and finally, south, east and north aare enfolded in the west. From this perspective the west can only unfold itself if it truly acknowledges and is empowered by the other three worlds enfolded within it.* We now turn to introduce the four steps of transcultural learning in more detail.

THE WEST NEEDS THE REST: FROM EXPERIENTIAL TO PRACTICAL

This dynamic up-hierarchy, from experiential grounding to practical effect, that is grounded in the 'south' and ultimately bearing fruit in the 'west', is different from the classical top-down one, whereby the 'west' controls everything below, without being empowered by any of it, that is by the 'rest' of the world. Such a spiral, which expands our being, becoming and knowing through ultimately doing, is free and unfettered. The transformational/transcultural learning spiral, representing and re-enacting the journey of mankind, regresses, and becomes distorted, if we are socially damaged in the way we handle the local (south) and global (west). So, to reiterate what has been said before in a new guise:

- Experiential: Experiential reality is the indigenous lived experience.
- Imaginal: Imaginal reality is significant indigenous-exogenous form and pattern that fuses together the knowledge of different worlds.
- Propositional: Propositional reality is the exogenously combined reference of concepts.
- Practical: Practical reality is exogenous-indigenous practice, building on everything that has come before.

Experience of 'being-in-the-world' is the ground of exercising imagination with its significant patterns of imagery. Both of these together underlie, and are a precondition for, subsequently global propositions, concepts or theories, as well as, ultimately, local practices. Experiential being is the ground of fourfold being-becoming-knowing-doing. Because of their relatively autonomous form, each of these – southern, eastern and northern – can function in a limited way without the other three, except for inclusively 'western' intentionality, so that practical action needs to be a culmination of the experiential, imaginal and conceptual. Intentional action (western) then is at the apex of the supportive pyramid of fourfold being (southern), becoming (eastern), knowing (northern), and doing, thereby actualizing all of these dimensions and bringing them to an integrated focal point. Such an integral approach is patently not the way that our monocultural political or economic world works today.

The four modes form the basis for a concerted and congruent set of behaviours that is honed through cyclical integration of all of them. It includes a centred integration, as a necessary condition of its continuing practice. Practice as such, fulfils all other modes. It fulfils them because it involves them all, integrates them, gives them human purpose, imbuing them with intentionality, and completes them by manifesting them. It is a declaration by concerted doing. What is important here is the word 'concerted': people acting together and interacting through consensus.

8.4 Cycles of Learning and Co-creation

STATIC INDIGENOUS TO DYNAMIC INDIGENOUS-EXOGENOUS KNOWLEDGE

At this time of writing, and under considerable duress, incumbent Zimbabwean President Robert Mugabe of ZANU PF and Morgan Tsvangirai of the opposition MDC are making a prolonged and strife-ridden attempt to reach political and economic consensus, and thereby turn power sharing into a reality. At one and the same time, little known to the world outside of the protagonists themselves, a naturally and culturally laden attempt at co-creation has been taking place in Zimbabwe. In this case a local rural community called Chinyika co-created together with Cairns Food, the country's leading food processing company, an innovative pathway out of starvation. The protagonists were the son of the local chief of the Chinyika community and the Human Resource Director of Cairns Food, both participants of our Masters Programme on Social and Economic Transformation. It was indeed during that Masters Programme, which is designed to bring about Social Innovation, that the following co-creative process unfolded. The case is particularly remarkable as it is staged in Zimbabwe presumably one of the most hostile environments for social innovation these days.

CASE: PAUL MUCHINERIPI AND STEVE KADA FROM ZIMBABWE

Paul (Chidara) Muchineripi, the son of a Zimbabwean chief in the rural area of Chinyika, upon entering our Transformation Masters Programme, in South Africa, immediately felt the pull of home, as we invited him to ground himself in his community. As a prominent management consultant, based in Harare, he had lost touch with his roots. Analogously, Steve Kada, Muchineripi's close colleague as an HR Director for the country's largest food processor, Cairns Food, felt the pull of the 'south'. It began to dawn on him that Cairns had become thoroughly westernized, despite the black African management now at the helm, and needed to re-experience its southern roots. Together, Steve and Chidara directed their transformational masters projects on a concerted campaign to reconnect with the indigenous foods, which had served the Chinyika community, which was then fighting starvation, in the past. That said, such a process of recognition, involved not only going back to the past, but also moving forward into the future. For that, Steve engaged his company's best agronomists in the process. In fact, he discovered that his CEO, unbeknown to him and to anyone else in the company, had gained his doctorate in the field of indigenous knowledge systems. In the course of a year, not only did the previously hungry Chinyika villagers have food in their bellies, but Steve and Chidara had now established an *Indigenous-Exogenous Knowledge Centre*, aiming to link indigenous agricultural wisdom with exogenous and modern agronomic know how and technology. This centre attracted the attention of the Minister of Agriculture. Together, in this new private, civic, public and environmental set up, they were planning to scale up indigenous production in Zimbabwe, with the support of exogenous farming techniques. This Zimbabwean case serves not only as an illustration for creative interaction of local and global knowledge, but also as a remarkable co-evolution of different types of organizations within a private-civic (and now also public) constellation. The following Table distils the innovative work of Chidara and Steve in our conceptual terms.

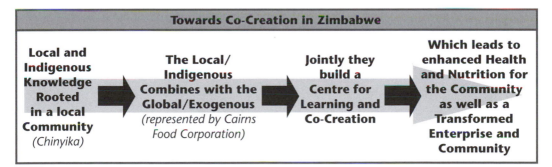

Towards Co-Creation in Zimbabwe			
Local and Indigenous Knowledge Rooted in a local Community (Chinyika)	**The Local/ Indigenous Combines with the Global/Exogenous** (represented by Cairns Food Corporation)	**Jointly they build a Centre for Learning and Co-Creation**	**Which leads to enhanced Health and Nutrition for the Community as well as a Transformed Enterprise and Community**

We have witnessed the effectiveness of this process and its capacity not only for transcultural learning and co-creation again and again in our Masters Programme in the Middle East, the UK and Southern Africa.

In summary, we have identified four co-creation and learning cycles (see Figure 8.5) that together make a strong case for transcultural innovation. Heron's rhythm is equally resonant with our Four World approach, as is the knowledge creation spiral of Nonaka and Takeuchi, that itself proved to be applicable for transcultural knowledge creation. The concluding, more popular cycle builds on the conventional wisdom of 'think global – act local' and transcends it into an authentic and integral local global approach to globalization.

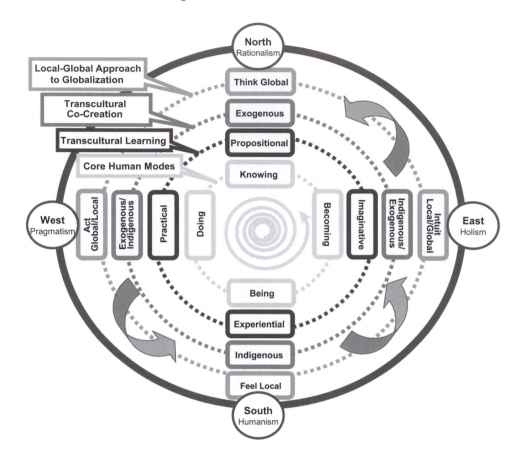

Figure 8.5   A cyclical perspective to learning and knowledge creation

We maintain that in each cycle all four elements are indispensable aspects. If even one is absent, the cycle is broken and incomplete. Knowledge then does not actualize itself into a stage where it can be used developmentally and applied societally, hence leading to social and economic transformation.

8.5 Conclusion: From Local Identity to Global Integrity

DYNAMIC INTERACTION OF THE INDIGENOUS AND THE EXOGENOUS

We argued in this chapter that for a well-rounded transformative potential to be transculturally actualized, the local needs the global and vice versa. In other words, the indigenous and the exogenous are in reciprocal need of one another.

We have traced a successively transcultural and transformative path through indigenous and exogenous wisdom as the initial sources of differentiation and integration in the individual, organizational, communal and societal processes of transformation. In other words, as local identity assumes a global integrity, the indigenous (local) and exogenous (global) need to be fused. Whereas modernization has involved a move from the indigenous to the exogenous, largely to the exclusion of the former, the transformative orientation advocated here requires a transcultural fusion of the two. Such an approach will involve a dialectical process of engagement rather than a smooth transition. But such co-creative dialectic is inevitable, if creative emergence needs to ensue. It is thereby important that the underlying grounds of reconciliation and trust are there, to provide a 'safe haven' for such turbulent interchange. But there is more to transformation than that.

BECOMING FOUR WORLDLY: FROM FEELING LOCAL TO ACTING GLOBAL-LOCAL

Individual, organizational and societal transformation needs to start out experientially in the 'south' and end practically in the 'west', rather than vice versa. This runs counter to conventional wisdom, or indeed to the logic of 'globalization', whereby the initial impetus arises from the west, and then makes its way through 'the rest'. In fact, the well-known adage in business circles – 'think global, act local' – means think of the west and then the rest can follow. We argue the reverse, that is feel local, act global/local and indeed 'intuit and think in between' the two.

How, in summary, does this take place? Evidently enough, it is not straightforward, or else the world as a whole would be a much better place. For as and when such authentic transformation arises, a process of 'undoing' needs to ensue, that is from within rather than without. This is what Nonaka characterizes as 'externalization', Heron incorporates as 'imagination', and we allude to as 'easterness'. This process of taking a society, organization or individual apart with a view to forming a new whole, falls somewhere in between 'de-construction', to use a postmodern term, and 'social construction', to use a phenomenological or hermeneutic one. Transformation is a necessarily dynamic process, but one which needs to emerge from within rather than be imposed from without. This leads ultimately to a new approach to globalization.

FUNDAMENTALLY RETHINKING GLOBALIZATION

The prevailing perspective on globalization is, in our view, fundamentally flawed, in 'thinking global' rather than 'feeling local' from the outset. Such an elite perspective does not constructively engage with cultural diversity and with transformative cultural forces. It ultimately represents an unhealthily monocultural force, with no stimulation whatsoever for transcultural learning and knowledge creation. The approach, which follows out of our argument, is fundamentally different.

Because the world has become a global village, each society is influenced from outside as well as from within. But because people and societies today are such a mix, the global nature and scope of such different influences are difficult to discern. Overall then, there is a lack of differentiation, prior to integration. So diverse influences are characteristically either:

- mixed together into one clearly constituted *melting pot*, as in the USA;
- blended into an undifferentiated *salad bowl*, as in Brazil, in which case, at one and the same time, one culture – usually white – remains implicitly dominant;

- a core culture, as in France, explicitly dominates the peripheral cultures; this might be termed the *dominator model*;
- the *multi-cultural model*, sometimes called a 'mosaic', where cultures are insulated from one other in nominally tolerated groups as in Canada or the UK;
- what Nelson Mandela has termed the *rainbow model* in South Africa, where each culture is celebrated for its richness, but not integrated as such.

What we are advocating here is an ultimately 'holographic model', where each part contains the whole, and vice versa.

As such, each of the 'colours' is clearly differentiated, with a view to their being integrated. The differentiation of colours, in our terms, means the promotion of 'local identity', which, as transformation takes place, serves to contribute to global integrity. Such a process works from the 'inside out', as opposed to the conventional 'outside in'. Ultimately, we call such a differentiated-integrated model on a societal level an integral society; on an organizational level, we call it an Integral Enterprise, the core focus of this book.

On a global, cultural scale, our approach represents a healthy antithesis of the still prevailing image of a 'clash of civilizations' and a by and large unipolar world. If societies rooted in their local identities, which provides them with access to the set of cultural capacity each culture has developed over time, engage with each other, then there is the possibility to jointly evolve so-called 'global integrity'. Such global integrity symbolizes the capacity of a particular society to contribute to the world at large, which results in a multipolar global society. Such a society builds consciously on its diversity; and diversity, as we have demonstrated earlier, is crucial for the survival of any living system.

The importance and value of diversity on a cultural level is equally crucial on a knowledge level. We are therefore moving now from a transcultural to a transdisciplinary perspective.

References

1. Nonaka, I. and Takeuchi, H. (1995). *The Knowledge Creating Company*. Oxford: Oxford University Press.
2. Flavier, J. (1996). *Recording and Using Indigenous Knowledge: A Manual*. IIRR Philippines.
3. Flavier, J. (1996). *Recording and Using Indigenous Knowledge: A Manual*. IIRR Philippines.
4. Flavier, J. (1996). *Recording and Using Indigenous Knowledge: A Manual*. IIRR Philippines.
5. Nonaka, I. and Takeuchi, H. (1995). *The Knowledge Creating Company*. Oxford: Oxford University Press.
6. Heron, J. (1992). *Co-operative Inquiry*. London: Sage.
7. Nonaka, I. and Takeuchi, H. (1995). *The Knowledge Creating Company*. Oxford: Oxford University Press.
8. Heron, J. (1997). *Feeling and Personhood*. London: Sage.
9. Bohm, D. (2002). *Wholeness and the Implicate Order*. London: Routledge Classics.

4 *The Third Fundamental of Transformation Management*

Transforming R&D
into Social Innovation

Core Theme within Transformation Management:
**Simulating Knowledge Navigation of the Enterprise
through Science and Technology
by Tapping into the Transdisciplinary Fields**

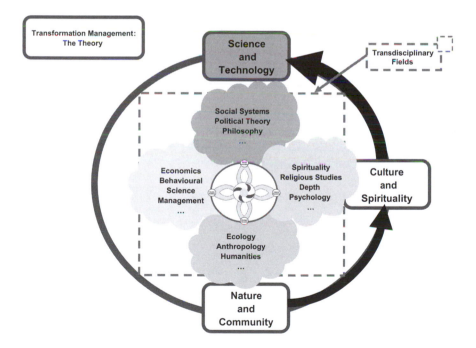

Transforming R&D
into Social Innovation

Core Outcome for the Integral Enterprise:
1. **Building an Innovative Organization**
2. **Releasing Scientific GENE-ius**
3. **Institutionalizing Social Innovation**

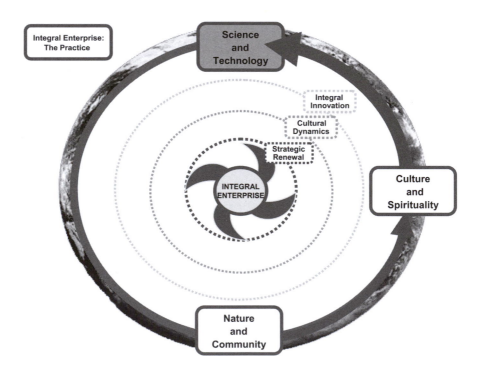

9 *Science and Transformation*

Expanding the Knowledge Base of the Enterprise

9.1 Introduction: From Transcultural to Transdisciplinary

In the previous chapters we illustrated how the engagement with cultural dynamics, within a particular culture and in between one culture and another, is crucial for co-creation. With the transcultural forces, underlying culture and spirituality, we introduced the second fundamental of Transformation Management, following the transformational flows, rooted in nature and community. Hence nature and culture laid the foundation for the transformational journey towards an Integral Enterprise. While, in our Four World terms (physical and human), nature is located in the south, culture is located in the east. We now move to the north, where science and technology are located. As such, the entire book follows the GENE flow, from grounding and originating in nature, to the emergent realm of culture. And from there to the more rational and explicit realm of science.

Science, in this context, covers all knowledge disciplines: the natural as well as the social sciences and humanities. We are entering the arena of articulated knowledge. But again, this is not a static world, but a dynamic one of continuous knowledge creation. The dynamic and creative aspect, as we see it, is again lodged in the 'trans'. It is the creative interaction between different knowledge perspectives, between various knowledge disciplines that ultimately leads to new knowledge. If we translate Ali Mazrui's general definition of civilization as a creative synthesis of cultures, then, more specifically, advances in disciplines are very much generated by an open interaction between various schools within a discipline, and, alternatively, between disciplines.

By starting in nature and culture we have, in addition, already discovered, a number of further knowledge fields relevant for the evolution of the enterprise. From the southern world of nature we include ecology and biology, if not also anthropology, while, from the eastern world of culture we re-discovered the relevance of disciplines such as anthropology, depth psychology, philosophy and history. The knowledge base of the enterprise has, therefore, by now significantly broadened.

While the second fundamental of transcultural forces enables us to see the importance of consciously engaging with cultural dynamics, in order to generate new knowledge we now need first to take a closer look at this new knowledge base, and second to introduce a process that builds on that new knowledge base, thereby fostering the creation of knowledge leading to innovation. We call this process 'Integral Research',[1] and it is designed to increase and renew on an ongoing basis the knowledge base of both education and organization. Integral Research will help both to generate the most relevant knowledge needed in order to address those burning social issues that academics and practitioners aim to address in society.

If we trace our progress in this book back to the Transformational Topography introduced in Chapter 6, we see ourselves as having evolved as follows. The societal core, where physical and human nature, as well as culture, arts and religion are lodged, is home to the transformational flows as well as to the transcultural forces. These forces, however, also form part of the bedrock of a society, influencing its core ideologies. The philosophies and methodologies that arise from, additionally, part of the scientific realm of a society, and hence relate to the transdisciplinary fields. These fields, however, also include all further social scientific disciplines – such as economics, management and politics – which are lodged in the subsoil of a society. These fields constitute the substance of the educational system of a society, and, based on such, institutions are built.

Figure 9.1 also illustrates that science and education (transdisciplinary fields) form the necessary knowledge bridge between nature and culture on the one hand, and a new functioning of the organization, leading ultimately to a renewal of its form. As nature is the starting point, we are also introducing a more organic metaphor of this process.

The tree of life depicted in Figure 9.1 is grounded in its roots (formed by nature and culture), emerges into a main stem (formed by culture and science). From there it reaches out and navigates through branches (various disciplines, education), ultimately producing fruits (a new enterprise functioning). Such a tree continuously goes through seasons and cycles, growing and evolving – and, when it dies, enriching the soil and forming the ground for new life. Modern day management, leadership and enterprise education focuses primarily on the functioning of the enterprise (fruits) and partly on

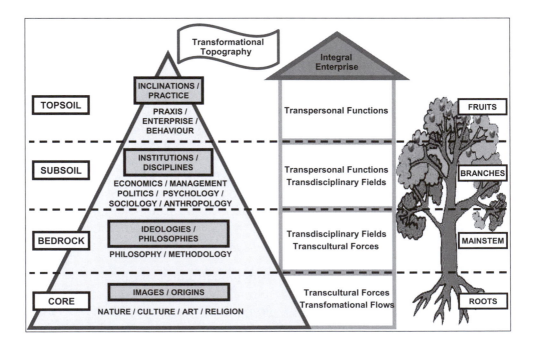

Figure 9.1 Fundamentals of transformation within the transformational topography

the evolution of the knowledge base (branches) – though as we illustrated in very narrow terms. However, it is disconnected from culture (main stem) and nature (roots). As such fruits and branches do not contribute to the sustainability of the entire organism.

It is such a disconnection that we attempt to re-establish with our approach. We are, therefore, moving now from nature and culture to a redefinition of science, as it is relevant for the enterprise.

As the transdisciplinary fields are lodged both in the bedrock and also in the subsoil of the society, we shall, in this chapter, look at both, as well as undertaking a critical review of social science in general, to which management and economics belong. We are therefore re-examining the knowledge base of the enterprise. Finally, we shall introduce a case of a remarkable enterprise, the Basque Cooperatives Mondragon that has indeed evolved through unlocking the transdisciplinary potential and integrated the four layers of the transformational topography.

9.2 Recreating Universities, Business Schools and Management Education

9.2.1 THE EMERGENCE OF THE UNIVERSITY BUSINESS SCHOOL

An initial historical and sociological perspective

We now focus on the ways in which our Transformation Management might overcome the lack of a transdisciplinary orientation in the fields of enterprise, leadership and management.

As such we illustrate historically how parts of the social sciences and almost all of the humanities have been excluded from the theory and practice of management. We reveal that it is economics rather than anthropology, technology rather than ecology that have triumphed.

As we saw in Chapter 1, while entrepreneurship draws almost exclusively on classical economics, and leadership on social psychology, management, though more eclectic than leadership and enterprise, is still somewhat narrowly based. Indeed, we have often asked our colleagues, when designing MBA or business studies programmes, why economics is a standard offering, whereas philosophy or psychology, anthropology or ecology, political science or theology, or even history or sociology, are not? We have never received a satisfactory answer to that question.

Harvard Business School's Associate Professor Rakesh Khurana maintains that in the initial formation stage of such schools at the turn of the last century a transdisciplinary orientation was evident. He describes that in his seminal and award-winning recent study and critique of American business schools, titled From Higher Aims to Hired Hands: The Social Transformation of American Business Schools and the unfulfilled Promise of Management as a Profession:

> Examining the emergence of the large corporation from a historical and sociological perspective, legal theorists, sociologists and organizational behaviour researchers . focusing on the social and political context of the late 19th and early 20th centuries, noted that the period saw a wholesale reconstruction of American society and its institutions. Thus, they argued, explaining

the rise of large corporations only in economic terms offers a limited view. They considered its implications for the law, the role of government, the position of labour, and the relationship between the economy and society. Debate centred on the nature of claims over corporate property, the economic and political consequences of separating ownership from control, class relations, democratic values and the public interest, as well as on the legitimacy of a new system of social authorities in the form of management and large-scale bureaucracy. The development of economic institutions, in other words, was not just a function of their efficiency; rather it resulted from the outcome of contests in the legal, political, social and cultural realms.[2]

Half a century later it was all change. A newly narrowly based 'management elite science' supplanted the hitherto, more broadly based approach to 'social science'.

Reverting to narrowly based western type

In the 1950s in America, the Ford and Carnegie Foundation reports into business education pointed the way toward a new 'management science' of decision making, heralding a new type of 'scientific' manager. The hoped-for result was a more dispassionate and rational manager whose decision making was not clouded by experience or sentiment, or indeed by moral or societal considerations. Such rational management and the underlying academic disciplines were clearly depicted by the doyens of The Principles of Management of that time, Harold Koontz and Cyril O'Donnell,[3] based at the Graduate School of Business Administration in Los Angeles. The various 'schools' or disciplines of management, for them, were grouped into:

- Operational School: an operational (or management process) school, drawing originally upon the American industrial engineer Frederick Taylor.
- Human Behaviour School: a human behaviour school drawn from human relations, leadership and behavioural science orientations.
- Empirical School: an empirical school based on the now famous Harvard case study method.
- Social System School: a social system school, with a sociological as well as systems perspective, the spiritual father of such being a reflective practitioner at America's General Electric Company in the 1930s, its then CEO Chester Barnard.
- Decision Theory School: a decision theory school which was both qualitative and quantitative, an outgrowth of the economic theory of consumer choice.
- Mathematical School: a mathematical school, which had both maths and statistics at its core, operating under the assumption that management is a logical process.

Together, engineering and economics, mathematics and systems theory, behavioural and social psychology, constituted the disciplinary fields upon which concepts of business management were based. While these were arguably interdisciplinary in their nature and scope, as we shall see when compared to the potential scope offered by the social sciences and humanities at large, the monocultural 'northwestern' foundations limited their disciplinary range. That having been said, right up to the 1970s, elite business schools like Harvard and Stanford were still organized around the goal of producing general managers, reflecting such an ideology of 'managerialism'. The MBA curriculum was intended to give the student a wide exposure to management. However, by the end of the century, this northwestern managerial orientation was becoming more exclusively 'western'. Again, in Khurana's words:

> Over the course of the 1970's and 1980's, and thereafter into the 1990's, leading business schools were transformed from training grounds for general managers into institutions that trained professional investors and financial engineers, especially in the area of investment banking, private equity and hedge funds. A powerful theory of the firm would come to be known as agency theory – rooted in the school of neoliberal economic philosophy at the University of Chicago – consolidating these ideas and contributing to a fundamental reconsideration of the purpose of corporations and the role of managers in realising this purpose. Lacking a general managerial orientation most faculty members also limited their research to a single function. The goal of producing deep knowledge of the functioning of the organization as a whole was displaced. In its place, as heroic individuals, were financial engineers, entrepreneurs and leaders.[4]

To explore the wider backdrop to such a 'western', economic reversion, we now turn from the emergence of the business school in America, to an overall examination of the role of the university in society, again from such an American perspective.

9.2.2 THE ROLE OF THE UNIVERSITY IN SOCIETY

Absence of vision

The American political philosopher Allan Bloom, writing a bestseller in the late 1980s on The Closing of the American Mind, thought profoundly about the university's role in the wider world.[5] Bloom was particularly focusing on the role of the 'liberal arts' based university. He controversially maintained (in the 1980s) that the university in America offered no holistic vision for the young person.

In short for Bloom there was no vision, nor was there a set of competing visions, of what an educated human being is. Further, for our purposes, there was no overall organization of the sciences, no tree of knowledge. The student got no intimation in the university of our day that great mysteries might be revealed to him or her, that new and higher motives of action might be discovered within, that a different and more human way of life could be constructed by what he or she is going to learn, that the world extended beyond the shores of America and Europe.

Inauthentic learning

Bloom maintained, and here lies the business or management rub, that no public career these days – not that of businessman nor doctor nor lawyer nor journalist – had much to do with authentic human learning. Most professors were specialists concerned only with their own fields. They were, therefore, interested in the advancement of those fields in their own terms, or in their own personal advancement in a world where all rewards are on the side of professional distinction.

For Bloom, academe had been entirely emancipated from the old structure of the 'liberal' university, where it was apparent, that specialists were incomplete, only parts of an undiscovered and unexamined whole. Even the greatest of American universities, which could split the atom, find cures for the most horrible diseases, conduct surveys of whole populations and produce massive dictionaries of lost languages, could not, he argues, generate a modest programme of general education for undergraduate students. This is a parable, Bloom reckons, of our modern times. Liberal education flourished when it prepared the way for the discussion of a unified, transdisciplinary view of nature and man's place in it, which the best minds debated on the highest level. It decayed when what lay beyond it were only specialities, like the MBA, the premises of which do not lead to any such vision.

Where natural science ends trouble begins

How then, for Bloom, do the disciplines today generally move forward? We distinguish between the big three disciplines that rule the academic roost and determine what is knowledge: natural sciences, social sciences and the humanities.

Natural science, to start with, is doing just fine, which is precisely why technological innovation proliferates, emerging out of a continuing stream of scientific discoveries. Living alone but happily, running along like a well-wound clock, it is as successful and useful as ever, at least in the developed world. Technological innovation proceeds apace; there have been great things discovered lately. Physicists have uncovered black holes and biologists the genetic code. Its objects and methods are largely agreed upon by the presiding academic community. Our way of life is utterly dependent on natural scientists, as is born out today, for example, by the politicians' call for technical innovation to overcome global warming. Only at the margins are there now questions and doubts as to the use of the results of research, such as is the case for nuclear weapons or genetically modified foods. As a result, technological innovation is all the rage and what we might term 'social innovation' falls desperately far behind.

So where natural science ends, trouble begins. It ends at man and, for us, management. To be exact, it ends at that part of man, which is not his body. All that is human lies outside of natural science. The trouble is that for the study of this alternative social theme, pertaining to (wo)man and their activities, there are two great divisions of the university, the humanities (human culture) and social science (human nature), while for bodies there is only one natural science (physical nature). The social sciences and the humanities do not cooperate, though they occupy much of the same ground. And hardly ever the twain meet at university. All our efforts to bring together the social sciences and humanities continually fall on polite but stony ground. In fact, now that the environment and sustainability are coming to the fore within management, the natural sciences are newly asserting themselves in that 'green' light.

Social science moreover – including management – hardly receives any recognition from natural science. And the humanities, a Cinderella discipline at most universities, has turned out to be selling diverse and ill-sorted antiques, decaying and becoming ever dustier. Social science has proved more robust, more in harmony with a world dominated by natural science. However, it has lost the inspiration and evangelical flavour it had in Europe in the eighteenth and nineteenth centuries, together with the capacity to promote innovation – just witness the birth of capitalism, perhaps the most prolific of contemporary social innovations, via Adam Smith in the later part of the eighteenth century. Humanities languish, because they don't suit the modern world, and are more identified with tradition, and indeed art and culture. Social science meanwhile, in a

European context, comes more out of the school founded by English political philosopher John Locke; humanities out of that founded by the Swiss-French social philosopher, Jean Jacques Rousseau. Let us now delve a little deeper into the social sciences.

Divide and rule: Locke and Rousseau

The social sciences work largely independently, and this, as we shall see, has a very damaging effect on the nature and scope of business and management, in a local as well as global context. Each of the social sciences makes a claim that the others need to be understood in its terms – economics arguing for the economy or the market, psychology for the individual psyche, sociology for society, anthropology for culture and political science for the political order. Moreover, in business and management it is economics and behavioural psychology that together, in splendid isolation, rule the roost.

The social sciences then represent a series of mutually isolated perspectives on the human world we see around us, a series that is not harmonious, for there is no agreement on what makes it up altogether. Recent progress with regard to such integration, characteristic of general systems and complexity theory, has not yet made its way into most of the halls of conventional academe. A further disagreement exists on what is to be termed 'science'. Economics, held to be the most successful social science, is the most mathematized. Many argue though that economic man ('homo oeconomicus') is an abstraction that simply does not exist.

Politics and economics versus culture and nature

What students actually see, should they (which is seldom actually the case) encounter social science as a whole, are two robust, self-sufficient and self-confident social sciences. These are, on the one hand, economics (embodying business and management and the 'modern' world); and on the other hand, it is cultural anthropology (representing community and society and the 'traditional' world). These extremes forming the antipodes, with nothing to say to each other, with the other social sciences falling in between. Locke and Smith, falling on the one side, have underpinned economics. Rousseau, on the other humanities side, has been left out in the cold. Rousseau does not have anywhere near the influence on economics and business administration, as do John Locke and Adam Smith.

For Locke, life, liberty and property are the fundamental natural rights, and the social contract is made to protect these. These 'western' principles agreed upon, economics comes into being as the science of man's proper activity, and the 'western' free market, currently triumphant in our turbulent world, as the natural and rational order. Rousseau argued that nature is good, and the 'white' man was far away from it. So the quest for the faraway origins becomes imperative, for Rousseau, champion of 'the noble savage', and 'southern' anthropology is by that very fact founded.

Business overtakes philosophy

So the glory days, for Bloom, of the liberal education that preceded the consolidation, if not the formation, of business schools are over. Gone are the days when political scientist Karl Marx, psychotherapist Sigmund Freud and sociologist Max Weber, philosophers and interpreters of the world, were king. Charles Darwin and Albert Einstein would be as relevant to social as to natural science, and modern literature. The latter could range from Fjodor Dostojevski or Franz Kafka in a European context, to Kahlil Gibran or Edward Said in an Arab one, to Confucius or Lao Tzu in a Chinese one, to Leopold Senghor or Chenua Achebe in an African one – providing insights that social science would systematize or prove. This is the path we are seeking to follow, resurrecting such a 'liberal', and now also 'transcultural' and educational past.

True liberal education, for Bloom, requires that your whole life and work be radically changed by it. Such 'liberal' education and research puts everything at risk. It requires you to not only to risk all but transforming all: ecologically, socially and economically. Philosophy is the key to this process. However, it is lost amongst the collection of natural and social science disciplines and the humanities. Such philosophy once proudly proclaimed that it was the best way of life to seek the first causes of things, and not only dictated its rules to the special sciences but constituted and ordered them.

Today our problems are so great, and their sources so deep, that to understand and resolve them we need philosophy more than ever. Just as in politics the responsibility for the fate of freedom in the world had devolved upon our governments, so the fate of philosophy in the world has devolved upon our universities. Universities, nowadays, are catering for both full- and part-time students; hence, the two, university and enterprise, are related as they have never been before. Ultimately, as we see it, the enterprise might even have a lead role to play in the transformation of university and business school. In fact, along our transformational journey, particularly through engaging in transdisciplinary fields, the enterprise becomes a social innovator, specifically to the extent that it engages in the full trajectory from fundamental research to transformative action. This trajectory is well known and established when it comes to technology. For example, virtually all the large pharmaceutical companies like Pfizer, Merck, Bayer and Novartis as well as high tech organizations like Siemens, Canon and Cisco, or food conglomerates from Nestle to Kraft, entertain huge R&D centers, which engage in fundamental and applied research, as well as ultimately in commercialization. The starting point, however, is fundamental research and we maintain that – by way of an analogy to the natural sciences – there is no full-fledged social innovation, if we fail to tap deep into the knowledge grounds of the social sciences. We shall illustrate, later in this chapter and in the chapter that follows, how several organizations, have consciously and purposefully engaged with such deeper layers of the social sciences in order to bring about social innovation. For now, we consequently turn from a critical review of the current state of our universities and business schools to the social sciences in general. We thereby also turn from Bloom to his compatriot Wallerstein.

9.3 Recreating the Social Sciences

9.3.1 HISTORICAL CONSTRUCTION OF THE SOCIAL SCIENCES

Immanuel Wallerstein is the founder of the World Systems Analysis group, based at the Braudel Centre at Suny University in New York State. Wallerstein, a sociologist and historian, draws on the research of the great French historian of civilizations, Fernand Braudel. In fact, in sponsoring the studies on *Opening Social Science*[6] as well as *Social Science for the 21st Century*,[7] the Portuguese based Gulbenkian Foundation was concerned with charting possible trajectories of the Portuguese nation at the dawn of the twenty-first century. Wallerstein then was invited to chair a group of international scholars – six from the social sciences and two from the natural sciences and humanities – from Africa, Asia, Latin America, Europe and America.

For Wallerstein, from the outset, social science is an enterprise of the modern world. Its roots lie in the attempt – full-blown since the sixteenth century, and part and parcel of the construction of our modern world – to develop systematic, secular knowledge about reality that is somehow validated empirically. At first, those who attempted to establish the legitimacy and priority of the scientific search for the laws of nature, made little distinction between science and philosophy. To the extent that they distinguished the two domains, they thought of them as allies in the search for secular truth. But as experimental, empirical work became ever more central to the vision of science, philosophy began to seem to natural scientists more and more a substitute for theology, equally guilty of a priori assertions of truth that were untestable. The term 'science' came to be associated primarily with natural science, with which the newly emerging social sciences felt the need to compare themselves and compete.

9.3.2 THE ESTABLISHMENT OF SOCIAL SCIENCE DISCIPLINES

Disciplinization and professionalization

The intellectual history of the nineteenth century is marked therefore, as Bloom previously intimated, by the disciplinization and professionalization of knowledge, that is to say by the creation of permanent institutional structures designed both to produce new knowledge and to reproduce the producers of knowledge. The creation of multiple disciplines in the social sciences was premised on the belief that systematic research required skilled concentration on the multiple separate arenas of reality. These were partitioned rationally into distinct groupings of knowledge, of which business and management studies recently formed one such, duly sub-divided into the separate business functions.

Social science as a response to social change

The backdrop to such was that in many countries, certainly in Britain and France, it was the cultural upheaval brought about by the French Revolution in the eighteenth century that forced a certain clarification of the social and political debate. If one were to organize and rationalize social change, one had first of all to study it and understand the rules, which governed it. There was then a deep social need for what we have come to call social science, and what has since been termed management science. Furthermore, it seemed to follow that if one were to try to organize a new social order on a stable basis, the more exact (or 'positive') the science, the better.

Natural science – social science – humanities

At one end lay, first, mathematics and next to it the experimental natural sciences. At the other end lay the humanities, starting with philosophy and next to it the study of formal artistic practices (literature, painting, musicology) closely related to history.

In between the humanities and the natural sciences, so defined, lay the study of social realities, history closer to the arts, and 'social science' closer to the natural sciences.

The creation of multiple disciplines of social science, then, was part of the general nineteenth century attempt to secure and advance 'objective' knowledge about 'reality' on the basis of empirical findings, as opposed to 'speculation'. However, at that stage, such disciplines were still not clearly differentiated. The overall intent, though, was to 'learn' the truth rather than to invent or intuit it. As such, by World War I, there was general consensus around a few specific names, the other vaguer social science candidates now being dropped. These names were primarily five: history, economics, sociology, political science and anthropology. In the Anglo-Saxon world, in particular, economics was making a name for itself.

The quartet of history, economics, sociology and political science, as they became university disciplines in the nineteenth century, and indeed up to 1945, not only were practised primarily in the five countries – France, Britain, Germany, Italy, America – of their collective origin but were largely concerned with describing social reality.

Anthropology and oriental studies frozen in history

As sociology had largely begun as the activity of social reform movements outside universities, so had anthropology largely started outside the university as a practice of explorers, travellers and officials of the colonial services of the European powers. Like sociology, it subsequently became institutionalized as a university discipline, but one that was quite segregated from the other social sciences, which studied the western world. While some early anthropologists were attracted to the universal natural history of humankind, the social pressures of the external world pushed them into becoming ethnographers of particular peoples.

All non-European people, however, could not be classified as such particular 'tribes'. Europeans had long had contact with other so-called 'high civilizations', such as the Arab-Islamic world and China. In the nineteenth century, oriental studies, whose original home was in the Church and whose original justification was an auxiliary to evangelization, became a more secular practice, eventually finding a place in the evolving structures of universities.

The institutionalization of such studies was preceded in the Mediterranean world by what the English called 'classics', the study of European antiquity. It actually constituted the prologue to modernity. By contrast, but following the same logic, other 'civilizations' had no autonomous history; they became the story of histories that were frozen. What became of interest to orientalists was not reconstructing historical development, as for European history, since this non-European history was not presumed to progress. What was of interest was understanding and appreciating the set of values and practices that created the civilizations which, while conceived of as 'high' civilizations, were nonetheless thought to be immobile. Geography, like history, in relation to 'developed' and 'developing' cultures was also problematic!

Geography and psychology: a place at the margins

Geography sought to bridge the gap between the natural sciences, through its concern with physical geography, and the humanities, through its connection with culture. In fact, geography was the one subject, pre-1945, which tried to be worldwide in its coverage. Probably as a result it remained a kind of poor relation often serving as a kind of adjunct to history.

Consequently, treatment of place and space, which is a keynote of the study of geography, and hence culture and nature, were neglected in the social sciences. For the most part such context, in management specifically as with the social sciences generally, was seen as a residual influence, which had to be taken empirically into account, but was not central to the analysis.

Psychology was another marginal case. Here too the discipline was only partially separated from philosophy. In practice, it came to be defined as lying not in the social arena, but rather in the medical one, which meant that its legitimacy was dependent on its close association with the natural sciences. Furthermore, the 'positivists', sharing Comte's preconceptions in seeking after hard facts, pushed psychology concertedly in this direction. Social psychology, therefore, was for the most part not successful in establishing a full institutional autonomy for itself, and suffered the same marginal status, vis-à-vis psychology, as history and culture in relation to economics.

Separation rather than integration

An essential element in the process of institutionalizing the disciplines, moreover, was the effort made by each of them to define what distinguished each from the other. Historians stressed they were interested in reconstructing past reality by relating to the cultural needs of others in an interpretive way. Anthropologists reconstructed modes of social organization of peoples that were quite different from western forms. They demonstrated that customs strange to western eyes were not irrational, but functioned to preserve and reproduce populations. Orientalist scholars studied, explained and translated the texts of non-western 'high' civilizations and were instrumental in legitimating the concept of 'world religions' to break the Christo-centric mould. Each one was intent on marking out its own disciplinary territory, to distinguish it from the other, thereby militating against the transdisciplinary.

Most of the positivistic social sciences – economics, political science, sociology if not also psychology – stressed first what distinguished them from history: an interest in arriving at general laws. Once social science was distinguished in this way from socially constructed history, the social scientists were anxious to take out their separate terrains as essentially different from one another. At the very moment that the institutional structures of the social sciences seemed for the first time fully in place and clearly delineated, the practices of social scientists began to change.

9.3.3 RECENT EVOLUTION OF THE SOCIAL SCIENCES

Political bias: investing in 'big science'

The overwhelming economic advantage of the US, on the one hand, in the 15 to 25 years following World War II meant that social scientific activity was located primarily in the United States to an unusual degree. This affected how priorities were defined by social scientists. On the other hand, the political reassertion of the non-European peoples meant that many assumptions of social science would be called into question on the grounds that they reflected the political biases of an era, which was now over or at least ending.

The major powers then, largely stimulated by the cold war, began to invest in big science. This investment was extended to the social sciences. The percentage allocated to the social sciences was small, but the absolute figures were still very high relative to what had been available until then. This encouraged the further scientization of the social sciences. Thus the economic expansion reinforced the worldwide legitimation within social science of the scientific paradigms that underlay the technological achievements behind it. At the same time, however, the ending of the political dominion of the western world over the rest of the world meant that new voices were entering the social science scene.

Emergent challenges to universalist 'western' social science

It is only when the political dominance of the west began to be significantly challenged after 1945, and when East Asia became a new, very powerful locus of economic activity in the 1970s, that the challenge to the cultural universality of western ideas began to be taken seriously. Moreover, this challenge was being made not merely by those who felt left out in the analysis of social science, but also within western social science itself. The self-doubts of the west, which had existed only among a minority before, now loomed much larger.

A major critique was initially made by feminists challenging a masculine orientation, accompanied by various groups challenging Eurocentrism. The call for inclusion, also with the advent of de-colonization, altogether represented a call for a transformation of power relationships. Scientific truth, it was also felt, is historical. The issue therefore is not simply what is universal but what is evolving, and whether that which is evolving is necessarily identifiable with progress. The natural sciences have long accepted the reality that the measurer intrudes on the measured. And yet this statement has remained controversial and in the social sciences where, if anything, it might seem more obvious. For Wallerstein, in the final analysis, some kind of universality is necessary to promote a community of discourse. But it is important to accept a coexistence of different interpretations in an uncertain and complex world. Only a universalistic pluralism will permit us to grasp the richness of the social realities in which we live and have lived.

9.3.4 WHAT KIND OF SOCIAL SCIENCE SHALL WE BUILD?

Restructuring the social sciences

The situation in the social sciences before us today is that of a dispersal of disciplines, more than compounded by the separation of the natural sciences, the social sciences and the humanities. Yet, of late there has been a growth of 'institutes of advanced studies' and other non-teaching structures, such as our own *Trans4m* Centre for Social and Economic Transformation, which in many ways have proved to be more evolved than the segmented university structures themselves. All these developments at least open up the question of whether, in the next 50 years, universities as such will continue to be the main organizational base of scholarly research.

What seems to be called for is less an attempt to transform organizational boundaries than to amplify the organization of intellectual activity without attention to current disciplinary boundaries. To be historical is after all not the exclusive purview of persons called historians. It is an obligation of all social scientists. To be sociological is equally an obligation of all social scientists, and economic questions, equally, are central to all social scientific analyses. In short, there are no monopolies of wisdom. Business schools, as separate entities, are antithetical to the growth of knowledge.

Where, therefore, do opportunities for creative experimentation lie? At one extreme lies the U.S., with the largest density of university structures, and indeed business schools, in the world, and strong pressure for the restructuring of the social sciences. At the other extreme lies Africa, where universities are of recent construction and traditional disciplines not strongly institutionalized. The paucity of public resources there has forced the social science community to innovate.

The U.S. has a long history of structural experimentation in university systems: the invention of graduate (including business) schools in the late nineteenth century, a modification of the German seminar system; the invention of free electives; of social science research councils; of area studies, and most recently of women's and 'ethnic' programmes. Perhaps the U.S. social science community can come up with imaginative solutions to the problems we have been citing. For Wallerstein himself, social science in the twenthy-first century will be very much influenced by the evolution of what he terms the 'world system' – for us transcultural – which is likely to substantively precondition the nature and scope of the social sciences in the future.

9.3.5 SOCIAL SCIENCE AND THE WORLD AS A WHOLE

The collapse of certainty

Modern science moreover for Wallerstein, that is Cartesian-Newtonian science, has been based on the certainty of certainty. The basic assumption is that there exist objective universal laws governing all natural phenomena, that these laws can be ascertained by scientific inquiry, and that once such laws are known, we can, starting from any set of initial conditions, predict perfectly the future and the past. The belief in such certainty is now under severe attack within natural science itself, a prominent example being Nobel Prize winning chemist Ilya Prigogine's book *The End of Certainty*.[8]

These new views of his, and many others' today, are called the science of complexity, partly because they argue that Newtonian certitudes hold true only in very constrained, simple systems. Also they maintain that the universe manifests the evolutionary development of complexity, and the majority of situations cannot be explained by assumptions of linear progress.

Human social systems, in addition, are the most complex systems in the universe, therefore the hardest to analyse. Furthermore, it is precisely in periods of transition from one historical system to another one, as is currently the case, Wallerstein argues – whose nature we cannot know in advance – that human struggle takes on most meaning. Or to put it another way, it is only in such times of transition that what we call free will outweighs the pressures of the existing system to return to equilibrium. Thus fundamental change is possible, albeit never certain, and this makes claim on our moral responsibility to act rationally, in good faith, and with the strength to seek a better historical system.

It is a time then for rigorous analysis of historical social and economic alternatives. It is a moment when social scientists have something important to contribute, assuming they want to do so. But it requires an unthinking of their past concepts. It is a task precisely for the next twenty-five to fifty years, one whose outcome will be entirely the consequence of the kind of input social scientists are ready and able to put in.

Social science must recreate itself

Today's social science, for Wallerstein, must recreate itself. It must recognize that science is not and cannot be disinterested, since scientists are socially rooted and can no more escape their minds than their bodies. It must recognize that empiricism is not innocent, but always presumes some prior assumptions. It must recognize that our truths are not universal truths and that if there exist universal truths they are complex, contradictory and plural. It must recognize that science is not the search for the simple, but the search for the most plausible interpretation of the complex. We must do all these things because social science really does have something to offer the world. What it has to offer is the *possibility of applying human intelligence to human problems, and thereby to achieve human potential*, which may be less than perfection but is certainly more than human beings have achieved heretofore.

It is as if we are tearing down the building in which we all have lived for some 400 years now, while at the very same time trying to build new pillars that will hold up some kind of roof over our heads, metaphorically the new one more open to the light than the old one. No wonder Prigogine argues that science is at its very beginnings. Social science, which is the effort to study the most complex systems of all, becomes not merely the queen of the sciences, but the most difficult one.

Are social scientists, including management practitioners, ready for such a central role? Far from it. Most social scientists are burrowing inward rather than exploding outward. The 'crisis' of continual splicing off into new specializations that are ever more overlapping with other such splices may not be a sign of loss of viability but rather a crumbling of the old structures. For under the weight of the epicycles we have been constructing we have not been ready to recognize the end of the Newtonian era. Can we also tear down the old structure of social science while constructing new pillars for some kind of roof? And will this roof be limited to just social science or else encompass a reunited single world of transdisciplinary knowledge that knows no divisions between humans and nature, no divorce between philosophy and science, no separation between the search for the true and the good? Can we unthink hitherto Eurocentric social science while reconstructing the structures of knowledge?

Eurocentricism and the social sciences

Social science has been Eurocentric (including the United States of America) throughout its institutional history, which means ever since there have been departments teaching social science within university systems. This is not in the least surprising. Social science is a product of the modern world, and Eurocentrism is constitutive of the geo-culture of such. The social science disciplines were actually overwhelmingly located, at least up to 1945, in just five countries – France, Great Britain, Germany, Italy and the United States. *Social science, including management, emerged in response to European problems, at a point in time when Europe and thereafter America dominated the world.* It was virtually inevitable that its choice of subject matter, of theorizing, its methodology and its philosophy all reflected the constraints of the crucible in which it was formulated.

However, in the period since 1945, the decolonization of Asia and Africa, plus the sharply accentuated political consciousness of the non-European world everywhere, has affected the world of knowledge just as much as it has affected the politics of the world system. One major such difference today, and indeed from some 30 years now at least, is that the 'Eurocentricism' of social science is under attack. To make progress, hereafter, social science must overcome its Eurocentric heritage that has distorted its ability to deal with the contemporary world, and it must overcome its attempt to impose the theory of progress. Over the past 70 years, the need to 'develop' the underdeveloped countries justified the involvement of social scientists of all political persuasions. Sad to say this hardly applied at all to the business and management disciplines.

What is specific in the modern world-system is the concept of 'two-cultures'. Such a divorce between science and philosophy/humanities is unprecedented in history, accompanied by the separation of the quest of the truth from that for goodness and beauty. It took three centuries before the split was institutionalized. Today it is fundamental to the geo-culture of our university systems. However, in the last 20 years or so, the legitimacy of the split has been challenged for the first time in a significant way. This is the meaning of the ecology movement, for example. And this is the underlying central issue in the public attack on Eurocentricism. If we are to construct an alternative world-system, or indeed form of management, to the one that prevails today we must treat simultaneously and inextricable the true and the good.

Social science and the quest for a just society

The biggest change in world social science in the 25 years after 1945 had been the discovery of the contemporary reality of the Third World. Thus was born the era of 'area studies', which changed the organization of the social sciences. Their work was based on the view that there exist stages through which societies go. Applied to the Third World this was 'modernization theory' or 'developmentalism'. The theory further assumed a general law of social development that was supposed to be progressive. Those states at an earlier stage of development would eventually become clones of the most 'advanced' states.

To deal with the colonized world of what were called 'primitive' peoples, a separate social science was constructed; out came anthropology, with its separate methods and traditions, though such has not infiltrated into the management curriculum. Meanwhile, in insisting on originality and objectivity, the research establishment militated against macro-scholarship. Originality required that each successive scholar says something new, and the easiest way to do that was to divide up the subject matter into subjects of ever smaller scope. It was the mentality of the microscope, and it pushed scholars to using ever more powerful microscopes. This fitted in well with a reductionist ethos.

There were thus, for each field, objective pressures that led scholars to narrow the scope of their research. One chose sites of data collection according to the quality of the data, not its relevance.

Science, overall then, is at its earliest moments. All knowledge, for Wallerstein, is ultimately social knowledge. And social science claims to being the locus of self-reflection of knowledge, a claim it makes neither against philosophy nor against natural sciences, but at one with them. Much as Wallerstein thinks that the next 25 to 50 years will be terrible ones in terms of human relations – the period of disintegration of our existing historical system and of transition towards an alternative. However, he also thinks that these years will be extremely exciting in terms of knowledge. The systemic crisis will force social reflection. A heyday for the social sciences approaches, if we choose, including the business schools, to grasp the nettle.

One person who did grasp such a nettle in the twentieth century was the founder of the famed Basque-Spanish cooperative group, Mondragon. We shall now introduce Mondragon as a showcase for an enterprise that successfully and purposefully engaged in fundamental research in philosophy, religion and the social science in general, in pursuit of a new innovative approach towards business in particular.

9.4 Towards a Transdisciplinary Enterprise: The Case of Mondragon

9.4.1 BRIEF OVERVIEW

In illustrating this transdisciplinary orientation to leadership, enterprise and management, we cite the case of the Mondragon Cooperatives in the Spanish Basque country and their founder, Father Jose Arizmendiarietta. The Mondragon Cooperatives, which are now central to the economy and community of the Basque region of Spain, were founded and continue to operate along the following lines:

- *Equality:* All human beings, for Mondragon, are deemed to have been created equal, with equal rights and obligations.
- *Solidarity:* Members of a given cooperative should rise and fall together; this principle also applies to relationships between cooperatives, and between Mondragon as an enterprise and the Basque community.
- *Dignity of Labour:* There should be integrity to any labour, blue or white collar.
- *Participation:* Members have the right and obligation to participate as much as possible in shaping the decisions that affect them.

In what follows we retrace the development of Mondragon – closely aligned with the evolution of the founder's ideas – with the help of the Transformational Topography. We shall demonstrate how the enterprise was built progressively on all four layers who, until today, remain interconnected. The case of Mondragon, in addition, beautifully articulates the engagement with the transdisciplinary fields. Figure 9.2 serves as an overview of this transformational journey.

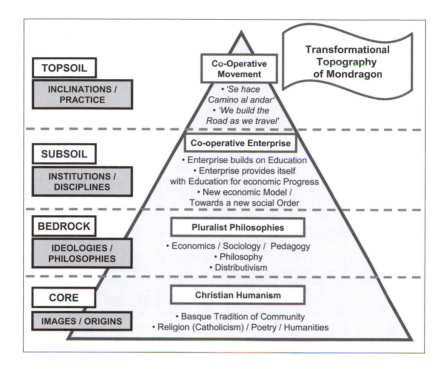

Figure 9.2   The transformational topography of Mondragon Group (Spain)

9.4.2 MOVING FROM CORE TO TOPSOIL: THE TRANSFORMATIONAL TOPOGRAPHY OF MONDRAGON

Core to bedrock: from Christian-humanist values to pluralist political philosophy

In his first writings, in the 1930s, the crisis of the times is seen as one of faith, according to a general system of Christian-humanist values. By about 1945 to 1950, Don Jose Arizmendi was centering his attention on 'the social question'. The nucleus of the crisis was not longer one of faith but that of the ownership and distribution of property. In his first years in Mondragon he had grappled with issues of housing and health, but now he focused ever more on the workplace.

Don Jose had several close friends and admirers amongst the clergy. However, the Catholic Church did not provide institutional support for his work or for the Mondragon cooperative movement. He was himself highly critical of religion in general and of his church:

In the name of religion, what barbarities have been committed? We must be on guard against any form of dogmatism. Religion has been well marketed, but what good has it done? It has led us to feel the importance of the universal and the abstract. Theologians, sociologists and philosophers have operated from the top down, when the correct way to think is in the opposite direction.[9]

This statement is an impressive argument for the bottom-up orientation of our Transformational Topography. It also indicates how allergic Arizmendi was to all isms, including cooperativism. 'Isms imprison and oppress us'. He described his political philosophy as pluralist:

> In the minds of the co-operators is the idea that future society probably must be pluralist in all of its organizations including the economic. There will be action and interaction of publically owned and private firms, the market and planning, entities of paternalistic style, capitalistic or social. Every juncture, the nature of every activity, the level and evolution of each community, will require a special treatment, but not limited to one from of organization, if we believe in and love man, his liberty, justice and democracy.

From bedrock to subsoil: education for transformation and the building of Mondragon

While teaching, Don Jose continued his education at a Social Seminary where his interest extended from economics and sociology to philosophy and pedagogy. He also saw the cooperatives as being built on a foundation of education, and in turn providing education for economic progress toward a new social order. He defined the cooperative experience as:

> An economic effort that translates itself into an educational action ... an educational effort that employs economic action as a vehicle for transformation. One is not born a co-operator, because to be a co-operator requires a social maturity, a training in social living. For one to be an authentic co-operator it is necessary to have learnt to tame one's individualistic instincts, through education and the practice of virtue.

Arizmendi was fully aware of the interdependence of education and institution building. Indeed, Mondragon itself had from the very beginning a very strong educational impulse, that it remained until today. Action research and action learning have always been core pillars of the organizational evolution of the enterprise.

He believed in learning cooperatively from experience:

> Life is a fabric of relations between the past and the present, and the future is not built in a vacuum; experience, that of others as well as our own, is enriching, a positive resource . we build the road as we travel.

The last phrase 'se hace camino al andar' (we build the road as we travel), quoted from Spanish poet Antonio Machado, recurs again and again in Arizmendi's writings.

From subsoil to topsoil: on the cooperative movement

Arizmendi considered growth inevitable and believed its disadvantages needed to be faced:

We must think in terms of inter-cooperative solidarity as a unique resource through which we can advance toward other problems of growth and maturity: we must think of providing living space adequate to the circumstances.

Later he wrote, with the advent of the knowledge-based economy:

Today the great industrial and economic battles are decided in the field of research and scientific discovery, and the various states turn to this field to support their dominant position.

9.4.3 THE COOPERATIVE ENTERPRISE OF MONDRAGON

Overall, the founder of Mondragon was influenced by the Catholic religion and by the Distributivist philosophy of French philosopher Mounier, by economics and sociology, and by poetry and the humanities, while at the same time having a sharp commercial eye. As a social innovator, Arizmendi created, together with kindred spirits, a new kind of Basque cooperative enterprise, built on the then forgotten traditions on community-based organizations that existed earlier in the Basque country. In Bloom's as in Wallerstein's terms, he was loath to separate art from science, philosophy from enterprise, business from community.

9.5 Conclusion: From Social Science to Integral Research

The Mondragon Cooperatives and particularly Don Jose Arizmendi himself are most unusual in that they have combined philosophy and business, sociology and economy, in a way that few enterprises today purposefully do. So the question remains why, in our terms, bedrock and core generally remain so disconnected from topsoil and subsoil. One of the main reasons, for us, is that conventional research method and methodology, a standard part of conventional business and management education, is taught instrumentally rather than substantively, as tools and techniques rather than philosophies and paradigms. Moreover, and added to this, innovation and knowledge creation, from a corporate perspective, is totally disconnected from social research within an academic environment. It is the purpose of this book to militate against both these tendencies.

We now turn from the social sciences to a new process, which we have developed in recent years, enabling, practically, an enterprise, to engage with transdisciplinary fields in a way that takes the enterprise all the way from fundamental research to transformative action. We call this process Integral Research.

References

1. Lessem, R. and Schieffer, A. (Forthcoming: 2010). *Integral Research and Innovation: Transforming Enterprise and Society*. Farnham: Gower.
2. Khurana, R. (2007). *From Higher Aims to Hired Hands: The Social Transformation of the American Business Schools and the unfulfilled Promise of Management as a Profession*. Connecticut: Princeton University Press.

3. Koontz, H. et al. (1955). *Principles of Management*. New York: McGraw Hill.
4. Khurana, R. (2007). *Higher Aims to Hired Hands, Social Transformation of the American Business Schools*. Connecticut: Princeton University Press.
5. Bloom, A. (1988). *Closing of the American Mind*. Chicago: Chicago University Press.
6. Wallerstein, I. (ed.) (1996). *Open Social Sciences*. Palo Alto: Stanford University Press.
7. Wallerstein, I. (1999). *Social Science for the 21st Century: The End of the World as We Know it*. Minneapolis: Minnesota University Press.
8. Prigogine, I. (1997). *The End of Certainty*. New York: Free Press.
9. Whyte, W. (1991). *Making Mondragon*. Ithaca New York: Cornell University Press.

10 *Research to Innovation*

Fundamental Research to Transformative Action

10.1 Introduction: Transformative Research

10.1.1 TOWARDS ACTION RESEARCH

In this second chapter on the transdisciplinary fields we reach a turning point in our book on (the) Transformation (of) Management. So far we have mapped out a path from the transformational onto the transcultural and transdisciplinary, which you – as an individual, organization or society, in a particular part of the world – can follow.

The social sciences began life in the early part of last century as a form of engaged political economy, aimed at social betterment. Only as they were split out into the various existing conventional disciplines and subjected to harassment and purges because their social and political activism – according to organizational anthropologists Greenwood and Levin[1] – offended the rich and powerful, did the social sciences become separated from the world of transformative action.

Up to this point we as authors have remained in the background, mapping out the transformational terrain and introducing you fellow travellers within it, but not purposefully acting as guides or pathfinders. Now it is time to change our tune and tone, from informative to transformative, from management educators and researchers, in conventional terms if you like, to process consultants and social innovators as well. In fact, whereas the overall terrain that this book spans is that of Transformation Management, the vehicle to transport you across such is embodied in *social innovation*. However, there is more to it than that.

Conventionally, higher education involves certified educational programmes, on the one hand, ranging from undergraduate to postgraduate, from certificate to diploma, which may or may not involve projects. Such projects or coursework serve to enhance the value of an individual participant's qualification, whether in business administration or community development. Such elements often add a practical or experiential foundation to an otherwise purely academic programme. In fact and on the one hand, although our own Masters and Doctoral Programmes in Transformation Management, accredited by the University of Buckingham in the UK, are ostensibly oriented towards self, organizational and societal transformation, the basis for accreditation is ultimately the academic performance of the individual. While we have recently introduced *Integral Research and Innovation*[2] to enhance the potential for social innovation, the individual and academically based form of accreditation limits that organizational, communal and societal potential.

On the other hand, when engaged in consultancy consignments or process interventions to ostensibly promote individual and organizational transformation, we have been similarly restricted. While drawing upon our richly transformational, transcultural and transdisciplinary 'tool-kit', the delivery mechanism involved is the conventional 'workshop'. While such a mechanism is well adapted to the immediate requirements of the 'busy practitioner', the limitations in time and scope inhibited any attempt at so-called social innovation. In fact the practitioner-based MSET and DSET programmes (Social and Economic Transformation) in which we have been engaged, in Europe, the Middle East and Africa involve education and research, process consultancy and social innovation, all in one.

The key that opened that social innovation door then was constituted of a combination of process intervention, in organizational terms, and project-based learning, in academic ones. Such action research draws upon the social sciences and on the humanities, rather than upon natural science. Why then do we draw upon action research as our basis for social innovation, albeit in somewhat different guise from the conventional action research wisdom?

10.1.2 ACTION RESEARCH TO INTEGRAL INNOVATION

We call for the social sciences to assume their rightful role in the twenty-first century, in helping to resolve the complex social and economic – including environmental – problems we face today. The argument we make is that the burning social – including the natural and cultural – issues of our day and age far outweigh the purely technologically based ones. Our call is for integral, as opposed to merely technological innovation. Integral Innovation includes equally social *and* technological innovation.

Ironically the path to such has been hidden by purist academics who have concealed such potential social innovation from view, in the esoteric guise of 'research methodology', as distinct from the more commonplace research and development, or now the more recently emergent knowledge creation. Such research methodologies, conventionally restricted to academic practitioners and students on doctoral programmes, are cast in such inaccessible terms to the everyday management practitioner, as in terms of so-called phenomenology or hermeneutics. Yet for us, as for renowned Japanese organizational sociologists Nonaka and Takeuchi through their *Knowledge Creating Company* (see Chapter 14), such methodologies are not merely an academic nicety, but a much more thoroughgoing and potentially prolific basis for social innovation.

While this is more fully spelt out in our companion volume, for our purposes here we provide an initial overview. Within such we reveal ways in which both process interventions (in organizations) and also research methodologies (in academe) can be fused together to promote social innovation. We start by introducing you to the key cast of characters that have been responsible for the birth and growth of action research, that serves as a bridge between research (reflection oriented) and innovation (action oriented) in the social sciences. By positioning these seminal influencers in our Four Worlds, philosophically, geographically and culturally, we serve to establish an 'integrated' form of action research that leads towards social innovation.

All of these formative influences on action research were social innovators, in both an academic and an organizational or communal context. They actually are the giants upon whose shoulders we stand. Together we are promoting social innovation, in the context of the management of transformation, in both educational and also organizational contexts. Within the context of such an educational and research 'laboratory', inclusive of process interventions, we hope to transcend the limitations of educators and consultants alike, in promoting all round social innovation. This approach is opposed to merely running courses for individuals, ranging from workshops to doctoral programmes, or solving organizational problems. We start with perhaps the best known of these seminal and inherently transdisciplinary influences, the American educational philosopher, political scientist and social psychologist, John Dewey.

10.2 The Evolution of Action Research

WESTERN – PRAGMATIC: JOHN DEWEY AND THE ORIGINS OF ACTION RESEARCH (AR)

John Dewey, based at the University of Chicago at the turn of the twentieth century, headed up the department of philosophy, psychology and pedagogy. In 1896, more specifically for our purposes, he founded the University Laboratory School, now better known as the 'Dewey School'. The Laboratory, for Dewey as a pragmatist, was a place for educational experiments. Theories and practices were developed, tested, criticized, refined and tried again. Dewey, as such, was not only a pragmatist, but also an arch democrat.

His Laboratory School was not the only site for educational research in Chicago at that time. Jane Addams and her work at Hull House, for which she eventually received the Nobel Prize, greatly influenced Dewey. There he met some of the most influential early feminists whose involvement in the political issues of the day, that is, at the turn of the twentieth century, was caused by massive immigration, the social and economic effects of urbanization and rapid technological advance. Dewey also mixed with workers, trade unionists and political radicals in the course of his research and indeed some of his most influential educational works, which have influenced generations of educators, if not also other professional practitioners since, emerged out of these laboratories. America's John Dewey, as such, was a major influence on central European Kurt Lewin, the second now more explicitly 'rational' founder of action research. Lewin then was more 'northern' in his socio-technical orientation than the more behaviourally oriented 'western' empiricist, Dewey. At the same time, like Dewey, he straddled various scientific disciplines, most particularly biology, sociology, psychology and political science.

NORTHERN – RATIONAL: KURT LEWIN AND HIS SOCIO-TECHNICAL DESIGN (STD)

Kurt Lewin was born in 1890 in Prussia (now part of Poland) as one of four children in a middle class Jewish family. In 1909 Kurt Lewin entered the University of Freiburg to study medicine. He then transferred to the University of Munich to study biology. Around this time he became involved in the socialist movement. His particular concerns appear to have been the combating of anti-semitism, the democratization of German institutions and the need to improve the position of women. With the political position worsening in Germany, he and his family settled in the USA in 1933.

There he also became involved in various applied research initiatives linked to the Second World War effort. These included exploring ways of improving the morale of the fighting troops, methods of engaging in psychological warfare and ways of reorienting food consumption away from that in short supply. He was also much in demand as a speaker on minority and inter-group relations, both of which subjects had been, for him, areas of major research. He wanted, overall then, to establish a centre to research group dynamics – and in 1944 this dream was realized with the founding of the *Research Center for Group Dynamics* at Massachusetts Institute of Technology in Boston.

Lewin is generally accredited with the coining of the term action research. For him research that produces nothing but books will not suffice and he was focused on designing and serving to effect 'socio-technical systems' that promoted human flourishing. He was also closely aligned with the views of John Dewey in their belief that democracy had to be continually invented anew, both politically, in society as a whole, and institutionally, that is within an organization. Developments in industrial democracy owe a great deal to Lewin's early efforts to promote such participative 'socio-technical' structures. It was actually John Heron, though a generation later, who took on from where Lewin and Dewey had left off.

EASTERN – HOLISTIC: COOPERATIVE INQUIRY (CI) AND THE RELEASE OF HUMAN POTENTIAL

Between the 1950s and the 1970s, there was a lull in the development of action research, as it became marginalized in America, because of its seemingly radical overtones. The renewal of such, interestingly enough during the 1960s, in this era of student revolution and 'flower power', emerged via philosophical and spiritual influences from the holistic 'east'.

John Heron was a pioneer in the creation of what he came to identify as 'participative spirituality', more commonly termed 'co-operative inquiry'. As such, he was the founder and director of the Human Potential Research Project at the University of Surrey in England from 1970 to 1977, and as such an educator, a depth psychologist and a philosopher of research. Within the context of the research methodology he invented, co-operative inquiry, individuals and institutions are linked in a generative web of communion with other people as well as the rest of creation, again both in educational and organizational settings. All ways of knowing – for Heron ranging from experiential to imaginative, from theoretical to practical – support your skilful being-in-the-world from moment to moment, your ability to act intelligently in support of worthwhile purposes. In other words, Heron, as we have done through our Four Worlds, broadened the base of inquiry from first theory (research) and second practice (action) to thirdly experience and finally imagination.

For him, such an action research-based process of co-operative inquiry, whereby research is conducted with rather than on others, is not only informative but also transformative. Specifically this may involve the transformation of social, political and economic structures, including the liberation of the disempowered; of a specific organization, turning bureaucracy into democracy; of amateurism towards professionalism, creating a culture of competence; and finally of personhood, involving an individual's personal growth. In each of these cases, such a process towards social innovation is both a political (the democratic involvement of co-researchers) and a knowledge based (combination of experience, imagination, theory and practice) process. We finally turn to participatory action research, where the influence of the 'south', now alongside 'east' (Heron), 'north' (Lewin) and 'west' (Dewey) becomes most apparent.

Before we do that, we, once again, emphasize, that the various forms of action research, which we introduce at level four in our research and innovation trajectory, have all, in themselves, a strong integral element. The higher the level of the trajectory, the stronger the interconnectedness between the south-east-north-west variations of that particular path. That is why we call this last action research oriented level one of 'integration', as well as 'transformation'. So, for example, John Heron, with whom we have been in contact, sees his approach to co-operative inquiry as inherently integral, to the extent that he has strong reservations about positioning any of the different action research approaches in singular worlds. Whereas we take his general point, within the fine nuances of our approach, we do regard PAR as more vividly relational and indeed communal than CI, and CI as more holistic and indeed spiritual, than for example, generic AR and socio-technical design.

SOUTHERN – HUMANISTIC: PARTICIPATORY ACTION RESEARCH (PAR) AND SOCIAL CHANGE

In 1975, a young Canadian adult educator named Budd Hall compiled a special issue of the American journal for community activists, Convergence, on the topic of what ultimately was termed participatory action research. Beyond Hall's expectations, this issue sparked an international network of educators, academics and activists interested in this area, which became known as the 'International Participatory Research Network'. This network would grow stronger and larger over the next two decades. The key protagonists, amongst such, were two sociologists and social activists, from respectively Colombia in Latin America and from Bangladesh in Asia, Orlando Fals Borda and M.D. Rahman. Furthermore, the best known exponent of PAR was Burkina Faso's Bernard Ouedraogo, of Six S's (*Se Servir de la Saison Seche en Savanne et au Sahel*) who ultimately, as an anthropologist, an agronomist, a sociologist, a political scientist and an economist, as well being as a social activist, involved 160,000 villages, in the 1970s, in rural development.

The beginning of this PAR story can be traced to Tanzania, where Hall worked from 1970 to 1974. At that time, under the leadership of President Julius Nyerere, Tanzania had launched an experiment in what is known as 'ujamaa socialism', in which such emergent participatory action research was involved. In Tanzania, Hall had the fortune of learning from many inspiring adult educators. Among them were Brazil's Paulo Freire and the Tanzanian President himself; Julius Nyerere was probably the only adult educator in the world who became president of a country. Through these experiences, Hall became acquainted with approaches to education and development based on the principles of self-reliance, active participation and dialogue. He also became interested in the potential of research to promote transformative learning, local development and social change. The focus then shifted, in this 'southern' humanist context, from individual (Dewey), interpersonal (Heron) and organizational (Lewin) to whole communities (Ouedraogo), as in the Burkina Faso and Tanzanian cases. We are now ready to some up this overall orientation to action research and social innovation.

INTEGRAL RESEARCH: TOWARDS INTEGRAL INNOVATION

The mode of process intervention (institutional)or project-based learning (individual) leading to social innovation therefore, thereby cutting across enterprise and academe, consultancy and education, organizational workshops and academic projects, is action research. Such action research becomes potentially integrated, thereby paving way for fully fledged social innovation, whereby it accommodates all four of our worlds, in this case spanning individual (pragmatic) and institutional (rational), interpersonal (holistic) and societal (humanistic). To appreciate the full nature and scope of such we need to consider each of these in turn, following the logic of social innovation. The four such paths towards Integral Innovation, each one containing four layers, we identify as:

1. the southern relational path – descriptive, phenomenological, feminist and PAR based;
2. the eastern path of renewal – narrative, interpretive, critical theory and CI based;
3. the northern path of reason – theory, critical rationalism, postmodernism, and STD based;
4. the western path of realization – experiment, empiricism, critical realism and AR based.

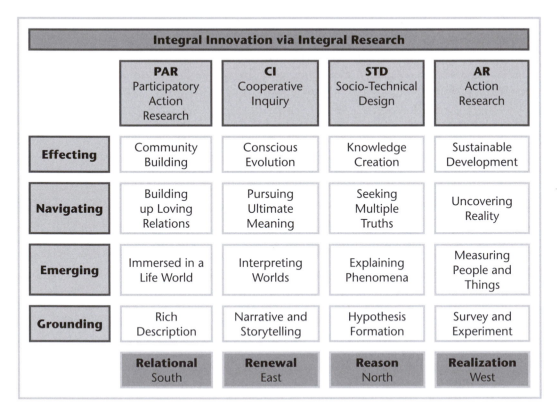

Integral Innovation via Integral Research			
PAR Participatory Action Research	**CI** Cooperative Inquiry	**STD** Socio-Technical Design	**AR** Action Research
Effecting Community Building	Conscious Evolution	Knowledge Creation	Sustainable Development
Navigating Building up Loving Relations	Pursuing Ultimate Meaning	Seeking Multiple Truths	Uncovering Reality
Emerging Immersed in a Life World	Interpreting Worlds	Explaining Phenomena	Measuring People and Things
Grounding Rich Description	Narrative and Storytelling	Hypothesis Formation	Survey and Experiment
Relational South	**Renewal** East	**Reason** North	**Realization** West

Again, each path evolves integrally from grounding to effect, thereby releasing GENE-ius. The composite or integral path is set out, in matrix form (show in the table above). The cast of characters who serve to illustrate the application of all of such are participants on our practically based masters in social and economic transformation. At the same time, moreover, as we shall see illustrated more specifically in the chapters that follow, such participants from the Middle East and Southern Africa have engaged with community building, conscious evolution, knowledge creation and sustainable development, with a view to evolving from a building society to society building. We then start with the Relational Path, connected with community building. In each of the four research to innovation paths, moreover, a progressive evolution through four layers, from individual and institution, to community and society, is involved:

- Layer 1: Individual Revealing
- Layer 2: Institutional Understanding
- Layer 3: Communal Immersion
- Layer 4: Societal Engagement (via Action Research).

In each such case, there is a southern, eastern, northern and then western perspective. Figure 10.1 gives an overview on the design of Integral Research. Figure 10.1 further illustrates how Integral Research is targeted to bring about social innovation, addressing the burning issues, organizations and societies are facing.

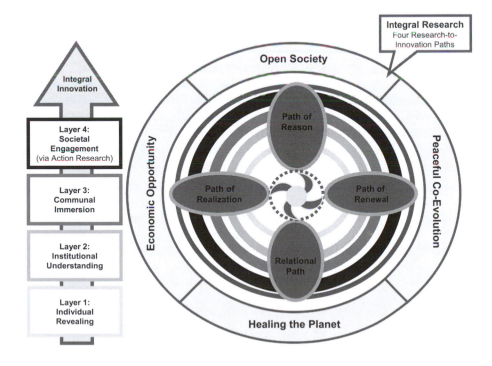

Figure 10.1 Overview of the Integral Research model

10.3 The Southern Relational Path towards Community Building

10.3.1 GROUNDED IN RICH DESCRIPTION: INDIVIDUALLY REVEALING

• Engage your total self in passionate involvement with the undertaking.
• Undertake comprehensive descriptions, vivid and accurate renderings of experience.

The 'southern' path of social innovation, via ultimately Participatory Action Research, is the first of our means towards a transformational end. Such innovation is promoted through either an institutionallybased process intervention, and/or through individually oriented project based learning, in each case underpinned by research and development. The process of engagement would be grounded in this *relational* case, in a rich description, or diarizing of everyday experience, both inwardly and outwardly, towards such a social innovation.

Case: Sue Jenkins – social worker

Sue Jenkins was a senior social worker, born and bred in Ireland, who was based in the Borough of Ealing, in West London. Possessing a natural empathy with the impoverished communities with which she worked, she became 'one of them' from the moment she became involved with her clients and communities. Having, moreover, a poetic touch, she was able to describe in a colourful and intimate way, the lives that they lived, in moving detail.

Starting out individually, there is a need to collectivize in the next step.

10.3.2 SET WITHIN A LIFE WORLD: INSTITUTIONAL UNDERSTANDING

• Focus on the subjective view of experience.
• Locate every uniquely local cultural history as an episode in the larger global story.

The facilitation of such individual description provides the initial grounding for a process intervention, or transformational project. Thereafter, such an intervention, with a view to, for example, consciously engaging in society building, needs to emerge out of a particular 'life world'. The research methodology to engage in such life world is termed 'phenomenology'. For its founder, the central European Edmund Husserl[3] early last century, such research involves putting the study of culture on a proper scientific footing. Such culture is the ultimate horizon of all human achievement. As conscious human beings, we always inhabit such a life world. It is pre-given in advance and experienced as a unity. The life world is the general structure, which would allow *community building*, in the Ealing case in point, to emerge.

Case: Borough of Ealing (UK) social work department

In the case of the social work department at the Borough of Ealing – a thoroughly multi-racial work environment – this involved getting inside the skin of the Irish, Indian and Polish communities in the Borough. While the Irish responded, in particular, to psychodrama, and the Indians to family based care, the Polish, in many cases, wanted to be taken care of by their own communities.

10.3.3 BUILDING UP LOVING RELATIONSHIPS: IMMERSED IN A COMMUNITY

- You aim to create social change.
- You see knowledge as a tool for liberation not domination.

The descriptive and the phenomenological – intentionally engaging with life worlds such as that of West London communities – provides the individual, immediate grounds and the wider, socially emergent reality. The point of emancipatory take-off, with a view to navigating a course towards social innovation in a more active and reflective guise, is, in this 'southern' case, through the development of loving relationships. Such an indeed 'feminist'[4] course of further research and development has a particular character. The social, rather than natural, sciences are seen as the new paradigm, or model, for all sciences, including the economic. Included in such is nature as active and complex, leading to an ecological or open systems approach. Finally, knowledge should be used as a tool for liberation not domination.

Case: RSCN Royal Society for the Conservation of Nature (Jordan)

The model of 'ecosophy',[5] developed by ex financier and economic philosopher Bernard Lietaer, may be the one for the Royal Society to go for in the future. Evolved out of 'mother nature' rather than 'father time', such an approach to finance and economics would lead to the development of natural as well as financial, social as well as spiritual capital. RSCN, which started out as a 'conservation agency', actually the largest one in the Middle East, has in recent years evolved new nature based economic enterprises to serve its local Bedouin populations.

We now turn ultimately to PAR, as the last step of our southern relational path.

10.3.4 EFFECTING SOCIAL INNOVATION THROUGH COMMUNITY BUILDING: ENGAGING WITH SOCIETY

- PAR involves the full and active participation of the community.
- Create awareness of people's own resources, mobilizing for self-reliant development.

Ultimately, the fusion of action and reflection in a social context culminates in community building, or indeed society building, through participatory action research.

For the co-founder of PAR, Colombia's Orlando Fals Borda,[6] the pursuit of such involves: *Collective research* obtained from groups through dialogue, discussion, argument and consensus in the investigation of social realities; a *critical recovery of history* to discover those elements of the past which have proved useful in heightening consciousness, using popular stories; *valuing and applying folk culture* whereby account is taken of art, music, drama, sports, story-telling and other expressions related to human sentiment and imagination; and ultimately the *production and diffusion of new knowledge* whereby different levels of communication are developed using sound, painting, mime, photograph, theatre, poetry, music, puppetry and exhibitions.

Case: Chinyika Community

The Chinyika Community in rural Zimbabwe, like many others in the new millennium, was suffering drastic food shortages under the debilitating Mugabe regime. Chidara Muchineripi, the son of a local chief, management consultant, and participant on our transformation programme, felt impelled, as a son of the African soil, to do something about it. Gathering together the elders of the community he and they reviewed, together, the history of Chinyika and uncovered the fact that they had traditionally been self-reliant, that is before the colonialists had discouraged the locals from growing indigenous foods. Enhancing their consciousness of such, and helped by a fellow participant on the programme, a director of a major food processing company in the country, Chinyika, over the course of a year, returned to food self-sufficiency.

We now turn from the 'south' to the 'east' and as such from socially oriented community building, to the interpersonally oriented conscious evolution of individual and group.

10.4 The Eastern Path of Renewal towards Conscious Evolution

10.4.1 GROUNDED IN NARRATIVE AND STORYTELLING: INDIVIDUALLY REVEALING

- The narrative mode leads to gripping drama, creative origination.
- Tying together potentials and possibilities of your respective beginnings.

The 'southern' humanistic path to social innovation, whether educationally or organizationally instigated, is only one, relational part of the integrated whole. Such a whole serves not only to build community but also to promote conscious evolution. We hence come now onto the path of renewal, which consciously promotes the further evolution of self and community, organization and society.

In moving on, from being to becoming we turn from description to narrative. Your *author-ity* as such, for Canadian Professor of English Literature William Randall,[7], with respect to your unfolding story, lies somewhere in between you. You are in a position to reconstruct – not so much the events or idea within your/its research and development story – but the plots whereby you/it make them into your own. A new plot means a new story, and a new story leads to a new individual, organizational or societal construction.

Case: Anisa Al Raisi

Anisa Al Raisi was born in Oman at a time when there was a virtually total absence of basic infrastructure, including schooling for girls. At the age of five she therefore asked a neighbour, who was a teacher, to educate her. In return, Anisa would look after the children. As per the local custom she was married at the age of 13, to a military man, and bore her husband three children, continuing her studies at the same time. Ultimately finding herself an administrative position at a bank in Muscat, she rose so fast up the ranks that she emerged as Director of the Omani World Trade Centre. While on our

Transformation Programme she was motivated to establish her own Transformation Centre.

We now turn from individual narrative to an interpretation of communal worlds.

10.4.2 INTERPRETING OR RE-INTERPRETING WORLDS: INSTITUTIONAL UNDERSTANDING

- Reconnecting with the source.
- Reconstructing self and society.

As we move on from the individual narrative to that of the organization or society, so narrative evolves into interpretive research, or so-called hermeneutics. This involves interpreting and thereby reconnecting different worlds, both past and present as well as one world with another. For a contemporary student of *The Hermeneutics of Africa*,[8] Eritrean-American social philosopher Tsenay Serequeberhan, liberation movements, for example, are born out of the 'fusion of horizons' of two broad segments of society, the urban and the rural. Each manifests in itself what the other does not have and is estranged from. The westernized urbanized native is acquainted with the 'global' world beyond the colony or neo-colony and the struggles of other peoples. The rural non-westernized native, on the other hand, is steeped in the broken 'local' heritage of his own particular past. In the fusion of these two fractured urban and rural 'worlds' the possibility of freedom is concretized or made tangible.

Case: Arab Educational Foundation

In establishing the Arab Educational Foundation in Muscat, Anisa was catering for the development needs, not only of the young men and women of urban Muscat, but also of those in the neighbouring rural areas. Based on her own life story, she had a profound empathy for people and communities coming from such rural areas. Indeed, and like Sultan Qaboos who had served to transform Omani society over 30 years, Anisa was a true disciple in that respect.

We now turn, more fully, towards individual and collective emancipation.

10.4.3 PURSUING MEANINGFUL ENTERPRISE: IMMERSED IN A COMMUNITY

- Analyzing specifically the suffering of people.
- Explicitly focused on promoting 'liberation'.

As is the case for the relational path, so in the path of renewal, reflection begins to turn towards action at the emancipatory stage. According to the so-called 'Frankfurt School' – the most famous of its members being psychotherapist Erich Fromm and philosopher Herbert Marcuse – founded in Germany in the 1930s, social science should strive to develop an independent and critical stance regarding institutions and modes of thought, and should call attention to the contradictions in the way society functions. The inherent restrictions and irrationalities that inform modern capitalist societies should be among the major subjects of research. Such an approach to research and development, in effect, termed *critical theory*,[9] may seem out of place in a process intervention, directed at a business – if not a social – enterprise, but not necessarily so. For Muhammad Yunus, his banking orientation emerged in Bangladesh and subsequently in other parts of the world out of just such a societally critical orientation.

Case: Omani business immersed in community

Profit for me is unashamedly biased towards capital. The poor work for someone who controls the productive assets. Why can't the poor control any capital? Because they do not inherit any capital or credit, nor does anybody give them access to capital, because we have come to believe that the poor are not creditworthy. But are the banks people-worthy? Grameen looked at conventional banks and turned everything upside-down. Success therefore, for us, is not measured by bad debt figures or repayment rates but whether the miserable lives of our borrowers have become less miserable.[10]

Anisa, in that respect, was a disciple of Mohammad Yunus, founder of Grameen. Like him she believed that the train of economic development had to be started from the rear, as it were, that is with the poorest of the poor. With that end in mind she continually engaged herself with local businesses, to turn their thoughts and actions in the direction of the young unemployed, to work with them to establish social and economic enterprises.

John Heron, to whom we now return, would be very much in sympathy with Yunus and with Anisa.

10.4.4 EFFECTING CONSCIOUS EVOLUTION VIA COOPERATIVE INQUIRY: ENGAGING WITH SOCIETY

- A politically-oriented process, involving a participative form of inquiry.
- A knowledge-oriented process – experiential, imaginative, theoretical and practical

Cooperative Inquiry, as we have seen, is both informative and transformative in orientation.[11] As such it is constructed through social participation in which there is a mutually enabling balance within and between people, of autonomy, hierarchy and cooperation. Reality for Heron moreover, in terms of his four modes, can then be understood as follows: the experiential is the mutual co-determination of you and your world; the imaginative is significant form and pattern; the propositional serves to combine sense and concepts; the practical is excellent practice.

Case: Team Jordan

The RSCN, to which we have already referred, was involved, through the participation of its Managing Director in the Transformation Management programme, designed by our Geneva centre TRANS4M and run jointly by the University of Buckingham and management consultants Team Jordan. The founder of TEAM, Maqbouleh Hammoudeh, herself a graduate of our programme, had based her doctoral studies with us on a cooperative inquiry into RSCN. Working with its senior management as co-researchers, they together applied a newly developed Islamic approach to management, based on the value of justice, to the organization. In the process they applied experiential, imaginative, conceptual and ultimately practical knowledge to the transformation of the enterprise.

We now turn from east to north, from the path of renewal to that of reason, from conscious evolution to knowledge creation.

10.5 The Northern Path of Reason towards Knowledge Creation

10.5.1 GROUNDED IN HYPOTHESIS FORMATION: INDIVIDUALLY REVEALING

- Regarding nature and social life as consisting of essential uniformities.
- The aim is to discover these uniformities, to find universal statements, or hypotheses.

The humanistic and holistic paths to social innovation are less in evidence in educational and in organizational contexts than both the rational path, which we consider now, and the pragmatic path of realization, which comes later. The path of reason is grounded in hypothesis formation, academically speaking, and the generation of ideas or concepts, more generally. For Anglo-Austrian Karl Popper,[12] the doyen of such a deductively based research orientation: you begin by putting forward a tentative idea, a conjecture, a hypothesis; then, with the help of other previously accepted hypotheses or assumptions, you reach a conclusion, or a number of conclusions; further, you examine the conclusions and the logic behind them, comparing this argument with existing theories to see if it constitutes an advance in understanding; if so you test the conclusion by gathering appropriate data, making the necessary observations or conduct the necessary experiments; if the test fails – if the data are not consistent with the conclusion – the 'theory' must be false and the original conjecture must be rejected, and if the conclusion passes the test, because the data are consistent with it, then the 'theory' is temporarily supported, that means it is corroborated, not proved to be true.

Case: Reza Moussavian

Reza Moussavian was Iranian by birth but had been brought up in Germany. After his business studies, he ended up as a management consultant, working mainly in the Middle East. Conscious of his heritage, while being a great admirer of the European Union, he conjectured that the Middle East would be much more prosperous and politically stable, if it was able to establish a political and economic union like the one that surrounded him in Germany, that is, the EU. In fact, and in this day and age, he posited that a network society, combining the social networks he observed in the Arab world with the communications technology with which he was concerned as a consultant, could prospectively enhance such a union.

10.5.2 EXPLAINING PHENOMENA THROUGH CRITICAL RATIONALISM: INSTITUTIONAL UNDERSTANDING

- Strong theory drives out the weak.
- Natural and social science are value neutral.

The underlying idea of Popper's theory of knowledge is that problems and attempts to solve them through hypotheses, theories or conjectures precede all observation. In fact for the eminent African philosopher, Paulin Hountondji[13] from Benin, in today's social sciences the decisive stage of investigation is neither the collection of data, nor the application of theoretical findings to practical issues, but what comes between them – the interpretation of raw information, the theoretical processing of the data collected, and the production of those particular utterances which we call scientific statements, or indeed theory building.

Case: Integrated social responsiveness

Reza, however, was unable to test his theory across the Middle Eastern region, not only because of its wide-ranging scope, but also because of the general turbulence in parts of the region. So he decided to narrow his focus from politics and economics to business in society, in the region, most especially in the Gulf States. He began to forge a new approach to corporate social responsibility, drawing on the Four Worlds approach to which he had been exposed. To that extent he invited the businesses with which he consulted to develop their business, academic, spiritual and communal engagement with a particular society. We now turn from the pursuit of one truth to many.

10.5.3 SEEKING MULTIPLE TRUTHS: IMMERSED IN A COMMUNITY

• Engage in multiple discourses rather than a following grand theory or ideology.
• Reconfigure history, focusing on discontinuity and rupture rather than continuity.

While the world at large is familiar with postmodernism, in terms of the post-industrial, knowledge and service based economy, epitomized by Apple and Google, its significance for financial services is less clearly apparent. Whereas a 'modern' approach to deductively based research sees useful knowledge as hypothesis shaped, the postmodern one that we consider now, in contrast, involves constructing specific accounts of the world, through discourse and culture.[14] In the last three decades of the twentieth century, all the disciplines of the social sciences have experienced a fundamental reappraisal of their basic assumptions, the most significant of such is the recognition that 'culture' deserves much more serious attention as an object of study in its own right. Together with this has been a focus on knowledge, arising out of culture, in the context of a post-industrial, knowledge based society.

Case: Mohammad Al Zoubi

Mohammad Al Zoubi, a senior administrator with Jordan customs, entered our doctoral programme with a view to pursuing an empirical study of the effect of customs duties on trade in the region. Having, however, been exposed to ideas on social and economic transformation, as well as to Integral Research, he instead decided to pursue a postmodern course. That led him to undertake an investigation of culture and globalization in Jordan, alternating between trade, communications and Islamic discourses. In the process he began to fundamentally challenge the prevailing beliefs in the value of free trade in Jordan, engaging with politicians in the process.

That ultimately involved a conscious socio-technical design for knowledge creation.

10.5.4 EFFECTING A SOCIO-TECHNICAL DESIGN FOR KNOWLEDGE CREATION

- The research and development is geared towards social betterment.
- Using a co-creative approach to organizational or communal development.

Institutionally based action research, aimed at a new socio-technical design, is framed as a democratic process supporting the creation of knowledge that potentially can be liberating.[15] Obviously then, the inquiry process has to aim to solve problems important to the organizational participants, and the knowledge produced by the research process must increase participants' control over their own situations. The participants, moreover, must be able to use the knowledge that emerges, and this knowledge must support the enhancement of the participant' goals. Such an approach to action research then centres on a co-generatively structured encounter between the worlds of practical reasoning and those of scientifically constructed knowledge. It is a social process in which professional knowledge, local knowledge, process skills, a research orientation and democratic values are the basis for knowledge creation and social innovation.

Case: From government to university

Mohammad then, upon completion of his doctorate, was invited to establish at his local university, a new department that dealt with the impact of globalization on culture, and vice versa. In that context commercial and social customs were fused together in the most unusual way. Moreover, Mohammad was encouraged to come up with a new design for his department, so that it simultaneously served the needs of individual students and the government department concerned.

This brings us primarily onto generic 'western' action research.

10.6 The Western Path of Realization towards Sustainable Development

10.6.1 GROUNDED IN SURVEY AND EXPERIMENTATION: INDIVIDUALLY REVEALING

- You are a good listener – not trapped by your own ideologies and preconceptions.
- You are adaptable so that newly encountered situations can be seen as opportunities.

Unlike descriptive, narrative and 'hypothesis building', each of which has gained relatively scarce attention in the social sciences (with psychology being to some extent an exception) hundreds of books and billions of dollars have been devoted to survey based, if not also experimental, modes of research. Not only that every minute in the day and all over the world undergraduate and postgraduate students will be attending classes on survey methods, ranging from interview methods and questionnaire design to focus groups and to statistical methods, but also market research and human resource practitioners will be engaging prolifically with these. Such is the predominance of the western world, at least in terms of basic research.

Case: Duke of Edinburgh Award Scheme

Samar Kildani was responsible for the Duke of Edinburgh Award Scheme in the Middle East. Through this scheme she brought together young people from the region, including Arabs and Jews, with a view to reconciliation through shared adventure based activities. She was particularly keen to compare and contrast the attitudes and behaviours of the young people, from different countries, and used a 'spectral inventory', developed by one of the authors (Ronnie Lessem) as a basis for such.

10.6.2 EMERGING THROUGH MEASURING PEOPLE AND THINGS: INSTITUTIONAL UNDERSTANDING

The empiricist uses induction to collect observational data and build theories to explain the observations.[16] Thus, the empirical method of induction involves two movements simultaneously: from the particular to the general, and from observed events to theoretical constructions. The method of induction, then, refers to a logical process of constructing knowledge about observed relationships between variables in particular instances. This can be taken as a basis for making universal generalizations in as yet unobserved, particular instances. The strength of such an empirical approach lies in its appeal to data collected through human senses, rather than perceived intuitively, or conceived abstractly, as a means of validating propositions. The explanatory power of this approach, moreover, is said to rest upon its predictive uses.

Case: Intrapreneurship

Having issued and collated an extensive number of inventories, 200 in all, Samar analyzed the data and discovered in terms of the 'spectral inventory', that the category of 'adventurer', and of 'agent of change', predominated amongst the young people. At the same time there were comparatively few 'enablers' and 'visionary' types, and the animateurs and entrepreneurs were in between categories. That having been said, she found there to be no significant differences across the different countries.

But this is not the end of the 'western' story bearing on social innovation.

10.6.3 NAVIGATING A PATH OF REALIZATION: IMMERSED IN A COMMUNITY

Whereas an experimental, and thereafter empirically based approach to social innovation is focused on experiences, attitudes and behaviours, on the surface, the so-called *critical realist* approach goes deeper, towards thereby uncovering reality. The most fundamental enterprise in science, for such critical realists, is to find the inherent mechanisms that generate events; it is these inherent properties they call 'causal powers'. The critical realists, with Anglo-Indian philosopher Roy Bhaskar as their founder,[17] distinguish three domains. First the basic, underlying one is the domain of the *'real'*. Here we find the generative mechanisms, existing irrespective of whether they produce an event or not.

When mechanisms produce a factual event, second, it comes under the domain of the *actual*, the next level up, that is third and finally, whether we observe it or not; when an event is finally *experienced*, we enter the surface domain of the empirical fact.

Case: Four Worlds

Our own Four Worlds typology, interestingly enough, we regard as a generative mechanism, in Bhaskar's terms in that it underlies, at philosophical bedrock, the more variegated attitudes and behaviours within and across cultures. As such the humanistic (south) and holistic (east), rational (north) and pragmatic (west), are for us more 'real' than the more surface inclinations, such as English 'reserve' or French culinary preferences. As such, the *real* depths of such Four World philosophies underlie more pervasive features of each culture.

Finally, we now come onto generic action research.

10.6.4 EFFECTING SUSTAINABLE DEVELOPMENT THROUGH ACTION RESEARCH: ENGAGING WITH SOCIETY

Action research (AR) generically, that is in its overtly 'western' and pragmatic form, focuses on specific contexts, demands that theory and practice are not separated, and is committed to the idea that the test of any theory is its capacity to resolve a problem in a real life situation. This focus on the world of experience, with its complexity and dynamism, means that AR distances itself from the purified world of conventional, social research with its friction-free, perfect information and 'others being equal' assumptions that make being an academic easier though at the cost of being irrelevant. The credibility-validity of AR knowledge is measured according to whether actions that arise from it solve problems (workability) and increase participants' control over their own situations.

Case: Anglian Water

Finally in this action research respect, with a view to turning SMVAC, the then Czech subsidiary of the UK's Anglian Water Group into a customer oriented company, in the 1990s, the HR Director Petr Svab tried a series of experiments, as part of his masters projects. He thereby experimented in particular with different approaches to customer service in different regions, using a range of American, Scandinavian and home-grown Czech approaches. Interestingly enough he found the Nordic approaches to service and relationships management worked better than the approach to empowerment adopted in the Anglo-Saxon world, and indeed the more conservative and hierarchical orientations adopted in the Czech Republic hitherto.

10.7 Conclusion: Research and Social Innovation

We have now completed the journey towards Integral Research, altogether culminating in southern participatory action research (PAR), eastern cooperative inquiry (CI), northern socio-technical design (STD), as well as western generic action research (AR). Each of these four had to undergo an evolutionary journey, from individual revealing to societal engagement, which involved different elements in each case.

Altogether, we encompass both the conventional and indeed unconventional research repertoire. We do that both vertically from individual revelation to societal engagement, and horizontally involving integral – southern and eastern, northern and western – action research. What we have done here is to take them out of the academic research closet and illustrate how they might apply in the context of an organizational process intervention, as well as in a project based academic programme.

In the final analysis, drawing once again on our Four Worlds and our GENE, we have charted the composite paths of research to innovation that we need to draw upon, to promote the Transformation Management that we seek. Now we turn to the next part of the book, to the fourth fundamental of transpersonal functions.

References

1. Greenwood, D. and Levin, M. (2007). *Introduction to Action Research*. London: Sage.
2. Lessem, R. and Schieffer, A. (Forthcoming: 2010). *Integral Research and Innovation: Transforming Enterprise and Society*. Farnham: Gower.
3. Husserl, E. (1970). *The Crisis of the European Sciences*. Chicago: Northwestern University.
4. Eisler, R. (2007). *The Real Wealth of Nations*. San Francisco: Berrett Koehler.
5. Lietaer, B. (2004). *The Future of Money*. New York: Century.
6. Fals Borda, O. (1991). *Action and Knowledge*. New York: Apex Publishing.
7. Randall, W. (1995). *The Stories We Are*. Toronto: Toronto University Press.
8. Serequeberhan, T. (1994). *Hermeneutics of Africa*. London: Routledge.
9. Held, M. (1980). *Introduction to Critical Theory*. London: Routledge.
10. Yunus, M. (2008). *Social Business*. New York: Public Affairs.
11. Heron, J. (1994). *Co-operative Inquiry*. London: Sage.
12. Popper, K. (2000). *Popper on Problem Solving*. London: Routledge.
13. Hountondji, P. (2002). *The Struggle for Meaning*. Buckingham: Open University Press.
14. Foucault, M. (2000). *Archaeology of Knowledge*. London: Routledge.
15. Greenwood, D. and Levin, M. (2007). *Introduction to Action Research*. New York: Sage.
16. Smith, M. (2004). *Social Science in Question*. Buckingham: Open University Press.
17. Danemark, B. (2002). *Explaining Society*. London: Routledge.

PART 5

The Fourth Fundamental of Transformation Management

> **Transforming**
> *the Functions of Management*

Core Theme within Transformation Management:
**Realising the Effective Enterprise
through Enhanced Economics and Management
by Building up Transpersonal Functions**

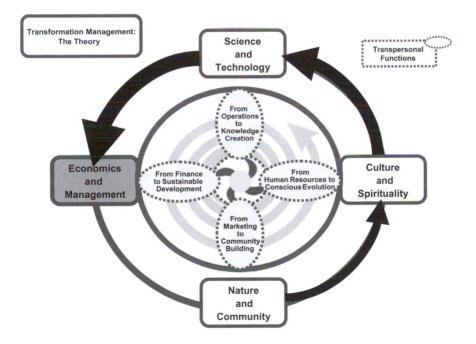

Transforming
the Functions of Management

Core Outcome for the Integral Enterprise:
1. **Building the Efficient Organization**
2. **Releasing Managerial GENE-ius**
3. **Institutionalizing Community Building**
   to Sustainable Development

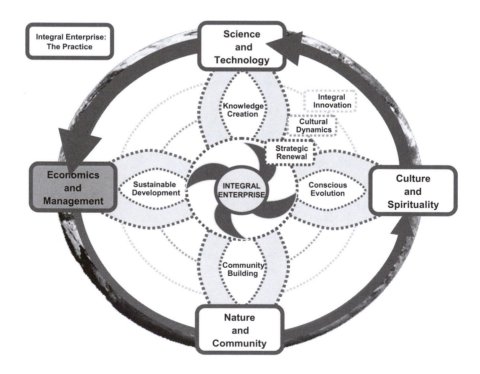

11 *Management and Transformation*

From the Evolution of Marketing to the Evolution of Finance

11.1 Introduction: Overview of the Four Core Functions of the Enterprise

ARRIVING IN THE WEST: THE TRANSPERSONAL FUNCTIONS OF THE ENTERPRISE

We now come to the fourth fundamental of Transformation Management, the transpersonal functions. In building the Integral Enterprise, we go through the four following steps:

1. *Nature (South):* Harnessing the transformational flows relevant for all living systems (from self, organization, community to society), altogether rooted in nature. On the level of the Integral Enterprise such an understanding and engagement with the transformational flows lead to a *transformation of competitive strategy into strategic renewal*, enabling the organization to continuously renew itself.

2. *Culture (East):* Building upon the transcultural forces within a particular social and cultural context and in between various cultures, crucial for each transformation process. In relation to the Integral Enterprise, an understanding of and engagement with the local and global forces, provides the basis to t*ranscend conventional organization development into cultural dynamics.*

3. *Science (North):* Understanding the transdisciplinary fields provides the basis for building a fundamentally new knowledge base for the organization. Integral Research, further, enables the enterprise to engage in a process of innovation, leading from fundamental research to transformative action. In relation to the Integral Enterprise, this prospectively leads to the institutionalization of an internal *R&D function, focusing on Social Innovation*. As such the organization lays the foundation to become a Social Innovator, addressing burning issues and serving core needs in a society. However, this foundation now needs to be translated into specific and differentiated organizational functioning, the functional management of the enterprise.

4. *Management (West):* In this fourth step, and only now, we are arriving in the west, where conventional management is lodged. Being enriched cumulatively by the prior three steps, *management, which deals with the functioning of the enterprise, is itself fundamentally transformed.* Each of the core functions of the enterprise now builds on nature, culture and science, and thereby plays an important part in forming the Integral Enterprise.

RETRACING STEPS: THE CONVENTIONAL FUNCTIONS OF THE ENTERPRISE

In this chapter we shall be dealing with the functioning of the enterprise. We will start by providing an overview of the conventional organizational functions, focusing on how they have evolved over time. Doing so, we lay the foundations for a subsequent transformation of these four functions, promoting thereby the progressive evolution of an ultimately integral and sustainable enterprise. This entire section on the transpersonal functions builds successively on the transformational flows, the transcultural forces as well as the transdisciplinary fields. In this chapter, in particular, we shall make continuous reference to the previous chapter on Integral Research.

The transformation of the core functions of the enterprise is not an easy task. It requires a purposefully innovative process, whereby the Integral Research trajectory, referred to in the last chapter, is instrumental. As we have demonstrated, it is important that organizations embody their research and development through the organization's evolved functioning, ultimately directed towards social innovation. Such institutionalized innovation is intrinsic to the Integral Enterprise. The final step in this journey is the most radical part of Transformation Management. It is when the enterprise gradually transforms its core functions – marketing and operations, human resources and finance – in a way in which they integrate person (self), organization and community/society. That's why we called it 'transpersonal'. At the same time, each such 'transpersonal' function evolves through applying the transformational GENE. Thereby, each function is becoming an evolutionary force itself.

The conventional enterprise consists of four core functions, plus a central one, called strategy. The four core functions are marketing, human resources, operations and finance. While we already dealt with strategic renewal earlier in this book, we shall have a close look at the other four specialist functions. As indicated in Chapters 2 and 5, the four functions of the enterprise correspond with the four vital functions of any living system:

1. *Marketing:* Marketing, for us, builds upon the southern function of a society, related to community and nature. The first products that were economically exchanged between human beings were natural products (like vegetables, meat, spices, etc.), and the place where they were exchanged were local markets. In conventional enterprise terms this is the domain of sales and marketing and customer relationships.
2. *Human Resources*: Human Resources draws upon the eastern functioning of a society, for us related to culture and spirit. This traditionally is the realm of art and religion rather than nature and community. In conventional enterprise terms this is the domain of skills and capacities, of talent and creativity.
3. *Operations*: Operations, for us, builds upon the northern functioning of a society, related to science and technology. Such functioning takes us back to 'homo faber', man the maker, and indeed to the stone, bronze and iron ages. It involves the structuring and systematizing of a living system. In conventional enterprise terms this is the domain of artefacts and inventions, of processes and systems.
4. *Finance*: Finance finally draws upon the western functioning of society, where economic and commercial activities come to the fore, taking us back to the ancient trade routes, and forward to the financial markets. In conventional enterprise terms this is the domain of financial management and accounting.

Figure 11.1 provides an overview on the conventional enterprise, positioning the four functions in Four World terms. The evolution of the conventional functions, historically, is our starting point, and focus of this chapter. Based on that foundation, we then introduce the necessary transformation of each function, each in one chapter.

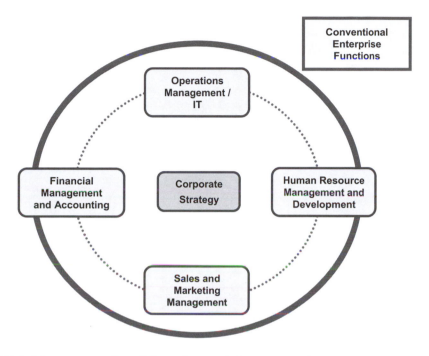

Figure 11.1 The conventional functions of the enterprise

By tracing the origins of each function, we can connect to the wider knowledge base each function builds upon. Integral Research, as such, represents a trajectory from fundamental research to transformative action: the enterprise, and in this case each of its functions, starts by re-searching and re-connecting to its origin and thereby to its relevant knowledge base, and works itself progressively towards transformative action. For us, this is an ultimately sustainable process, from local grounding to global effect. Such a process enables the organization to build and evolve its own knowledge and innovation base from the ground up. This is a fundamental shift away from applying alien, external concepts, which make the enterprise not only dependent on external input, but also, much more important, prevents it from becoming a social innovator itself. The following table connects the four functions with their relevant knowledge bases (disciplines) and the respective research-to-innovation path, enabling the transformation of each function.

Functions, Disciplines and Research Paths		
Functions	**Disciplines**	**Research Paths**
Marketing	Sociology, Psychology, Economics, Anthropology, Ecology	**Relational Path**
Human Resources	History, Geography, Depth Psychology, Religious Studies	**Path of Renewal**
Operations	Philosophy, Systems Science, Environmental Studies, Operations Research	**Path of Reason**
Finance	Economics, Political Science, Mathematics and Statistics	**Path of Realization**

You will actually find in this chapter that particularly the more recent evolutionary trends in each function give indications of the ultimate transformation of the functions that we are setting out in the four following chapters.

We now turn to the first of these functions, which is marketing. You will notice how marketing evolved over time from its anthropological and economic origins towards a psychological and social, if not also a technological, function.

11.2 Marketing: The Southern Function of the Conventional Enterprise

11.2.1 EXPERIENTIAL AND ORIENTED TOWARDS THE RELATIONAL

Of all four of the major functions, it is marketing that is the most relationally and community oriented. It is the most grounded, the most experientially oriented and, ultimately, the most humanistic of the functions.

In other words, the relational research path, together with its grounded, experiential and humanistic overtones, constitutes the inner character of the marketing function, serving to ultimately transform it into community building (see Chapter 12). However, before we take that transformative leap, and as we do with all four functions in the next chapters, we take you through a brief history of the evolving nature and scope of marketing, bearing in mind that all of such is lodged in private – as opposed to public, civic or animate (environmental) – enterprise, which has never undergone a similar evolution. In fact, this is similarly the case for all the, therefore, 'business' functions, most of which have since been transplanted into the other sectors, with manifold 'rejection' along the way.

11.2.2 BUSINESS EXISTS TO CREATE A CUSTOMER

For the redoubtable Peter Drucker in the 1950s, as we saw in Chapter 4, in a modern business context: 'The purpose of a business is not to make a profit. Rather a business exists for its economic contribution. Its purpose is to create a customer.'[1] What has proved problematic is the lengths to which some businesses will go to create such a customer, fuelled by the growing power of the advertising and public relations industries. Indeed, the individualistic orientation of sales and marketing is a recent 'western' invention.

11.2.3 THE ADVENT OF SALESMANSHIP

For if we look for the communal origins of salesmanship, which is not too difficult if we reach back into indigenous sources, we shall find them in the market places of antiquity. For wherever there is buying and selling, marketing of the most basic kind is going on. In fact trade, by way of barter, preceded economic exchange, mediated by money, by thousands of years. When, on my (Ronnie Lessem) last trip with my family to the Victoria Falls in Zimbabwe, the affable sculptor by the roadside offered me a wooden elephant, he was continuing a sculpting tradition that stretches back thousands of years, if not also a trading one. Having sensed that my need for his carving was not all that great, and that British-made tee shirts were easy for me to come by (but difficult for Zimbabweans to acquire), he made his proposition that we exchange his sculpture for my tee shirt. In the event my little boy accepted, on our behalf!

Returning to salesmanship, young children acquire experience of 'primal marketing', or indeed 'relationships management', long before they learn how to handle money. When one of the authors' young nephew 'sold' his friend Linus the idea of 'playing' monopoly, having previously ascertained that Linus was bored and needed stimulus, he was already marketing – in a primal way. Indeed, a French Canadian management consultant, Jean Marc Chaput, has written a book called *Living is Selling*[2] in which he elaborates on this social theme. Such a theme changes once we move onto contemporary salesmanship.

Harry Turner, in his book *The Gentle Art of Salesmanship*[3] indicates that a good salesman has two particularly dominant personality traits, *ego drive* and *empathy*. These, incidentally, correspond very nicely with the hard material (ego drive) and soft social (empathy) traits that are a feature of such formative exchange. Ego drive is the urge to succeed (*preneur*). If it is not balanced by empathy between (*entre*) one person and another, it can be a destructive force. Such empathy then involves sensitivity to the reactions and feelings of others. In fact, very few people have both these qualities, that is ego and empathy, in equal proportions. Strong empathy and reduced drive means less cutting edge, which will make the closing of sales difficult. Too much ego drive and too little empathy produce the killer instinct. I (Ronnie Lessem) was always struck, when accompanying our former head of sales on his business rounds in our family business in Zimbabwe where our men's clothing factory had been based, of the overwhelmingly friendly nature of his selling orientation. He actually treated all his retail customers as his friends.

A more 'western' authority on such salesmanship in Britain, Heinz Goldman[4], introduced us to 'AIDA', well known in salesman's circles! AIDA means that the successful salesman needs to:

- *A:* *arouse the* attention of the customer;
- *I:* *make him personally* interested in the offer; and
- *D:* *increase his* desire to buy the product; in order to
- *A:* *stimulate him into the* action of buying.

As we can see, there is something of a conflict between communal exchange and individual salesmanship. The resolution of that conflict is more likely to be attained as salesmanship turns into service consciousness, something that has been picked up most thoroughly by our Indian colleague at the University of Buckingham in the UK, V.S. Mahesh, in his *Thresholds of Motivation*.[5] There, with an unusually 'eastern' service touch, he aligns an 'evolution of consciousness' to the evolution of sales into service. However, the mainstream orientation towards the customer, albeit inclusive of sales and service, is marketing management.

11.2.4 MARKETING MANAGEMENT

As America in particular developed into a 'modern' society, so family and community, as both an economic and a social unit, was no longer the predominant force that it traditionally used to be. Social goods and services, identified in terms of economic activity, now become produced and 'marketed'; and needs were actively and analytically exploited through 'marketing management'. Marketing management, established in American in the 1960s, has continued to predominate around the so-called developed world ever since. The high priest of marketing is the American academic, Philip Kotler, who defines marketing as follows:

> *Marketing is the analysing, organizing, planning and controlling of the firm's customer – impinging resources, policies, and activities with a view to satisfying the needs and wants of chosen customer groups at a profit.*[6]

As we can see the abstract world of resources and customer groups replaced the concrete salesman's world of people and things. In our terms, marketing embodies the economic and commercial more heavily than the social and communal.

As such management had come a long way from its origins, substituting analytical cut and thrust for the emotionally based ego drive. Actually, by the 1970s marketing had become the most intellectually demanding of the business functions. Then, in the course of the 1980s and 1990s, it began to change as its rationally based principles were somewhat supplanted by a newly interactive, somewhat more developmental approach.

11.2.5 RELATIONSHIPS MANAGEMENT

It was the Hollander Bernard Lievegoed who, already in the early 1970s, came up with the notion of 'relations management'.[7] Supplanting marketing and human resource management, this function, as the organization moved out of its predominantly rational phase, reunited with its social and relational origins, albeit still in somewhat analytical guise. However, it was now relating to both employees and customers. The 'Nordic School of Services', based in Finland and Sweden, went a step further, replacing the old concept of analytical marketing with a new 'interactive' and relationships oriented one.

Marketing was now seen in terms of relationships. It was thereby aligned with the management of services, creating, developing and maintaining a network in which the firm thrives. Such a network was interactive, that is involving bilateral and multilateral supplier-customer relationships, to produce goods and services. For Sweden's Evert Gummerson,[8] as for Finland's Wikstrom and Swede Normann,[9] these relationships are long term. For them, relationships management:

- needs time to be built and to be maintained, so as to generate knowledge and value;
- stresses relationships rather than promoting products or satisfying needs;
- extends beyond customers to suppliers, distributors and investors, clients and communities, patients and students;
- is viewed as a node in an ever-widening pattern of interactions.

You can already see, how marketing, in its recent evolution, is moving closer to the community, internally (within the enterprise) and externally (within society). For a further evolution of such a relationships orientation, we need to turn further south. We shall do so in Chapter 12. However, we first turn – in this overview of the functions – to the east, from marketing to human resource management.

11.3 Human Resource Management: The Eastern Function of the Conventional Enterprise

11.3.1 IMAGINATIVE AND ORIENTED TOWARDS RENEWAL

The second of the major functions is Human Resources, which for us, as we shall see, is aligned with the research path of renewal. Human Resources is also the most holistic of the functions.

In other words, the path of renewal constitutes the inner character of the human resource function. It serves to ultimately transform it, as will become apparent in Chapter 13, into 'eastern' conscious evolution. However, before we take that transformative leap, let us again take you through a brief history of the evolving nature and scope of this function.

11.3.2 THE ADVENT OF PERSONNEL

Elements of the human resource function first began to appear in Europe and America, at the turn of the twentieth century, in reaction to the harsh behaviour of autocratic businessmen like Henry Ford. As such the emerging Human Resource Management (HRM) completely bypassed centuries, if not millennia, of 'human relations', including 'relations with nature', in traditional societies. It was not until the 1970s and 1980s, however, like most of the business functions, that it began fully 'rational' shape and form, as a now human 'resource'. In the process, however, it missed out on its creative as well as convivial origins, lodged within, or indeed restricted by, the personality of the entrepreneur, for whom, in different ways, 'business is people'.

11.3.3 BUSINESS IS PEOPLE

Enterprising man

In 1964, Orville Collins[11] and his fellow sociologists at the University of Michigan, concluded that entrepreneurship involves, most essentially, 'the bringing together of people into new and profitable combinations'. Although their book *Enterprising Man* was a classic in its time, it completely bypassed the human resource establishment.

The tough and 'macho' approach to influencing people was actually introduced to us many years ago by the American doyen of public speaking, Dale Carnegie. Although his book *Winning Friends and Influencing People* is not normally incorporated into a management curriculum, it is a classic in its own right. Subsequently, though, the prolific sports promoter, Mark McCormack, wrote the definitive antidote to the rationally based management of human resources. Its appropriate title is *What they Don't Teach You at Harvard Business School*.[12] For McCormack the management of people, as insiders or as outsiders, involves the same basic approach. 'Whether I'm selling or buying; whether I'm hiring or being hired; whether I'm negotiating a contract or responding to someone else's demands, I want to know where the other person is coming from. I want to know his real self.' Of course McCormack is merely putting into words what entrepreneurs round the globe may have been thinking for centuries. However, not only has he taken the trouble to articulate his thoughts so that they now become codified knowledge, but his focus on the self gives it a particular western flavour.

It is also important to point out that the tough and masculine McCormack is naturally self-interested. He is neither philanthropic nor is he paternalistic. He is a businessman who knows that business is people. And he is also a man. Mary Kay, conversely, is a woman.

P&L also stands for profit and love

Actually, business entrepreneurs have traditionally been viewed as men, and thus in some cases paternalistic. Yet Mary Kay in America has developed a multi-million cosmetics company, called Mary Kay, in thoroughly maternal fashion. We also know that Nigerian market women, as we shall see later in this chapter, exercise a great levelling influence on economic life.

For Mary Kay and for the market women in Nigeria, no matter how much profit a company makes if it doesn't enrich the lives of its people it will have failed. For Mary Kay then: 'To me P&L doesn't only mean profit and loss – it also means people and love. When all our people come to understand one another, a family-like atmosphere remains intact and the customer is better served. The most important justification for being in business is to fulfil a need.'[13]

For Mary Kay, who had no need of a human resource manager, the source and destination of business is people – both within the company and out in the market place. For them it is the tender side of people management that takes hold, albeit intermingled with something of a tough-minded business orientation. Ironically, many human resource managers, by way of comparison, are not innately 'people people'. The reason is that they are cut off from their primal selves. Having acknowledged such a heritage though, via such influential practitioners as Mark McCormack and Mary Kay, we are in a more powerful position in moving on to a more rational domain.

11.3.4 ANALYTICAL BASED HUMAN RESOURCE MANAGEMENT

The evolution of HRM

As businesses grew in size and scope, during the early part of the twentieth century, entrepreneurs were no longer able to cope on their own. While some fell by the wayside others were astute enough to take on 'scientific' advice. The evolution of a rationally based, human resource function can be traced historically. It developed together with the growth and evolution of an individual enterprise. Such a development of a rational as opposed to holistic approach to human resource management, as we will argue later (see Chapter 13), was because of the lack of a wholehearted 'eastern' touch to it.

The advent of bureaucracy

In the early days of management's evolution, attempts to rationalize production and organization were tentative and ad hoc. However in the first decades of the twentieth century, businessman did come under the influence of engineers. Such 'social engineers' sought to substitute rational, 'scientific management' for the highly personalized, idiosyncratic style of the owner manager. Some of the earliest efforts at substituting rational procedures for intuition and family traditions simply involved better record keeping, for which purpose many personnel departments were first established. Personnel records indicated such information as when the employee was hired, educational background, succession of jobs, and provided a record of time and production for payrolls. These were relatively routine clerical tasks. This concern with methods was one precursor of personnel's concern today with training. It also represented an irrevocable and powerful drive towards increasing specialization.

The development of industrial psychology

In the last years of the 1920s rationalization and efficiency were the watchwords. The need to rationalize production arose from the new kinds of problems created by competition and demand, and from inventions in machinery and techniques. Many jobs were broken down. In order to rationalize, manufacturing combines were formed and amalgamations took place. Planning and efficiency in all aspects of a business became essential. Rationalization brought complexity with it. Selection assumed increasing importance during the 1920s because of the requirements of efficiency and the demands of complexity. As a result of government experience of classifying recruits during World War I, psychologists were brought into industry to help pick out the most able workers. They developed testing techniques for assessing individual differences, and personnel began concentrating on selection methods.

The emergence of industrial relations

The influence of personnel expanded during the 1930s and 1940s. With their title changed to Industrial Relations many personnel departments began to take charge of hiring, firing, wage determination, handling union grievances and deciding who should be transferred and promoted. The personnel department suddenly gained so much power, partly because of management's widespread recognition of the importance of the human element, but chiefly because of the threat of unionism. Personnel managers were now called upon to be negotiators, drawing on tough primal qualities of stamina and risk taking. Unfortunately, though, the industrial relations manager's foe was not the external competition but the internal labour force.

The advent of professionalism

By the end of World War II, in Britain and America, the functions of a personnel department could be clearly differentiated between employment, wages, joint consultation, health and safety, and education and training. By 1939 the perception of the range of personnel activities was fairly clear to the boards of larger, more highly organized companies, but the specialist sectors of the work were not always well coordinated. In fact, this remains the situation in many companies today.

However, all this resulted in many organizations, such as America's IBM and Britain's Marks and Spencer's, in a much fuller functioning of human resource management. Within a few years half a dozen of its component parts were distinguished, each with its own theory forming behind it and its own skills being defined. Recruitment, training, performance appraisal, industrial relations and personnel administration each became sub-disciplines in their own right. As a profession 'human resource management' was coming of age.

11.3.5 THE MANAGEMENT OF CHANGE

Human relations

Human resource management, by the 1950s and 1960s was seen to be relevant to the whole work situation: to the interrelationship between the work to be done, the individuals and the groups carrying it out, and the environment in which the whole activity took place.

A new phase of professionalism began then in the middle 1950s, with specialists developing in depth certain elements of personnel management, and identifying new approaches with the help of the social sciences. The application of sociology, as well as psychology, to the management of organizations, had been initiated by such people as Elton Mayo[14] in America in the 1920s and 1930s. It has continued in America and in Britain, as well as latterly via Japan, ever since.

The planning of change

The origins of what ultimately came to be called 'organization development' lie in the 1950s, when two distinct aspects of the personnel function had become identified. On the one hand, there are the processes of analyzing the existing conditions and resources in the light of the requirements of the enterprise, of diagnosing and defining its problems, of prescribing and executing the appropriate action to bring about change. This may be regarded as a predominantly creative and dynamic aspect. On the other hand there are the routine administrative duties involved in the execution of established policy, the solution of minor problems as they occur, the maintenance of healthy relationships, and the provision of personnel services.

In similar guise, America's Warren Bennis distinguished bureaucratic structures from structures of freedom. 'Bureaucracy was a monumental discovery for harnessing muscle power via guilt and instinctual renunciation. In today's world it is a prosthetic device, no longer useful. For we now require organic/adaptive systems, as structures of freedom, to permit the expression of play and imagination and to exploit the new pleasure of work.'[15] Some large companies, like Texas Instruments in the United States and ICI in Britain, tried to introduce Bennis's ideas in the 1960s and 1970s. However, those early attempts were often only half-hearted, partly because organization development had not yet come of age. In the meanwhile, and during the 1970s, there had been some very interesting developmental work going on in Holland, led by the social psychologist Bernard Lievegoed. His book *The Developing Organization*[16] has influenced many people since that time. For Lievegoed has a much more thorough understanding of development than his better-known Anglo-American counterparts.

Manager self development

Anticipating such a development already in the 1930s, was the renowned Mary Parker Follett. Based at Harvard's School of Government, Follett, a very influential figure with captains of industry at the time, was, in her turn, strongly influenced by the German philosopher Hegel. For Follett the individual and the organization are considerably enriched by collaboration. The business world, she was already arguing then, will never again be directed by individual intelligences, but by intelligences interacting and ceaselessly influencing each other. There is of course always competition between large forms but cooperation between them, she maintained, is coming to occupy a larger and larger space. She proclaimed:

> *The surge of life sweeps through the given similarity, the common ground, and breaks it up into a thousand differences. This tumultuous, irresistible flow of life is our existence. The unity, the common, is but for an instant, it flows to new offerings, which adjust themselves anew in more varied, richer syntheses. This is the process of evolution.*[17]

In the 1960s a new movement emerged that potentially might have taken HR out of its overly 'rational' cul-de-sac. It ultimately didn't. However, a *personal growth* or *self-development* movement emerged, assuming a more sophisticated and cerebral form than the 'self improvement' orientation that had preceded it. Central to it were the National Training Laboratories in America, which, though dating back to 1947, came into full bloom in the 1960s. The idea behind the laboratory was that participants, staff and students would become both experimenters and subjects in the study of their own interpersonal and group behaviour. The seminal influence in the creation of these laboratories was Kurt Lewin[18] who also built on the notion of the organization as a 'field of force'. At the same time, of course, the Jewish Armenian emigrant to the U.S. Abraham Maslow, was making his mark with his work on 'self-actualization'.- In the process, depth psychology took over from social and behavioural psychology in its influence on the development of people.

However, since the 1960s and 1970s, the heyday of what has become identified as organization development, human resource management and development, arguably took a backward turn. In the 1980s and 1990s, and on into the new millennium, human resource practitioners were increasingly called upon the 'serve the bottom line', and have become involved in 'down sizing' and 'right sizing' in the process. Therefore, while on the one hand there have been ever growing calls for 'empowering people', alongside the resurgence of literature on 'leadership', this is all done to increase business productivity and profitability, harking back to the predominantly 'northwestern' orientation of such HRM. In its stead, as will be illustrated in Chapter 13, we have turned to the 'east', as a source of inspiration for conscious evolution, in the process taking on from where people like Abraham Maslow have left off. Here and now, in our first overview of the functions, we turn to operations management.

11.4 Operations Management: The Northern Function of the Conventional Enterprise

11.4.1 CONCEPTUAL AND ORIENTED TOWARDS REASON

The third of the major functions is operations, which for us is aligned with the northern research path of reason. It is the function of operations, moreover, which initially was clearly identified with so-called classical 'scientific' management, and subsequently was strongly influenced by communications technology and organizational learning. Finally, unlike all the other business functions with their overall northwestern orientation, operations has been strongly influenced by the Japanese east.

That having been said, the path of reason, together with its navigational, conceptual and rational overtones, constitutes the inner character of the operations function. It serves, as we shall see in Chapter 14, to ultimately transform it into 'northern' knowledge creation. Before we take that transformative leap, let us take you through a brief history of operations management.

11.4.2 HOMO FABER

Man (or woman) in this case is a technological animal. Hence he (generally rather than she) is sometimes called *homo faber*, man the maker. Other animals have technologies (beavers construct dams and birds build nests), but only for man or woman are tools a central factor in his or her existence.[20] Only (wo)man has evolved culturally to the point where s/he can consciously alter his or her physical environment and biological make-up. In fact, one of the reasons that Great Britain was the first country to undergo a modern industrial revolution was its innate affinity with technology.

Such an affinity also underlies the technical curiosity and acumen, which is associated with today's computer buff or indeed 'nerd' or 'techie' and the modern engineer. Such a formative drive, to tinker with physical things and physically to fashion an environment, is more of an innate than an acquired skill. However, skills of craftsmanship, with wood or metal, textiles or plastic, can indeed be acquired. In northern European countries like Germany this is associated with traditional forms of apprenticeship and originally with medieval guilds.

11.4.3 QUALITY CIRCLES

Germany alongside of Japan – like the Great Britain of yesteryear – has a particular strong reputation for craftsmanship. Such is reinforced by its solidly based apprenticeship schemes. Production and engineering skill is acquired on the job, backed up by personal example. It is the immediate and tangible experience, reinforced by personal supervision that counts. Zen Buddhist traditions, in Japan, have had a similar effect on its working population, inculcating a desire for perfection that has been largely absent in America and Britain in recent years. What was new about engineers in their heyday, as they started to develop as a profession, was the delight they took in thinking of themselves as saviours of mankind.[21] Since the lot of the common man had been one of unrelenting hardship, engineers looked upon their works as man's 'ultimate redeemer from despairing drudgery and burdensome labour. The engineer's works, as such, would also contribute to brotherhood by literally bringing men closer together.

For American social philosopher Robert Pirsig, quality- or its absence does not reside in either the subject or the object. It lies in the relationship between the people who produce the technology and the things they produce, which results in a similar relationship between the people who use the technology and the things they use. The major vehicle, in Japan in the latter part of the last century, for maintaining quality production has been the quality circle. Interestingly enough, rationally based techniques for quality control were imported from America after the war, which, combined with primarily Japanese features, were woven into its unique form. For Ishikawa, a Japanese production engineer, the quality circle is a small group, performing quality control activities voluntarily within the same workshop, carrying on continuously as part of a company-wide programme, focusing on mutual development, with all members participating.[23] The basic ideas behind quality control, Ishikawa says, involve contributing to the improvement of the enterprise, building up a worth-living-in, happy and bright workshop, exercising human capacities fully and serving to promote overall quality management.

11.4.4 OPERATIONS MANAGEMENT

While Ishikawa paved the way for a more wholesome approach to manufacturing management, once we get fully there, the tone changes completely. As probably the best-known professor of operations management in the UK, Ray Wild,[24] puts it, an *'operating system is a configuration of resources combined to provide goods or services'* (see Figure 11.2).

Bus and taxi services, motels and dentists, tailors and mines, fire services and refuse removers, retail organizations, hospitals and building contractors are all operating systems. They all convert inputs in order to provide outputs that are required by a customer. Physical inputs will normally predominate. Hence operating systems convert these inputs, using physical resources, to create outputs, the function of which is to satisfy consumer wants, which is to provide some utility for the customer. The bulk of any rationally based operations management text will contain mathematical and statistical techniques for such functions as facilities location and material handling, work study

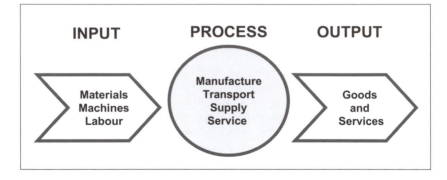

Figure 11.2 A simple operating system

and measurement, activity and project scheduling and inventory control. However, there is a rationally based and qualitative logic that underlies it all, divided between overall function and structure.

The nature of the operations manager's job will to some extent depend on the nature of the system being managed. All such systems, as is illustrated in Figure 11.2, may be seen to comprise inputs, processes and outputs. Such an operational model, still in its heyday when one of the authors was at Harvard in the 1960s, has since been eclipsed in more progressive enterprises by the emergence of knowledge management.

11.4.5 KNOWLEDGE MANAGEMENT

The late Will Abernathy and his production-minded colleagues at the Harvard Business School called in the 1980s for the technology based revitalization of large-scale manufacturing enterprise. In the process he exposed the limitations of the conventionally analytic approach to operations management. The task today, he maintained in the mid 1980s, is to incorporate particular new technologies and heightened product variety into high volume manufacturing systems and to do so without the luxury of long lead times.

> *What is therefore needed is a view of production as an enterprise of unlimited potential, an enterprise in which current arrangements are but the starting point for continuous organizational learning. No omniscient engineer ever handed down a design for product or production that could not stand improvement. Only when grafted on to a production system dedicated to ongoing learning and communication, only when used in tandem with a skilled and responsible workforce, can new technologies realise their potential as competitive weapons. Only when such a workforce is truly engaged in the enterprise and encouraged to learn and excel, can a company hope to introduce competitively successful new products in a timely fashion.*[25]

Another Harvard Professor in the late 1980s, Shoshana Zuboff, subtly traced a path from the formative world of the craftsperson to the 'informating' rationality of the 'informated' organization.[26] Zuboff stated that the work of the skilled craftsman may not have been intellectual, but it was knowledgeable. These nineteenth-century workers participated in a form of knowledge that had always defined the activity of making things. It was knowledge, she says, that accrues to the sentient body in the course of its activity;

knowledge inscribed in the labouring body – in hands, fingertips, wrists, nose, eyes, ear, skin, muscles, shoulders, arms and legs – as surely as it was inscribed in the brain. It was knowledge filled with intimate detail of material and ambiance – the colour and consistency of metal as it was thrust into the blazing fire, the smooth finish of clay as it gave up its moisture.

The agenda for scientific management was to increase productivity by streamlining and rationalizing. Efficiency was the goal, and to achieve efficiency it would be necessary to penetrate the labour process and force it to yield up its secrets. In order that such effort be rationalized, workers' skills had therefore to be made more explicit. This knowledge, for the scientific manager, was carefully and systematically collected and the data so obtained were classified and digested until the knowledge was instantly available whenever a problem is presented to management.

With the evolution of computer technology, Zuboff maintains, you centralize controls and move away from the actual physical process. If you don't have an understanding of what is happening and how all the pieces interact it is more difficult. You need a new learning capability because when you operate with the computer you can't see what is happening. There is a difference in the mental and conceptual capabilities that you need – you have to do things in your mind. You have to be able to imagine things that you have never seen, to visualize them. The 'informated' organization therefore is a learning institution, and one of its principle purposes is the expansion of knowledge, not knowledge for its own sake (as an academic pursuit) but knowledge that comes to reside at the core of what it means to be productive. We now turn from the rationality of such informated operations to the networked, somewhat more holistic, 'eastern' influenced operations that is so-called 'lean' production.

11.4.6 NETWORKED OPERATION AND LEAN PRODUCTION

In an illuminating book written in the latter part of the 1980s, American business academics Cohen and Zysman argued that *Manufacturing Matters*[27] in a way that simplistic arguments about post-industrial societies fail to reveal. For them, services are not a substitute or successor for manufacturing. One needs the other. The process of reformation is not one of sectoral succession but instead it is one of increased sectoral interdependence, driven by an ever more extended and complex division of labour. Manufacturing, in days gone by, was conducted by individual craftsmen, or by small groups of workers, engaged in cottage industries. This was the era of primal production. For the last hundred years, though, in industrialized countries, mass production has taken over as the rationally dominant mode. It is only recently, with the advent of flexible manufacturing systems facilitated by the microprocessor revolution, that this stable model is being reformed. The French, in the early 1980s, used the word 'filiere' (net) to refer to the fact that there are critical interrelations in pieces of the economy. The more advanced or modern the production process, the longer and more complicated the chains or networks of linkages.

For the Japanese in fact, as embodied in 'lean production', we can now think of functions as the hills and mountains forming the valley for the value stream. Their knowledge washes down to those working alongside the stream to create value and speed its flow. If functions then create a valley for the stream flowing past and through many firms, what purpose does the firm itself serve? Firms provide the link between streams. They are the means of crossing from one valley to the next in order to make maximum use of the technologies and capabilities accumulated by each of the firm's technical functions. They also provide the means of shifting resources from value streams that no longer need them to other streams that do. From this it follows that most firms will want to participate in multiple value streams. The great challenge for westerners, Womack and Jones[28] maintain in *Lean Thinking*, is to overcome their 'every firm for itself' individualism in which each organization along the value stream optimizes its own stretch while sub-optimizing the whole. This tendency of Anglo-Saxon management is exacerbated by the industrial finance system, which asks each firm to optimize its short-term performance but ignores the value of sustainable development as a whole. In fact, the American Gary Hamel and his Indian colleague C.K. Pralahad in their book on *Competing for the Future*[29] took off from where lean production left off. They thereby turned Michael Porter's economically oriented strategic orientation into a more technologically oriented approach to promoting 'core competence'.

On the one hand then such 'Strategic Intent', for Hamel and Pralahad, involves establishing the institution as the intellectual leader in an industry, influencing the direction and shape of its transformation. The accompanying strategic architecture must be grounded in a deep understanding of potential discontinuities, competitor intentions and evolving customer needs. A core competence in that respect is a bundle of skills and technologies that enables an enterprise to provide a particular benefit to customers. At Fedex, for example, the benefit is on-time delivery and core competence logistics management. In their case these competencies descend from meta-competencies (logistics) to core competencies (package trading) to constituent skills (bar coding).

What inhibits the development of core competence is a reversion to pragmatic and rational type which does not take account of the long-term needs of the customer and the enterprise alike. As such the following risks need to be faced: opportunities for growth will be needlessly truncated; no mechanisms for ensuring the best talent gets aligned behind the best opportunities; with fracturing into smaller units, competencies may become fragmented; in focusing only on end products the organization may fail to invest adequately in new core competencies, unwittingly relinquish valuable skills when they divest an underperforming business. In the final analysis, competencies that are most valuable are those that represent a gateway to a wide variety of potential product markets. Sony's unrelenting pursuit of leadership in miniaturization, for example, has given it access to a broad array of personal audio products. We now turn from such strategic intent aligned with lean production, to contemporary virtual operations.

11.4.7 THE VIRTUAL ORGANIZATION: TOWARDS THE NETWORK ECONOMY

For America's Kevin Kelly,[30] a child of the 1960s, and now the editor of 'Wired', the new economy has three distinguishing characteristics: it is *global*, it favours *intangible* things – ideas, information and relationships – and it is intensely *inter-linked*. Unless, for Kelly, we can understand this distinctive logic of networks, we cannot profit from the economic transformation now under way. Until this moment our economy has been in the multi-cellular stage. Our industrial age has required each customer or company to almost physically touch one another. Our firms and organizations resemble blobs. Now, by enabling the invention of silicon and glass neurons, a million new forms are possible. Kelly sees four new rules as particularly important:

1. *Plenitude not Scarcity:* Two fundamental axioms we inherited from the industrial age and from classical economics are that value comes from scarcity and, second, when things become plentiful they become devalued. In a network economy, value is derived from the plenitude of open systems more than the scarcity of closed ones.

2. *Follow the Free:* In the information age, consumers quickly have come to count on drastically superior quality for drastically reduced price over time. Expanding knowledge makes computers smarter; as computers get smarter we transfer some of that intelligence to the production line, lowering costs and raising perfection.

3. *No Harmony, All Flux:* As we know from recent ecological studies, no balance exists in nature; rather, as evolution proceeds, there are perpetual disruptions as new species displace old, as natural biomes shift in their make-up and as organisms and environments transform each other. Within a network perspective then companies are indefinite groupings of fluctuating firms, in a state of continual flux.

4. *Opportunities before Efficiencies:* Frederick Taylor revolutionized industry by using his scientific method to optimize mechanical work. But in the network economy, where machines do most of the inhuman work of manufacturing, the question is not how do I do the job right, but what is the right job to do?

In this historical overview, the drive of the northern function of operations management towards knowledge creation becomes, in part, already tangible. Before we engage in the transformative process for this function in Chapter 14, we first turn from this 'northern', technology based function, to the currently predominant and 'western' function of finance.

11.5 Financial Management: The Western Function of the Conventional Enterprise

11.5.1 PRACTICAL AND ORIENTED TOWARDS REALIZATION

The final and currently most influential of the major functions is finance, which for us is aligned with the western research path of *realization*. In other words, the path of realization, together with its effective, practical and pragmatic overtones, constitutes the inner character of the finance function. As such, it serves to ultimately transform it into sustainable development (see Chapter 15). However, before we take that transformative leap, we take you through a brief history of financial management. We start out, anthropologically so to speak, with the advent of trade, set in the context of the primal marketplace.

11.5.2 STARTING OUT WITH TRADE

We commence then with the origins of finance as a specific function, and indeed economics as an overall discipline. The work of Suzanne Guiterrez, a former Mexican-American doctoral student of ours in the 1980s, gives us a first clue of the original importance of trade rooted in local markets for the evolution of the finance function. In her research, she focused on the market women of Nigeria:

Market traders have had to rely on their verbal skills to wheel and deal since childhood. The importance of their oral history, their richness in cultural expression and oratory, has contributed to their self-assurance in face to face communication. Furthermore, the close connections which make or break the extended family will have drawn out skills of diplomacy for people that enhance their social and economic communications.[31]

What emerges in the local marketplace is a role of 'leveller' between profit and people – as has equally been the case of America's Mary Kay, through her cosmetics company run by and for women[32] – that is between home and work, between cooperation and competition, between the personal and interpersonal, and between oneself and another.

11.5.3 FROM COMMUNITY TO ENTERPRISE

In more recent times, though, and especially in the 'west', individual enterprise has gained precedence over the communal variety. People, moreover, who are instinctively adept at making money – be it a Alan Sugar or a Donald Trump – are driven by the instinct to survive, and thereby to 'make it' through life. Long before the Industrial Revolution, traders bought in one country, sold in another, and sometimes even built up commercial empires. Moreover, they followed their hunter predecessors in venturing out into the unknown.

Entrepreneurship then is an energetic and disruptive force, keeping everyone on their toes, and constantly breaking up the old order by introducing new ideas and products. The function of enterprise is not only to introduce something new, to invent, to discover, and to diversify products and services, but also, for the Austro-American political economist Joseph Schumpeter, to spread new methods of operation, and to adopt and popularize the inventions of others.[33] It does not confine itself to the efficient management of the existing economic system according to traditional rules, but at each moment, through initiative taking and bold faith in the future, it threatens the habits of customers and therefore the sources of economic or social profits of more conservative competitors.

In fact, in the 1980s and 1990s, especially in Britain and America, the notion of 'intrapreneurs', that is entrepreneurs within large organizations, became popular. Self-selection, for Gifford Pinchot, in his book on *Intrapreneuring,* is the first great divide between treating people as mere employees and treating them as so-called 'intrapreneurs'.[34] Some organizations, he says, paternalistically plan job assignments as if they were a religious act. But intrapreneurs don't fit this mould. They passionately appoint themselves executors of their ideas and then find ways to get the corporation to give them the tools to do so. In taking an enterprise through from idea to action, there are a series of cumulative phases, including a solo phase during which the vision is being formulated; a network phase, during which the entrepreneur begins to share her/his idea with trusted friends, colleagues and customers; the 'bootleg' phase, when an informal team is formed around the idea, as was for example the case with the original IBM PC; the formal phase, when an official project team is set up to carry the idea forward. To that extent – for American management thinker Gifford Pinchot as for his British economist colleague Norman Macrae in *The Coming Entrepreneurial Revolution*[35] – such enterprise is alive and well within the newly 'intrapreneurial' large scale organization.

The evolution from enterprise to finance through financial accounting involves a progression from financial trading and free enterprise, to financial management, and thereafter, as we shall see, to intellectual capital.

11.5.4 FINANCIAL CONTROL

Management control

Whereas the proverbial entrepreneur or leveller, like a Mary Kay (Mary Kay) on the one hand, or the late Anita Roddick (Bodyshop) on the other, sees personal psychology and business finance as intimately linked, in the realms of financial control they are worlds apart. This is the case particularly within conventionally rule bound management accounting. In fact, the entire discipline of accounting has grown up – notwithstanding double-entry bookkeeping's origins through Pacioli in the Italian Renaissance – as an abstract and impersonal tool of business.

Such conventional bookkeeping is the systematic recording of economic transactions in a manner which enables the financial relationship of an enterprise with other persons to be clearly disclosed, and the cumulative effect of the transactions on the financial position of the business itself to be ascertained.[36] Such transactions comprise the exchange of value, either in the form of money or of goods and services, which are measured and expressed in terms of money. Double entry accounting, then, enables a financial department to gauge at any time the institution's financial position, and its 'financial relationship with other persons'. Thus an abstract relationship takes over from a concrete one. Precise, rationally derived measurements overtake emotionally laden bonds of trust, or mistrust.

Stable financial accounts then, and corresponding managerial accountability, supplant 'back of the envelope' records of transactions. Similarly, an accountant may overtake a craftsman, technician or salesman at the head of the company. Subsequent developments of the financial function, often mathematically based, have extended its rationality and impersonality. Discounted cash flow, capital budgeting, portfolio analysis, financial model building and simulation, as well as financial derivatives have added further degrees of intellectual sophistication to an already analytically refined discipline.

From financial to intellectual capital

In the new millennium, alongside the so-called knowledge based economy, has been the growth of interest in so-called 'intellectual capital'. Such intellectual capital emerges as a composite measure of performance, rationally as well as developmentally befitting the knowledge era. The charter of Sweden's Scandia Financial Services, for example, was to grow and develop the company's Intellectual Capital as a visible, lasting value that would complement the balance sheet.[37] The operation was also to forge a link between other company functions, such as business development, human resources and information technology. In the process it was to develop new measurement tools and metrics as well as implement new programmes to speed knowledge sharing.[38]

Such intellectual capital was initially defined as the knowledge, applied experience, organizational technology, customer relationships and professional skills that provide Scandia with a competitive edge in the market. As such, and aside from financial capital, so-called *human capital* firstly represented the combined knowledge, skill, innovativeness and ability of the company's individual employees to meet the task at hand. It also includes the company's values, culture and philosophy. Such human capital, at the same time, cannot be owned by the company.

Structural capital, secondly, is comprised of the hardware, software, databases, organization structure, patents, trademarks, and everything else of organizational capability that supports those employees' productivity. Structural capital also includes customer capital, or relationships developed with key customers. Unlike human capital, structural capital can be owned and therefore traded. It includes such factors as the quality of reach of information technology systems, company images, proprietary databases, organizational concepts and documentation, and such traditional constituents of intellectual property as patents, trademarks and copyrights.

In fact, and further to such intellectual (also now incorporating environmental and socio-psychological capital) one of the authors,[39] already in the mid 1970s, was speculating on ways and means of accounting for an enterprise's overall well-being, using principles of reciprocity and double-entry to apply to psychological and ecological as well as to economic accounting. We now turn from enterprise and finance towards comparative advantage, where the economic and the financial are strategically aligned.

11.5.5 COMPARATIVE ADVANTAGE

When one of the authors was at Harvard Business School in the late 1960s, so-called long range planning was coming of age at the leading intellectual edge of business. At that time the major thinkers on corporate strategy – George Steiner, Igor Ansoff and Russell Ackoff – were all central European emigrants. However, 20 years later, and in the wake of Tom Peters's call for business to go 'back to basics', a parallel regression and progression took place.

For on the one hand Harvard economist Michael Porter returned to his competitive roots, becoming the father of independently *Competitive Strategy*,[40] while on the other hand he evolved his thinking towards interdependently based 'business clusters'. In this respect he got, for example, intensely involved with Singapore's Economic Development Board. Like Peters, Porter was of Anglo-Saxon heritage, but unlike his compatriot, his thinking evolved significantly in midlife.[41] Writing first in the 1980s then, Porter as an economist maintained that the essence of formulating competitive strategy involved relating a company to its environment, though primarily to an economic rather than a social, technological or cultural one. The key aspect of the firm's environment is the industry or industries in which it competes. The goal of competitive strategy is to find a position in the industry where the company can best defend itself against his famous 'five forces' or influence them in its favour:

1. Threat of new entrants.
2. Industry competitors.
3. Rivalry among existing firms.
4. Bargaining power of suppliers and buyers.
5. Threat of substitute products.

What we have now done here, overall, is to illustrate how, particularly in more recent times, an increasingly quantified, and footloose form of investment finance, and, of late, of hedge funds and private equity finance, has served to mark out its own terrain, virtually independent of the functioning of public and private, civic and animate enterprise as a whole. Most recently, such development culminated in the 'credit crunch' that has arisen in 2008, out of rogue ventures in the 'sub-prime' housing market.

11.6 Conclusion: Towards the Transformation of the Functions of the Enterprise

11.6.1 FUNCTIONAL IMBALANCE

The most recent economic recession reflects the functional imbalance that we currently face, and that we shall serve to alleviate in the following chapters. This imbalance reflects a lack of a transformational, transcultural, transdisciplinary, and ultimately transpersonal orientation. From a transformational perspective, first, the 'business' functions are neither rooted in nature, generally, nor do they serve, as such, to release natural and cultural, as well as technological and economic GENE-ius. This is what we shall be attempting to do – see Chapters 12 to 15 – in this section of the book.

Second, from a transcultural perspective, the functions are predominantly 'northwestern'. With the one exception of the operations function, which has drawn upon the influence of the Japanese 'east', the west and the north exercise by far the greatest influence. Third from a transdisciplinary point of view, economics together with behavioural psychology rules the roost. Anthropology hardly gets a look in, and political science and sociology, ecology and depth psychology, are very much second class citizens, functionally speaking, Fourth, and from a transpersonal perspective, the functional focus on the organization eclipses person (self), community *and* society.

The recent pre-emphasis on personalized leadership – as opposed to depersonalized management – has meant that an individual orientation has eclipsed an organizational, if not also a societal orientation. As such, the functioning of enterprise has stopped evolving, indeed from the 1990s onwards. In the rest of the book we will seek to redress this regressive influence on the evolution of management.

11.6.2 ANTECEDENTS OF FUNCTIONAL TRANSFORMATION

We now come onto functional transformation. It is at this ultimate stage of our new approach to management that we see the completion of our overall GENE-cycle:

- *G:* transformational grounding in nature and community   → Flows
- *E:* transcultural emergence through culture and spirituality   → Forces
- *N:* transdisciplinary navigation through science and technology   → Fields
- *E:* transpersonal effect through economics and management   → Functions

Only now, at the end of the cycle we are coming to the western domain of economics and management, now in a significantly enriched way. Building progressively and accumulatively on the southern, eastern and northern worlds of the GENE cycle, western management is now about a fundamentally new functioning of the enterprise. As such, we shall now start to move transformatively:

- From Marketing to Community Building.
- From Human Resources to Conscious Evolution.
- From Operations to Knowledge Creation.
- From Finance to Sustainable Development.

Such a Transformation (of) Management can be distinguished from other related concepts, which have recently entered into the management, leadership and enterprise discussion, as we first intimated in Chapter 1. Whereas social enterprise, including social entrepreneurship, corporate social responsibility and social business have their place in promoting all round sustainability, none of these have transformed the overall structure and functioning of the management processes that underlie these. That is where Transformation Management comes in, essentially building upon prior humanistic and holistic, natural and cultural foundations to establish rational and pragmatic, socio-economic systems and structures.

The same goes for self-transformation or indeed transformative leadership, where a newly transformative ethos has generally been applied to individual functioning, but not to the specific functioning of organizations or communities. Finally, and to complete our transformative overview, social innovation, as an activity analogous to technological innovation, is yet to see the light of day; our companion volume on *Social Innovation in Enterprise and Society*.

11.6.3 RELEASING THE TRANSFORMATIONAL GENE-IUS OF EACH FUNCTION

Following overall transformational lines, each function releases its full GENE-ius, that is through its grounding and emergence, navigation and effect. In the transformational process, therefore, a continual interweaving of the indigenous and the exogenous, of tradition and modernity, is required. Interestingly enough, that was the key to Japan's economic miracle in the latter part of the twentieth century. This miracle ended in the bubble burst in the 1990s, when global market speculation overtook local Japanese productive spirit.

That having been said, our transcultural and transformational course follows our Four Worlds. As such we reposition marketing, first in the natural as well as communal 'south', where mankind's journey began. Second, we relocate human 'resources' outside of such a so-called resource, and within, instead, 'eastern' consciousness, that is along the reformative path of cultural and spiritual renewal. Third, operations, for us the embodiment of reason and indeed of management as a 'science', we relocate specifically in the 'northern' realm of knowledge, aligned with such science and technology. Finally, we reposition finance within the path of 'western' realization, thereby removing it from its singular isolation, and, instead, repositioning it as a force for functional integration, or indeed all round sustainable development, purposefully building on all that has come before.

Such a transformational and transcultural approach to an enterprise's functions is, necessarily, fully transdisciplinary. In other words first, a marketing function that is rooted in nature and community is underpinned now by ecology, anthropology and the humanities, rather than by classical economics and behavioural psychology. Second, a spiritually and culturally infused HR function is founded upon depth psychology and comparative religion, rather than more narrowly based behavioural and social psychology. Third, an operations function building upon science and technology, draws upon the natural sciences, ranging from pure maths to applied engineering, as well as the social sciences, most specifically sociology and communications theory. Finally, finance draws upon economics primarily, but secondarily, also, on environmental studies as well as political science.

Ultimately, we identify the functions in the context of (the) Transformation (of) Management as transpersonal. What is the significance of that? Functional management, over the course of the twentieth century, primarily in America, was developed, as Peter Drucker has stated (see Chapter 1), very deliberately. It was an attempt to evolve a depersonalized approach to managing large-scale organizations, to enable them to outgrow the personalized approach of individual entrepreneurs or leaders. In fact, as we have already intimated, the recent reversion to leadership and entrepreneurship is, in such evolutionary terms, a backward step. *The transpersonal approach we adopt here, involves three distinct, though interrelated, steps. First it represents an evolution of the personal and impersonal towards the simultaneously individual and communal. Second, therefore, it serves to interrelate the functioning of self, organization and society. Finally, it applies to all forms of enterprise – public and private, civic and animate – without the private (business) functions predominating.*

Figure 11.3 provides an overview of the core functions of the enterprise and their transformative trajectory. The model is embedded in a depiction of the earth, illustrating that the transformation of the functions happens in interaction with the particular

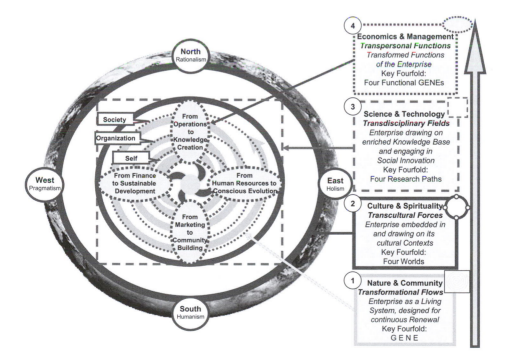

Figure 11.3 The transformative trajectory of the functions of the enterprise

societal and cultural context of the enterprise. The spiral represents the transformational flow (nature), the three squares symbolize the interconnected levels of self, organization and society, while the outer square represents the newly defined transdisciplinary fields of the enterprise.

We shall now address the transformation of each function, one by one, in a separate chapter. We start out with the transformation of marketing into community building.

References

1. Drucker, P. (1979). *Management*. London: Heinemann.
2. Chaput, J. (1975). *Living is Selling*. Montreal: Habitex Books.
3. Turner, H. (1985). *The Gentle Art of Salesmanship*. London: Fontana.
4. Goldman, H. (1971). *How to Win Customers*. London: Pan.
5. Mahesh, V.S. (1993). *Thresholds of Motivation*. New Delhi: McGraw Hill.
6. Kotler, P. (1968). *Marketing Management*. Connecticut: Prentice Hall.
7. Lievegoed, B. (1990). *The Developing Organization*. Oxford: Blackwell.
8. Gummerson, E. (1987). *The New Marketing*. Long Range Planning, Volume 20, 4.
9. Wikstrom, S. (1994). *Knowledge and Value*. London: Routledge.
10. Peters, T. et al. (1982). *In Search of Excellence*. New York: Harper and Row.
11. Collins, O. et al. (1964). *Enterprising Man*. Michigan: University of Michigan.
12. McCormack, M. (1984). *What They Don't Teach You at Harvard Business School*. London: Collins Hardback.
13. Kay, M. (1996). *Mary Kay on People Management: Doing Well by Doing Good*. New York: Prima Publishing.
14. Mayo, E. (2007). *The Social Problems of an Industrial Civilisation*. London: Routledge.
15. Bennis, W. (1969). *Organization Development*. New York: Addison Wesley.
16. Lievegoed, B. (1990). *The Developing Organization*. Oxford: Blackwell.
17. Parker Follett, M. (1998). *New State*. Philadelphia: Pennsylvania State University.
18. Lewin, K (1997). *Resolving Social Conflicts*. New York: American Psychological Association.
19. Maslow, A. (1998). *Maslow on Management*. New York: John Wiley.
20. Ferkis, V. (1969). *Technological Man*. London: Heinemann.
21. Florman, S. (1984). *The Existential Pleasures of Engineering*. New York: New Library.
22. Pirsig, R. (1976). *Zen & the Art of Motorcycle Maintenance*. Burnet, USA: Swan.
23. Ishikawa, K. (1985). *What is Total Quality Control?* New Jersey: Prentice Hall.
24. Wild, R. (1980). *Essentials of Operations Management*. New York: Holt Rinehart.
25. Abernathy, W. (1984). *Industrial Renaissance*. New York: Basic Books.
26. Zuboff, S. (1989). *In the Age of the Smart Machine*. London: Heinemann.
27. Cohen and Zysman (1987). *Manufacturing Matters*. New York: Basic Books.
28. Womack, J. and Jones, D. (1995). *Lean Thinking*. Cambridge, Mass.: HBS Press.
29. Hamel, G. and Pralahad, C.K. (1994). *Competing for the Future*. New York: Harper Business.
30. Kelly, K. (1999). *The New Rules of the New Economy*. New York: Fourth Estate.
31. Gutierrez, S. (1986). *The Market Women of Nigeria*. PhD Thesis, London: City University.
32. Kay, M. (1985). *On Managing People*. New York. Pan Books.
33. Schumpeter, J. (1961). *Theory of Economic Development*. Cambridge: Cambridge University Press.
34. Pinchot, G. (1981). *Intrapreneuring*. New York: Harper and Row.

35. Macrae, N. (December 1976). *The Coming Entrepreneurial Revolution*. London: Economist.

36. Bigg, W. et al. (1963). *Book-keeping and Accounts*. London: HFC.

37. Edvinsson, L. (1997). *Intellectual Capital*. London: Piatkus.

38. Kaplan, R. et al. (1995). *The Balanced Scorecard*. Cambridge: HBS Press.

39. Lessem, R. (1974). *Accounting for an Enterprise's Wellbeing*. London: Omega Journal for International Management Science.

40. Porter, M. (1982). *Competitive Strategy*. New York: Macmillan.

41. Porter, M. (1994). *Competitive Advantages of Nations*. New York: Macmillan.

12 *Transforming Marketing into Community Building*

From Reciprocity and Exchange to Workplace Democracy

12.1 Introduction: Transforming the Southern Function

12.1.1 TRANSFORMING MARKETING, MARKETS AND COMMUNICATION

A keynote of our transpersonal orientation is a correlation between the personal (self), the organizational (enterprise) and the communal (society). Marketing, as such, is a distinctly depersonalized, organizational function; in that guise, it is taught on hundreds, if not thousands, of MBA and business studies programmes. In depersonalized isolation, though, it is cut off from physical and human nature, which, in this 'southern' instance we align with natural and social reciprocity.

Actually, as we move from individual (communication) and organizational (marketing) to the societal, we locate 'markets'. Such markets, in turn, because of the predominance of neo-classical economics today, have been cut off from their roots in human as well as natural reciprocity. The imperilled nature of our planet today then, not to mention the escalating costs of energy and rocketing food prices constitute the price we are now paying for our ignorance. By aligning communication, marketing and markets, we are seeking to heal such a damaging divide.

12.1.2 MARKETING TO COMMUNITY BUILDING VIA SOCIAL BUSINESS

In Chapter 11 we identified how, from an evolutionary perspective, marketing emerged out of primal forces of what might be termed social and economic exchange, rooted in physical nature and human society, reaching back millennia. It was only when salesmanship took hold as a specific business activity, alongside the notion that 'the customer is king', that such social as well as economic exchange was supplanted by an individualized form of economic activity. That was further reinforced by the emergence of a somewhat depersonalized marketing management as a business function, as opposed to a public, civic or animate one.

The subsequent development of relationships marketing, as well as, to some extent, service management, served to remind us of the originally communal and natural scope of physical and human exchange. In transforming marketing into community building, we are revisiting those communal and natural grounds, building upon ecology and anthropology, albeit now in twenty-first century guise. Such a community building function, as opposed to marketing is equally applicable to the public, civic and animate, as it is to the private enterprise.

Finally as will be so for all the functional cases, we build on a local cultural force; in this southern case, we build on the African philosophy of Ubuntu, introduced earlier in this book.

12.1.3 SOUTHERN UBUNTU: I AM BECAUSE YOU ARE

We have selected as our 'cultural southern force' Ubuntu. In Chapter 6 we had briefly introduced this vital force from Sub-Saharan Africa, whose spirit is best captured with the famous expression 'I am because you are'. The South African Peace Nobel Laureate Bishop Desmond Tutu provides us with an intimate perspective into Ubuntu in the prelude of his acclaimed book *No Future without Forgiveness*.[1]

'When we want to give high praise to someone ...' Tutu asserts, 'we say *Yu, u nobuntu: a person is a person through other persons. I am human because I belong. I participate, I share.* A person with Ubuntu is open and available to other, affirming of others, does not feel threatened that others are able and good, for he or she has a proper self assurance that comes from knowing that he or she belongs in a greater whole, and is diminished when others are humiliated or diminished, when others are tortured or oppressed, or treated as if they are less than who they are.'

In short, and in the words of our South African colleague and Member of Parliament Mfuniselwa Benghu, Ubuntu is an 'African fundamental life philosophy, often considered the primary foundation of the African social-giving ethos.'[2]

It is the southern force of Ubuntu that can act as a powerful enabler to reconnect humankind with community, for the Africans the touchstone of life. This touchstone is, till today, most tangible on an African market, and, as we will show, it is exactly the traditional significance of markets within a community, that will provide the grounding for the southern function.

In the following we will guide you through the GENE of the southern function, from southern *reciprocity and exchange* to eastern *justice and reconciliation*, up to the northern concept of a *social business* (social combined with business) to western *workplace democracy* (workplace combined with democracy). Figure 12.1 illustrates the transforming fourfold of the southern function.

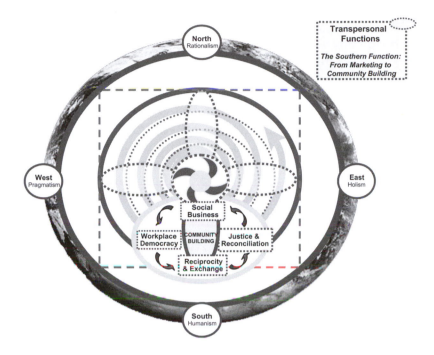

Figure 12.1 The transforming fourfold of the southern function

12.2 Southern Formative Grounding: Reciprocity and Exchange

12.2.1 HUNTER-GATHERER ANTECEDENTS OF MARKETS, MARKETING AND COMMUNICATION

Some 15 years ago, one of the authors published his *Global Management Principles* in which he analyzed the roots, main stem, branches and fruits of management in the four corners of the globe. Reviewing the roots of such in the 'south', Ronnie Lessem identified cultural anthropology, alongside the market economy, as a formative influence on such socio-economic foundations of enterprise.

'The primal roots of management, relatively close to the – secondary – surface, lie in economics, and in Adam Smith's market economy. Through the "market", resources are allocated and controlled. Deeper down, within the historical soil, the primal – or indeed primary – roots reach cultural anthropology, inside primordial, Stone Age communities. Through "culture" physical and human nature is cultivated and values are exchanged and shared. The human being also evolves a sense of place.'[3]

Hundreds of thousands of years ago, then, our ancestors, the ape-men, lived out in the wild as nomads, barely able to communicate with their fellows, or to settle in one place.

Then, some 10,000 years ago, Neolithic men and women began to settle in particular abodes, in one 'oikos' or another. Oikos is the ancient Greek term for household, house or even family. At this late dawn of history a village society had emerged in which life seemed to be unified by a communal disposition towards work, its products, as well as the exchange of such, within and between one community and another. *The primal roots of business, of enterprise and of management, are therefore to be found in such gathering rather than in hunting. Not surprisingly, as we have said, the modern term 'economics' derives from the Greek term 'oikos', a sense of place, and also the source of 'ecology'.*

In fact, it was not until the seventeenth and eighteenth centuries, Adam Smith's *Wealth of Nations* appearing in 1776, that economics and enterprise were transformed, and gradually lost their homely connection, one that the 'social entrepreneur' today may be seeking to rediscover. The business entrepreneur, then, and the derivative business enterprise, visibly evolved from hunting origins. Such an entrepreneurial tradition has lived on since, most evidently in 'western' guise, and has gained force recently, in both developed and transitional societies. Thus the original hunting image, stretching back to Neolithic times, retains much of its primal force and identity.

12.2.2 THE GATHERER'S ROLE AND EVOLUTION TOWARDS SOCIAL BUSINESS

The communal, ecological tradition, on the other hand, has undergone an ironic transformation. The gatherer has been thrust out of classical economics, despite the original 'oikos'. She reappears in the nineteenth century in Marxian guise. By this point the gatherer is sitting outside, and in opposition to, business. In the twentieth century this results in the Russian and Chinese revolution, and now of course we have, in these two countries, a kind of backlash. Whereas, then, in the twentieth century the stage was set for a clash between 'capitalism' and 'socialism', both of which bypassed the 'gatherer', in the twenty-first century capitalism has reasserted itself, and again the gatherer is left out in the cold. What we are doing here is to bring her back into the picture. We do so in newly 'southern' communal guise, set in the context of social and economic exchange, and embodied in the recently emerging 'social entrepreneur'. Grameen's Mohammad Yunus and Cashbuild's Albert Koopman, as we shall soon see, are cases in point. However, we are jumping the gun. Let us return to anthropological economics.

Karl Polanyi,[4] whom we will meet later in the context of his 'great transformation' from market to society, was an unusual mixture of economist and anthropologist. Polanyi was Anglo-Saxon (English resident) and central European (Polish born). Economics, for him, had two meanings. The first 'formal' meaning related to the 'economizing' function, which we identify as 'western', relating to the allocation of scarce resources. The second 'substantive' meaning points to the fact that human beings, like other living creatures, cannot exist for any length of time without a physical and social environment that sustains them. It is the second, often neglected function, which brings the gatherer – today termed a social entrepreneur – into the foreground. This substantive meaning is derived from man's dependence for his livelihood on nature and upon his fellows. It draws, originally, from Neolithic, matricentric societies.

The American social ecologist Murray Bookchin in *The Ecology of Freedom* characterizes such horticultural communities as 'procreative in their relationship with the natural world, touching the earth and changing it, but with a grace, delicacy, and feeling that may be regarded as nature's own harvest'.[5] The social and economic imagery of the time, therefore, shifted from the predator to the procreator, from the campfire to the domestic hearth, and from cultural traits associated with the father to those related to the mother. The role of 'gatherer' as collector, grower, carrier and maker of useful things, superseded that of hunter. In our transformational terms, 'southern' functioning supplanted 'western' functioning; and civic and animate enterprise taking precedence over public and private.

The substantive view of economics, as embedded within the norms and values of the community at large, continued to be held for thousands of years. Aristotle, in ancient Greece, saw the role of barter in society to be that of returning society to self-sufficiency, rather than that of securing profits or gains. He saw the need to set rates of exchange, through law and custom, in such a way that the natural friendliness that prevails among members of a community maintained. At the same time he likened the labour process not to a form of production, but to one of reproduction, not to an act of fabrication, but to one of procreation. In fact Ghana's statesman-philosopher, Kwame Nkrumah, referred to Aristotle in his *Consciencism*: 'Aristotle's humanism was a co-operative one, in which each man, perceiving a different aspect of the truth, contributed to the common whole. But whereas Aristotle stood for co-operative humanism, the second Renaissance humanism was an atomistic one.'[6]

12.2.3 EXCHANGE AND RECIPROCITY

Actually, such principles of social and economic exchange as well as of reciprocity are alive and well in parts of Africa today. Susanne Guiterrez pointed out in her research in the 1980s on the market women of Nigeria: 'There is a clear reflection of European commercial and philosophical influences – in the emerging impersonal, formal and specialised attitude – in today's African institutions. In the marketplace, however, women are able to transcend these influences and bring to their daily lives the historical African sense of family and community. Regardless of the sophistication of the surrounding community, no matter how urbanised and industrialised it may become, the market-place prevails as a centre of trade and communication, whether the traders are dealing in cement, tomatoes, or television sets.'[7] In fact, the cultural anthropologists Ellis and Ter Haar have more recently given us a new perspective on money and markets in an African context:

> *Throughout West Africa, the morality of exchange has been associated with the markets. West African markets are real meeting places, not just virtual or technical places of exchange. Some are regulated by sophisticated conventions on the pricing and sale of goods. They are rather like the 'agora' of the ancient Greeks, places to meet friends and talk as well as to do business; they are places of fundamental social importance.*[8]

Indeed, and in concluding our grounding of this function in 'southern' social and economic exchange, where the words of the gatherer of old, and the social entrepreneur of today, meet, we are made aware of thousands of years of tradition, where enterprise and community have come together in a shared 'oikos'. However, as our 'southern' GENE-ius unfolds, we shall become aware of the fact that this is only the grounding of our journey through marketing to community. We turn now to 'southern' emergence through healing and reconciliation, with Nelson Mandela to lead the way, taking us on from the private and civic to also public enterprise. As we can see, such a communal perspective further transforms individual marketing.

12.3 Southern Reformative Emergence: Justice and Reconciliation

12.3.1 FROM EXCHANGE TO RECONCILIATION

The grounding in economic and social exchange is as old as the hills. The reformation that has taken place, in recent years, most poignantly so in South Africa, is the turning of such exchange and reciprocity, into healing and reconciliation. In fact, the South African academic theologian John De Gruchy, in the context of South Africa's 'Truth and Reconciliation Commission', in his book on *Reconciliation – Restoring Justice*, has pointed out that:

> *The Greek words translated in the New Testament by 'reconciliation' or 'reconcile' are compounds of the Greek 'to exchange', and this in turn is derived from the Greek word meaning 'the other'. The words thus carry with them the sense of exchanging places with 'the other' and therefore being in solidarity with rather than against such 'another'.*[9]

This indeed serves to cast 'exchange', whether economic or social, in a new light. It also serves to *reinforce the original context of the 'marketplace' as a place of social as well as commercial interaction.* If we therefore de-construct 'market-ing' in that light, something new emerges – an idea which resonates with justice and reconciliation. Reconciliation, in this context, begins to become a reality when, without surrendering our individuality, but opening ourselves up to the 'other', we enter into the space between. It is here, in the 'space between' that we exchange places with the other in a conversation that takes us beyond ourselves. Furthermore, in the process, our self-understanding begins to change. The aim of each step in the process is to break through the barriers of the past, discern common interests, and so break open new possibilities that can take the process of exchange, supply and demand as well as profit, further than we currently understand.

What we are arguing here is that most developing or transitional societies have recently experienced injustices both within their national boundaries and in an international context. In fact, and at the time of writing (summer of 2008), as knife crime proliferates in local UK urban centres and global terrorism continues to proliferate, we are reminded of the effects of such injustice on a world stage. Moreover, the need for a healing force in relation to (wo)man and her or his environment is becoming all too evident. *Marketing and exchange, in this reciprocal vein, emerge as a force for the healing of nature and society. In the process, together, they become a force for good, as well as a means of exchange of goods and services.*

12.3.2 COVENANTING TOGETHER TO RESTORE JUSTICE

Nelson Mandela declared in his inaugural speech to the South African public in May 1994:

We enter a covenant that we shall build a society in which all South Africans, both black and white, will be able to walk, without any fear in their hearts, assured of their inalienable right to human dignity – a rainbow nation at peace with itself and the world.[10]

Such reconciliation is about building bridges, about allowing conflicting stories to interact in ways that evoke respect, about building relationships including economic ones, and helping restructure power relations. This means that we have to go beyond a political, social or economic agreement to co-exist across those rivers that divide, and find ways to engender common endeavour, including that between producer and consumer. A covenantal relationship, in other words, goes further than a social or business contract because it is concerned about animate-civic-public reconciliation rather than mere private or commercial reconciliation, in financial and economic terms. It involves building up 'equity', not only in a financial and economic sense, but also in a social and communal one.

12.3.3 MARKET TO RESTORATIVE ECONOMICS

Restorative economics – restorative justice

The South African Peace Nobel Laureate Bishop Desmond Tutu, in his evocative book *No Future Without Forgiveness* written in the latter part of the 1990s, builds upon the notion of 'restorative' justice. He contrasts it with market economics, also building upon notions of exchange and reciprocity, for a South African process of reconstruction and development (RDP):

> *In South Africa today, the resources of the state have to be deployed imaginatively, wisely, efficiently and equitably, to facilitate the reconstruction process in a manner which best brings relief and hope to the widest sections of the community, developing for the benefit of the entire nation the latent human potential and resources of every person who has directly or indirectly been burdened with the heritage of the shame and the pain of the country's racist past ... to take into account the competing claims on resources, with regard to the 'untold suffering' of individuals.*[11]

The whole process of reconciliation has been placed in jeopardy by the enormous disparities between rich and poor, between the mainly rich whites and the mainly poor blacks. The rich provided the class from which most of the beneficiaries and perpetrators came from, and the poor produced the bulk of the victims. This is why Tutu has exhorted whites to support the transformation taking place in the lot of blacks. For unless houses replace the hovels and shacks in which most blacks live, unless blacks gain access to clean water, electricity, decent health care, decent education, good jobs and a decent environment – we can just kiss reconciliation goodbye. As things have actually turned out in the country, spiralling crime, arising at least in part out of a lack of economic reconciliation, has been a massive deterrent on the overall development of markets and communities.

In our terms here, South Africa mirrored the world at large. And in terms of reconciliation means also that social and economic exchange is the experiential base for markets and for justice. Indeed, a further journeying is required, for every business to evolve through its society, as well as for every society to evolve through its business. The problem has been that the proposition, or business concept, that can bring into full light of day the economics of reconciliation has been missing. To bring such a concept of enterprise to light, we turn from 'southern' grounding (reciprocity and exchange) and emergence (justice and reconciliation) to navigation (social business).

12.4 Southern Normative Navigation: Social Business

12.4.1 INTRODUCING SOCIAL BUSINESS

Mohammad Yunus has by now gained international renown, including the award of the Nobel Peace Prize, for his work on micro lending in Bangladesh (which we locate here in the 'south'), through the Grameen Bank. We were made aware of Grameen, in Chapter 5, through Yunus's earlier work on *Banker for the Poor*. We now turn to his latest work, following on from where De Gruchy, Mandela and Tutu in South Africa have left off, in *Creating a World without Poverty*.[12]

Mainstream free-market theory, which South Africa, for example, was obliged to conform to in the 1990s, suffers, for Yunus, from a 'conceptualization failure', a failure to capture the essence of what it is to be human:

> *In the conventional theory of business, therefore, we have created a one-dimensional human being to play the role of business leader, the so-called entrepreneur. We've insulated him or her from the rest of life, the religious, emotional, political and social. He is dedicated to one mission only – the maximization of profit. And today's world is so mesmerized by the success of capitalism it does not dare doubt the systems underlying such economic theory. Yet the reality is very different. People are not one-dimensional. They are multidimensional. This is where the social business comes in. Entrepreneurs will set up a social business not to achieve limited personal gain but to pursue social goals.*

12.4.2 THE PMB VERSUS SOCIAL BUSINESS

By insisting that all businesses must be profit-maximizing (PMB), we have ignored the multi-dimensionality of human beings and, as a result, business remains incapable of addressing many of our most pressing social problems. Yunus, in turn, offers, based on his experiences with Grameen, the model of a social business. In its organizational structure, for Yunus, it is basically the same as the PMB, but it differs in its objectives. It employs workers, creates goods and services, and provides these to customers at an amenable price; however, its objective is to create social benefits for those whose lives it touches. It is cause-driven rather than profit-driven, with the potential to act as a change agent for the world. A social business, however, is not a charity. It concentrates on creating products and services that create a social benefit, and recovers its costs in the process, for example through:

- providing nutritious foods to poor and underfed children;
- designing and marketing health insurance policies to provide affordable medical care to the poor;

- developing renewable energy systems and selling them to rural communities at a price they can afford;
- recycling garbage, sewage and other waste products in poor and politically powerless neighbourhoods.

Once the social-objective-driven project overcomes the gravitational force of financial dependence, it is ready for a space flight. As the social business grows, so do the benefits it provides to society.

A social business, moreover, has owners who are entitled to recoup their investments, but the surplus generated is reinvested in the business. The bottom line of the social business is to operate without incurring losses while serving the people and the planet – particularly the disadvantaged – in the best possible manner. *Unlike philanthropy, the social business is self-sustaining, investors get their money back, and business people can leverage their skills to solve social problems.*

12.4.3 WHERE WILL SOCIAL BUSINESS COME FROM?

Humans moreover, for Yunus, have an instinctive, natural desire to make life better for their fellow human beings if they can. Given the chance people would prefer to live in a world without poverty and disease. These are the causes that lead people to donate billions, and the same drive will lead people to create social businesses, once this new path is widely recognized, so that:

- existing companies wanting to launch their own social business as a way of exploring new markets to help the less fortunate;
- foundations may create social business funds, continually replenishing the foundation's ability to support good works;
- individual entrepreneurs may branch out into social business;
- international and bilateral development donors may choose to create dedicated funds to support social-business activities;
- government may support such projects;
- young people fresh out of college may choose to launch social businesses.

We are then multidimensional creatures and the business models we recognize should be equally diverse.

12.4.4 THE EFFECTS OF SOCIAL BUSINESS

For Yunus, Bangladesh today is a living laboratory. It represents the story of one of the world's poorest countries that is being transformed by innovative social and business thinking. Over the past two decades:

- the poverty rate has fallen from 74 per cent (1974) to 40 per cent (2005), as measured by the World Bank;
- the country's rapid economic growth (6.7 per cent in 2006) has not been accompanied by growing inequality;

- population growth has fallen sharply from 3 per cent in the 1970s to 1.5 per cent in 2000, driven by improvements in healthcare;
- the percentage of children completing the 5th grade has increased from 49 per cent in 1990 to 74 per cent in 2004; more girls now attend secondary schools than boys;
- between 1980 and 2004 the Human Development Index increased by 45 per cent compared to 39 per cent in India.

We now turn from social business in general, to a particular expression of such, again in South Africa, which has drawn explicitly on the southern African philosophy of Ubuntu – I am because you are – as originally illustrated in Chapter 7. Albert Koopman and Cashbuild, our case in point, are individual and institutional catalysts for Ubuntu like economic and social exchange, culminating the process of 'southern' transformation of marketing into community building.

12.5 Southern Transformative Effect: Workplace Democracy and the Case of Cashbuild in South Africa

The Cashbuild case is unique in South Africa to this day. With Albert Koopman at the helm of this provider of building supplies in the rural areas of the country, the company was not only ultimately transformed into a workplace democracy, but became distinctively profitable, socially as well as economically. Moreover, this initially took place in apartheid South Africa, where the conditions for such social and economic reconciliation could not have been worse. How then did Koopman manage such an ultimately successful process of mutual development, between business and society, including conflict resolution, duly incorporating the advance of human rights with such a profitable enterprise? Let Koopman tell his own story.

12.5.1 I ENTERED LIFE AS A MORAL FIGHTER

'I was raised as a street fighter. My mother died when I was 13 and my father lived in Mozambique, 1240 miles from me. Set free at a very early age I had to learn to survive in my community. That meant dealing with people, including people who had hang-ups, and people who wanted to do me in for what I believed. The one thing that I learnt as a result was that I was going to enter my life as a clean, moral fighter, someone who sterilised his bicycle chains before he entered the fight of interpersonal relationships.'[13]

12.5.2 UNCOVERING THE DIVINE WILL OF AFRICA

'Cashbuild was started as a wholesaler in 1978 and became a very successful business in a short space of time. Situated predominantly in the rural areas of South Africa and focusing on the black housing market, our staff consisted of 84 per cent black, 13 per cent white and 3 per cent Indian. However by mid 1982, with 12 outlets, profits started sliding. Everything "northern" was in place – systems, procedures, technology, combined with a booming market – but something was going wrong and I did not know enough about the south, at that point, to recognise where to start looking.

Key questions went through my mind. Why do the workers actually work? What is their social or Divine Will? What went wrong in Cashbuild with respect to capital and labour? What were we actually trying to achieve as a business organism? How do we bring together the rights of people, their spiritually based humanity and the economic process as represented in the workplace? Subsequently I conducted a succession of brainstorming sessions to uncover the purpose of Cashbuild's existence. It soon became clear to us that one purpose existed in management's head and another in the workers'. Management "up north" was pulling one-way and the people "down south" another. There was no transcendent purpose linking one with the other.'

12.5.3 INTRODUCING OUR CARE PHILOSOPHY

'I was therefore forced to seek a way in which we could spell out and determine our objective common interest in the production of commodities – customer service (southern) – to replace capital's pure interest in increasing profits (western). Lots of meetings, small group activities, discussion groups and open two-way communications had to form as much of the way we ran our business as did the work itself. Everything had to be focussed upon the common interest of creating wealth and fostering an understanding amongst workers that the correct management of capital benefits the organization as a whole. This correct management, in turn, could only occur if the worker was democratically involved in contributing towards the overall success of the organization. I visualised that in this manner so-called capitalist exploitation (of the "southern" community) would no longer be able to exist.

Exploitative capitalism demands quotas, productivity and quality, all as part of a commodity outlook on life. People remain part of the production-distribution-consumption process, without their spiritual work or social ethos being recognized. The protagonists of class-consciousness, meanwhile, became a rallying point in the name of social justice, without actually giving expression to the human face. We promptly decided at Cashbuild to pursue our own course.

We needed a social form that could accommodate the freedom to be enterprising, as well as harnessing the spiritual consciousness of all our employees. This incorporated our CARE philosophy – Cashbuild's Aspirations with Regard to Excellence. A CARE philosophy designed by the people for the people spelled out how our workplace should be regulated, and set out the rules of the business game. Some of the salient points were:

- a commitment to joint decision making at all levels, with everyone playing their part in finding solutions to problems;
- an open and free culture with everyone in the organization having access to any line manager;
- a team consisting of different races, sexes and cultural creeds, none of which were to be discriminated against;
- a belief in the "Extra Mile" concept both for organization and individual;
- after the philosophy was translated into seven languages and a little booklet given to each and every employee to read, we felt we could start moving into the future;
- whilst our CARE horizon extended over five years I found, however, after only eighteen months, that resistance to change had become an inordinate obstacle.

- "I have no power. Although my people voted me in I cannot get my manager to act on their requests. He simply is not interested."
- "The company has cheated us for so long. Why is it suddenly changing? We don't believe in it."
- "What happens to my family if I die?"'

12.5.4 THE ADVENT OF VENTURECOMM

'It was time to look at the whole situation again. We were sure that our belief in raising spiritual consciousness was valid, but we could now see our employees expressing their "southern" social selves as apart from the "western" economic process. While they perceived their labour power as intimately associated with themselves as human beings, they still saw the company as viewing their labour content as part of the production – distribution – consumption process. They were being treated as commodities. Our CARE structures, as representatively democratic, were still separating management and worker. What they were crying out for was for participatory democracy, thereby integrating their economic and social selves, so as to relieve labour power of its commodity character. It dawned upon me as a result that:

- No one can demand productivity from anyone, but I can create a climate within which social man is willingly productive.
- I cannot manage people, only things, but I can create a climate within which people take responsibility and manage themselves.
- One cannot demand quality from people, but I can create conditions at work through which quality work is a product of pride in workmanship.

A convention of some 200 workers was held and the ground rules were established:

- Respect human dignity and individual freedom of speech.
- Allow everyone to have access to company results and performance standards.
- Give everyone a role in developing company policy.
- Improve the quality of life of all employees outside the work sphere through active community involvement.

It was proposed that a governing body of five people be constituted to each outlet – the VENTURECOMM – with each person being democratically elected to hold a portfolio, save for the manager who was appointed to the operations portfolio, based on his or her expertise. This portfolio was concerned with the "hard" variables whereas the safety, labour, merchandise and quality of work-life portfolios were the "soft" ones.

Moreover, each of these managers was continually assessed by lower levels in the hierarchy. In fact this Cashbuild VENTURECOMMM system was socialistic in that it instated social justice and offered security against destitution. It was likewise capitalistic to the extent that individual expression was given its due reward, and group development its due recognition. Our system thus gave expression to the work ethic and also to the enterprising spirit of people.'

12.5.5 TOWARDS WORKPLACE DEMOCRACY

'I could now see that if I recognised and restored the dignity and pride of the workforce I could achieve a new human spirit that would drive the enterprise for the betterment of all. I would therefore be able to change, not by losing my individual competitive value system but by finding "southern" solidarity as Managing Director with all the people in the organization. To do this I had to go "north"! This entailed at a technical level:

- taking Cashbuild employees on a journey, strengthening their relationships with management;
- turning all employees into stakeholders of the organization;
- aggressively addressing the distributive aspect of the business, through profit sharing, in the ultimate interest of the business, its workers and their families;
- promoting excellence of quality and productivity, within the organization, and fostering a communal climate for its achievement;

At the structural level I had to restore meaning into people's lives, by constructing a code of ethics around which people could be rallied for the common purpose. This entailed developing:

- a superordinate goal for the enterprise through the people themselves – bottom up;
- a philosophy of social justice and equality pride and dignity within every employee.

I found later that this last point was in fact the spark for all endeavours, and took precedence over any of the other technical systems, rewards, or structures we introduced. It reflected the Divine Will of Cashbuild, which in its turn manifested the parallel will of the communities, which the company represented. It further reflected the difference between competitive, north-western "having" and co-operative "south-eastern" being, as fundamentally different modes of life.'

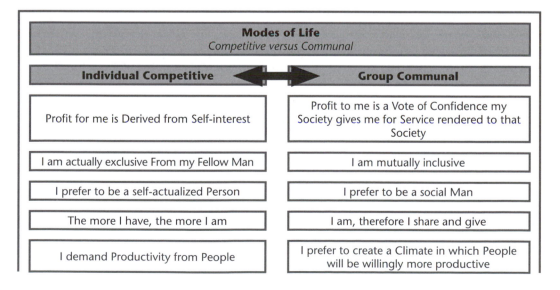

Modes of Life *Competitive versus Communal*	
Individual Competitive ⬅ ➡	**Group Communal**
Profit for me is Derived from Self-interest	Profit to me is a Vote of Confidence my Society gives me for Service rendered to that Society
I am actually exclusive From my Fellow Man	I am mutually inclusive
I prefer to be a self-actualized Person	I prefer to be a social Man
The more I have, the more I am	I am, therefore I share and give
I demand Productivity from People	I prefer to create a Climate in which People will be willingly more productive

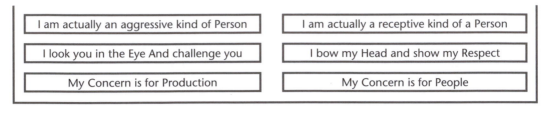

We are now ready to conclude marketing's transformation into community building.

12.6 Conclusion: Towards Community Building

12.6.1 THE REST FOLLOWS BEHIND THE WEST

Cashbuild in today's South Africa is still a thriving commercial business, with a well-developed marketing model, but, with Koopman and his protégé Haumant having long gone, it is no longer, in Yunus's terms, a 'social business'. The fate of Cashbuild is replicated across the world's stage. Because the 'western' model of free-market capitalism, economically, and the model of the shareholder controlled, market oriented corporation, commercially, is so universally predominant, that marketing can hardly evolve, as was the case for Cashbuild in Koopman's time, into community building on a sustainable basis. In fact, a similar question might be raised for Grameen, that is what will happen to this 'social business' when Yunus is no longer at the helm.

12.6.2 THE WEST NEEDS TO BUILD ON THE REST

It was patently obvious for us to see, that while Koopman and his protégé were at the helm, then marketing as community building, at least within Cashbuild, and as such the promotion of social business (as an extension of Ubuntu, as it were) proceeded accordingly. As such Cashbuild became a 'mutual', in the best possible sense.

However, because the surrounding economic, social and intellectual environment was not supportive of all of such, it withered on the establishment vine. To that extent markets, as opposed to communities, marketing as opposed to community building, and individual competitiveness as opposed to social cooperation reasserted themselves.

12.6.3 CONCLUDING THE SOUTHERN GENE-IUS

In a concluding review of this chapter, we retrace once more the four core steps of the southern GENE-ius, serving to transform the southern function:

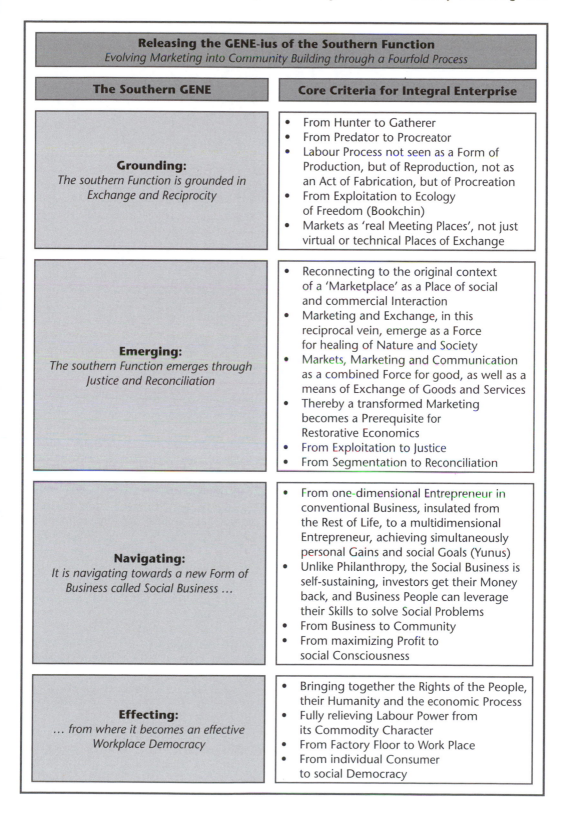

Releasing the GENE-ius of the Southern Function
Evolving Marketing into Community Building through a Fourfold Process

The Southern GENE	Core Criteria for Integral Enterprise
Grounding: *The southern Function is grounded in Exchange and Reciprocity*	• From Hunter to Gatherer • From Predator to Procreator • Labour Process not seen as a Form of Production, but of Reproduction, not as an Act of Fabrication, but of Procreation • From Exploitation to Ecology of Freedom (Bookchin) • Markets as 'real Meeting Places', not just virtual or technical Places of Exchange
Emerging: *The southern Function emerges through Justice and Reconciliation*	• Reconnecting to the original context of a 'Marketplace' as a Place of social and commercial Interaction • Marketing and Exchange, in this reciprocal vein, emerge as a Force for healing of Nature and Society • Markets, Marketing and Communication as a combined Force for good, as well as a means of Exchange of Goods and Services • Thereby a transformed Marketing becomes a Prerequisite for Restorative Economics • From Exploitation to Justice • From Segmentation to Reconciliation
Navigating: *It is navigating towards a new Form of Business called Social Business …*	• From one-dimensional Entrepreneur in conventional Business, insulated from the Rest of Life, to a multidimensional Entrepreneur, achieving simultaneously personal Gains and social Goals (Yunus) • Unlike Philanthropy, the Social Business is self-sustaining, investors get their Money back, and Business People can leverage their Skills to solve Social Problems • From Business to Community • From maximizing Profit to social Consciousness
Effecting: *… from where it becomes an effective Workplace Democracy*	• Bringing together the Rights of the People, their Humanity and the economic Process • Fully relieving Labour Power from its Commodity Character • From Factory Floor to Work Place • From individual Consumer to social Democracy

We now turn from 'south' to 'east', identifying how one needs to build on the other.

References

1. Tutu, D. (2002). *No Future Without Forgiveness*. New York: Doubleday.
2. Bhengu, M.J. (forthcoming). *Economic Humanism*.
3. Lessem, R. (1989). *Global Management Principles*. Connecticut: Prentice Hall.
4. Polanyi, K. (1977). *The Livelihood of Man*. Burlington: Academic Press.
5. Bookchin, M. (1982). *The Ecology of Freedom*. Oakland: AK Press.
6. Nkrumah, K. (1970). *Consciencism*. New York: Monthly Review Press.
7. Gutierrez, S. (1986). *Market Women of Nigeria*. PhD Thesis. London: City University.
8. Ellis, S. et al. (2004). *Worlds of Power*. Johannesburg: Wits University Press.
9. De Gruchy, J. (2000). *Reconciliation – Restoring Justice*. Canterbury: SCM Press.
10. Mandela, N. (1994). *The Long Walk to Freedom*. Grand Rapids: Abacus.
11. Tutu, D. (2002). *No Future Without Forgiveness*. New York: Doubleday.
12. Yunus, M. (2008). *Creating a World Without Poverty*. Public Affairs. New York.
13. Koopman, A. (1991). *Trans-cultural Management*. Oxford: Blackwell.

13 *Transforming Human Resources into Conscious Evolution*

From Individual Consciousness to Self-Organizational-Societal Co-Evolution

13.1 Introduction: Transforming the Eastern Function

13.1.1 TRANSFORMING HUMAN RESOURCES, LABOUR FORCE AND CONSCIOUSNESS

As we move from marketing to human resources, in conventional functional terms, so we turn from community building to conscious evolution, in our transformative context. In the process, we change our worldly orientation from 'southern' to 'eastern'. In this case we are not drawing on African Ubuntu, but on Japanese Kyosei, as an exemplary cultural force.

Moreover, our moving from depersonalized HRM to such a transpersonal people oriented approach, enables human consciousness (person), human resources (organizational) and indeed the societal labour force to come 'transpersonally' together.

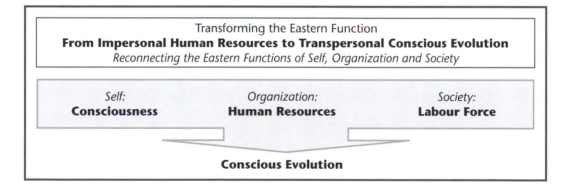

As we indicated in Chapter 11, since the 1960s and 1970s, so-called HRM, as it developed into the 1980s, took a backward, ever more 'western' turn. Having been influenced particularly by the 'east' through the personal growth and organizational development movements, it then reverted to narrowly western type. For all the talk on servant leadership, organizational learning and people as 'our greatest asset', the HRM function has become very much a servant of the bottom line. Further, it has become ever more involved in 'down sizing' and 'right sizing'. In order to renew, if not transform, the HR function, we have turned to the 'east' as a source of inspiration. In this process we are taking on from where people like Mary Parker Follett and Abraham Maslow (see Chapter 11) left off.

In focusing upon the 'east', we shall pay particular attention to the Indian Near East, and the Chinese and Japanese Far East. Each is richly endowed with philosophies and practices of raising consciousness. At the same time we shall again be traversing a wider eastern world, incorporating in particular central-eastern Europe. In the process, the very nature of 'western' human capacity building becomes transformed in the light of a more conscious evolution of the person. We thereby draw on such indigenous cultural forces as Dharma (Indian – life path), Tao (Chinese – the 'way' or nature's way) as well as Japan's Kyosei (co-existence) and Ba (spirit of place) to transcend the ultimately material limitations of 'human resources'. In that respect, conscious evolution emerging out of the 'east', builds on the prior grounds of community building, pre-eminently located in the 'south'. In the process, labour is removed from its commodity status.

13.1.2 REMOVING LABOUR FROM ITS COMMODITY STATUS

For eastern European polymath and social philosopher Rudolf Steiner, 'labour' needs to be removed from the economic process of production, distribution and consumption. As such people in organizations are no longer viewed as a human resource, nor as a factor of production, but rather they are self-conscious human beings. What Steiner had to say in *Towards Social Renewal* at the turn of the last century was:

> *The modern worker abhorred instinctively the fact that he or she had to sell labour power to an employer in the same way that commodities are sold in the marketplace. It is not possible therefore to divest human labour power of its commodity character without first finding a means of extracting it from the economic process. Efforts should therefore not be devoted to transforming the economic process so that human labour is justly treated within it, but towards extracting labour power from the economic process and integrating it with social forces which will relieve it of its commodity character.*[1]

Furthermore, for his German follower, Folkert Wilken, in *The Liberation of Capital*:

> *The continual inventiveness of human beings is ultimately the source, and actually the only source, of capital. In such a context capital is an intellectual, cultural, even 'spiritual' force originating in continuing innovation. As such it creates both the possibility of, and the desire for, a liberation of the person from physical labour, to find his or her 'true' place in a world of mental and cultural activity.*[2]

In fact, it was the renowned American follower of Buddhist philosophy, Robert Pirsig, in his classic work on *Zen and the Art of Motorcycle Maintenance,* who said: 'You can find the Godhead just as easily in the gears of a motorcycle transmission as in the heavens above.'[3]

And it is human beings who fit the gears into the transmission. We have always been uneasy with the way human 'labour' is bought and sold, as if we humans were mere chattels. From that perspective we have been amazed, for example, that Britain's 'Labour Party' retains its old denomination, while claiming to be 'New Labour'. We also had the strong feeling that when Personnel, as a business function, transformed itself in the 1970s and 1980s into 'Human Resources', it was signing its death knell, by officially confining itself to the status of a classical economic 'resource', as labour along with land, and capital. For we, in our Four World capacity, for Steiner and Wilken as central-eastern Europeans, and for Japan's Nonaka and Takeuchi, all of us as somewhat 'easterners', are dedicated to *remove labour, human resources and capacity building from their commodity status*.

13.1.3 EASTERN KYOSEI: CO-EXISTENCE AND CO-EVOLUTION

As our 'eastern cultural force' we have chosen the Japanese philosophy of Kyosei, usually translated as 'co-existence' or as 'co-evolution'. As a cultural force, Kyosei was, like Ubuntu, not conceived of in a vacuum. From about 1500 to 1640 Japanese traders were among the most successful in the world. Merchants travelled to China, Thailand, Indonesia and the Philippines. As people came together to exchange goods, however, cultural differences led to conflict. So a successful merchant teamed up with a Confucian scholar and developed a set of guidelines known as 'shishu kiyuka'. The guidelines said that trade must be carried out not only for one's own benefit, but also for the benefit of others. For Canon's late Chairman Kaku, as we shall see at the end of this chapter, this policy sowed the seeds of Kyosei today.

We now turn from such 'eastern' gene-ius to the GENE that underlies 'conscious evolution' for self, organization and society. Specifically we consider the grounding, emergence, navigation and effect of each. As such we shall be drawing on the Japanese example, for it has been most prolifically evolved its large scale manufacturing enterprise, though less self and society. In fact, the absence of societal and cultural renewal has ultimately proved to be Japan's Achilles heel.

In the following we shall guide you through the GENE of the eastern function, from southern *spiritual consciousness* (grounding) to the eastern *evolutionary spiral* (emerging), catalyzing consciousness raising, up to the northern systematization of the *conscious organization* (navigation) to western *co-evolution* (effect). Figure 13.1 illustrates the transforming fourfold of the eastern function.

13.2 Eastern Formative Grounding: Spiritual Consciousness

13.2.1 THE BACKDROP OF HUMAN CONSCIOUSNESS

We draw here upon 'eastern' human consciousness, as opposed to 'western' human resources, for two reasons. First, as Steiner has intimated, it is damaging to the human spirit to identify the human being as 'resource'. Second, the Indians, the Chinese and the Japanese have been studying consciousness for some 3,000 to 5,000 years, well before the 'west' or 'north' started out on that journey. Moreover, such 'consciousness raising' techniques, ranging from martial arts to meditation, had an enormous influence on the 'west', individually if not also organizationally, in the 1960s, greatly influencing the so-called OD (organizational development) movement, before it receded in the 1970s and 1980s as indicated. Third, and one of the reasons such an influence has since receded,

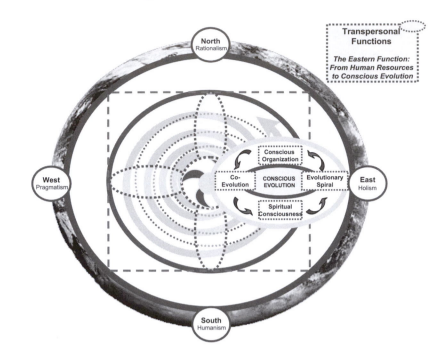

Figure 13.1 The transforming fourfold of the eastern function

at least within organizations, is that the conventionally recognized human resource function, today, unlike the other three functions, has no major institutional support base on a societal level in 'western' or 'northern' society.

For whereas, in the 'west' the customer is increasingly king, and all powerful stock markets prevail in the financial domain, while there is an equally powerful 'northern' scientific establishment that supports science and technology, the human being is all too often left out in the cold, duly unsupported by society at large. Indeed it was Matsushita's (life President of Mitsubishi) recognition of such a comparative lack of human concern, in 'western' as opposed to Japanese enterprises, which served to distinguish the Japanese economic miracle in the latter part of the twentieth century. Today Toyota – which overtook GM as the world's largest and most profitable automobile manufacturer – is a reflection of such, albeit along with other, more technically oriented considerations.

We now probe more deeply into such a Japanese approach to conscious evolution, applied as we have said, most particularly to the large scale manufacturing organization, and less so to the individual – where India is pre-eminent – and society, where conscious renewal is yet to take place.

13.2.2 JAPANESE BASHO: ANTECEDENT OF KYOSEI

The backdrop for conscious evolution within large scale manufacturing enterprise has been provided by the work of Kitaro Nishida, Japan's leading twentieth- century philosopher. His logic appears in various forms, but most directly in the Japanese term 'basho', literally 'place', and by extension 'field', 'matrix', 'medium' and even 'world'.[4] In this sense there are for Nishida distinct 'basho', each having their place in the final enveloping 'basho', or 'place of no-thingness', or indeed 'every-thingness'. Each of these 'worlds' presupposes and exhibits the contradictory identity of objectivity (explicitly known) and subjectivity (tacit knowing). Nishida, by his own admission, follows in the footsteps of Germany's notable philosopher and phenomenologist of 'being' Martin Heidegger and France's renowned existentialist philosopher Jean-Paul Sartre. Moreover, his philosophy has much in common with ancient Vedic wisdom.

For all such philosophical systems, first, the physical or biological world is at one end, while the psychological human-historical world is at the other. Each such human-historical world has its own 'basho' or locus of self-transformation. Each one is dynamically formative, organic and teleological, these properties being absent from the physical world. Its self-organizing, self-transforming character becomes an analogue of the 'creative act' in the existential mode of human awareness. Nishida relates such to the 'I-Thou' relationship of Jewish philosopher Martin Buber. The abstractions of science can never get away from their own basis in individual experience of the historical world.

In human-historical life, second, there is always a dialectic of the affirmative and the negative: the former, for Nishida, is the world of matter and the latter is the world of consciousness. The former is the world of objects; the latter is the world of intentional acts. What the Japanese organizational sociologists Nonaka and Takeuchi have done with their approach to conscious organizational evolution, in terms of 'knowledge creation', is to transform Nishida's 'worlds', basho, (not human resources) into fields of knowledge – Ba.

13.3 Eastern Reformative Emergence: Evolutionary Spiral

13.3.1 THE EVOLUTIONARY SPIRAL

Nonaka and Takeuchi[5] draw substantively on Nishida, as well as upon the central European philosopher of *Personal Knowledge*, Michael Polanyi.[6] Their 'eastern' evolutionary spiral is a continuous, self-transcending process through which you transcend the boundary of the old self into a new self by acquiring a new context, a new view of the world, an evolved consciousness and knowledge, indeed a new social construction. In short, it is a journey 'from being to becoming'. You also, in the process, transcend the boundary between self and other, through interactions among individuals or between them and their environment.

It is important to note that the movement through such modes of development forms a spiral, not a circle or a straight line. In such a developmental spiral, the knowing interaction between tacit (subjective knower) and explicit (objective known) is amplified through these – as we shall see – four levels of meaning, which correspond with our Four Worlds. These four modes of development or knowledge are socialization (S), externalization (E), combination (C) and internalization (I). As the so-called SECI spiral, they visualize the knowledge creation process, which lies at the heart of a knowledge creating organization. The spiral becomes larger in scale as it moves up and through these levels, expanding horizontally and vertically across organizations.

It is a dynamic process, starting at the individual level and expanding as it moves through communities of interaction that transcend sectional, departmental, divisional and even organizational boundaries. Development, as such, or indeed conscious evolution, is a never-ending process that upgrades itself continuously. This interactive spiral process takes place both intra- and inter-organizationally, transferred beyond organizational boundaries. Through dynamic interaction, one organization's development can trigger that of outside constituents such as consumers, affiliated companies, universities or distributors. For example, an innovative new manufacturing process may bring about changes in the suppliers' manufacturing process, which in turn triggers a new round of product and process innovation within the organization. As such it is a self-transcending process, in which you reach out beyond the boundaries of your own existence, transcending the boundary between self and other, inside and outside, past and present, building altogether upon Ba.

13.3.2 BA: SHARED CONTEXT IN MOTION

Ba in general

Based on the philosophy developed by Nishida, and subsequently further developed by Shimizu,[7] Ba is here defined as a shared context in which being and becoming, and thereafter knowing and doing are communicated, created and utilized. Generation and regeneration of Ba, or indeed consciousness, is the key, providing the energy, quality and place to move along the evolutionary spiral. Ba then means not just a physical space, but a specific time and space. The key concept in understanding Ba, then, is 'interaction'. Development, or transformation, alludes to a dynamic and indeed dialectical human process, as opposed to 'labour force', human resources or even human capacity. The former are committed to socially constructing Ba through action and interaction.

Four types of Ba

There are then four types of 'Ba'. In our Four World terms, these are originating Ba (southern), dialoguing Ba (eastern), systemizing Ba (northern) and exercising Ba (western). These, altogether, are defined by two dimensions of interaction. One dimension is the 'type' of interaction; whether the interaction takes place individually or collectively. The other dimension is the 'media used' in such interactions; whether the interaction is through face-to-face contact or virtual media such as books, manuals, memos, e-mails or teleconferences:

- *Originating Ba is defined by individual and face-to-face interactions.* It is a place where individuals share experiences, feelings, emotions and mental models. From such originating Ba emerges care, love, trust and commitment, for us, 'southern', the ground for evolution within and among individuals and organizations.
- *Dialoguing Ba is defined by 'eastern' collective and face-to-face interactions.* It is the place where individuals' mental models and skills are shared, converted into common terms, and articulated as concepts. Dialoguing Ba is more consciously constructed than originating Ba, involving the conscious use of metaphor and analogy, as well as negation and affirmation, to make the tacit explicit.
- *Systemizing Ba is defined by 'northern' style depersonalized and virtual interactions.* Information technology, through on-line networks, groupware, documentation and databanks, offers a virtual collaborative environment for the creation of systemizing Ba.

- *Exercising Ba is defined by personalized, individual as well as virtual 'western' style interactions.* Here, individuals embody explicit facts and concepts communicated through virtual media, such as written manuals or simulation programmes, making the explicit tacit.

Figure 13.2 illustrates the four types of Ba, a philosophy evolved by Nishida, which served as the philosophical background for the renowned knowledge creation spiral of Nonaka and Takeuchi (SECI). Together the four types form an integral (Four Worldly) representation of knowledge creating interactions, set in a particular 'shared context' and space.

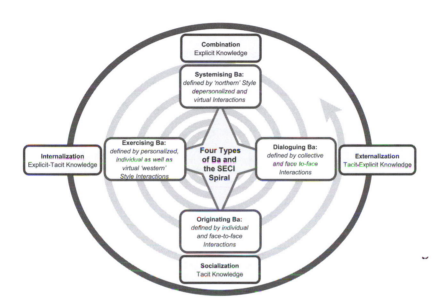

Figure 13.2 Four types of Ba and the SECI spiral of Nonaka and Takeuchi

The emergent, reformative world of Japanese style evolutionary spiral, arising out of an eastern, consciousness-based perspective – alongside the other worlds – is like a half-way house between 'southern' community building and 'northern' knowledge creation, in this case focused on the conscious evolution of organizations. For a more individually as well as organizationally oriented eastern approach, we now turn to Richard Barrett and his *Liberation of the Corporate Soul*.[8]

13.4 Eastern Normative Navigation: Conscious Organization

13.4.1 LEVELS OF CORPORATE CONSCIOUSNESS

Richard Barrett introduces a systematized, hierarchical, and thereby more 'northern' concept of consciousness, relating it to the corporate world. For him, organizations like individuals – and, for us, also societies – have the potential to evolve through seven levels of consciousness. These seven levels are derived, directly, from the ancient Indian Vedic wisdom to which Barrett subscribes. The consciously evolving organization, as such, becomes a living entity with a distinct personality, as illustrated in Figure 13.3.

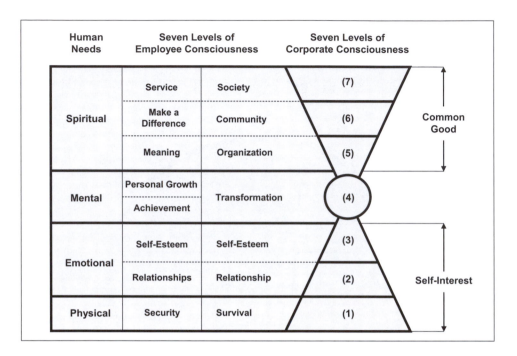

Figure 13.3 The conscious organization

Barrett starts with 'survival consciousness', which, from this eastern perspective on conscious evolution, can be related to a developing person (consciousness raising), to an organization (organizational development) or to a society (societal renewal). Each case serves to transform levels of individual-institutional-societal consciousness. From such an 'eastern' perspective, the evolution of individual and organizational consciousness go hand in hand. We begin with 'survival consciousness', and end with societal consciousness:

1. *Survival Consciousness:* The first need for individual and enterprise is financial survival. Without profits or access to funds, organizations quickly perish. However, when they become entrenched in survival consciousness, they develop an exclusive preoccupation with the bottom line, and a deep-seated insecurity about the future.
2. *Relationship Consciousness:* The second need for an individual as well as for an organization is for harmonious interpersonal relationships. In the case of the enterprise, without good relationships with employees, customers and suppliers – or indeed their equivalent for a public or civic enterprise – organizational survival is compromised.
3. *Self-Esteem Consciousness:* The third need is self-esteem, reflected in an enterprise's desire to make its mark on the world, to be the biggest and the best at what they

do. Consequently they are very competitive, and are consequently seeking ways to improve their cost-effectiveness, and overall image.

4. *Transformation Consciousness:* This, fourthly, is the bridge that institutions must cross if they are to build organizational cohesion and shift their belief systems from self-interest to the common good. The principal focus at this level of consciousness is self-knowledge and renewal.

5. *Organization Consciousness:* The primary focus of organizations at this fifth level of evolved consciousness is internal connectedness, achieved through the development of a positive culture that supports employee fulfilment. Values such as transparency and equality become important, as was the case for Cashbuild in our 'southern' case.

6. *Community Consciousness:* The primary focus of organizations at this sixth level is external connectedness. From our perspective this involves a fusion between the public and private, civic and animate functioning of the enterprise, achieved by creating partnerships between commercial and social, cultural and environmental constituencies within and without the institution.

7. *Societal Consciousness:* Ultimately, at this seventh level of conscious evolution, the institution serves humanity and the planet. There is recognition of the interconnectedness of all of life and the need for both individuals and enterprises to take responsibility for the welfare of the whole. Canon, as we shall see later, is our point in case.

Organizations, like individuals and societies, rarely operate from a single level of consciousness. Most business enterprises in America, according to Barrett for example, are strongly focused on the bottom three levels of profit consciousness [level 1], customer satisfaction [2] and productivity [3]. Many organizations get stuck exactly at this level. In further transforming the organization and in moving towards ultimately contributing to the wider society [7], Canon has adopted the spirit of Kyosei.

We now turn in more detail to the 'eastern' case of Canon.

13.5 Eastern Transformative Effect: Co-Evolution and the Case of Canon in Japan

13.5.1 CANON'S BEGINNING

Mitarai to Kaku

Canon is well known[9] in the world for its cameras, photocopiers and printers. What is less well known is its very distinctive heritage. Of particular interest to us is the way it has been consciously evolved in both its early and later years. Created by a devout Buddhist, it was taken over in its early years by Takeshi Mitarai, a highly ethical medical practitioner, who remained attached to the hospital he established throughout his working life. Subsequently in Canon's history, Ryuzabaru Kaku came to the helm, a unique combination of philosopher and businessman, who introduced the path of Kyosei (co-existence) into the company.

Kannon to Canon: Buddhist idealism and Business realism

November 1933 saw the newly founded SKK Seiki Kogaku Kenkyusho (Precision Instruments Laboratory) set up shop in a suburb of Tokyo. Started by a former employee of Yamaichi Securities, Saburo Uchida, together with his brother-in-law Goro Yoshida, neither knew much about cameras. But Uchida's belief was that the only way resource-starved Japan could compete on the international markets was through investment in high technology and intelligent planning to complement this strategy.

Uchida's greatest success may have been that he brought his friend Takeshi Mitarai on board, the first member of a family that, along with many talented researchers, would take Canon into the forefront of Japanese industry. Today Fujio Mitarai is still represented on the board. Takeshi himself had studied medicine, before working in obstetrics and gynaecology at the Japanese Red Cross in the 1930s. His career in medicine had stimulated his interest in medical imaging. He became fired up by the prospect of beating the Germans in this area, and was persuaded by his friend Uchida to invest in SKK. In those early years, and even when he ultimately became President of the company, he saw himself primarily as a medical man, continuing his medical career throughout his life.

It was indeed Yoshida, the originator of SKK, who had the upper hand in the early years. He decided to name the first cameras produced after the Buddhist Goddess of Mercy, Kannon, and the range of lenses after the Buddhist wise man, Mahakasyapa. He even designed the first company logo of this supposedly high tech enterprise in line with his Buddhist path, represented by the image of the thousand-handed Kannon amidst flame shaped lettering. Uchida took the opposite line, keen to operate more like a genuine, modern business, and gradually his realism took over from Yoshida's idealism. He came upon the idea of changing indigenous Kannon to exogenous Canon, the latter defined as 'a standard to judge by'. In this sense, he was evolving rather than dissolving the indigenous-exogenous connection. It was actually during the late 1930s that Japan began to catch up with, and even overtake, many countries in areas of high technology.

Profitability alone is not enough

In 1942, Mitarai took charge of what was now Canon, while continuing to run the new hospital he had established. Ushida finally severed his ties five years later. Under the leadership of Dr Mitarai, the company began to take on the form and philosophies recognizable in Canon today. Thirty-seven years later Takeshi Mitarai explained it in this way: *'We have a responsibility to our stockholders to make a profit. But I feel profitability alone is not enough. We also have an obligation to lend our strength to society's betterment.'* Canon today has the following major product groups: office imaging products, peripheral products, bubble jet products, chemicals and optical products. Almost all are the result of the pioneering efforts of Dr Mitarai. In line with his philosophy, almost everything made by Canon has a value to society that is more than simply economic.

13.5.2 THE HEART OF THE ENTERPRISE

Dr Mitarai selected his employees very carefully. Once he had these in place he was able to concentrate on the philosophies and policies that would distinguish Canon from most other companies. The most basic of these, handed down very early in the company's history, was called the *Three J's: 'ji-hatsu', 'ji-kaku' and 'ji-chi' (self motivation, self awareness and self management). The harmony of the company, its members and their family members is essential to the well-being of all. Every aspect of Canon's personnel administration is intended to reinforce these three qualities.* In fact, until 1943, what is thought of as the Japanese-style one-family-system did not exist, and Canon was a pioneer in that respect, making every employee a member of the Canon family.

Alongside Takeshi Mitarai's Three Js philosophy and his demand for the equal treatment of all employees, was this New Family policy. Indeed the English word 'employee' does not truly describe the Japanese situation. Their word 'sha-in' is better translated as 'member of the firm'. There is a feeling of mutual responsibility. Mitarai said, *'we do not fire employees when times are hard, but expect them to share the burden with us'*. When a union was first recognized in 1946, Dr Mitarai made it clear that it would be seen as a partner by corporate management, not as an opponent. To sum up then *'the spirit is the most important part of the company. If the heart is good, business will be good'*. But the mind, embodied in research, was important too!

13.5.3 THE MIND OF THE ENTERPRISE

If the Three Js represent the heart of Canon, the Fuji-Susono Research Park embodies its mind. Built in the 1980s, it is now home to 1,000 of Canon's leading researchers, working mainly in areas connected to electro-photography, a core Canon technology with applications in over 70 per cent of Canon's products. Few companies, Japanese or non-Japanese, could have designed such a centre. Fewer could have taken such care to minimize the effect on the natural environment, and fewer still would have taken such time and trouble to harness Japan's most famous beauty spot, Mount Fuji, for the development of individuality and creativity. For its Research Director, Dr Takashi Nakagiri, the role of the centre is to develop technologies that will carry Canon profitably into the future. The company is currently working in such areas as long-term memory, optical LAN devices, large-screen flat displays and bioremediation. Many of these products, though now in the early stages of development, will have huge effects on the way people will live in the coming decades.

'Our mission is to nurture the seeds for the future crops of Canon technologies.' In many western countries, a great deal of basic research is done in universities, but that does not happen in Japan. The education system is such that creative thinking does not emerge, so all must be done at a corporate level. And that is why, for Takashi Nakagiri, the cultivating of creative freedom is so important at Canon, while, simultaneously working together for the common good. This brings us to Kyosei.

13.5.4 KYOSEI AT CANON

Working together for the common good

Ryuzaburo Kaku as company Chairman in the 1970s and 1980s was addressing the fact that many companies around the world felt a moral duty to respond to global problems like Third World poverty, the deterioration of the environment and endless trade battles. But few had realized in his view that their very survival depended on their response. Global corporations relied on educated workers, consumers with money to spend, a healthy natural environment and peaceful co-existence between nations and ethnic groups. As such, Kaku wanted to 'resource' business in society, saying that global companies had no future if the earth had no future. How then were such companies to promote peace and prosperity, while at the same time enhancing their profitability?

The answer, for Canon, at least while Kaku was at the helm, lay in the path of Kyosei, a 'spirit of co-operation', or indeed co-evolution, where individuals and organizations work together for the common good.

A company practising Kyosei establishes harmonious relations with its customers, suppliers and competitors, as well as with the government with which it deals, and the natural environment. When practised by a group of corporations, Kyosei can become a powerful force for social, political and economic transformation.

The five states of Kyosei

For Kaku, *Kyosei begins with laying a sound business foundation, and ends in political dialogue for global change.*[10] The strength of each layer, as is the case for Barrett's Conscious Organization, depends on each level before it. However, Kaku starts from the immediately and locally practical, and works his way towards the more far reaching and global 'life-world'. Conversely, we see the global in the local, and vice versa. Whereas Kaku's perspective, like Nonaka's, is devoid of cultural-societal context, ours is fully imbued with this dimension.

Stage 1 – Economic Survival
Companies at the survival stage work to secure a predictable stream of profits and to establish strong market positions in their industries. They contribute to society by producing needed goods, purchasing locally produced raw materials, and employing workers to realize business goals. However, they tend to exploit workers. For Kaku, making a profit is only the beginning of a company's obligations. As a company matures, it needs to understand that it plays a larger role in a global context. 'Two years before Kaku became President, in 1975, Canon was losing money. He had to set aggressive targets for each division, reorganize around the main product lines, and invest heavily in manufacturing, marketing and R&D. Today it is one of the market leaders in copiers and desktop printers, and, in the 1990's, net profits grew, over 10 years, 20 per cent per year.'

Stage 2 – Cooperating with Labour
A company enters a second stage when management and workers begin to cooperate with each other. The two sides are in the same boat, sharing the same fate. This stage is well known in Japan, but is more inward than outward looking. Canon started cooperating with its employees well before other companies. It had no distinctions between factory and office workers: we are all 'sha-in', members of the company. Because employees tend to spend their entire lives with the company it invests heavily in them.

Stage 3 – Cooperating outside the Company
At this stage, customers are treated respectfully and reciprocally, suppliers are provided with technical support in return for high quality materials. Competitors, moreover, are invited to form partnerships for mutual gain, while the company links up with community to solve local problems. At this point, the focus is still more local than global.

Aside from getting close to its customers and suppliers, Canon, for Kaku, contributes its technological know-how to the general public and communities.

Stage 4 – Global Activism
By cooperating with foreign companies, large corporations can reduce trade frictions by building local plant; they can set up R&D facilities in foreign countries to upgrade their local know-how; and they can improve the living standards of people by paying and training them well. And by developing and using technology that reduces pollution, companies can help preserve the global environment. So, for Kaku, firstly, Canon addresses trade imbalances by situating production facilities in countries where Japan has the greatest trade surpluses; it creates employment in poor countries by building manufacturing plants there; to protect the environment Second, Canon has a major recycling initiative in 21 countries for photocopiers and laser copiers. Third, it is involved in developing bioremediation products, which break down microbes in chemical pollutants, which will enable Canon in the future to generate profits and help the planet.

Stage 5 – The Government as a Kyosei Partner
When a company has established a worldwide network of Kyosei partners it is ready to move onto the final stage. Fifth stage companies, for Kaku, are very rare. They urge governments to rectify global imbalances. Overall then, and substantiated by Canon's ever-increasing investment in R&D, it is committed to neither support military activities nor harm the environment. It encourages cooperation, worldwide, not duplicating work of others.

Kyosei in perspective

Today, some 400 years after the origins of Kyosei, multibillion-dollar corporations control vast resources around the globe, employ millions of people, and create and own considerable wealth. As such they hold the future of the planet in their hands. Although governments and civil society need to play their part, they do not possess the same degree of wealth and power. So Kaku's point is this:

> *If corporations run their businesses with the sole aim of gaining more market share, and earning more profits, they may well lead the world towards economic, special and environmental ruin. But if they work together, in a spirit of Kyosei, they can bring food to the poor, peace to war-torn areas, and renewal to the natural world. It is our obligation, Kaku maintains, as business leaders, to join together to build a foundation for world peace and prosperity.*

13.6 Conclusion: Towards Conscious Evolution

13.6.1 THE SOUL OF CANON

When Kaku retired from the Chairmanship of Canon, Hajimi Mitarai, from the original Mitarai family, took over the reigns. After only two years, though, he suddenly died and Fujio Mitarai then replaced his cousin at the top. All the time, Kaku remained a dominant figure in the company, best described as the soul and conscience of Canon, rather than as a businessman. He was now above the fray of day-to-day business, and simply studied and philosophized about the future.

Fujio Mitarai, meanwhile, had spent many years in America, before he took the helm. While he saw America as individualistic and a lonely place, Japan was a typically Confucian island nation. Responsibility is shared. Each country has what the other lacks. America has raw energy and vitality, Japan has a philosophical view. Mitarai's ability to distil such a hybrid management style, combined with his modesty and humour, could be the key to Canon's success in the future.

13.6.2 THREE INTO JAPANESE ONE DID NOT CONSCIOUSLY GO

Today of course, fully into the new millennium, Canon is no longer quite the Kyosei force it once was. This is for two main reasons. First, of course, Kaku is no longer at the helm. Second though, and more significantly, the co-evolution of Canon, as an organization, has not been accompanied by the Japanese individual (consciousness raising) on a significant scale, and by that of Japan as a society (societal and cultural renewal). In fact, turning to a recent study of *The Credit Crunch* by British economist, Graham Turner, the following was said about Japan:

> *At the turn of the 1990's Japan was the envy of the world. The people of Japan were enjoying untold prosperity as the stock market. Unemployment was negligible. Companies everywhere were trying to emulate the Japanese way of doing business. It seemed that Japan could do no wrong. The swift reversal of Japanese fortunes was a classic illustration of the damage inflicted by excessive speculation, allowing property prices to soar out of control, and then not tackling the threat of debt deflation early enough. In fact advice from abroad reflected a popular belief that Japan's problems would not be so endemic if it had adopted the Anglo-Saxon model. In reality it was the last thing Japan needed.*[11]

The point Graham is making means for us, in the overall context of 'eastern' conscious evolution, is that such a co-evolution of self, organization and society has not taken place. In fact, Canon, as an organization, has been overtaken by both indigenous and exogenous events, that is the Japanese internal propensity for speculation set alongside that of the financial markets in the external west.

Further, in observing what is happening today in China and India, we find that such a 'western' material orientation has overtaken the 'eastern' spirituality almost completely. Though this is very good for the economy of both these countries, the split between matter and spirit, which is arising, is matched by the growing economic inequality between the rich and the poor, the urban and the rural, in both countries. Interesting enough, for Turner as for us, such inequality is at the root of today's credit crunch, in the same way as we argue that an imbalance between western material energy and eastern spiritual consciousness is doing untold damage to the world.

> *Globalization predicated on unfettered markets is going awry. The housing bubbles were not an accident, spawned simply by careless regulatory oversight. They were a necessary component of the incessant drive to expand free trade at all costs. Dominant corporate power became the primary driving force for economic expansion. Profits were allowed to soar. A growing share of the national income was absorbed by companies at the expense of workers.*[12]

For Turner, such growing inequality has served to decrease the purchasing power, in developed countries, of the majority of the population, and hence the rise of levels of debt, in order to support individual and national incomes. Such are effects of global imbalances.

13.6.3 CONCLUDING THE EASTERN GENE-IUS

In a concluding review of this chapter, we retrace once more the four core steps of the eastern GENE-ius, serving to transform the southern function:

Releasing the GENE-ius of the Eastern Function *Evolving Human Resources into Conscious Evolution through a Fourfold Process*	
The Eastern GENE	**Core Criteria for Integral Enterprise**
Grounding: The eastern Function is grounded in *Spiritual Consciousness*	• Going beyond the Human as a 'Resource' to re-sourcing the Human • Linking to the philosophical Base of a Society and its Spirituality (e.g. Japan – Basho/Ba)
Emerging: From such rootedness in a Spiritual Consciousness, the eastern Function engages in an *Evolutionary Spiral*	• Engaging in a self-transcending Process • Intense Interaction with other Human Beings, other Organizations and other Societies within a 'shared Context'
Navigating: From there Individual/ Enterprise/Society navigate through the *Conscious Organization …*	• Organization is viewed as a living, evolving entity with a distinct Personality • Self, Organization and Society co-evolve through Stages of Development and ever greater Complexity
Effecting: … becoming thereby increasingly effective in the Art of *Co-evolution*	• Co-Evolution includes Customers, Suppliers, Competitors, Government and Environment • 'Profitability alone is not enough. We have a responsibility to lend our strength to society's betterment' (Kaku of Canon) • Continually letting go and transcending • Evolving from ego- or ethno-centric to world-centric

We are now ready to turn from the east to the north. We are moving forward, being aware of the foundations that community building and conscious evolution have laid for the northern function of the enterprise. Southern community building and eastern conscious evolution are an integral part of the transformation of operations into knowledge creation.

References

1. Steiner, R. (1974). *Towards Social Renewal*. Sussex: Rudolf Steiner Press.
2. Wilken, F. (1981). *The Liberation of Capital*. London: Heinemann.
3. Pirsig, R. (1975). *Zen and the Art of Motorcycle Maintenance*. New York: Black Swan.
4. Nishida, K. (1990). *An Inquiry into the Good*. Connecticut: Yale University Press.
5. Nonaka, I. (33/2000). *SECI, Ba and Leadership*. London: Long Range Planning, International Journal of Strategic Management.
6. Polanyi, M. (1974). *Personal Knowledge*. Chicago: University of Chicago Press.
7. Shimizu, H. (1995). *Ba-principle: New Logic for the Real-time Emergence of Information*. Holonics, 5 (1).
8. Barrett, R. (1998). *Liberating the Corporate Soul*. Woburn: Butterworth-Heinemann.
9. Sandoz, P. et al. (1997). *Canon*. New York: Sponsored Publishing.
10. Kaku, R. (1997). *The Path of Kyosei*. Harvard Business Review. July-August.
11. Turner, A. (2008). *The Credit Crunch*. London: Pluto Press.
12. Turner, A. (2008). *The Credit Crunch*. London: Pluto Press.

14 *Transforming Operations into Knowledge Creation*

From Open Society to Open Source

14.1 Introduction: Transforming the Northern Function

14.1.1 TRANSFORMING OPERATIONS, TECHNOLOGY AND COMPETENCE

We now turn from community building and conscious evolution to knowledge creation as a transformation of operations. This is our 'northern', science and technology based function, forged out of and serving to combine science and technology on the level of society, operations on the level of the organization and personal competence on the level of the self. The resulting combination of the three interdependent levels and their subsequent transformation altogether leads to an evolution of operations into knowledge creation.

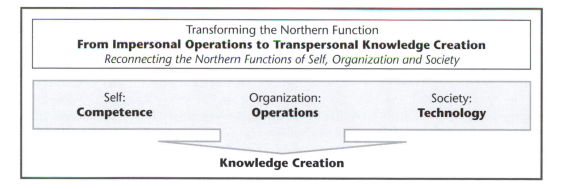

There has been lots of talk on knowledge management and knowledge creation in the past decades. However, as we see it, the Achilles heel of the new move toward a so-called 'knowledge based society', is that such 'northern' knowledge creation does not build on the prior grounds of 'southern' community building, and of 'eastern' conscious evolution. Once again the north and the west dominate over the rest, which results in an impoverished world, on the one hand, and a technical and economic pre-emphasis, over and above nature and culture, on the other hand.

In other words, we need to transform technology, operations and competence in a knowledge creating, northern light, through building on the prior southern, and eastern, transformations. Indeed, one of the reasons that so-called 'knowledge management' today is so dominated by technology, is that the more social and cultural influence in this area that came from Japan has waned, and the influence of the south, embodied in so-called indigenous knowledge systems which are deeply rooted in nature and culture, has been minimal.

14.1.2 HOMO FABER TO INFORMATION TECHNOLOGY

That having been said, the progressive transformation of materially based operations into information based knowledge systems has probably been more marked than in any other of the functional cases. Actually, the only other major function that was added to marketing, human resources and finance, over the course of a whole century, has been information technology, as an adjunct of operations.

It was also the operational function alone, which was significantly influenced by a culture and society outside of the 'west' and 'north', that is by the 'east' in the specific guise of Japan. In fact it was this fusion of western and eastern orientations which gave rise to the new push towards organizational learning that first emerged out of the operations function in the early 1980s, paving the way for the subsequent pre-emphasis on knowledge management. Indeed, the most prolific moves to integrate enterprise and IT, as we shall see, have come from Scandinavia. We actually turn now to the Scandinavian north.

14.1.3 NORTHERN NARINGSLIV: ENTERPRISE AND ENVIRONMENT

We have selected as our 'cultural northern force' – as we saw in Chapter 7 – the Swedish notion of Naringsliv, which literally means *'nourishment for life'*. Interestingly enough, it is used to connote what the west terms 'business'. This is of utmost significance for us here. Moreover, Naringsliv encompasses 'enterprise and environment' as an integrated business-societal entity.

In other words, whereas in the south the local community ('I am because you are') is the touchstone of life, and in the east it is global consciousness ('I am the universe'), in the north organizations-and-environments are together key, thereby providing an institutional, as opposed to a cosmic or communal orientation. Finally, it is no accident that we have chosen a Nordic country for the cultural, northern force, as the Fins, the Norwegians, the Swedes and the Danes seem to carry a uniquely differentiated rational and ethical, northern impulse.

In the following we shall guide you through the GENE of the northern function, from southern *open society* (grounding) to the eastern *communications networks* (emerging), up to the northern *knowledge creating enterprise* (navigation) to western *open source* (effect). Figure 14.1 illustrates the transforming fourfold of the northern function.

We now turn to the transformative journey from operations to knowledge creation, starting on the northern 'ground', that is with open society.

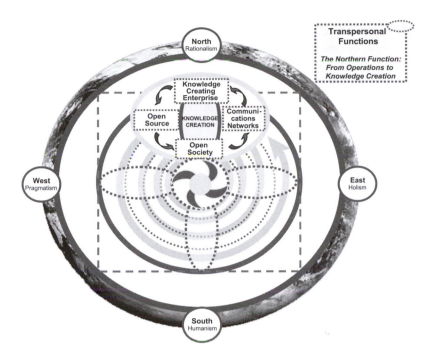

Figure 14.1 The transforming fourfold of the northern function

14.2 Northern Formative Grounding: The Open Society

14.2.1 THE PHILOSOPHY OF OPEN SOCIETY

Austria's Popper and Hungary's Soros

The term 'open society', which serves to ground the European 'north', was first significantly evolved by Austria's Karl Popper, the originator of 'critical rationalism'. Popper argued in his book *Open Society and its Enemies*[1] that open society is threatened by universal ideologies, like capitalism and socialism, that claim to be in possession of the ultimate truth. Both Karl Popper, as well as his follower George Soros, escaped from a totalitarian system. Whereas Popper, a Jew, had to flee to England from Nazi Austria, Hungarian born George Soros, also Jewish, had to flee from communist Eastern Europe to the UK and thereafter to the USA. While Popper became one of the pre-eminent philosophers of our time, Soros became a noted international financier as well as philanthropist.

In Soros's view,[2] whereas communism sought to abolish the market mechanism and to impose collective control over all economic activities, market fundamentalism seeks to abolish collective decision-making and to impose the supremacy of market values over all political and social values. Both extremes, for Soros, are wrong. We need to recognize, he argues, as does his mentor Popper, that all human constructs are flawed. As such he chooses to focus upon:

- the concept of *reflexivity* and the image of human *fallibility*;
- a *critique of market fundamentalism* for neglecting the socio-economic;

- the *difference between centre and periphery* in global capitalism;
- ultimately developing a *new political and financial architecture.*

14.2.2 TAKING HUMAN FALLIBILITY INTO ACCOUNT

Technological innovation to the fore

Open society, for Soros, falls short of perfection; however, it has the great merit of assuring freedom of thought and of speech, giving ample scope to experimentation and creativity. Nothing is more fundamental to our thinking than our concept of the truth. Instead of a one-way street, we find a two-way feedback mechanism – reflexivity.

We must content ourselves with a form of social organization that falls short of perfection but holds itself open to improvement. Linux will be the illustrating organizational case for such, which we introduce later in this chapter. This is the concept of an open society: a society open to improvement. Therein lies its superiority over a closed society, which seeks to deny its own imperfection even while the world around it changes. Recognition of our fallibility is the key to progress towards an open society. Such recognition, however, is fundamentally lacking in conventional economics and in the classical sciences, which are based on the objectively derived convention of 'rational man'.

The limits of classical science

Classical economic theory is the child of the enlightenment. The Enlightenment sought to establish the authority of reason by treating reality as something passively waiting to be understood. Its outstanding accomplishment, as we have seen, was Newtonian physics, and economic theory sought to imitate it. As such, economic theory takes the market participant's preferences as givens. Under the guise of this methodological convention, it tacitly introduces certain assumptions about values. The most important of these is that only market values – as opposed to social, cultural and environmental ones – should be taken into account.

This is justified when the objective is to determine the market price, but it ignores many such values, as noted above, that do not find expression in market behaviour. Generally speaking, for Soros, *only individual preferences are studied; collective needs are disregarded. This means that the entire political and social realm is left out of account.* We now turn from Hungarian born Soros to Spanish born Manuel Castells, who has been as much concerned with politics as with economics, with technology as with society.

14.3 Northern Reformative Emergence: Communications Networks

14.3.1 FROM INDUSTRIALISM TO INFORMATIONALISM

Manuel Castells is a Spanish sociologist, currently resident in the west coast of America. In his recent trilogy, which culminated in the *End of the Millennium*, in which he focused on the emerging 'network society' in contrast to the formerly industrialized one, he stressed:

By industrialism I mean a mode of development in which the main sources of productivity are not the quantitative increases of factors of production – labour, capital and natural resources – together with the use of new sources of energy. Rather, by informationalism I mean a mode of development in which the main source of productivity is the qualitative capacity to optimise the combination and use of factors of production on the basis of knowledge and information. The last quarter of the 20th century has been therefore marked by the transition from industrialism to statism, and from the industrial society to the network society.[3]

This emerging technological and organizational development, arising out of an open society, sets the stage for what is to follow.

14.3.2 THE NET AND THE SELF

A new world, for Castells, is taking shape at the end of the last millennium. It originates in the historical coincidence around the late 1960s and mid 1970s of three independent processes: the information technology revolution; the economic crisis of both capitalism and statism, and their subsequent restructuring; and the blooming of cultural social movements, such as libertarianism, human rights, feminism and environmentalism. The interaction between these processes and the reactions they triggered brought into being a new dominant social structure: the network society; a new economy; the informational, global economy; and a new culture, the culture of real virtuality. The logic embedded in this economy and society and culture underlies all institutions in an interdependent world. Particularly important is IT's role in allowing the development of networking as a dynamic, self expanding form or organization of humanity, as per 'open source'. This prevailing networking logic transforms all domains of social and economic life.

For Castells, therefore, societies today are constituted of the interaction between the global 'net' and the local 'self', the global network society and the local power of identity. Yet unless the two – in our terms the local indigenous and the global exogenous – are fused together, the latter serves to fragment rather than to reconstitute society. People's experience remains confined to simple, segregated locales, while global elites retrench within immaterial palaces made up of communication networks and information flows. *Therefore a long march is required from communities built around local resistance identity to the heights of new local as well as global project identities, sprouting from the values nurtured in these. For this transition from resistance to project identity, a new politics will need to emerge.* This will be a cultural politics that connects to values and experiences that spring from local people's life experience, while simultaneously connecting up with global issues and development.

The promise of the Information Age, for Castells, is the unleashing of unprecedented capacity by the power of the mind: 'I think therefore I produce.' The dream of the Enlightenment that reason and science would solve the problems of mankind is within reach. *'Yet there is an extraordinary gap between our technological over-development and our social under-development. Our economy, society and culture are built on interests that, by and large, limit collective creativity, confiscate the harvest of information technology, and divert our energy into self-destructive confrontation. If people are informed, active and communicate; if business assumes its social responsibility; if the media become the messengers rather than the message; if all this is made possible by our informed, conscious, shared decision, while there is still time, maybe then, we may, at last, be able to live and let live, love and be loved.'*

Castells's 'network society', building upon the 'open society' grounds to which Soros has alluded, needs a particular vehicle, an operational concept, at both a macro and a micro level. As we move from such an emerging economy and society towards the kind of institution that arises from it, we come, again, but now in more 'northern' guise, upon Nonaka and Takeuchi's knowledge creating enterprise. In such, network transcends hierarchy, in the newly normed 'hypertext organization'. Working with and through knowledge in a fundamentally new fashion transcends employment per se, via a 'knowledge crew', set within a knowledge creating enterprise.

14.4 Northern Normative Navigation: Knowledge Creating Enterprise

14.4.1 KNOWLEDGE CREATION TO CONTINUOUS INNOVATION

Nonaka and Takeuchi maintain[4] that the path taken by a knowledge creating enterprise is in essence, to turn knowledge creation into continuous innovation, so as to gain subsequent comparative advantage. A first step for a knowledge creating enterprise is to define the 'field' or 'domain' that gives a mental map of the world in which a Canon or Sony lives, and provide a general direction regarding what kind of knowledge they ought to seek to create. Most organizations only have products and services in mind when formulating strategy. Such products and services have clear boundaries. In contrast, boundaries for knowledge are more obscure, helping to expand the organization's economic, technological and social scope. A case in point, for example, is Matsushita's knowledge based vision in 1990:

- We are in the 'human innovation business', a business that creates new lifestyles based on creativity, comfort and joy in addition to efficiency and convenience.
- We produce 'humanware technology', technology based on human studies such as artificial intelligence, fuzzy logic, neuro-computers and networking technology.

Nonaka and Takeuchi identify three key 'enabling conditions' for the knowledge creating enterprise:

- first, develop intentionally the organizational *capability to acquire, create, accumulate and exploit knowledge;*
- second, *build up autonomous individuals and groups*, setting their task boundaries by themselves to pursue the ultimate intention of the organization;
- third, provide employees with *a sense of crisis – as well as a lofty ideal –* such so-called 'creative chaos' increases tension within the organization.

How then does the so-called 'hypertext' organization serve to promote such?

14.4.2 THE HYPERTEXT ORGANIZATION

The project layer

Nonaka refers to a 'hypertext' organization, because of its layered nature and scope, which serves to develop, channel and distribute knowledge through the duly formed networks. The top stratum of this kind of enterprise is comprised of the 'project team' layer (see Figure 14.2). Multiple project teams engage in knowledge creating activities such as new product and systems development. In all such cases the team members are brought together from a number of different units across the business system, and are assigned exclusively to a project team until the project is completed.

The bureaucratic system

Alongside this project layer, but occupying a lower order of knowledge creating significance, is the conventional 'bureaucratic system' with its normal hierarchy of authority. The project layer, on the one hand, is engaged with developing new knowledge through self-organizing groups. The hierarchical system, on the other, is primarily concerned with categorizing, ordering, distributing and commercializing or operationalizing such knowledge. In terms of the Nonaka and Takeuchi's knowledge spiral (SECI) introduced earlier (Chapter 8): whereas the project layer is primarily focused upon 'southern' socialization and 'eastern' externalization, the hierarchical system is more engaged with 'northern' combination and 'western' internalization. Underlying both project layer and business system, for Nonaka and Takeuchi, is a 'knowledge foundation'.

The knowledge foundations

This third layer does not exist as an actual organizational entity, but is embedded in corporate vision, organizational culture and technology. Of course, in our context here, societal culture is of even greater significance than the corporate one. The vision arises from these spiritual, aesthetic and scientific knowledge grounds. If made explicit, it provides the direction in which the enterprise should develop its social as well as technological innovations. Moreover, it clarifies the overall 'field' in which it wants to play. Furthermore, while vision and culture provide the experiential and imaginal base to tap tacit knowledge, technology taps the explicit knowledge generated in the other two layers.

A knowledge creating enterprise ultimately must have the organizational ability to acquire, accumulate, exploit and create knowledge continuously and dynamically. Moreover it must be able to recategorize and recontextualize it strategically for use by others in the organization or by future generations. As Nonaka and Takeuchi have indicated, a hierarchy is the most efficient structure for the acquisition, accumulation and exploitation of knowledge, while a task force is the most effective for the creation of new knowledge.

This corresponds exactly with the findings of the Austrian physicist and ecologist Fritjof Capra, when he talks in *The Hidden Connections*[5] about the emergence of novelty in human organizations. Human organizations always contain both designed and emergent structures. The designed structures are the formal structures of the organization, as

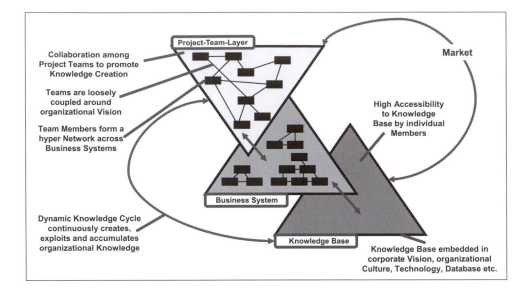

Figure 14.2 The Hyptertext Organization (according to Nonaka et al.)

described by its official documents. The emergent structures are created by an organization's informal networks and communities of practice. The two types of structures are very different, and every organization needs both. Designed structures provide the rules and routines that are necessary for the effective functioning of the organization. They enable a business organization to optimize its production processes and to sell its products through effective marketing campaigns. Emergent structures, on the other hand, provide novelty, creativity and flexibility. They are adaptive, capable of changing and evolving. We now turn to the so-called 'knowledge crew', as opposed to conventional managers and employees, who run such a hypertext organization.

14.4.3 THE KNOWLEDGE CREW

What is seldom recognized is the way in which Nonaka and Takeuchi have dissolved the notion of 'labour', or even 'human resources', and replaced these terms with knowledge creators. *Such a transformation from 'labour' to knowledge is distinctly absent from the 'western' literature on knowledge management, which is much more strongly rooted in technology.* For the Japanese organizational sociologists there are three kinds of knowledge creators: knowledge practitioners, knowledge engineers and knowledge officers.

Knowledge practitioners

Knowledge practitioners consist of 'knowledge operators' like technicians who interface with tacit knowledge for the most part, and 'knowledge specialists' like computer programmers, who interface primarily with explicit knowledge. Such practitioners develop a strongly personal perspective, a strong degree of openness to discussion and debate, as well as a variety of experience inside and outside the organization from and through which they are able to learn. They also acquire a high degree of specific skill based competence, and functional management knowledge, as well as skill in interacting with colleagues and customers.

Knowledge engineers

Knowledge engineers, constituting the heart of the knowledge creating enterprise, are responsible for converting tacit knowledge into explicit and vice versa, thereby facilitating the four modes of knowledge creation. As such they mediate between the 'what should be' mindset of the senior management and the 'what is' mindset of the frontline employees by creating mid-level business and product concepts. Such middle managers synthesize the tacit knowledge of both frontline employees and executives, make it explicit, and incorporate it into new products and technologies. Such knowledge engineers become proficient in employing metaphors and in developing story lines, to help themselves and others imagine the future. They become adept at communication whereby they encourage dialogue, and grow their competence in developing new strategic concepts. They are able to develop methodologies for knowledge creation, and become equipped with project management capabilities.

Knowledge officers

Knowledge officers, finally, are responsible for managing the total knowledge creation process at the organizational level. They are, therefore, expected to give an enterprise's knowledge creating activities a sense of direction by articulating grand concepts – like sustainable development – on what the organization might be, establishing a knowledge vision in the form of a policy statement, and setting the standards for justifying the value of the knowledge that is being created. In other words, knowledge officers are responsible for articulating the company's 'conceptual umbrella', the grand concepts that in highly universal and abstract terms identify the common features linking disparate business activities into a coherent whole. In short, knowledge officers direct the entire process of knowledge creation. They create chaos within the project team, for example, setting challenging goals for would-be leaders, and they have responsibility for selecting the right project leaders or knowledge engineers in key areas. Finally, they need to be able to interact with team members on a hands-on basis and solicit commitment from them.

We are now ready to present with Linux a case that builds accumulatively on the notions of southern open source, eastern communications networks and northern knowledge creating enterprise. We are drawing on Linux and its co-founder Torvalds as the 'northern' equivalent to southern Cashbuild and eastern Canon. The case of Linux, a 'living system' par excellence, represents Naringsliv (nourishment of life) at work. In fact, and analogously, the Latin roots of the English world 'company' derives from 'com panis' that is 'the sharing of bread'. Linux, as an 'open source' company is a real embodiment of such.

14.5 Northern Transformative Effect: Open Source and the Case of Linux in Finland

Linux, as of today, is a fully-fledged unix-type operating system, programmed by a community of thousands of people on the Internet. It is distributed by the terms of the GNU Public License, which means it is free. It is used by several million people, organizations and companies worldwide. Linux started in the bedroom of the then student of Helsinki University, Linus Torvalds, who – to his own surprise – initiated the formation of the biggest collaborative project in the history of the world. But let us listen to Linus Torvalds in his own words.[6]

14.5.1 CHILDHOOD AND YOUTH: BIRTH OF A NERD

'I don't actually remember the first time I saw a computer, but I must have been about eleven at the time. It must have been in 1981, when my grandfather bought a new Commodore VIC-20. Getting into computers started slowly, and grew on me. I would sit on grandfather's lap, and would type in his handwritten programmes into the computer. I gradually grew comfortable with the keyboard, something my grandfather never did. Then I started reading the manuals. There were simple games you could programme yourself. I started writing my own. It's the greatest feeling.

I come from a Swedish immigrant family in Finland. My maternal great-grandfather was a poor farmer, who had six sons, two of whom got PhDs, a product of Finland's free university education. One of the six sons was my maternal grandfather. My paternal grandfather was named Torvalds. He was a journalist and a poet. There are only 21 such Torvalds's in the world.'

14.5.2 ESTABLISHING AN OPERATING SYSTEM: FRIENDS CHIP IN

'I was always searching for something interesting to do. So I wrote programming tools for myself. And then I got interested in operating systems. One of the things I hated about the QL is that it had a 'read-only' operating system, so you couldn't change anything. So I had the Sinclair for three years, and then we were ready to part ways. All the signs were not pointing towards the PC.

Everyone has a book that changed their life, like the Holy Bible or the Qu'ran. The book that launched me to new heights was Andrew Tanenbaum's *Operating Systems – Design and Implementation*. In this book Tanenbaum, a university professor in Amsterdam, discusses Minix, which is a teaching aid he wrote for UN11. Soon after reading the introduction, and learning the philosophy behind UNIX and what the clean, beautiful operating system would be capable of doing, I decided to get a machine to run UNIX on.

At Helsinki University, where I was still studying in 1990, we were all babes in the UNIX woods, with a UNIX course that was being made up as we went along. But it was obvious that there was a unique philosophy behind UN11. It has a set of fundamental ideals. Everything that does anything in it is a process. And you can build up just about everything out of six basic system calls. It's clean and beautiful.

Of course much of the initial work for UNIX had been done in the sixties and seventies. This was technical flower power. It was a time of rampant idealism. Revolution. Freedom from authority. Free love. And the relative openness of UNIX was born out of this spirit. In 1991, I went along to hear Richard Stallman at our university. He is the God of Free Software. He pioneered the notion of free source-code availability, the way it happened with the original UNIX open development, but this time purposefully. So Stallman created the Free Software Foundation. He started creating the alternative to UNIX, called GNU, which became associated with GPL (General Public License). He was a typically longhaired, hacker type. We don't have them in Helsinki. I must have seen some kind of light, because I ended up using GPL for Linux. But I'm getting ahead of myself.

In 1991 I bought my new computer, with a cut down version of DOS, on which I could run Minix, the UNIX variant. I spent the next month playing Prince of Persia on it, and, in between, reading books that would help me understand the new computer I had bought. There was a lot wrong, I soon discovered, with Minix, which was basically developed as a teaching aid, and that's all. I spent most of my time in my bathrobe, huddled over my unattractive new computer, with thick black window shades shielding me from the sunlight, not to mention the outside world. I had absolutely no money, so friends started to chip in, to pay off my new computer. I'm getting choked up. That's how Linux got started.'

14.5.3 CREATING A WORLD

'I'm personally convinced that computer science has a lot in common with physics. Both are about how the world works at a fundamental level. The difference, of course, is that while in physics you are supposed to figure out how the world is made up, in computer science you create the world. If you're good enough you can be God, on a small scale. You get to create your own world. It is a combination of art and engineering, an exercise in creativity. You can do anything you want, but as you add complexity, you have to be careful not to create something that is inconsistent, within the world you have created. For it to be beautiful it can't contain flaws.

When you create an operating system you're creating the world in which all the programmes running the computer live. It's like creating the constitution of the land you live in, and all the other programmes are like the common laws.

My original goal was to create an operating system that would eventually replace Minix, to so do some of the things I cared about that were already part of it, as well as other things that were not. Privately I called the new system I was generating Linux, but to release it publicly would have been too egotistical. Once I had a few rudimentary things going I informed a handful of people by private mail. I remember the date. It was September 17, 1991. Ari Lemke, one of the people, named my posting pub/OS/Linux. It wasn't yet useful. It was just a speciality for a few people interested in creating new operating systems.

Suddenly, then, there were people switching from Minix to Linux. At the time, it did not do everything Minix did, but it did the things people cared about. In this same period the notion of 'shareware' was coming to light, where you downloaded a programme and were supposed to send a nominal amount to the writer. I preferred to receive postcards to money, to tell me where people were using Linux. They came in from all over the world.

Of course, and in time, Tanenbaum and the Minix users became not too pleased that their system was being supplanted. Minix, in fact, was compiled as a 'microkernel', which meant that its operating system was complicated. So you try and get some of the complexity out by modularising it a lot. So you split up the problem space. I thought that was stupid. The interactions in fact make it far more complex than it would be if many of the services were included in the kernel itself, as with Linux. Think of your brain. Every piece is simple, but the interactions between them make for a complex system.

In 1992 Linux graduated from being mostly a game to something that had become integral to people's lives, their livelihoods, commerce. A hacker named Orest Zborowski created a socket interface for Linux, which not only enabled us to have windows, but also to network with other computers. Networking, though, is a nasty business, and it ended up taking us two years to get it right. Yet, by the fall of 1992, tens of thousands of people were participating in our news group, and I emerged as the leader.

Just as I never planned for Linux to have a life outside my own computer, I also never planned to be the leader. It just happened by default. At some point a core group of five developers started generating most of the ideas in the key areas of development. It made sense for them to serve as the filters and hold the responsibility for maintaining those areas. The best leaders, I discovered, enable others to make decisions for them. Otherwise the Linux development model would never have become an intricate web of hundreds of thousands of participants, with maybe 4,000 projects being undertaken at any one time. Hackers, in fact, working on Linux and other open source projects, forgo sleep because they love programming. And they love being part of a global collaborative effort – Linux is the world's largest collaborative project – dedicated to building the best and most beautiful technology that is available to anyone who wants it. And it is fun.'

14.5.4 HELSINKI TO SILICON VALLEY: WHY OPEN SOURCE MAKES SENSE

'The birth of a fully developed Linux, what we called version 1.0, as opposed to 0.1 or 0.5, for example, meant something new – the need for public relations. Others volunteered to do it, as it wasn't my scene, and it worked. The computer sciences department of the University of Helsinki, and not my bedroom, was the chosen site for publicity. It was the first time I got to see myself on TV. In the talk I gave, as has been the case pretty well ever since, I spoke not so much about the technology but about Open Source. The launch put Linux above the radar zone in Finland, and started generating publicity elsewhere. Corporations that had been interested in UNIX came to me. Novell, in 1994, paid me to visit them in the U.S. By the spring of 1995, our kernel had grown to 250,000 lines of code, the new magazine Linux Journal claimed a 10,000 person circulation, and Linux was capable of running on Intel, Digital and Sun processors. That was a big step. By 1995, I had been promoted from a teaching to a research assistant, and I was completing my Masters degree, which was about porting Linux to different architectures.

At the end of 1996, having eventually completed my masters, I decided to work for Tramsmeta Corporation in Silicon Valley. The first thing I ended up doing, once I got there, was to fix up some of the problems they were having with their Linux software. My deal with Tramsmeta, moreover, was that I could work on Linux, for our own community's purposes, during work hours, and I took full advantage of that. By 1998 Sun Microsystems declared it would become the first major hardware vendor to join what we now called Linux International, and then came IBM, who declared they would support Apache, the most popular commercial Linux version used for Web servers. In fact both companies were following the lead set by advocacy newsgroups, who by now had decided that Linux was the darling of the world's operating systems. By 2001, IBM was spending $1 billion on Linux. Then Oracle followed suit.

While all these news were very gratifying it did not change my life. I had a lovely wife and two young, adorable daughters. Most of the action was taking place in the corporations, who were swayed by the sheer technical attributes of Linux. Moreover, people hate to have to do things the way that Microsoft or anybody else tells them. Like Microsoft though, in one respect, Linux does not have a niche, it flows everywhere. At the same time the best and the brightest of the young generation are using it, because we are the thing that excites them. By August 1998, Forbes had discovered our little world by putting a picture of me on the cover with the words: peace, love, and software.

Linux had captured the planet's heart, like some improbable Olympic gold medallist from an unrecognizable third-world nation. I was the poster boy. The press, meanwhile, was playing up the dichotomy between the idealists and the pragmatists. For me it was a non-issue. Without commercial interests, how would Linux flow into new markets? How else could it create opportunities for innovations? How else would it be able to reach people who want an alternative to the bad technology out there? Open source is about letting everybody play, and of having fun in the process.

Moreover, as the poster boy, holder of the Linux trademark, maintainer of the Linux kernel, I felt a growing sense of responsibility for the fact that millions of people now relied on Linux, and it was important for me to help corporations understand what it was all about. There was no war, as far as I was concerned, between greedy corporations and altruistic hackers. It was important for me to be trusted both technically and ethically. Meanwhile my method of managing the project with hundreds of thousands of developers was the same as that when I coded in my bedroom: I wait for people to volunteer to take over things. So why, in the end, did things turn out that well?

If you try and make money by controlling a resource, you'll eventually find yourself out of business. This is a form of despotism, and history overflows with examples of its ill effects. That's why Microsoft's strategy of bundling software is bound to fail. Open source products, on the other hand, cannot possibly be used in a despotic manner because they are free. What started out, for me, in my messy Helsinki bedroom, has grown to become the largest collaborative project in the history of the world. It began as an ideology shared by software developers, who believed that computer source codes should be shared freely, with the General Public License – the anti-copyright – as the movement's powerful tool. It evolved to become a method for the continuous development of the best technology. And it developed further to gain widespread market acceptance, as seen in the snowballing adoption of Linux as an operating system for Web servers.

What was inspired by ideology has proved itself as technology and is working in the marketplace. The theory behind open source is simple. In the case of an operating system the source code – the programming instructions underlying the system – is free. Anyone can improve it, change it, and exploit it. But these improvements, changes, and exploitations have to be made freely available. The project belongs to no one and everyone. When a project is opened up there is rapid and continuous improvement. With teams of contributors working in parallel, the results can happen far more successfully than work being conducted behind closed doors. And when the money rolls in, as numerous value-added services are introduced, people get convinced. One of the least understood pieces of the open source puzzle is how many good programmers would deign to work for absolutely no money. Folks do their best work, at least in a society where survival is more or less assured, when they are driven by a passion, and having fun. This is as true for playwrights and sculptors as it is for entrepreneurs and software engineers. The open source model gives people the opportunity to live their passion.

Science was originally viewed as something dangerous, subversive and anti-establishment – basically how software companies sometimes view open source. And just as science wasn't born out of an effort to undermine the religious establishment, open source was not conceived in order to detonate the software establishment. It is there to produce the best technology and to see where it goes. Science, on its own moreover, does not make money. It has been the secondary effects that create wealth. The same goes for open source. It allows the creation of secondary industries that challenge established businesses. Like science itself, open source's secondary effects are endless. By not controlling the technology you are not limiting its uses. People use it as a launching pad for their own products and services.

People don't quibble with the need for free speech. It is a liberty that people have defended with their lives. And the same is true of openness. It's a difficult stand to take, but it actually creates more stability in the end.'

14.6 Conclusion: Towards Knowledge Creation

14.6.1 OPEN SOCIETY AND OPEN SOURCE

In conclusion, as we digest the enormity and indeed unpredictability of Linux's achievement, we cannot but be struck by the degree of 'northern' resonance. If Karl Popper were alive today, he would undoubtedly be delighted by the tone of 'open source', and its connectedness with his own 'open society'. Similarly George Soros, with his emphasis on fallibility and reflexivity, coupled with his emphasis on feedback processes, is likely to applaud such an 'open source' world.

Further, Manuel Castells, who sees Europe leading the networked way, is likely to consider 'open source' as part and parcel of the networking revolution he sees unfolding before us. Furthermore, the notion of a knowledge creating company or community is conceptually completely aligned with that of Linux, with Torvalds providing the underlying knowledge based vision, and enabling conditions for its realization, ultimately through open source. Finally, in comparing the western American with a northern European way, Linux represents the latter in the same way as Microsoft represents the former. Moreover it has turned out to be the major rival to Microsoft, technologically and commercially.

14.6.2 FROM LINUX TO NARINGSLIV

The puzzle we are left with is why is Linux such an isolated case, albeit that it is the biggest collaborative project in the history of the world? We would argue that its rarity is based on two factors. First, 'open source' represents the best of the 'north', and there are many lesser elements weighing it down, like bureaucracy and hierarchy. Second, 'northern' knowledge networks are disconnected from 'eastern' conscious evolution and 'southern' community building.

That having been said, and to set the Linux in a broader Nordic context, we have adopted 'Naringsliv' as our cultural force. The term has resonance, for us, with open society and with open source, set in the overall context of technology that has social meaning. In fact, Leif Edvinsson, the architect of the so-called 'knowledge navigator', has used it during the time he spent at Scandinavia Financial Services, developing ways and means of assessing its *Intellectual Capital*.[7] Indeed Edvinsson and his Swedish countryman Erik Sveiby[8] played a major role together in managing and measuring know-how. Edvinsson, in addition, also did some speculative work on the development of an IC (Intellectual Capital) Index, to supplement that of the financially based stock markets. And it is to finance and sustainability, that we finally and functionally now turn.

14.6.3 CONCLUDING THE NORTHERN GENE-IUS

In a concluding review of this chapter, we retrace once more the four core steps of the northern GENE-ius, serving to transform the northern function:

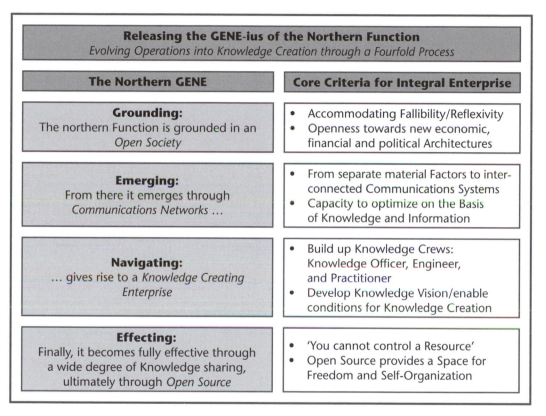

Releasing the GENE-ius of the Northern Function *Evolving Operations into Knowledge Creation through a Fourfold Process*	
The Northern GENE	**Core Criteria for Integral Enterprise**
Grounding: The northern Function is grounded in an *Open Society*	• Accommodating Fallibility/Reflexivity • Openness towards new economic, financial and political Architectures
Emerging: From there it emerges through *Communications Networks …*	• From separate material Factors to inter-connected Communications Systems • Capacity to optimize on the Basis of Knowledge and Information
Navigating: … gives rise to a *Knowledge Creating Enterprise*	• Build up Knowledge Crews: Knowledge Officer, Engineer, and Practitioner • Develop Knowledge Vision/enable conditions for Knowledge Creation
Effecting: Finally, it becomes fully effective through a wide degree of Knowledge sharing, ultimately through *Open Source*	• 'You cannot control a Resource' • Open Source provides a Space for Freedom and Self-Organization

We are now ready to turn from the north to the west. We move forward, being aware of the foundation that community building, conscious evolution and knowledge creation have laid for fundamentally revisiting the domain of the western function of the enterprise. Finance is, at the time of writing this book, perhaps the single most distorted organizational and societal function. In the course of the next chapter, which concludes the transformation of the functions, it will become evident how southern community building, eastern conscious evolution and northern knowledge creation, together, form an integral part of the transformation of finance into sustainable development. The current financial and economic crisis is a reflection of the fact that such an enriched backdrop is not yet in place.

References

1. Popper, K. (1945). *Open Society and its Enemies*. London: Routledge.
2. Soros, G. (2000). *Open Society*. New York: Little Brown.
3. Castells, M. (2000). *End of the Millennium*. Oxford: Blackwell.
4. Nonaka, I. and Takeuchi, H. (1995). *The Knowledge Creating Company*. Oxford: Oxford University Press.
5. Capra, F. (2002). *The Hidden Connections – A Science for Sustainable Living*. New York: Anchor Books.
6. Torvalds, L. and Diamond, D. (2001). *Just for Fun*. Mason: Texere.
7. Edvinsson, L. (1997). *Intellectual Capital*. New York: Harper Business.
8. Sveiby, K.E. and Lloyd, T. (1988). *Managing Know-how*. London: Bloomsbury.

15 *Transforming Finance into Sustainable Development*

From Life Instinct to Self-Organization

15.1 Introduction: Transforming the Western Function

15.1.1 TRANSFORMING FINANCE, CAPITAL AND CAPACITY

We now turn to the transformation of the final and 'western' function, which is finance. This function is forged out of and serves to combine the notion of capital on the level of society, finance on the level of the organization and capacity on the level of the self. The resulting combination of the three interdependent levels and their subsequent transformation altogether leads to an evolution of finance into sustainable development.

15.1.2 CREDIT CRUNCH TO CREDIT WORTHY: THE WEST AS 'SERVANT LEADER' TO THE REST

This chapter is being completed in the latter part of 2008, when the so-called 'credit crunch', alongside 'peak oil' and 'food insecurity', are seemingly holding the world to ransom. Whereas for many these may appear as separate and isolated phenomena, the one financial and the other environmental, for us they are all connected. We share this perspective with futurists and financiers such as Belgium's Bernard Lieater and America's Dee Hock. At this point, we may also recall Bangladesh's Mohammad Yunus saying in

Chapter 1, that *mainstream free market theory suffers from a 'conceptualization failure', that is a failure to capture the essence of what it is to be human.*

This last functionally oriented chapter is a tricky, as well as a crucial, one. For we are dealing with the financial function, the one that, in its more insular 'western' orientation, leads to narrowly based 'market fundamentalism'. Yet for us it should serve as 'servant leader' to the south, east and north. In that way it would 'serve' to culminate our functionally based transformation, building upon the transformational, transcultural and transdisciplinary fundamentals that have come before. Therefore, the practical 'west' needs to cumulatively build upon the conceptual north, the imaginative east and the experiential south. That builds upon what John Heron (see Chapter 8) has said:

> *Practical knowing is the consummation of the knowledge quest. It is grounded on and empowered by all the prior forms of knowing, and is immediately supported by propositional knowing which it celebrates and affirms at a higher level ... It affirms what is intrinsically worthwhile, by manifesting it in action.*[1]

In terms of this book, the final realization – building purposefully on what has come before – of both 'self-hood' and 'society-hood' as well as the evolving 'institution-hood' (as per Broad and Sekem as we shall see in the next chapter) as an integral part of it, is lodged in the practicality of the archetypal 'west'. However, it is a 'western-ness' that is able to take into account all that has come experientially (community building), imaginatively (conscious evolution) and conceptually (knowledge creation) before it. In the process, this integral pragmatic outcome has to incorporate the humanistic 'south', the holistic 'east' and the rational 'north'. This all sounds a bit of a tall order. And yet it is possible. In our review of the developing finance function, in Chapter 11, we have illustrated how narrowly based economic enterprise, from an evolutionary perspective, has evolved toward more broadly based intellectual capital. In fact at the very same time as the credit crunch has raised its ugly head, a new financial order has been unfolding before our eyes, albeit that it cuts across the mainstream.

15.1.3 WESTERN INDIVIDUATION: FINANCE, CAPITALISM AND THE SELF-MADE MAN

Such mainstream, finance based capitalism, and the characteristically self-made man that go with it – hedge fund impresarios being good such cases in point – have made a comeback in the aftermath of the Reagan-Thatcher years. These heroic individualists are something of a throwback to the nineteenth-century past. The twenty-first-century future, from such a self-made 'western' perspective then, is more about individuation than about individualism. What is the difference between the two?

Individuation, in Maslow's terms, is to do with self-realization that is actualizing your unique self. In business terms, it is more like a Dee Hock than a Donald Trump. In acting terms this is more a Meryl Streep than a Jack Nicholson. In politics we are talking about a Nelson Mandela rather than a Margaret Thatcher. In scientific terms this is an Einstein rather than an Edison, and in cultural terms a Beethoven rather than a Mozart. In other words, we are talking of people in midlife rather than in their young adulthood who are engaged on a spiritual as well as a material journey. As such, for American development psychologist Daniel Levinson, as we saw in Chapter 5:

A major developmental task of middle adulthood is to find a better balance between the needs of self and the needs of society.[2]

We now turn from an evolving 'western' identity, focused on self-actualization or individuation as a transformative force, to the recently emerging principle of self-organization, emerging in particular from Santa Fe Institute in New Mexico. Though having a strong western pedigree in such places as the Santa Fe Research Institute with its pioneering work on chaos and complexity,[3] such a new approach has strong resonance with the 'north' and 'east', and also with the 'south'.

15.1.4 FREE ENTERPRISE TO LIVING SYSTEMS

The 'western' tradition in the late modern era has been strongly identified with democratic freedoms, on the one hand, and with free markets, together with the 'free enterprise', on the other. This orientation has been established in opposition to the totalitarian regimes and centralized planning that were identified with 'eastern' communism. To the extent that such free market capitalism has been challenged, the automatic response tends to be that 'centralized planning has been proved not to work'. As if that was the only alternative! (see our forthcoming book *Integral Economics*) The very reason we have established our more rounded Four Words is to counter this overly simplistic argument, which contrasts, in our terms, 'western' capitalism against, for us, 'northern', and for the world at large, 'eastern' socialism. As if nothing else in the world existed. Underlying a newly emerging 'west', then, is not only mature individuation, as opposed to youthful individuality, but also mature 'self-making' or 'self-organization', as opposed to immature self-made man.

In the last two decades, moreover, there has been a new development spearheaded from the 'west', in physics and biology[4] as well as in management,[5] towards what has been termed '*self-organizing systems*', where the emphasis has been less upon free enterprise, than upon '*living systems*'. In the process, 'self-making' or indeed a 'self-organizing universe' takes over from 'self help'. The so-called 'natural laws' of the 'market mechanism' (if ever there was such a contradiction in terms) are now overtaken by laws of natural life.

15.1.5 INTEGRATING INDIVIDUATION AND SELF-MAKING

In linking such an evolving 'western' culture – one that serves to integrate, rather than isolate or dominate the 'south', 'east' and 'north' – the Israeli peace activist Jesaiah Ben-Aharon, in outlining *America's Global Responsibility*,[6] draws once again on the work of Austrian polymath Rudolf Steiner.

Beginning in the nineteenth century, the ability of the modern 'western', adult mind to portray the universe, nature and human nature – including the economic universe – as wholly devoid of creative intelligence and spiritual-moral purpose was actually a positive, most courageous evolutionary step. Physical and human nature could be rediscovered in far greater radiance than was possible to the ancient, atavistic, clairvoyant cognition. The human, passing through the eye of the needle of individuation, was given the opportunity to discover within him or herself the inner creative source of the external universe. In creating a next industrial revolution, as Paul Hawken will later describe, we find the expression of the economic ideals – in Rudolf Steiner's terms – of the now mature 'western mysteries' of the earth, which build on prior, native Indian wisdom. Indeed the term 'economy', as understood in such 'natural' terms, is a seed of a new conception of western civilization.

This kind of economy brings forth the stems, branches, leaves and fruits of political and cultural life as naturally as a fruit grows in its wholeness from healthy seed and fertile soil. Legislation, human rights, arts and culture, religion and science receive unmistakeable ecological and communal meaning in the new economy. Ben-Aharon argues that the American economy, grasped in this sense, bears in itself the sources of vital cultural and spiritual reality, because it is rooted in the native American talent to use generously the gifts of great Mother Nature. Life then is a perpetual process of becoming, evolution and transformation. This, for Ben-Aharon, is the potentially unique contribution of the 'west' to global culture. Yet, we seem to be far away from such an evident western contribution.

In the following we shall guide you through the GENE of the western function, from southern *life instinct* (grounding) to the eastern *sustainable abundance* (emerging), up to the northern new economic framework of a *restorative economy* (navigation) to western *self-organization* (effect). Figure 15.1 illustrates the transforming fourfold of the western function.

We now turn to these new 'western' grounds of life instinct, underlying enterprise.

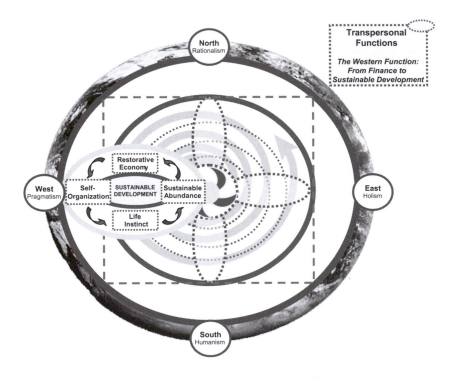

Figure 15.1 The transforming fourfold of the western function

15.2 Western Formative Grounding: Life Instinct

15.2.1 FROM DOMINATION TO STEWARDSHIP

The alternating life and death instincts

The American social philosopher Jeremy Rifkin, in comparing and contrasting the American and *The European Dream,*[7] maintains that globalizing technologies like 'open source', in compressing space and time, draw the human family together in tight webs of interdependent relationships. We become more aware of the many connections that make up the larger living systems within which we dwell. But if that technologically facilitated awareness is not balanced with intimate, face-to-face relationships, our journey to self-realization will be inhibited. Our relational selves will be more of a technological than of a truly human nature, only prolonging the older journey of what Rifkin terms 'the death instinct', which he identifies with his (USA) country's recent history. What does he mean by death instinct, and how does it compare with life instinct? For it is now this 'life instinct', as opposed to the traditional free enterprise, that, for us, constitutes the new grounding for western GENE-ius.

No one, and especially no Americans, Rifkin asserts, would deny that they are the most voracious consumers in the world. They forget, though, that *consumption and death are deeply intertwined.* The term 'consumption' dates back to the early fourteenth century and has Latin, French and English roots. Originally 'to consume' meant to destroy, pillage, subdue, exhaust. It is a word steeped in violence and until the twentieth century had only negative connotations. Still in the early 1900s, the medical community and the public referred to tuberculosis as 'consumption'. Consumption only metamorphosed into a positive term at the hands of twentieth-century advertisers who began to equate consumption with choice. How then can the life instinct be rekindled?

> *The life instinct can be rekindled only by really living life, and living life means deep participation in the life of the others that surround us. By choosing deep reparticipation with nature, by stewarding the many relationships that nurture life, we surround ourselves with a life-affirming environment.*

From dominion to stewardship

For Rifkin, if Americans could redirect their deeply held sense of personal responsibility from the more narrow goals of individual material aggrandisement to a more expansive commitment to advancing global ethics. From there they might yet be able to remake the American Dream. Barack Obama perhaps symbolizes such.

For most of Christian history, the concept of dominion has been used to justify the ruthless detachment from and exploitation of the natural world. Now, a new generation of religious scholars and a growing number of believers are beginning to redefine the meaning of 'dominion'. They argue that since God created the heavens and earth, all of his creation is imbued with intrinsic value. God also gave purpose and order to his creation. Therefore, when human beings attempt to undermine the intrinsic value of nature, or manipulate and redirect its purpose and order to suit their own self-interests, they are acting in rebellion against God himself. The idea of 'dominion' is being redefined to mean 'stewardship'. Human beings are to serve as God's caretakers here on earth, ultimately promoting sustainable abundance.

15.3 Western Reformative Emergence: Sustainable Abundance

15.3.1 THE PLACE OF MONEY IN THE HUMAN PSYCHE

A multifaceted perspective

Bernard Lietaer has a unique multifaceted perspective on the past, present and future of economics and money.[8] Such perspective arose out of the depth and breadth of his financial experience. In effect, he developed the first models of global currency management for multinational corporations. Subsequently he has consulted with developing countries on four different continents about improving hard currency earnings. His academic history includes a Professorship of International Finance at the University of Louvain in Belgium. Then, for five years he was head of the Organization and Planning Department at the Central Bank of Belgium, where he was President of the Electronic Payment System. Finally, he served as general manager and currency fund manager of the most successful offshore currency fund of his time. All these took place during his early adulthood.

In midlife and maturity, Lietaer, in the course of realizing himself, has turned to transforming the functioning of money, in theory and also in practice. As we shall see, he thereby linked an immature 'yang' attitude towards money with a more mature 'yin-yang' one. In this process, he has been influenced by the 'east' and the 'south', most particular by Chinese philosophy and Jungian psychology. As such, he has reached back into ancient civilisations, historically, and into our 'collective unconscious' archetypally. From the outset, *money is conceived of by him as a cultural and social artefact rather than as merely an economic and financial mechanism*. We start out, then, with Lietaer's root imagery, drawing upon 'the soul of money'.

Archetypal origins and psychological destinations of money

Lietaer describes in his forthcoming book entitled *The Soul of Money*[9] how money systems, from their prehistoric origins onward, were attributed primarily to the Great Mother archetype. As western societies were characterized by a systematic repression of this archetype they developed financial systems that embodied what he describes as the 'shadows', or repressed parts, of that archetype, reflected in effect in 'elite globalization'. These shadows turned out to be none other than the collective emotions of *greed and fear of scarcity*. All professional operators, brokers, fund managers, and financial experts will confirm, according to Lietaer, that financial markets are primarily driven by these two collective emotions.

Greed and fear of scarcity are therefore not an indelible reflection of human nature, as is explicitly assumed in classical and neo-liberal economic theory. Instead, the current money system itself, by providing a systematic incentive to save in the form of money, is constantly creating and reinforcing those two shadow emotions. The real issue, then, is the monopoly accorded to this type of contemporary currency, not leaving any choice in the medium of exchange to be used, regardless of the purposes of the transactions and the relationships involved.

Masculine and feminine money

Lietaer's claim is that *significantly different money systems manifest themselves, depending on whether the feminine is honoured in society or not.* He can of course only verify such a hypothesis in societies that have advanced at least to the point of having developed the concept of money in the first place. But in classifying such 'advanced' societies according to whether they repress the feminine or honour it, suddenly an intriguing pattern in money systems emerges for him:

- Whenever the feminine archetype has been repressed, as has been the case in almost all of western history, a monopoly of currencies that play simultaneously the role of medium of exchange and of store of value tends to emerge. They could be called *patriarchal 'yang' currencies.*
- When the feminine has been honoured in an 'advanced' civilization, *complementary monetary systems* have appeared, and one of these currencies invariably had an unusual feature that actively discouraged the accumulation of wealth in the form of that currency. In short, this latter currency operated as a pure means of payment and exchange, and was not used as a store of value. These he defines as matriarchal 'yin' currencies.

Money is one of those cultural forces that has remained mostly invisible to the conscious 'western' mind. It is therefore to a civilization as the DNA code is to a species. It replicates structures and behaviour patterns that remain active across time and space for generations. We now turn, with Lietaer, to sustainable abundance.

15.3.2 FROM ECONOMICS TO ECOSOPHY

Our traditional bank-debt national money, which underlies conventional financial management, has, according to Lietaer, been designed from a monopoly of legitimacy for a Yang perspective. Until now, independently of whether one is a man or a woman, a 'macho' way of thinking has been needed to succeed in business and economic life. *Reaching what he terms 'sustainable abundance' is going to require giving equal weight to a feminine perspective on money systems and economics. It is not that the male perspective is 'wrong' in itself. On the contrary, it is an indispensable ingredient. But problems arise when it wants to impose a monopoly on legitimately interpreting and directing human activity. In fact the combined concepts of 'finance' and 'economics', for him, are ripe for transformation.*

For Lietaer then 'ecosophy' is about how to live wisely together. Such ecosophy recognizes that our *monetary, business, economic and political constructs interact with and affect our sociological, psychological and ecological constructs* and, as a result, our collective presence on the planet. Such a global mind-shift, for Lietaer and other kindred spirits, involves three overlapping waves:

1. *Value Shift Wave:* a value shift wave from modernist to integrative;
2. *Information Wave:* an information wave, enabling unprecedented access to knowledge for vast numbers of people;

3. *Money Wave:* and most particularly in this case here, though least evident in the world at large, a money wave, whereby new money systems are being conceived of, and to a small but significant degree adopted, complementing the old ones.

For Lietaer, the old scarce national currencies had never been designed to support an explosion of creativity. However, it is *only by liberating the extraordinary potential of human creativity of all humans rather than of a small minority, that there is any hope for Planet Earth.* Less than 30 per cent of the world's population has full-time jobs. This could free the vast majority to dedicate themselves to the 'work' they feel most passionate about, that is if we were able to reconfigure our economic system. From today's perspective it looks as if our species was asked to engage in a race blindfolded with feet and hands bound. Our blindness is caused by the disconnect between economy and society, between economic trade and social reciprocity.

15.3.3 TOWARDS THE 'YIN AND YANG ECONOMY'

Financial and social capital

The fact is there is enough work to be done for everyone in our community to be kept busy for the rest of his or her life. So what can we do to redress the current situation, where we have, at least in the developing world, mass unemployment? The answer, Lietaer suggests, is to *create complementary currencies designed to fulfil social functions that the national currency cannot or does not fulfil, so that one currency would produce financial capital, and the other social capital.* They can then operate in symbiosis with each other.

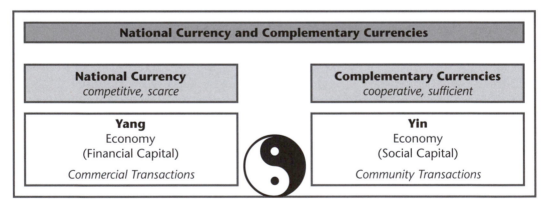

Ultimately, Lietaer proposes that we create a 'four level' monetary system.

15.3.4 A FOUR LEVEL MONETARY OPERATION

The four level operation of the monetary system in 2020 could be:

*   a global reference currency;
*   three main multinational currencies;
*   some national currencies;
*   local complementary currencies.

What then does this involve?

- A *Global Reference Currency* evolving through the emergence of barter, which has been around since the dawn of mankind, into a major industry today. In this regard, two significant trade organizations (International Reciprocal Trade Association – IRTA, and the Corporate Barter Council – CBC) are notable examples. Lietaer envisages over the next 20 years the convergence of the barter and cyber economies.
- *Multinational Currencies*, with the advent of the Euro are likely to build up irresistible pressure to create a Yen Yuan Asian Currency zone, and finally a NAFTA American/Canadian/Mexican dollar.
- *National Currencies* will continue to play an important part, especially for countries that are not members of multinational currency zones, such as Switzerland, but they will no longer be a monopoly.
- *Community Currencies* finally are proliferating today. Indeed, already in the 1930s, in Western Europe and North America, as well as in Mexico, literally thousands of communities started their own currency systems in the aftermath of depression and hyperinflation, though the central governments ultimately snuffed out all but one, the WIR System in Switzerland. In more recent years there has been a resurgence of such.
- That having been said they pale into insignificance when compared to the power and influence of the international financial markets, the WTO, IMF and World Bank. We now turn to the navigation of financial transformation, via natural capitalism, which offers a new conceptual approach towards a restorative economy.

15.4 Western Normative Navigation: Restorative Economy

15.4.1 THE NEXT INDUSTRIAL REVOLUTION

Capital stocks: financial to human

Paul Hawken, together with Amory and L. Hunter Lovins (economist, sociologist and physicist in turn) are seasoned environmental campaigners in America. They have reconceptualized business in an ecological light, with a view to promoting sustainable development. For Ben-Aharon, they are part of an alternative, ecologically based 'western' orientation to life and to 'self making'. *What is required, Hawken suggests, is the diligence to understand when and where western style markets are dysfunctional and misapplied, and to choose the correct targeted actions to help them operate more holistically while retaining their pragmatic vigour and efficiency.*

Hawken and his colleagues[10] thereby seek to ensure that what for them are four distinct capital stockholdings – financial and manufactured, natural and human – are as prudently stewarded as money is by the corporate finance director. This would lead to what we term, not a purely financially oriented free market, but ultimately a more holistically based market integration of all of the capital stockholdings, as outlined above. The next industrial revolution after the digital revolution, for Hawken and the Lovins's, has a particular structural, as well as processal, base to it. Within it, four kinds of 'capital stock' (structural) would be recognized, each one manifesting itself in four types of interconnected 'capital flows' (processal). These capital stocks are constituted of natural and human, as well as manufactured and financial capital. The flow forms enable companies and communities to engage in sustainable development. This means technically productive, biologically integrative, economically facilitative and ecologically restorative development.

Capital flows: productive to restorative

Enhancing productivity
Hawken believes, as far as the flow of capital is concerned, that *radically increased resource productivity is required to 'kick-start' natural capitalism.* Indeed, using resources more effectively has three major benefits: it slows resource depletion at one end of the value chain, lowers pollution at the other end and provides a basis for increasing worldwide employment.

Promoting bio-mimicry
Reducing the wasteful throughput of materials – thereby eliminating the very idea of waste – can be accomplished by redesigning industrial or utility-based systems along biological lines. This serves to change the nature of industrial processes and materials, enabling the newly sustainable company to maintain and develop a constant use of materials in continuous closed circles. A knowledge creating ecology then needs to be uncovered and promoted, so as to recast knowledge management in a contemporary, biodynamic light. In fact Interface Carpets in America, and its CEO Ray Anderson, are a notable example of such.

Service and flow
In calling for a fundamental change in the link between production and consumption, Hawken advocates a third *shift from an economy of goods and purchases to one of service and flow.* This entails a new perception of value, a shift from the acquisition of goods to the purchase of services, whereby quality, utility and performance is continually sought to promote natural and social well-being.

Restorative economics
Finally, a reversal of worldwide planetary destruction is required, through *reinvestments in sustaining, restoring and expanding stocks of natural and social capital.* As a result the biosphere will be able to produce more abundant ecosystem services and natural resources.

15.4.2 TOWARDS AN INTEGRAL PERSPECTIVE ON CAPITAL

Hawken's concept of natural stock comes close to a Four World perspective. In his capital stocks he distinguishes between a natural (southern), human (eastern), manufactured (northern), as well as financial (western) form of capital. His four capital flows have a strong emphasis on our south (biologically integrative and ecologically restorative), and further include a northern (technically productive) and a western perspective (economically facilitative). The one dimension, which is underrepresented, again, is the cultural and spiritual one – in our terms, the east. It is exactly this gap, which one of our doctoral students, Sam Rima from Bethel University in the USA, is currently trying to close, in his research on spiritual capital.[11] Linking Sam Rima's and Paul Hawken's work with our Four Worlds, an integral perspective on capital and finance suggests a balanced interaction between natural capital (south), human/spiritual capital (east), manufactured/intellectual capital (north) as well as financial capital (see Figure 15.2).

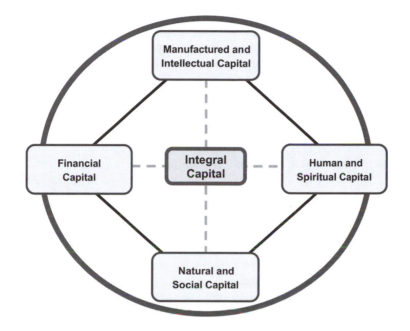

Figure 15.2 A Four World perspective on capital – towards integral capital

In fact this notion of spiritual capital has since been evolved into a prospectively new economic and financial discipline, which Sam Rima has termed *Pneumenomics*, based on the ancient Greek *Pneuma* (spirit, life, breath) and *Nomics* (economics). Such a new form of finance economics, rooted in the life and spirit of different cultures and societies, represents an evolved 'western' economic form.

We now turn in this evolved 'western' case to Dee Hock's Visa. It is important for us to stress, though, that Visa today is not what it was, in terms of a self-organizing system, two decades ago. That is also why its founder Dee Hock retired from the company and community he created. Our focus then is on that original creation and the early days of its development.

15.5 Western Transformative Effect: Self-Organization and the Case of Visa in the USA

15.5.1 VISA AND THE BIRTH OF THE CHAORDIC AGE

On Visa

Visa today is viewed as a hugely successful commercial venture, reaching, through its renowned credit card, across the banking sector and the whole world. What is not generally known is that its origins are very particular, in fact they are unique.

On Dee Hock and the redefinition of chaos and order

Dee Hock, the founder of Visa Card, would be another American who Steiner or Ben-Aharon would recognize, together with Hawken and the Lovins, as embodiments of the 'ecologically laden western stream'. In 1984 he retired from the business he created to tend the land. Thereafter he formed the *'Chaordic Alliance'* to promote his new business philosophy. His whole approach to enterprise and to finance was inspired by principles of life and of self-organization.[12]

His Chaordic Alliance has been established to address some fundamental questions. The core questions to which he returns to again and again are:

- Why are organizations everywhere, whether political, commercial or social, increasingly unable to manage their affairs?
- Why are individuals, everywhere, increasingly in conflict with and alienated from the organizations of which they are part?
- Why are society and the biosphere increasingly in disarray?

But let's listen to Dee Hock in his own words.

A philosophy of interconnectedness

'The whole thing behind the creation of Visa has not been about banks or merchants or credit or cardholders. It's not been about data or information or computers. It was about connections. It was about the dissolution of the notion of boundaries between separate, connected things. It was about relationships and growth; about all things growing from one another, and everything growing from some indefinable essence that is; about all things being inseparably interrelated. Imbued with that spirit I found myself, in the early seventies, taking the lead in launching a new banking venture, ostensibly to create a new type of credit card, although the way it eventually turned out was very different from what had been anticipated. What started out as closely held by a few, major banks, turned into a much more open system.'

Acting together for a common purpose

'However, no single bank could accomplish what was required. No hierarchical stock corporation could do it. No nation-state could do it. In fact no existing organization as yet conceived of could do it. It would *require a transcendental organization, linking together in wholly new ways an unimaginable complex of diverse institutions.*

My shift in organizational perception, meanwhile, was profound. I knew that no bank could create the world's premier system for the exchange of value, no nation-state, and no organization I could think of. I therefore wondered what if a fraction of the financial resource of all the financial institutions in the world, and a fraction of the ingenuity of all the people who worked there, could be applied jointly? But how might this occur, I wondered? So I came up with some organizational principles:

* it should be equitably owned by all participants
* participants should have equitable rights and obligations
* it should be open to all qualified participants
* power, function and resources should be distributed to the maximum
* authority should be equitable and distributive
* no participant should lose out to any new concept of organization
* to the maximum degree possible, everything should be voluntary
* it should induce, not compel change
* it should be infinitely malleable yet extremely durable

No one had thought that banks in America would voluntarily surrender a portion of their autonomy and act together for a common purpose. No one believed that such a horizontal grouping of competitors could exist within the spirit and constraint of anti-trust laws. And no one dreamed the emerging ideas would bring together in common ownership and enterprise people and institutions of every race, language, custom and culture – every economic, legal, philosophical and religious persuasion in the world. Each time that I fell into despair and wanted to give up in the face of the enormity of this enterprise – and it happed often – something softly whispered "not now". For there was an inexpressible, compelling sense that in some profound way, existence would lose its meaning if I didn't persist.' If only Hock had been able to persist in today's crisis laden financial world.

15.5.2 FROM BIRTH TO GROWTH

Quasi-governmental, quasi-for-profit, quasi-not-for-profit

'In 1968 the Visa community was no more than a set of beliefs and a vague concept. In 1970 it was born. Thirty years later its products are created by 22,000 owner-member financial institutions and accepted at 15 million merchant locations in more than 200 countries. Three quarters of a billion people use Visa products to make 14 billion transactions producing annual income of US$1.25 trillion – the single largest block of consumer purchasing power in the global economy.

Visa was effectively a quasi-governmental, quasi-for-profit, quasi-not-for-profit, quasi-consulting, quasi-franchising, quasi-educational, quasi-social, quasi-commercial, quasi-political alliance. The financial institutions that created its products were, at one and the same time, its owners, its members, its suppliers, its customers. Visa spawned new industries and new ventures in tens of thousands, creating conditions by which members can connect with one another without permission or limitation. Since it had no interest in controlling or owning technology or participants, the unlimited ingenuity and creativity of thousands of external entities was freely brought in to bear on the needs and opportunities of the system. The entirety, like millions of other chaordic organizations, including those we call body, brain, forest, ocean and biosphere, was largely self-regulating. A staff of fewer than 500, scattered across more than a dozen countries on four continents, coordinated this system as it skyrocketed past a hundred billion dollars providing product and systems development, global advertising and electronic communication systems.'

An archetype from which to learn

'Judged by orthodox measures of objective measurement – growth, size, profit, market share and volume – Visa has been a phenomenal success. By the standards, though, of what Visa might have become, and what it ought to be for, I feel a strong sense of failure. As a small staff with limited resources, my team and I faced incredible industry problems and insatiable demands on their time. Legal depositions were long and wearing, causing stress and depression. For more than a decade, until I left the company I had founded, in 1984, I was working in the midst of ever increasing complexity. At the end, I was reporting to more than 100 directors from dozens of countries comprising six boards, meeting on nearly every continent as the sales volume rocketed past one hundred billion dollars, with virtual certainty it would increase eightfold each decade, well into the next century. But such success was only part of the story. In spite of my pride in all that Visa demonstrated about the power of a chaordic concept of organization I do not now believe that Visa is a concept to emulate. It is merely an archetype to learn from and improve upon.'

15.6 Conclusion: Towards Sustainable Development

15.6.1 THE WEST OVERCOMES THE REST

Ultimately then for Hock and for Visa, what we have is a hugely imbalanced organization, not in the way it was designed, but in the way it turned out. It is not surprising that Hock retired to his new farm in the prime of his midlife. For Visa started out by being deeply influenced by natural principles of self-organization. But, as Hock intimated, there was a paradox: the more economically successful Visa became, the more that its other functions fell away. This has been explained in his more recent book *From One to Many*.[13] In other words, *Visa's huge success as a private enterprise over the course of time served to inhibit its development as a public and civic enterprise, which is where it started*.

Moreover, despite the chaordic principles that Hock followed from the outset, Visa remained and developed as a financial facility rather than as a natural one. Moreover, notwithstanding Hock's amazing personal capabilities and the incredible financial scope of Visa's growing operations, it never evolved as a societal force, building creatively on its initially integral quasi-governmental, quasi-for-profit, quasi-not-for-profit, quasi-consulting, quasi-franchising, quasi-educational, quasi-social, quasi-commercial, quasi-political alliance nature and scope. In our terms, and in Visa's case, the west overcame the rest rather than vice versa.

In other words, the life instinct from which Visa initially emerged served to realize sustainable abundance in the narrow sense, as a hugely successful private enterprise, but not as an integrated – public and private, civic and animate – one. The fact of the matter is that a singularly private enterprise without such enhancement, as it grows, will face great difficulties, if not impossibilities in its prospectively sustainable development.

15.6.2 TOWARDS AN INTEGRATED ENTERPRISE AND SOCIETY

What does that all mean in the final analysis? For us, the ultimate resolution to the credit crunch or to peak oil is not to regulate the banks more tightly or to seek new sources of renewable energy. These, for us, are mere economic and technological fixes, which fail to address the natural and cultural blindspots, or indeed the political and economic power imbalances, which are leading the world astray. A Transformation (of) Management, for us then, is required that starts from nature and culture and, building upon such, evolves technologically and economically.

What this involves from a micro perspective is that such an enterprise has integrated its core functioning at a new level, as we have demonstrated in the previous four chapters. Such an integral enterprise would then have an authentic public and private, civic and animate dimension, which we will outline in the final part of this book. Such an integral enterprise would resurrect the *quasi* cause that Visa, post Dee Hock, left behind. In that respect, structurally, the Sekems and Broads (see Chapter 16) of this world would become the integral norm. In contrast, the private enterprises Microsoft and the Quantum Fund, for example, alongside the civic-minded Bill Gates and George Soros would be the disintegrated exceptions. At the same time, functionally, community building would triumph over marketing, conscious evolution over human resources, knowledge creation over operations, and sustainable development over finance. For us, long term, this is the way to overcome the credit crunch.

For all of this to materialize, we need to respect the Four Worlds, north and south, east and west, in a concerted way that has never been done before, thereby making the case for a Transformation (of) Management.

15.6.3 CONCLUDING THE WESTERN GENE-IUS

In a concluding review of this chapter, we retrace once more the four core steps of the western GENE-ius, serving to transform the western function:

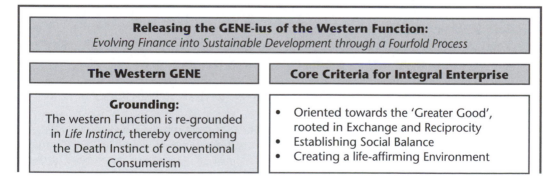

Emerging: From there a new perspective on *Sustainable Abundance* emerges, overcoming the conventional Concept of Scarcity	• Revisiting Money as a cultural and social Artefact, as well as a economic and financial Mechanism • From immature Yang-Currencies to mature Yin-Yang Currencies • From Economics to Ecosophy
Navigating: Such gives rise to a new financial and economic Framework for the Enterprise to navigate in, called *Restorative Economy*	• Radically increased Resource-Productivity • Redesigning Processes along biological Lines • Shift from Economy of Goods and Purchase towards one of Service and Flow • Investments in sustaining, restoring and expanding stocks of natural and social capital • Towards Integral Capital
Effecting: Finally, this Function becomes fully effective through a wide Degree of *Self-Organization*	• Rooted in chaordic Principles • Building a 'transcendental Organization' • From Institution to Alliance • Acting together for common Purpose, based on common Ownership

The trajectory from life instinct, to sustainable abundance, onto restorative economy to self-organization enables the Integral Enterprise not only to evolve its finance function into sustainable development, in narrow financial terms. Such an evolution, moreover, has led the western function to promote sustainability and balance equally on a natural and communal (southern), cultural and spiritual (eastern), technological and political, as well as on a financial level. Balance on a higher level is re-established; finance becomes a force for community development and against inequality in wealth distribution, which is a major source of conflict in our day and time.

Such a transformation of finance reconnects the evolved western function with all other organizational functions, which by now have been reintegrated. Sustainable development (west) then becomes an immediate driver of community development, as our late friend and colleague, the development economist Norman Reynolds, has successfully demonstrated with his People's Agenda in Southern Africa. That may serve as a concluding theoretical and practical illustration for the ongoing, spiralling nature of the GENE-cycle, thereby, renewing self, organization, community and society.

15.6.4 CONCLUDING THE TRANSFORMATION OF THE FUNCTIONS

We now conclude the functional transformation, completing the fourth and final element in building the Integral Enterprise. As we have introduced a circular process, the journey, that we have introduced, is a continuous one. This fourth step in the cycle, the western effect of our GENE, needs to fully reconnect to the grounds of self, organization and society. From there the GENE-cycle starts anew.

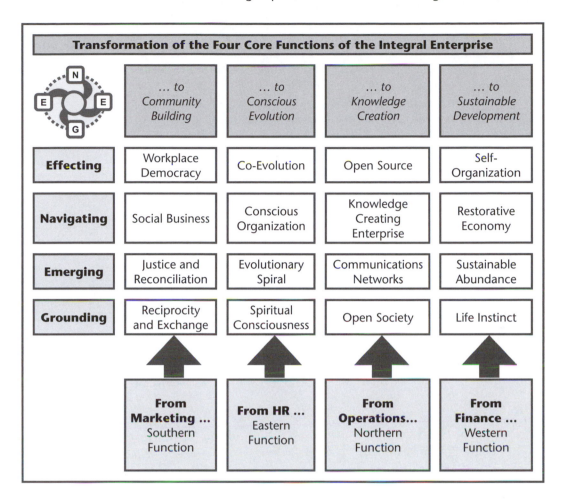

Transformation of the Four Core Functions of the Integral Enterprise

	... to Community Building	... to Conscious Evolution	... to Knowledge Creation	... to Sustainable Development
Effecting	Workplace Democracy	Co-Evolution	Open Source	Self-Organization
Navigating	Social Business	Conscious Organization	Knowledge Creating Enterprise	Restorative Economy
Emerging	Justice and Reconciliation	Evolutionary Spiral	Communications Networks	Sustainable Abundance
Grounding	Reciprocity and Exchange	Spiritual Consciousness	Open Society	Life Instinct
	From Marketing ... Southern Function	**From HR ...** Eastern Function	**From Operations...** Northern Function	**From Finance ...** Western Function

The functional transformation is indeed a very difficult task: one, which requires much further development in the future. In fact we encourage you to take a further transformative journey, together with us, to advance the theory and practice of the four transpersonal functions, to promote the ongoing transformation of management.

References

1. Heron, J. (1997). *Co-operative Inquiry*. London: Sage.
2. Levinson, D. (1979). *Seasons of Man's Life*. New York: Knopf.
3. Kauffman, S. (1993). *The Origins of Order*. Oxford: Oxford University Press.
4. Prigogine, I. (1997). *The End of Certainty*. New York: Free Press.
5. Stacey, R. (1993). *Strategic Management and Organizational Dynamics*. London: Pitman.
6. Ben-Aharon, J. (2002). *America's Global Responsibility*. Herndon: Lindisfarne.
7. Rifkin, J. (2004). *The European Dream*. Harmondsworth: Penguin Group.
8. Lietaer, B. (2001). *The Future of Money*. London: Century.
9. Lietaer, B. (Forthcoming). *The Soul of Money*.

10. Hawken, P. et al. (2000). *Natural Capitalism: Creating the Next Industrial Revolution*. London: Earth Scan.
11. Rima, S. (forthcoming). *Towards Pneumenomics: Spiritual Capital as a Catalyst for Holistic Relational Economics*. Dissertation. Buckingham: Buckingham University.
12. Hock, D. (2002). *Birth of the Chaordic Age*. San Francisco: Berrett-Koehler.
13. Hock, D. (2006). *From One to Many*. San Francisco: Berrett-Koehler.

Transforming CSR
into Society Building

Core Theme within Transformation Management:
**Applying all Four Fundamentals
of Transformation Management
thereby Re-integrating Enterprise and Society**

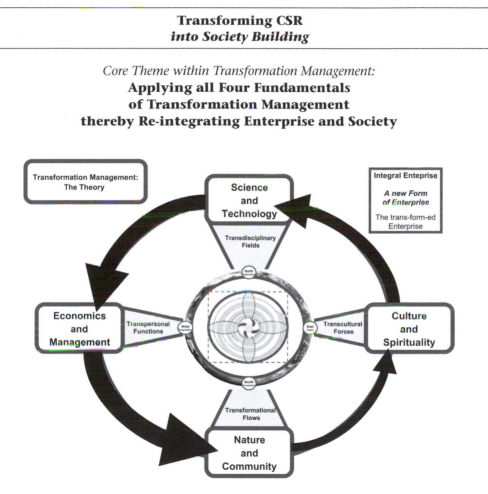

Transforming CSR
into Society Building

Core Outcome for the Integral Enterprise:
1. **Building a Resilient, Developing, Innovative and Efficient Organization**
2. **Fully Releasing Natural, Cultural, Scientific and Managerial GENE-ius**
3. **Becoming a Society Builder**

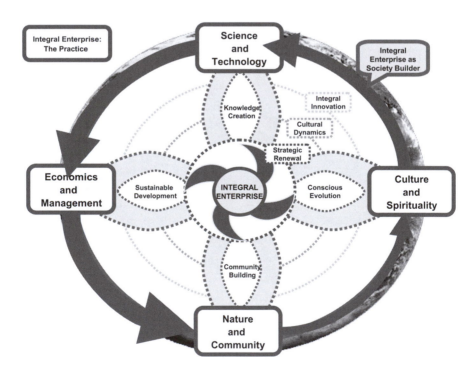

16 *Enterprise and Transformation*

Integral Theory and Practice

16.1 Summing up: The Integral Enterprise in Theory

16.1.1 THE TRANSFORMATION MANAGEMENT JOURNEY TOWARDS THE INTEGRAL ENTERPRISE

In the transformational journey we have undertaken in this book, we have now, finally, come full cycle.

From the very outset we have purposefully talked about transformation, not about change. We argued that mere change is not enough. We rather need to work towards a new organizational and societal form, within a specific cultural and communal context, where the formerly fragmented perspective of organization, self and society is altogether overcome.

A merely economic perspective on organizations and even on societies is still by and large the norm. All too often, for example, there is a tendency to use the terms economy and society even as equivalent terms, in which case we overlook the other equally important aspects of society, which are its environment (nature), its culture (civic sector), it public (political) sector and, of course, its economic (private) contexts. This general oversight is a clear expression of how imbalanced we have become in defining ourselves, our organizations and societies in purely economic terms.

In the beginning and throughout this book we have fundamentally challenged the prevailing monocultural (the west dominates), monodisciplinary (economics is key) and monosectoral (private sector leads) orientation of the current theory and practice of management, leadership and enterprise.

We have demonstrated the degree to which we suffer from a fragmented perspective upon the world as a whole, where the west, at least in the past few hundred years, has invariably taken the lead. A totally unbalanced globalization has been the result, dominated mainly by the west and primarily by economics as the result. And we have become painfully aware, especially today, how we are missing out in environmental, cultural and socio-political respects. Huntington's *Clash of Civilisations* is seemingly only one of the scenarios that seems to have been born out. It is high time that we develop a more integrated perspective, and we have shown here that it is not merely conceptual beauty that is driving us, but that there are farsighted organizations all over the world, that lead the way along such an integral path, and, by doing this, deliver extraordinary results.

We have, hence, presented in this book a number of case studies of organizations, such as Visa (USA), Linux (Finland), Canon (Japan), Cashbuild (South Africa) and Grameen (Bangladesh), and latterly – as will be cited in our epilogue – Virgin (UK) among others Two more case stories, Sekem (Egypt) and Broad Air Conditioning (China) follow in this final chapter.

A new integral, sustainable enterprise design is desperately needed. A design of an enterprise, that is sustainably lodged in its society; an enterprise, that is not only focusing on its own economic progress, but also on its ecological, cultural, social and public impacts; an enterprise that is thereby ultimately contributing to the evolution of community and society as a whole. But we need to go even further. Even more important, a new educational approach is required, which embodies, teaches and evolves the new knowledge base that organizations and the people who run them, need. And that knowledge base, overall, and as we indicate in the epilogue to follow, must transcend the capitalist cul-de-sac in which current forms of enterprise are lodged. In this book we have started out to lay the foundation for such a new micro discipline. We called it Transformation Management, ultimately aiming to transcend the prevailing management education.

The objective of Transformation Management is to enable organizations to build an Integral Enterprise. It is integral because it has developed the capacity to keep a dynamic balance between the major constituencies of a living social organism: nature and community, culture and spirituality, science and technology, as well as economics and management.

In other words, an Integral Enterprise is primarily rooted in a specific nature and community and equally in the cultural context within which it is active. Through our making nature and community, culture and spirituality the starting point, we fundamentally change the perspective on enterprise design. We have illustrated in this book that a deep understanding of the transformational flows underlying nature and community, as well as of the cultural dynamics (or transcultural forces) underlying culture and spirituality, constitutes the basis of an organization that is not only to be sustainable on a long-term base, but is to fully release its own gene-ius. It is like the individuation of the self: if you do not know your own nature, if you are not related to your own inner world as well as to those human beings that surround you (nature and community), if you are not aware of your deepest value and belief system (culture and spirituality), you can not consciously evolve.

In Transformation Management, we bring nature and culture back to the forefront of the interdependent development of self, organization and society, and from there progress to build a fundamentally new knowledge basis of the enterprise (science and technology). In touch with its own nature and culture, the enterprise can now creatively engage in knowledge creation and innovation. Through these three steps, we have now built a new foundation for transformative action; now the pragmatic west, enriched and empowered by the south, east and north, can pursue its now integral economic course.

If the enterprise engages in the full cycle of the Four Worlds, it can release its full gene-ius; or, in other words, and borrowing a term from the renowned researcher on creativity Mihaly Csikszentmihaly,[1] the enterprise is now 'in flow'. Furthermore, with self, organization and society now aligned, it is also 'in tune' with society and its needs. We now have a new approach towards business in society, specifically, and of a particular enterprise in a specific society, generally. Indeed, as we have illustrated again and again, Transformation Management as a discipline is equally relevant for organizations from all sectors of society. Following the four fundamentals of Transformation Management, we have now worked ourselves progressively through:

1. Nature and Community and the underlying Transformational Flows.
2. Culture and Spirituality and the underlying Transcultural Forces.
3. Science and Technology and the underlying Transdisciplinary Fields.
4. Economics and Management and the underlying Transpersonal Functions.

In this concluding chapter, we shall retrace our steps once more, providing you with a final overview on the journey. We then introduce the cases of two enterprises that have come a long way towards building an Integral Enterprise: Sekem in Egypt and Broad Air Conditioning in China. In the final part of this chapter we offer suggestions on how you, your organization and your community can take the journey of building an Integral Enterprise actively forward.

16.1.2 TOWARDS STRATEGIC RENEWAL: GROUNDING IN NATURE AND COMMUNITY

We started our transformational journey by learning from nature's transformational principles. Thereby we located our individual, organizational and societal being in nature and community. As such the starting point, as per conventional business administration, is not reflected in 'strategic doing', but in 'being vital'. In such a new 'natural' and 'communal' light, the conventional wisdom on organizational strategy got fundamentally transformed. By grounding the enterprise in nature (and its transformational principles) as well as in community, the purpose of the organization and its subsequent strategy became closely aligned with a specific nature and community. Conventional strategy was turned into strategic renewal. Such strategic renewal is not linear, as most organizational strategies are conceived of and executed, but circular, if not also spiralling. The circular and spiralling rhythm we introduced in this chapter was the GENE, which could be described as the inner transformational force of the organization. Embracing such a fourfold rhythm of self-renewal, from southern grounding, to eastern emergence, onto northern navigation and to western effect, is key for the sustainable evolution of the enterprise. The continuous and circular as well as spiralling return to its southern grounds enables the organization to align its strategic orientation with the real needs of the community and society in which it is lodged. This is further enhanced by simultaneously addressing the transformational flows of self, organization and society, whereby the Integral Enterprise serves as bridge between individual and community. While the following table provides a distilled overview of the first fundamental of Transformation Management, Figure 16.1 illustrates visually this initial part of the transformational journey.

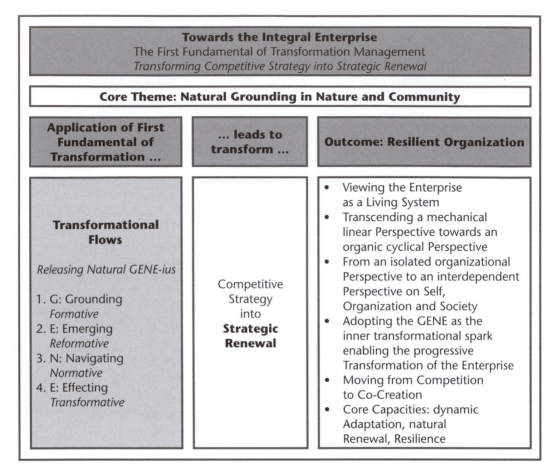

Towards the Integral Enterprise
The First Fundamental of Transformation Management
Transforming Competitive Strategy into Strategic Renewal

Core Theme: Natural Grounding in Nature and Community

Application of First Fundamental of Transformation ...	**... leads to transform ...**	**Outcome: Resilient Organization**
Transformational Flows *Releasing Natural GENE-ius* 1. G: Grounding *Formative* 2. E: Emerging *Reformative* 3. N: Navigating *Normative* 4. E: Effecting *Transformative*	Competitive Strategy into **Strategic Renewal**	• Viewing the Enterprise as a Living System • Transcending a mechanical linear Perspective towards an organic cyclical Perspective • From an isolated organizational Perspective to an interdependent Perspective on Self, Organization and Society • Adopting the GENE as the inner transformational spark enabling the progressive Transformation of the Enterprise • Moving from Competition to Co-Creation • Core Capacities: dynamic Adaptation, natural Renewal, Resilience

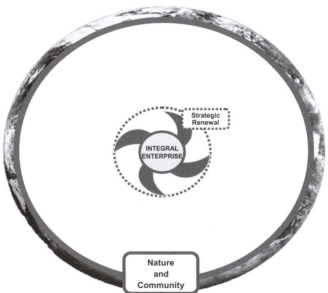

Figure 16.1 First fundamental – strategic renewal

16.1.3 TOWARDS CULTURAL DYNAMICS: EMERGENCE THROUGH CULTURE AND SPIRITUALITY

We continue our transformational journey by drawing on our own indigenous culture, as well as the 'exogenous' culture of a relevant other. Thereby we promote self, organizational and societal renewal. As such the starting point, as per conventional business administration, is not reflected in 'organizational behaviour', or even 'corporate culture', but in 'cultural fusion'. In such a new kind of 'local' and 'global' light, the conventional wisdom on organizational behaviour got fundamentally transformed. Conventional organizational activity was turned into transcultural interactivity. Embracing such a fourfold rhythm of self-renewal, from southern humanism, to eastern holism, onto northern rationalism and to western pragmatism, is a keynote of authenticity. While the following table provides a distilled overview of the second, transcultural fundamental of Transformation Management, Figure 16.2 illustrates this part of the transformational journey.

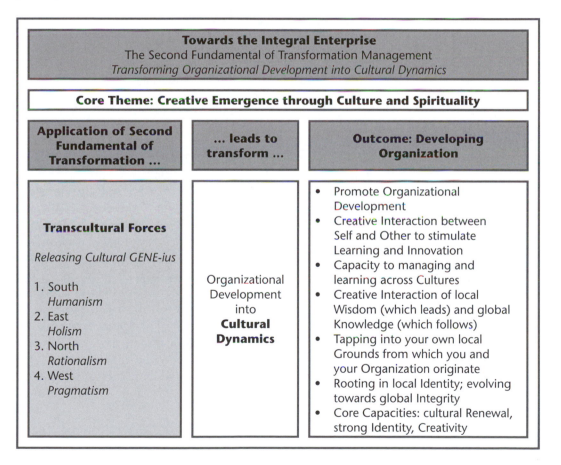

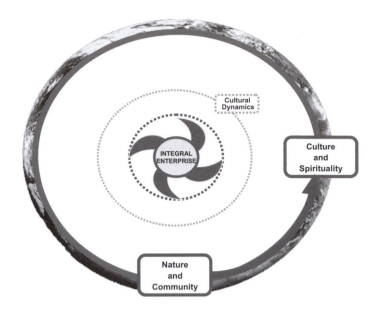

Figure 16.2 Second fundamental – cultural dynamics

16.1.4 TOWARDS INTEGRAL INNOVATION: NAVIGATION THROUGH SCIENCE AND TECHNOLOGY

We continue our transformational journey, building on nature and culture, by now focusing on science and technology, in our case from a 'social' perspective. Thereby we turn research methodology into a means of Integral Innovation, building up from fundamental research towards transformative action. As such the starting point, as per conventional research method, is not reflected in 'survey methods', or even 'empiricism', but in a combination of research paths: relational, renewal, reason and realization, via a social foundation and emancipation: 'cultural fusion'. By drawing upon economics and anthropology, philosophy and history, sociology and psychology, political science and theology (our transdisplinary principles), we span the social sciences as a whole. Conventional individual research, moreover, is turned into organizational and communal innovation. While we, in this book, focus primarily on the social component of what we term 'Integral' Innovation, set in the context of the Integral Enterprise, such *Integral* Innovation is ultimately both technological and also social. While the following table provides a distilled overview of the third, transdisciplinary fundamental of Transformation Management, Figure 16.3 illustrates visually this third part of the transformational journey.

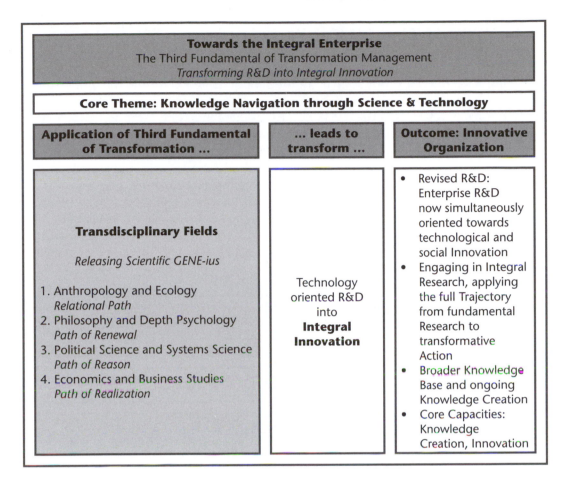

Figure 16.3 Third fundamental – integral innovation

16.1.5 TOWARDS TRANSFORMED FUNCTIONS: THE EFFECTIVE ENTERPRISE THROUGH ENHANCED ECONOMICS AND MANAGEMENT

We culminate our transformational journey, prior to establishing the fully-fledged Integral Enterprise, and indeed society, through our final fundamental, embodied in the transpersonal functions. On the one hand each of these functions is *transpersonal,* in that it accommodates self (individual), organization (enterprise) and society (community). On the other hand, each of these newly evolved functions, builds from the ground up, subsequently emerging, navigating and effecting, in the context of one particular entity (self, organization, society) or another. In that overall respect, marketing is transformed into community building; human resources into conscious evolution; operations into knowledge creation; finance into sustainable development. Moreover, whereas community building has specifically southern overtones, and conscious evolution eastern ones, knowledge creation has a northern ring to it, and sustainable development a western one (see Figure 16.4).

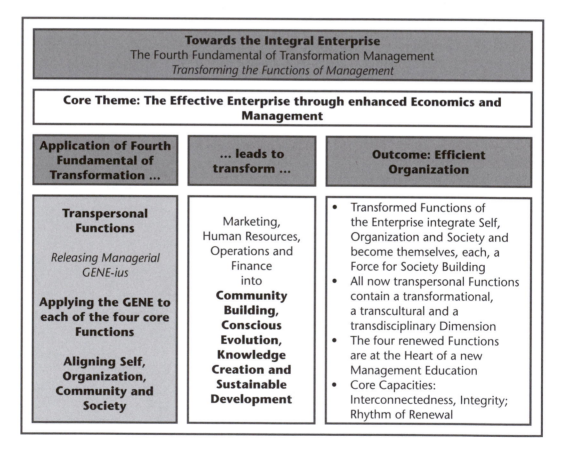

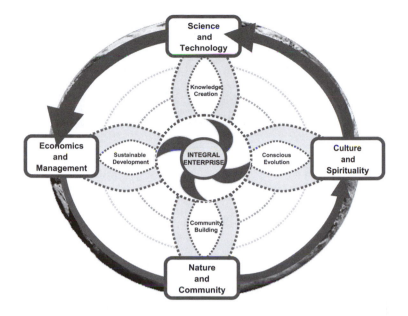

Figure 16.4 Fourth fundamental – transformed functions

16.1.6 TOWARDS SOCIETY BUILDING: THE INTEGRAL ENTERPRISE

The destination reached by the transformation journey, that is the actualization of the four fundamentals – transformational and transcultural, transdisciplinary and transpersonal – is the Integral Enterprise, set within an Integral Society. Such a fusion of public and private, civic and animate (environmental) enterprise is today the exception rather than the norm. We anticipate, over the course of this century, that it will become the norm rather than the exception that is if our world is to survive and prosper. Such enterprises are deeply embedded within society, and, by their very nature, society builders. There is no further need for a separate function called (corporate) social responsibility, as the very design of the Integral Enterprise makes the organization responsive to its societal, cultural and natural environment. We shall cite two prominent examples of such integrated enterprises in this chapter. However, and to the extent that such an enterprise serves to address the alleviation of poverty, the build up of open society, peaceful co-evolution between peoples, and the ultimate healing of the planet, a new kind of macro economy has to emerge, serving to unite the spirit of a particular place with the nature and scope of economic activity in general.

The Integral Enterprise Applying the Four Fundamentals of Transformation Management *Transforming CSR into Society Building*		
Application of Four Fundamentals of Transformation ...	**... leads to transform ...**	**Outcome: Integral Enterprise** *(Resilient, Developing, Innovative & Efficient Organization)*

Transformational Flows Releasing Natural GENE-ius
 	
Transcultural Forces Releasing Cultural GENE-ius
 	
Transdisciplinary Fields Releasing Innovation GENE-ius
 	
Transpersonal Functions Releasing Managerial GENE-ius
	Conventional Management, Leadership and Enterprise into
	Transformation Management
	
	* * * *
	
	Corporate Social Responsibility (CSR) into
	Society Building
		• Integral Enterprise is simultaneously a resilient, learning, innovative and effective Organization
		• Integral Enterprise fully embedded in Society, thereby acts as a Society Builder
		• Integral Enterprise holds dynamic Balance between:
		  – Nature and Community
		  – Culture and Spirituality
		  – Science and Technology
		  – Economics and Management
		
		• Thereby, Integral Enterprise is able to address burning Issues of Society and to contribute to:
		
		  – Healing the Planet
		  – Promoting Peaceful Co-Evolution
		  – Building an Open Society
		  – Alleviate Poverty
		
		• Doing so, the Integral Enterprise becomes a Social Innovator

In the process of becoming an Integral Enterprise, organizations, sooner or later, would need to start redefining the particular positions that the respective senior management hold. A title, like 'Head of Human Resources' simply does not make sense any more in such a transformed and integral organizational context. As each organization, according to its size, orientation, sector or cultural context, may be organized in a different way, there is, of course, no such thing as completely standardized title. However, at this stage, we would like to stimulate some reflection on how a newly integral organizational chart, may appear. In Figure 16.6 we give an intimation of such 'transformed' role descriptions. With this illustration we leave this conceptual summary of the Integral Enterprise and move on, to Egypt and China, towards integral practice.

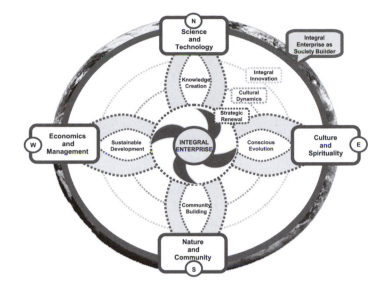

Figure 16.5 The Integral Enterprise – transforming CSR into society building

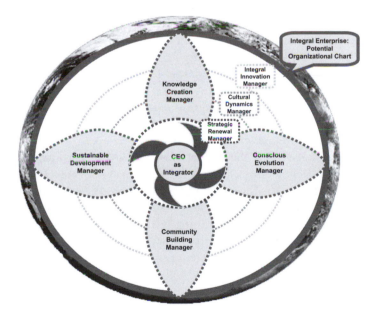

Figure 16.6 The Integral Enterprise – transformed positions

16.2 Looking Forward: The Integral Enterprise in Practice

16.2.1 SEKEM IN EGYPT

16.2.1.1 Sekem: an overview

We now turn to Sekem and its founder Ibrahim Abouleish, suitably based at the centre of our Four Worlds, in Egypt. Sekem was the first business enterprise to be awarded the prestigious Right Livelyhood Award, also called 'The Alternative Nobel Price'. Again, we will present this case primarily in Ibrahim Abouleish's own terms, as expressed in his book *Sekem – A Sustainable Community in the Desert*.[2]

Ibrahim Abouleish, having spent his childhood and youth in Egypt, pursued his doctoral studies in Austria, before taking up a senior research post at a pharmaceutical laboratory there. In his early forties, though, now married to an Austrian, and with two children, he felt the urge to return to his homeland, to make a contribution to his country in need.

16.2.1.2 Grounding of Sekem in nature and community

The birth of Sekem: cultivating the Egyptian desert
'After arriving in Egypt I went to see the Ministry of Agriculture, and told them I was looking for a patch of desert, which I wanted to cultivate using organic methods. I was shown a patch in Belbeis, where the quality of ground was very bad and water supply difficult, but I knew I wanted it. If biodynamic farming could thrive in this wasteland, then it would be possible to transfer this model to easier environments. So I bought the land and moved over, leaving my family behind in Cairo. Most of the time I was alone, with only now and then a Bedouin with goats wandering over. They could not understand my idea, but they saw it develop before their eyes.

All my experience showed me the importance of moral deeds as an example for people living primarily with their feelings. The Prophet says every one of you is a shepherd, and everyone is responsible for those under your protection. For those living with their feelings, a concrete step is to establish social forms. This starts with elementary principles: starting punctually, getting up and catching a bus. After I had positioned the first roads and plotted the fields, the next task was to drill two wells. I myself did not know how to do this so I was in the lucky position of having to employ people. We terraced the entire ground and dug canals for the water to flow to the fields.'

Islamic stewardship of the earth
'Allah says in Islam that the earth and the ground are only given to us to take care of. He alone owns the ground. It is the same with capital; we can only manage it for the good of the people. He says that whoever enters into trade works together with Allah and, following his principles, should give the proceeds to the poor. In the light of such I consider modern joint stock companies to be dysfunctional, as they act as if God's legacy was their own. The interest and the riches they receive are not their own achievement, because even intelligence and abilities are the gifts of Allah.

The Qur'an relates, how Adam and Eve lived in paradise before satanic whispers led them to the forbidden tree and they were expelled. But the Qur'an promised to return the Garden of Eden to believers as a most beautiful reward for their devoutness – the god fearing will live forever in gardens. The greatest source of joy for people living in arid surroundings is green gardens, shady oases, flowers and trees. It also gave me the greatest fulfilment to watch Sekem flourishing.'

In an article in 2003, on 'Engineering a Social Renaissance' 26 years after the birth of Sekem, the journalist Yasmine El-Rashidi, has described the Sekem, as it was at the time:

> *Two hours outside of Cairo, at a point on an unremitting, winding desert road, in an area where one might not have known that the desert existed, a white textured wall framed at its base with grass, indicates arrival at the 70 acre expanse comprising the Sekem community. The multi-level landscape in which it is set leads through sand pits, jungles of fruit trees, open fields of grass, fruits and herbs. Within it kindergarten children clamour and squeal with delight, while older children engage hands and minds with clay and wood. The nearby vegetable fields give way to streamlined, low-rise blocks housing ATOS pharmaceuticals. It is here that natural extracts from organically grown herbs and plants are engineered and integrated into a line of phytopharmaceuticals, including 'Safamood', a natural antidepressant, commonly known as 'St John's Worth'. Besides herbs, teabags are being stuffed and jars sealed: from Sekem's network of biodynamic agricultural farms around the country raw materials are processed, and packaged to produce foodstuffs, including cereal, fresh and frozen fruits and vegetables, noodles, honey, jam, spices, teas, coffees and herbs. The walls are shades of lime, green and violet, and the air conditioning is natural. The furniture is wooden, the curtains vibrant colours, woven from organically grown cotton threads manufactured on site. The kindergarten toys are all natural. No plastic, rubber or synthetic concoctions. The final products made by the company come under such brand names as Conytex, Cotton People, Nature Tex, Under the Nile, and Alana – organic garments, home textiles, and dolls.*

How then did Sekem become what it is today? How did it culturally emerge, as Dr Ibrahim Abouleish himself saw it?

16.2.1.3 Creative emergence of Sekem through culture and spirituality

On the borders of tradition and modernity
'My wish had been to build a community for people of all walks of life. It had to be built, for cultural reasons, on the borders of civil society. To begin with there was just a two-man team, Mohamed and myself. Mohamed was a local villager who came to me when he was walking around the local area, put his hand on my shoulder, and said, 'I am with you'. There was no infrastructure, no energy, nothing. The two of us began the reclamation and greening of the land, and people started coming. It was clear to me by that time, in the late seventies, that the implementation of my dream was a life's task. In fact it would probably take many generations to progress. Because the whole initiative was, from the outset, a cultural as well as a natural one, I had to generate capital. Such necessary cash flow started with the sale of the extract of a medicinal plant, which we exported to the United States. Then we moved on from there.'

Healing the soil through the vitality of the sun
'During my initial years in Austria I had absorbed much of European culture. Through this crosscultural exchange I could perceive my own roots, as well as Islam, from a totally

different perspective. This kindled the first flame of my vision. After much consideration I chose the name Sekem for it; the reason being that the Egyptians had recognised the light and warmth of the sun as well as a life giving force, permeating and enlivening the earth's entire being. The name "Sekem" portrays this.

The economic life of Sekem begins at a practical level to "heal" the soil through biodynamic methods. In partnership with close friends and colleagues in Europe, and local partners in trade, we marketed our products, through what we terms "the economics of love". Our cultural life, in the course of such, is nurtured and cultivated by the Sekem Development Foundation (SDF), educating the children, youth and adults in cognitive and practical skills, while enhancing their free will. While offering health and therapeutic care, Sekem initiates research into all aspects of life, searching for solutions to major questions.'

Uniting the spiritual with the material

'In uniting the material with the spiritual aspect of our lives, we gather 2000 plus Sekem employees in "circles" at least once a day. In the morning they gather together to share their achievements of the previous day and their plans for the following one. During the morning circles they chant together "Goodness of the heart, light of truth, love of the people". This is a means whereby people express themselves and take responsibility. They all stand together; from the manager to the man that cleans the floor. For that one period of the day they are all equals, and they are all as human beings given that dignity, to feel every job is important, and that they are all part of the community.

People did not come here, of course, and fall in love with it straight away. It took time. Now they feel a sense of belonging. They are being taken care of, they eat together, they watch their children learn and play. This is a model for a society. It is sustainable and feeds itself. As Goethe wrote: "Neither time nor any power destroys forms, which develop in a living way." People become so caught up with the pace of city life that they forget to absorb the sounds, the smells and colours of the earth. Sekem has an orchestra and books to read. And if people get bored I have Allah to work for – the 99 names of God inscribed on the wall in front. Being an Islamic initiative, Sekem follows the principles of "learning by working and working by learning", and puts the social community at the centre of its actions.'

16.2.1.4 Navigation of Sekem through science and technology

From natural and cultural to technological and economic

We now turn from Ibrahim Abouleish's own words, to what has been more generally documented about Sekem. As we have seen, and taking its name from the hieroglyphic transcription meaning 'vitality of the sun', Sekem was the first entity to develop biodynamic farming methods in Egypt. These are based on the premise that organic cultivation improves agro bio-diversity and does not produce any unusable waste. All products of the system can either be sold or reused in cultivation. Moreover, to ensure that the democratic rights, duties and values of co-workers are absorbed and adequately implemented, Abouleish founded the Cooperative of Sekem Employees.

It was Abouleish's wish for this initiative to embody itself as a community; a community in which people from all walks of life, from all nations and cultures, from all vocations and age groups, could work together, learning from each other and helping one another, sounding as one in a symphony of harmony and peace. Over time and from within the bounds of the community a 'Council for the Future' was born. Its goal was to strengthen Sekem's direction and simultaneously renew it according to contemporary needs. To do this Sekem drew its inspiration from spiritual and natural science, from religion and art. Added to this, the 'Council for the Future' has created a network based on communication and cooperation between Sekem, its friends and partners, co-workers and supporters, as well as scientists and artists from all over the world. Over the past 28 years Sekem founded various institutions based on economic, social and cultural life, striving to inspire, aid and develop our natural resources.

Towards 'Economics of Love'
Overall, Sekem declares:

- We build our cultural, social and economic activities to invigorate each other.
- We intend to restore the earth through implementing and developing biodynamic agriculture.
- We want to provide products and services of the highest standards to meet the needs of the consumer.

The intertwined natural and economic realms of activity within Sekem's group of companies begin on a practical level, as we have seen, by healing the soil through the application of biodynamic farming methods. Through this method, it has raw material at its disposal and is able to develop and manufacture natural medicine and a wide range of other products. It always adheres to the highest possible quality standards, which conform to the true needs of its consumers. In partnership with its friends and colleagues in Europe and its local partners in trade, Sekem strives to market its products, moreover, employing what it calls the 'economics of love'.

16.2.1.5 Sekem as an effective Integral Enterprise

The fourfold structure of Sekem
We now turn finally to the transformative economic impact of Sekem, building on what has come naturally, culturally and technologically before. Of particular interest for us is Sekem's now constituted fourfold structure and orientation, as well as its explicit emphasis of the importance of research. The Sekem fourfold reads as follows:

- *Restoring Nature:* We restore the earth through developing biodynamic agriculture.
- *Peaceful Cooperation:* We cooperate peacefully with all interested parties.
- *Researching Life:* We strive through our research to meet the questions of all aspects of life.
- *'Economics of Love':* We wish to build a long-term, trusting and fair relationship with our partners.
- *Integral Perspective:* We build our natural, cultural, social and economic activities to invigorate each other.

What then are Sekem's economic strategies for achieving such?

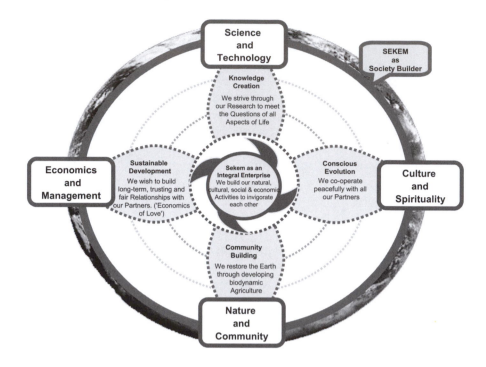

Figure 16.7 Fourfold Sekem

Strategy and structure

Sekem is formed by three closely interrelated entities: the Sekem holding company, with eight constituent companies, each one responsible for an aspect of its business value proposition; the Sekem Development Foundation (SDF), responsible for all cultural aspects, and the Cooperative of Sekem Employees, responsible for human resource development. Working together they have produced a modern corporation based on innovative agricultural products and a responsibility towards society and environmental sustainability. The eight companies are Atos (phytopharmaceuticals and health products), Libra and Hator (fresh fruits, vegetables and herbs), Conytex (organic textiles), Isis (organic food), Lotus (organic herbs and spices), Mizan (organic seeds, plantlets and seedlings) and Salis (agricultural info, technology and services).

Sekem has grown exponentially in the past decade to become a national market leader in organic products and phytopharmaceuticals. It has established export links with European and US customers and built up a strong local market, with 55 per cent of domestic sales. Its commitment to innovation, moreover, has led to the nation-wide development of biodynamic methods to control pests and improve crop yields. The company's most significant impact, locally though, has been through the Egyptian Biodynamic Association (EBDA), an NGO established in 1990 as a means of conducting R&D into biodynamic agriculture in Egypt and training farmers in its methods. In collaboration with the Ministry of Agriculture, Sekem deployed a new system of plant protection in cotton farming, which led to a ban of crop dusting throughout Egypt. By 2000, according to the UN and FAO reports, pesticide use in cotton fields had fallen by 90 per cent, annual yields having increased by over 30 per cent.

The Sekem 'mother farm' and processing facilities are located on 300 hectares of land near the town of Belbeis, 60 kilometres from Cairo. After successful implementation of the biodynamic method, in the area, neighbouring farmers started to cooperate. Today some 800 farmers from Aswan to Alexandria are applying the international guidelines for biodynamic agriculture on 8,000 hectares. In 1990 Sekem facilitated the establishment of the Centre for Organic Agriculture in Egypt (COAE) as a regulator and certification body, heeding to European guidelines. This already alludes to how the company relates to its wider society.

Outlook: towards a council of the future of the world
Today, 2,000 people work in the organization. Revenues have grown from 37 million Egyptian pounds in 2000 to 130 million in 2005. It has received support from the European Commission, Acumen Fund, the International Finance Corporation, Ford Foundation, DEG, PSOM and US Aid. It has begun to share its experience with countries like Turkey, Tunesia, Senegal, Uganda, Iran, Sudan, Tanzania, India and South Africa.

Sekem is starting to have a place in a worldwide association of people and initiatives who are concerned with a healthier more humane future on earth. The net of life created by Sekem and its initiatives is becoming connected to a larger, worldwide net. In this new phase our achievements are multiplied and perceived globally through international forums. For Abouleish then:

> *My vision now has a new, further level; to found a 'council of the future of the world' together with other institutions striving towards developing a better world. This council would not be an abstract term, but carry a concrete message into the world: there is nothing more powerful than the invisible net of life, which connects people with their hearts. Its fabric is woven deeper than our understanding, and long before we first shake a hand we have moved along its threads. The net of life is more real than the most dangerous weapon, and unattainable for all outer violence. Only from it can real peace radiate. He who counts on its effectiveness is practising the most effective form of social art, because without using power or thoughts for advantage, he can trust he will be carried by his energy and endurance. To learn to see the threads and to be able to form them determines the art of social networking.*

In the final analysis, Sekem's whole reason for being, in duly promoting 'the vitality of the sun', was to nurture and enhance nature. In effect, it has now established a new Heliopolis University to that end. We now turn from Sekem in Egypt to Broad Air Conditioning in China, which is similarly engaged with nature, culture, technology and economics.

16.2.2 BROAD AIR CONDITIONING IN CHINA

16.2.2.1 Broad Air Conditioning: an overview

Company background
Broad Air Conditioning Co Ltd ('Broad') in Changsha in China's Hunan Province is the world's largest and most technologically advanced absorption chiller manufacturer. Established in 1988, Broad is a privately owned company, with current assets of approximately US$2.2 billion and around 1,800 employees. Broad's growth had been internally funded and the company claims to be debt-free since 1995. Broad has operations

in more than 30 cities in China and overseas subsidiaries in Paris and New York. Broad's domestic offices are located in more than 20 cities in China.

'The company was established in 1988 by the Zhang Brothers and had developed quickly ... It grew from a 'family' company in 1992 (50 employees and assets of USD 240.000) to a 'nationwide' company in 2002 (more than 1.600 employees and accumulated net assets of USD 205 million).'[3]

Broad's systems, centrally controlled from a high tech monitoring station in Changsha, are found in more than 25 countries. The company's headquarter has been shifted to Beijing in recent years, while the manufacturing base is still situated in Changsha.

Broad's 'Nomen est Omen': The Chinese Word for Broad comprises two syllables, meaning: far and big; or 'designed to last long' and 'designed to grow'. Its founder and CEO, Zhang Yue, is a former teacher who started designing environmentally friendly air conditioners in his own garage, before founding Broad. Now, Broad is one of China's most successful private companies and an important player for raising China's environmental awareness.

We shall now explore the dynamics behind Broad's simultaneous development of its private (economic/business), public (political, public, knowledge engagement), civic (cultural engagement) and natural (environmental protection/bioorganic farming/ community building, etc.) activities. Doing so, we continuously demonstrate the local and the global dimension of Broad's activities. From the very beginning, the organization strived to equally contribute to the local community, to the Chinese society as a whole, but also to the world at large. We start with Broad's nature and community oriented activities.

16.2.2.2 Grounding of Broad in nature and community

Environmentally friendly technology
Broad's technology has a strong environmental impact. The company specializes in manufacturing absorption chillers and heaters using lithium bromide and water as the refrigerant agent, respectively. Absorption chillers use heat rather than the mechanical energy to provide cooling and are considerably more energy efficient than traditional mechanical air conditioning systems. Broad has won a number of awards for its contribution to the protection of environmental, including China's Gold Medal for ozone protection. Broad has also been China's first environmental protection case listed and read at Global Compact Learning Forum (United Nations).

Broad Town: home of the community
The estate where the company is located is called Broad Town, reflecting that the place is not built for people just to work, but that they are part of a community. Every employee has a place on campus to stay overnight, with special houses for men and women. This is not an obligation but an option. Most people stay overnight during the working week and only go to their families for the weekend. At a corner of the campus, Broad's CEO lives with his family.

In addition to accommodation, the basic needs for all staff, include clothing and food. All employees wear uniform clothing at work. While workers are all dressed in blue, office workers are all dressed in black trouser (skirt) and white shirt (blouse). Meals are provided in the staff canteen for free. Staff can buy further items in the company owned supermarket. There is no cashier in the supermarket. Employees pay cash-free using their employee tag and by scanning all items at the electronic cashier themselves. This system is therefore fully based on trust. In various interviews employees highlighted the significance of 'trust and honesty' within the Broad Community. Vital expression of this attitude is that the private rooms of the employees are not locked. There isn't even a locker. If convicted of stealing, an employee would lose his or her job immediately.

The sense of community comes alive in a number of examples, for example, while everyone has a clear job description and responsibility, all employees are encouraged to support others wherever possible. In the company's brochure on its values, it is stated: 'In an era of indifferent interpersonal relationships, unbalanced economic ecosystem and money worship, Broad has focused on creating more values for customers, caring for employees and being fair to partners. Love is more important than anything else.'[4] Broad's company song expresses the company's conscious inclusion of love in its vocabulary.

Broad's company song: linked to the year's seasons and to 'Mother Earth'
Broad's approach to nature and how the company puts itself in relation to its employees, to the nation (China) and to mankind as a whole is also expressed in the Broad Song, which had been developed by Zhang Yue. All employees meet every morning before 8.00am for a flag raising ceremony. Employees sing together the Broad song, facing flag posts, where the Broad flag, the Chinese flag and the national flags of company visitors are raised. The core refrain is:

Broad Song:

I love Spring for my young Heart

I love Summer for my Enthusiasm ardent

I love Autumn for my good Performance

I love Winter for pure Character

I love my Company hoping her flourishing Business

I love my Customers bringing them more added Values

I love my Motherland, wishing her Civilisation and Prosperity

I love Mother Earth, blessing her with Beauty and Health

Green campus

The entire area of Broad (360,000 square metres/89 acres) is a green campus rather than a typical industrial estate. The cleanliness of the entire area is surprising. Cars are hardly used on the estate. Employees walk or use bicycles. Visitors are driven around in electric golf carts. Recycling plays an important role. One example is that packaging materials based on wood are recycled into floors and other housing construction parts.

One, of course, will also notice the fleet of luxury cars reserved for prominent visitors, as well as the on-sitehelicopter. And among the company achievements of the year 1997, Broad also listed proudly, that it was China's first company to own its business jets.

Bioorganic farming

Broad is also engaged in bioorganic farming. Various types of vegetables are grown on the campus or on nearby fields. 'Company owned' pigs are fed with rice straw from Broad's own rice fields. The dung of the pigs is used as fertiliser. These vegetables are served in the company's canteen.

Hosting of the UN Environmental Programme

Broad's environmental engagement is not limited to the scope of the company. In December 2003, the United Nations Environment Programme (UNEP) held its Global Environmental Forum in Broad Town. The meeting brought government officials, scientists, members of the business community and environmentalists from 10 countries together.

The Broad environmental proposal

Broad has submitted an environmental proposal where it states its viewpoint on environmental protection. [5] Here it states: 'No matter where you live, China or India, the US or Switzerland, Nigeria or Brazil, we must work together to protect our world'. In this paper a large number of suggestions is made on how each individual can contribute to a cleaner environment; in particular factory workers, farmers, architects and building designers, product designers, scientists, teachers, journalists, commuters, mayors, parent are addressed. The statement ends with the following pledge:

> Today, we at Broad Town, Changsha, China make this proposal to people all over the world: for the sustainability of an earth that has existed 4 billion years, and for the sustainability of all the plants and animals that depend on this earth, and for the sustainability of mankind, let's make a joint pledge: We will protect our environment – everyone of us will play his or her role – we will all start now.

Replica of a Pyramid of Gizeh to host a public environment museum

Next to the entrance of Broad Town a large replica of an Egyptian Pyramid will surprise any visitor. Referring to one of the most ancient and long lasting civilizations of the world, the pyramid is built to host an environmental museum. This museum will be open to the public. It is one of Broad's contributions to create awareness for environmental protection in the Chinese society.

16.2.2.3 Creative emergence of Broad through culture and spirituality

Creating a learning environment for all employees
Broad seems to take the issue of developing its employees very seriously and provides (on campus) ample opportunities for self and group development. Every new employee starts with a seven-day introduction to the company and its principles. There are extensive learning facilities at Broad Town. In the lobby of the staff education centre, visitors are greeted by Leonardo da Vinci's quote: 'Whatever others can do, I can do, too.' On a Sunday night, at 10.00pm, the centre was filled with employees attending classes, studying in small groups or alone.

The standard is high, and jobs at Broad are very sought after. In 2001 and 2002 Broad was listed in the Top 20 most admired companies in China. Employees who do not develop themselves and do not perform are asked to leave.

Broad management school
Perhaps the most astonishing building on the campus is the newly built management school, which strongly reminds us of a small version of the famous castle of Versailles, though the architect included architectural elements from other epochs and cultures. It is meant not only to become the home of a recognized management school, bringing teachers from all over the world, to develop Broad's staff, it is also meant to hold open courses for the public.

Global architecture, art and wisdom
The entire company area is a most astonishing composition of global architecture. As already mentioned, one can find a replica of an Egyptian pyramid next to a replica of the Chateau of Versailles.

The green areas between the buildings are filled with bronze sculptures of outstanding individuals, from Aristotle, Alexander the Great, Diogenes, Confucius and Zhang Heng as well as Robespierre, Adam Smith, Napoleon Bonaparte, Jean Jacques Rousseau, Leonardo da Vinci, Franz Schubert, Honoré de Balzac, Charles Darwin, Thomas Edison and Abraham Lincoln up to contemporary figures such as Deng Xiaoping, Peter Drucker and Jack Welch.

The lobby and rooms of Broad's own company hotel also reflect the achievements of all cultures. Rooms are named after famous personalities from Chinese history. And a huge sign can be found in front of one of the factory buildings: *'Broad: We build Civilisation.'*

Zhang Yue has said that he wants to unite the best and highest achievements from all cultures and actively encourages his staff to think beyond their own culture.

16.2.2.4 Navigation of Broad through science and technology

Creating internal knowledge
Broad itself has developed all its technologies with over 70 patented rights. And the company claims to have never copied any other manufacturers. All absorption chillers of Broad are CE market, UL and ETL listed and ASME certified; they are CCMS approved, including TÜV-ISO9001 of Germany, SGS-ISO14001 of Switzerland.

The list of Broad's achievements in creating new knowledge is long. The company continues to develop innovative technologies. Selected successes are:

- 1999: Development of the world's first power heat recovery exhaust chiller.
- 2001: Development of the world's first multi-energy direct-fired chillers.
- 2001: Development of the world's first two-stage solar chiller.

Zhang Yue has a clear view on how Broad will continue to create innovative products and will stay ahead of the industry. He introduced his 'new knowledge cycle' starting with Broad's owns engineers, who are in constant interaction with engineers from all over the world, most of them based with the clients. They will then work with them in order to develop the products to exactly the clients' needs. The clients themselves are in constant touch with the top management of Broad and vice versa, to improve cooperation and explore the needs for new products, which then internally are discussed and explored at Broad.

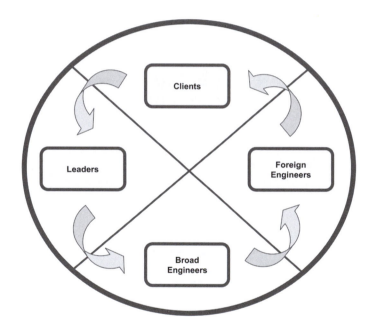

Figure 16.8 Broad's knowledge cycle

Zhang also mentioned that he still feels that Broad's innovations do not have enough impact on the world at large. He stressed the enormous potential of energy savings. His goal is to produce better and better products, until it become so evident to business and politicians all over the world, what impact on energy consumption they can make with the right kind of energy. He used the metaphor, that he sees himself as the fire in the middle of the knowledge cycle, to keep it turning over and over again. In conversations Zhang uses cyclical pictures over and over again: he speaks about knowledge cycles, value and life cycles, as well as of recycling.

16.2.2.5 Broad as an effective Integral Enterprise

Strong commitment to be the market leader
While acknowledging the wide-ranging animate-civic-public reach of Broad, one should not overlook the commitment towards economic success. Broad has clearly spelled out in one of their principles which they call 'Hard and High' that they want to be market leader in their field: 'Striving to be the No.1: We bear in mind constantly we were No.1, this is not self-complacent but a self-encouragement. No.1 is the most beautiful word in human languages. It is the most shining part of Broad corporate culture, which reflects our staff's wisdom, the company's dignity, our social responsibility and our client's values. This lights the road ahead of us and encourages us to overcome our failings and always strive to be the No.1.'[6] This attitude is also reflected in the following observation: According to Chinese regulations, employees officially work eight hours per day. However, at Broad everybody is asked to self-organize the work on a daily base, meaning setting him or herself a daily work target. This work target should be met by the end of the day. If a specific task group, e.g. within the production line, sets a target, no member of the group will leave before the group's daily target is met.

Until now, Broad has been economically very successful. In 2002, for example, the company was No.1 taxpayer among Chinese private companies according to China National Bureau' statistics. And in the same year, Zhang Yue was listed as the twenty-sixth richest person of China, according to a Forbes ranking.

Guiding principle: environmental protection
Broad understands environmental protection as one of its guiding principles. 'In an era of global warming, environmental degradation and ozone depletion, Broad specialises in absorption chillers powered by clean and recyclable energies. Broad chillers also use non-polluting refrigerant. The company has a continual goal of enhancing energy efficiency and minimizing pollution. Protecting our future is more important than profit.'[7]

Strong proponent of environmentally friendly technology
Zhang had announced in meetings that Broad would never make electric air conditioners, unless nobody else made them but people still needed them for an emergency. 'In that situation we will make it. But when the social responsibility conflicts with economic benefits, I will put responsibility and the company's reputation first.'

It is important to see that Broad's environmental vision unfolded gradually. Zhang himself stated in 2006 that it took him a number of years after Broad's foundation, to see what enormous environmental impact he could make, and realizing more and more the problematic situation of China and the world in relation to energy resources:

> *Since 1996, Broad had gradually turned into a strong proponent of safe energy sources and environmental protection. The company attempted to influence and inform the government, electric companies, heat source companies, end-users of air conditioners in society in general about the prospect of heat-source powered air-conditioners in regard to protecting the environment and improving the efficiency of resource utilization. Broad was making great efforts to find a way to harmonize the relationships between improving the quality of life, benefiting the company and protecting the environment.[8]*

The world in 2015: an integrated political, cultural, economic and environmental manifest
The employees of Broad do not regard Zhang simply as their CEO. They see him as CEO, innovator and artist at the same time. As in his perspective on management introduced earlier on, Zhang is continuously looking for a 'broad perspective', for the 'big picture'. It is from this perspective that Zhang has also written a kind of fictitious plot, imagining the world in 2015. In there he alludes to a new form of economy, which he called a 'Sustainable Economy'. Looking back at Ibrahim Abouleish's vision for an 'Economics of Love', we can see the strong commitment of both these social and economic visionaries towards a fundamental change in the economic system and of society at large. Both hold a strong vision for a future integral society. In the epilogue of this book, we introduce the first elements of such an integral society, providing the necessary economic and societal macro conditions for the Integral Enterprise to strive.

BROAD: Elements of an Integral Enterprise		
Local Activities *Rooted in China*	**&**	**Global Activities** *Reaching out to the World*
Environmentally friendly Technology/Broad Town/Green Campus/Bioorganic Farming/ Company Song, linking the Evolution of Employee and Customer (Self), Community, Society and Planet Earth	**Nature and Community**	Public Environment Museum (Egyptian Pyramid Style) Hosting of UN Environmental Programme/ Broad Environmental Proposal
Creation of a Learning Environment/Broad Management School	**Culture and Spirituality**	Integrating Global Architecture/ Building on Global Art and Wisdom
Continuous Creation of Internal Knowledge (New Knowledge Cycle)	**Science and Technology**	Engagement for IPR-Regulations and Execution in China/Bringing New Knowledge to Society
Strong Commitment to be Market Leader (No.1)/However, no Compromise to guiding Principle: Environmental Protection	**Economics and Management**	Broad as strong Proponent for Chinese and Global Industry of Environmentally Friendly Technology/The World in 2015 (an integrated political, cultural, economic and environmental manifest)/Towards a 'Service Economy'

In summary, Broad is an example where its animate, civic, public and private dimensions are built on each other. The ecological, civic and public/technological engagement of Broad within and beyond the company borders are related to its business.

16.3 Starting Your Journey: Making the Integral Enterprise Happen

We remember well, when we met Sekem's founder Ibrahim Abouleish for the first time, two years ago in Egypt, talking about the enormous achievements of his enterprise and his people, he shared his frustration that while many admire what Sekem has realized over the years hardly anyone understands the processes the organization went through to ultimately reach its current stage. His frustration was aimed in two directions: on the one hand, he claimed that without understanding the deeper processes behind the transformational journey of Sekem, any attempt to create a second Sekem, will be a futile imitation, not an impactful origination. On the other hand, Abouleish feared that if the deeper meaning of the Sekem story is not understood within the organization itself, then its own sustainability is endangered.

These ambiguous feelings of Abouleish underline what we have come to learn in our work: Each social innovator, in his or her attempt to create an Integral Enterprise needs to go his or her own, unique path. Such a unique path needs to release the particular gene-ius of the individual, community, culture and society in which any new enterprise is lodged.

If you are committed to engage in transforming your own organization into an Integral Enterprise, you will need to identify and pursue your and your organization's as well as your society's unique path. The pioneering work of an Ibrahim Abouleish from Sekem in Egypt, a Zhang Yue from Broad in China, a Linus Thorvalds from Linux in Finland, a Ryuzaburo Kaku from Canon in Japan, an Albert Koopman of Cashbuild in South Africa and a Muhammad Yunus from Grameen in Bangladesh, are extremely useful signposts. They help us to understand the core elements of the fundamentals of Transformation Management. But ultimately each agent of transformation needs to undertake the journey her- or himself. It is the journey of:

- rediscovering and assimilating the transformational flows of nature and community, thereby regrounding your enterprise in society;
- engaging with the transcultural forces of culture and consciousness, thereby enabling your self, enterprise and community to renew itself;
- creating new knowledge, thereby contributing to the transdisciplinary fields of science and technology; and ultimately
- aligning self, organization and society through transpersonal functions, to bring about Integral Innovation, through community building, conscious evolution, knowledge creation and sustainable development.

We now finally turn to our epilogue.

References

1. Csikszentmihaly, M. (1990). *Flow: The Psychology of Optimal Experience*. SOS Freestock.
2. Abouleish, I. (2005). *Sekem – A Sustainable Community in the Desert*. Edinburgh: Floris Publishing.

3. Zhi, Y.H. and Beamish, P. (2004). *Broad Air Conditioning and Environmental Protection*. Unpublished Case Study: Richard Ivey School of Business, The University of Ontario.
4. Broad (2002). *Internal Document on Organizational Values*. Changsha.
5. Broad (ed.) (2005). *Thinking of Our Future. The Broad Environmental Proposal*. Unpublished Discussion Paper. Changsha.
6. Broad (2002). *Internal Document on Organizational Values*. Changsha.
7. Broad (2002). *Internal Document on Organizational Values*. Changsha.
8. Broad (2002). *Internal Document on Organizational Values*. Changsha.
9. Zhang, Y. (2002). *The World in 2015*. Changsha: Unpublished Play.

> ## Towards
> ### *the Integral Enterprise and Society*

Core Questions:
How do we Build Integral Societies
that Support the Evolution of Integral Enterprises?

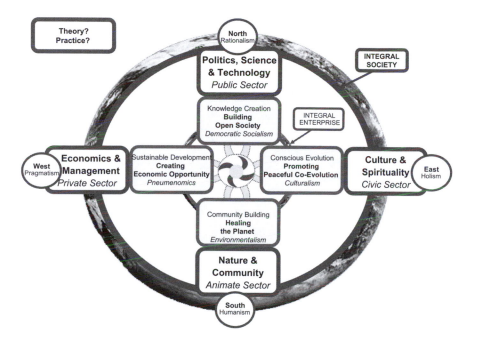

Epilogue: Towards the Integral Enterprise and Society

What an astonishing thing it is to watch a civilisation destroy itself because it is unable to re-examine the validity, under totally new circumstances, of an economic ideology.

Sir James Goldsmith

Re-Examining Economics: Entering Virgin Territory?!

We conclude this book by pursuing the notion that an Integral Enterprise needs an Integral Society in which to thrive. Such an Integral Society refers to the overall political economy, to use a traditional term, which a society chooses to adopt. Of course, no economy, and no society, acts in isolation. In fact, and at the time of our writing this epilogue, in the autumn of 2008, the turmoil in the financial markets around the world and the worldwide banking crisis, has all immediately been caused by wayward financiers in America. If ever there was, simultaneously, an indication of our global interdependence, on the one hand, and of the vagaries of financial capitalism within a disintegrated society, on the other, this is it.

Ironically though, amidst all this turmoil, not only in the financial markets but also in energy and food supplies, a light has appeared in this all too dark economic tunnel. For almost two decades now, an ex participant on one of our UK based Masters Programmes, and now one of Richard Branson's leading protégés, Jayne-Anne Gadhia, had been making the business headlines as co-founder of Virgin Direct, the Virgin Group's initial financial arm, and now as recently appointed CEO of what has become Virgin Money. In referring to Jayne-Anne, in his most recent book on *Business Stripped Bare*,[1] Branson wrote:

> ... *when the imminent collapse of Northern Rock hit the headlines Jayne-Anne's response was (in a note to Gordon McCallum, our Virgin Group MD): on the one hand I know this all sounds batty, but on the other hand ... discontinuities in the system make it right for change ... and I think we could do something ... if Richard was to speak to Alistair Darling or Gordon Brown to ask how we can help ...*

Though the Northern Rock bid, headed up by Jayne-Anne, ultimately failed – when the British government decided to nationalize rather than accept the Virgin bid – such a 'failure' was auspicious for both Jayne-Anne and for ourselves as TRANS4M. For it was at this point that we were asked to work with Virgin Money, with a view, as it turned out, to transforming the building society that Northern Rock was into a *society builder* that Virgin Money now intended to become. True to our (integral) Four World credentials, with which Virgin Money's top team was very familiar, the declaration of Society Building intent arose out of a workshop undertaken through our Social Innovation Laboratory. Associated with such were the following four visionary goals (to which we add here the transformed management functions we have introduced in this book):

- We want to build excellent and *enduring financial products* (finance to sustainable development).
- We want to develop *beautiful banking processes* (operations to knowledge creation).
- We want to infuse *banking and bankers with significant new meaning* (human resources to conscious evolution).
- We want to build societies through *uniting communities* (marketing to community building).

What a step towards the building of an Integral Enterprise. And, again, it becomes clear, that the systemic change our systems and societies so desperately need, will, to a large extent, be stimulated by such emergent society builders. But let us now turn to Richard Branson himself.

Towards New Economics: From Virgin Unite to Gaia Capitalism

Branson has come a long way since the time he launched his student magazine in the 1960s, to the Virgin Group he created since, in the latter part of the last millennium, to where he is now. From the outset moreover, Branson states in his new book:

> ... business is not about winning, about 'the bottom line', and about trade or commerce, or any of the things conventional business wisdom maintains. Rather business is what concerns us. If you care about something enough to want to do something about it, you're in business. Branson proclaims, therefore, that he had never been interested in being 'in business' in a conventional sense, that is 'making money'. Rather, he's been interested in creating things. Creating things shouldn't be something outside of yourself ...

More significant for our purposes here, Branson goes on to reflect on his work and life, divided such into two major periods:

> I spent the first half of my life creating businesses I could be proud of, so that Virgin ultimately became the most respected brand in the world. On the back of that early work, I have spent the second half of my career creating 'war rooms' to tackle environmental problems and disease, for the good of humanity.

This transformative shift in emphasis, from survival and growth, to, in our terms 'healing the planet', has been marked by a shift in organizational emphasis, whereby:

> Through my travels, over the last couple of decades, I have started to realise that the only way we are going to drive the scale of change we need in the world is if we pull together some very unlikely partnerships: with business, charities, governments, NGO's and entrepreneurial people on the front lines ... if, together with all of these, we really wanted to make a difference with

some of the tougher issues facing humanity, we had to start pulling together everything we were doing. I knew that this would only work if we put social responsibility at the core of what Virgin is. Virgin Unite has now become the entrepreneurial foundation of the Group, working with its businesses and partners to develop new approaches to tackle tough societal issues.

We can see here intimations of the *Integral Enterprise* with Virgin Unite at the centre. What then about, in Richard Branson's terms, the *Integral Society* to sustain it?

... capitalism as an ideology needs work and reform. It has to be more than the survival of the fittest. I call it 'Gaia capitalism'. Human behaviour and human capital have to work with our planet.

Branson ultimately falls short of conceiving of a new kind of *integral* economics, to supersede capitalism, but he does anticipate, duly inspired by environmental scientist and inventor James Lovelock, a new kind of economy that respects people and the planet. Jayne-Anne Gadhia and the top team at Virgin Money, together with ourselves, have taken Branson's business and societal argument on from there, drawing upon our Four Worlds.

The Vision of an Integral Society: From Twofold to Fourfold

The essence of our Four World Model is that it, from the very beginning, builds on an integral perspective of society as well as of enterprise. Indeed, as we have illustrated in Chapter 2, the original development of human communities and societies followed a fourfold rhythm. Tens of thousands of years ago, when the first human communities were forged, they started a deep and immediate relationship with nature. It was only much later, that cultural artefacts were added to such communities, initially most likely through burial rites. From there communities started to organize themselves more systematically, and developed initial simple structures, roles and positions. Thereafter it took a long time, until such communities started engaging in trade with other communities. These initial differentiations mirror, to this day, the core life giving functions of human communities and societies; a 'southern' function focused on nature and community, an 'eastern' function focusing on culture and spirituality, a northern function focusing on systematic knowledge (science), technology, politics and governance structures, and a western function focusing on economics (including trade) and management.

With a view to promoting an Integral Society, we return to this origin and ask the question, to what extent new economic and societal frameworks can be informed by such an integral perspective.

Let's recall the status quo. The conventional perspective sees 'business and society' as twofold, business *and* society. The first, that is business or the 'private' sector, in our globalizing and privatizing age, generally takes precedence over society, conventionally understood as the 'public sector'. Usually, business and society, private and public enterprise remain separate from one another, though at times, especially now in the wake of the credit crunch, they may share common stakeholders. In recent decades moreover, a new societal force has emerged, called 'civic society', cited by Philippine social activist Nicanor Perlas as 'the most important social innovation of the 20th century'.[2] Perlas, one of the key proponents of an alternative approach to globalization and internationally recognized – winning the Right Livelihood Award – builds on the threefold perspective on society of his late mentor, Austria's Rudolf Steiner. For Steiner,[3] the twofold division of society is replaced by a *threefold commonwealth,* incorporating now public (political-governmental), private (economic-business) and civic (cultural-communal) realms of activity.

The civic sector, however, is generally seen in opposition to business, partly also in opposition to the public sector. In short, the civic sector seems to act as a kind of 'correcting force' within society, challenging conventional practices of the business and the public sector. In recent years, the three sectors started to move from opposing each other to various forms of public-civic-private partnerships. This seems to be a step in the right direction, as no single sector can itself address the complexity of today's challenges. However, as we see it, such partnership does not go far enough, partly because it does not explicitly involve the 'animate' – environmental – dimension.

What we have done in this book is that we have introduced a 'fourfold organism', based on our Four World Model. Explicitly, we have added an 'animate', environmental dimension or sector, both at a micro and a macro level. What then does this actually mean?

The integral fourfold process dynamically balances what are potentially opposites: so sustainable economic development and conscious evolution of the spirit, for example, serve to balance out, rather than exclude, one another. So each of our four elements reinforce one another, in a virtuous circle, or indeed vital spiral. This is illustrated in Figure E.1.

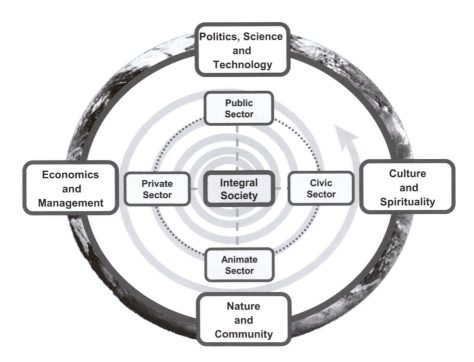

Figure E.1   Constituencies of an Integral Society

The problem we are facing in our time is that fundamental transformation on the micro level, which occasionally occurs, as we have cited in the Sekem, Broad and – to some extent – Virgin cases, needs, in order to be fully actualized, to be supported by a similar transformation at the macro level. In Four World terms that would, for example, mean, that:

- the economic power of the financial markets to build up *economic opportunity* for all;
- is politically complemented by democratically elected governments, that is *open society;*
- as much as by cultural (civic) power to promote the *co-evolution of peoples;*
- and environmental (animate) developments, with a view to *healing the planet.*

This patently is not the case today!

If we reflect on the macro forces prevailing, what we observe, to a massive degree, is a kind of splitting, or fragmentation that promotes autonomy in isolation of, rather than connected with, interdependence. In fact, at the forefront of this trend are economic forces, recently embodied in the vagaries of the financial markets, that predominate over all else (which is what gave rise to Marxism in the twentieth century, and, arguably, to Islamicism in the twenty-first). On the whole, *because the microorganism is set within the wider context of the macro-organism, the former is ultimately dependent upon the latter.* So during the 1990s when economic materialism, under the neo-liberal Anglo-Saxon ascendancy of the time, reached its greatest heights, the Cashbuilds and the Canons, the Visas if not also the Linuxs began to wane, at least overtly as public and civic entities. Though they remain economically and technologically vibrant, they have seemingly lost their political (Cashbuild), civic (Canon) and animate (Visa via Dee Hock) authority. At the same time, at least in the decade thereafter, 'western' financial markets, and their rampantly self seeking financiers, have wreaked havoc on the world.

Indeed, for political historian Halim Barakat, in his seminal book on *The Arab World*[4]:

> the triumph of capitalism in Eastern Europe has led many western leaders and intellectuals to prematurely declare the triumph of capitalism, while overlooking its western shortcomings. Even liberalism may no longer have a place on the world map. The mainstream has shifted from the centre to the right. What is lacking is a balance between freedom and equality. In their search for democracy, the Arabs, the great majority of whom suffer from poverty, cannot afford to accept the western democracy if it excludes equality and social justice as constituent elements. What remains certain is the determination of Arabs to transform their society and determine their place in history.

And, as we saw in the last chapter, people like Ibrahim Abouleish have made their due mark in that respect.

Such determination to identify alternative approaches can be found from more and more voices around the world. For example, in September 2007, in his address to the United Nations Assembly in New York, the President of Ecuador, Rafael Correa, himself trained as an economist, stated:

The best strategy to reduce poverty levels with dignity is to alleviate social, economic, territorial, environmental and cultural differences. Thus, one of our government's main goals is diminish inequalities in an endogenous development framework, and to enhance economic inclusion as well as socio-territorial cohesion domestically as well as worldwide.[5]

So how do we go from here to there? We vigorously maintain that capitalism has neither been the beginning, nor is it the end of the story, but is ripe itself (this for us is the real meaning of the recent credit crunch) for a fundamental transformation. And indeed, we have identified substantial forces that might promote such transformation. For us, such forces are primarily coming from the 'south', represented by environmentalism (nature and community) and from the 'east', represented by our version of culturalism (culture and spirituality). These, then, are to be followed, rather than preceded, by voices from the 'north', represented, for example, by movements that promote democratic socialism, and ultimately from the 'west', where economic opportunity beckons. In that respect, China and India are the latest, and most prominent, economies to 'westernise'. While all these voices have their part to play, they, together, represent again a highly fragmented picture. We believe that our approach towards an Integral Society may provide a valuable way forward, as it is designed to bring the Four Worlds – environmental, cultural, social, economic – into dynamic and creative interaction. So let us review some core trends from the Four Worlds of socio-political and economic theory in general.

We again start in the south, in nature and community, and see, how we can, by moving on to the east and then to the north, develop an enriched approach to hitherto western style economics, that not only transcends a narrow neo-liberal approach to capitalism that has been so predominant since the fall of the Berlin Wall, but also provides a dynamic balance between economics (west), politics (north), culture (east) and nature (south).

Environmentalism: Towards Healing the Planet

On countless occasions we have had conversations with 'progressive' management thinkers, organization developers, or agents of change within enterprises and communities, consultancies and universities, who have advocated 'transformation'. Whether in the form of new forms of spiritual consciousness, new kinds of organization structure, new approaches to corporate responsibility, or new varieties of communications technology, the one thing you can guarantee is that none of these approaches touches the underlying ideology, that is capitalism and the financial markets that serve to support it. In fact, when we have challenged such a 'head in the sands' orientation, the conventional response will be twofold. On the one hand there are those who argue that capitalism is sacrosanct, and cannot be questioned, unless we are advocating, like some latter day Don Quixote, state socialism once again. The other conventional response, perhaps like that of a Bill Gates or a Richard Branson, is that modern-day capitalism is something lamentable, and is therefore in need of reform, leading, as such, to *creative* capitalism, for Gates, and *Gaia* capitalism for Branson. Re-form not trans-form, is their progressive capitalist mantra. We have to say that we find both responses somewhat bizarre, although the latter is far preferable to the former.

Of late though, *environmentalism* has been rapidly coming into its own. For American environmentalist and social activist, Paul Hawken, author of *Natural Capitalism*, in his more recent *Blessed Unrest: How the Largest Movement in the World Came into Being*,[6] reveals how environmental activism, social justice initiatives and indigenous cultures' resistance to globalization have become intertwined, to collectively express the needs, in the new millennium, of the majority of people on earth. In fact, Peter Senge and his colleagues, in *The Necessary Revolution: How Individuals and Organizations are Working Together to Create a Sustainable World*[7] takes the story on from there. For them the industrial age has brought extraordinary improvements in public education, human rights and material well-being, but it has destroyed ecosystems and swallowed up traditional cultures that has thrived for centuries, and created a way of life that cannot continue for much longer. In this sense, climate change is a particular sort of gift, a time clock telling us how fast the industrial age is ending.

That said, while such environmentalists pay a lot of attention to cultural, as well as natural, diversity, they fail to draw on the particularities of each culture, whether Southern African or Northern European, Shona or Swedish, and how such cultural specificity has, in each case, its unique contribution to make to our world. Mexico then is such a case in point.

Culturalism: Towards Peaceful Co-Evolution

We are continuing from where Hawken and Senge have left off, albeit now in more 'south-eastern' guise. Mexico's renowned social activist Gustavo Esteva, and Penn State's Indian born Professor of Education Madu Prakesh, view the inevitable breakdown of the industrial age, in terms that: 'terrorize modern minorities, thereby being transformed by non-modern majorities into opportunities for regenerating their own traditions, their cultures, their unique indigenous and other non-modern arts of living and dying'.[8] In telling their 'non-modern' stories the authors encourage these societies to learn from their communal ingenuity and cultural arts, so as to go beyond the monoculturalism of the modern world, inspired to weave the fabric of their evolving epic: to retain and regenerate their culture, despite the odds that threaten their lives and spaces. However, in our own 'culturalist' terms, it is the juxtaposition of tradition and modernity, the local and the global, the indigenous and the exogenous that is the key to peaceful co-evolution between peoples, and indeed to societal renewal. In fact, while indigenous societies in Latin America today – Bolivia, Ecuador, Peru, Venezuela – are newly asserting themselves, perhaps the best known example of such renewal, which is taking place through the exposure, on an enormous scale, of hitherto marginalized peoples to classical music in Venezuela, is an example of such.

The programme is the brainchild of Venezuelan conductor José Antonio Abreu, 66, who in 1975 envisioned classical music training as a social service that could change the lives of lower-income, at-risk, and special needs children. From 11 young musicians at the first rehearsal in a Caracas garage, his vision has grown into a national treasure, with 240,000 children as young as two – some deaf, blind or otherwise disabled – now studying and performing in orchestras and choruses nationwide. Hundreds of them tour to international acclaim. The programme, moreover, has spurred the creation of similar programmes in 22 other Latin American countries. Within five years, Abreu aspires to involve 1 million Venezuelan youngsters to take part.

In a more techno-economic and 'north-eastern' context, the Japanese miracle, in the latter part of the last century, had a 'culturist' tale to tell, when the term 'Japanese Spirit-Western Technique' became something of a buzzword in business circles. Why has this island nation, Japanese social philosopher Taichi Sakaiya[9] asked then in the 1990s, suddenly become the world's purest industrial society? Since the Meiji period Japan has acquired many technologies from Europe and America. Without this knowledge, industrialization would not have proceeded. But the Islamic world, India and China also came into contact with such. Why then did these countries not develop similarly, at least now until very recently? If contact with knowledge, technology and systems were enough every country would be a modern industrial state. Europe underwent years of conflict between competing aesthetic and ethical systems from the Renaissance onwards before industrial civilization took root. Developers of new technologies were sometimes burnt as witches.

Japan accepted modernization more quickly than any other nation had done, in 40 years. The country had never become accustomed to the religious mode of thinking which says that cultures are self-contained systems that must be accepted or refuted in their totality. Instead they looked at events as discrete and unconnected, making piecemeal adoption of new ideas. This has been a defining characteristic of Japan through history. A history that begins with community oriented rice cultivation is quite different from one that springs from hunting and herding. In a rice cultivating agricultural society individuals and families could not survive independently of the group. Having never engaged in animal husbandry, Japan lacked experience with relationships of dominance and submission. It is therefore not surprising that the Japanese developed a culture of working together and a strong focus on the importance of the group. What Japan looked for in its leaders was neither decisiveness nor foresight but the gentleness that helped rice cultivation proceed smoothly and a spirit of self-sacrifice. Today, Japanese very jealously seek to maintain equality.

Japan, furthermore, has long-standing traditions that facilitate the embrace of foreign technology and systems and their digestion. Virtually all Japanese have a Shinto marriage and a Buddhist funeral. They visit Shinto shrines for the New Year's prayers and Buddhist festivals for the Festival of the Dead, while meditating in Zen temples and even perhaps celebrating Christmas. In Korea, Confucians, Buddhists and Christians intermingle, but their believers are distinct. In most countries people believe in one religion at a time. This phenomenon then, whereby religions are fused together, is the same one that enabled the Japanese to accept western civilization so easily. Prince Shotoku, a political genius in the seventh century, discovered a way to reconcile Buddhism, Shinto and Confucianism. He proclaimed that adding something new did not negate the old. The advanced technology accompanying Buddhism and the rituals of ancestor worship their parents had practised were worth combining. And just as Prince Shotoku's reconciliation of Buddhism, Shinto and Confucianism eliminated deep religious conflicts from Japan, fervent belief in religions themselves was also eradicated. In that sense the Prince gave Japan the world's first 'freedom from religion'. He also may have been the first political figure, in history, to deliberately adopt what we term 'culturalism', that is purposefully evolve a society.

We now turn from nature and culture to the socio-political, before ending up, rather than beginning, with economics.

Democratic Socialism: Towards Open Society

For the contemporary Eastern European philosopher based in the UK, in the 1930s,[10] Karl Polanyi, there are two organizing principles in society. The one, which we shall come to next, is that of economic liberalism (shareholder capitalism), relying on the support of the trading classes, using free trade; the other was the principle of social protection (democratic socialism). The latter aimed at the conservation of man and nature as well as productive organization, using protective legislation, restrictive association and instruments of intervention, something that characterizes the Nordic societies today, and has been a key constituent of the Finnish economic miracle, from the 1990s onwards.

In fact, for contemporary Spanish sociologist Manuel Castells[11] – note that both Polanyi and Castells are both continental European, what we term 'northern' – trade unions do not disappear in what he terms the postmodern network society. But, depending on their strategies, they might become trenches of resistance to economic and technological change, or powerful actors of innovation on the new meaning of work and wealth creation in a production system based on flexibility, autonomy and creativity. The network society, as such, is manifested in a *transformation of sociability*. Internet users are more social, more socially and politically active than non-users. Similarly, new forms of wireless, mobile and SMS communication increase sociability. People fold the technology into their lives. Productivity growth in the last ten years has been largely associated with three processes: generation and diffusion of new micro-electronic/digital technologies of information and communication, on the basis of scientific research and technological innovation; transformation of labour, with the growth of highly educated, autonomous labour that is able to innovate and adapt to a constantly changing local and global technology; diffusion of new form of organization around networking. Only when these three conditions are fulfilled in a firm, a sector, a region or a country, does productivity rise substantially.

More often than not it happens that the necessary adaptation of the workforce to the new conditions of innovation and productivity is manipulated by companies to their advantage. For Castells, that is ultimately self-defeating, as it distances the workforce from the enterprise. Indeed, for Polanyi as for Castells, a narrow conception of self-interest, such as a liberal and positivist one must lead to a warped world vision of social and political history. For no purely objective and monetary definition of interests can leave room for that vital need for subjective interest and social protection. For Nonaka and Takeuchi, as earlier illustrated, the process of 'socialization' starts off the knowledge creating process, which thereby is an essentially communal affair (see Chapter 14). Moreover, as is clearly apparent in all societies, the state, or public sector, has a major role to play in establishing schools and universities, where knowledge is generated and disseminated.

Pneumenomics to Mnothonomics: Creating Economic Opportunity

For our ultimate, 'western' and economic port of call, we have completely departed from the norm, so that rather than attaching ourselves to yet another 'ism' – like environmentalism, culturalism or democratic socialism – and now departing fundamentally from 'capitalism', we introduce you to *pneumenomics*. In other words, rather than introduce yet another ideology, on the one hand, or restrict ourselves to an old one, capitalism, on the other – be it natural, creative or even evolved capitalism – we are effectively setting out to create a new discipline. Such a new discipline in the wake of our contemporary financial as well as energy and food crisis, for us heralding the demise of capitalism, has been co-created, at least in its current embryonic form, by our own doctoral community, based at Buckingham and Bethel Universities in the 'west', while encompassing our Four Worlds.

Initiated by Englishman Andrew Lightbowm, a disenchanted hedge fund manager, now committed to co-creating economic opportunities with a rural community in Uganda, the term was in fact conceived of by Dr Sam Rima (of dual European and Native American heritage), who runs the Doctoral Programme in transformational leadership, at the Bethel University Seminary, in Minnesota. The term consists of *pneuma,* which is the ancient Greek for 'spirit' or 'life', and *nomics.* The Greek original of *economics* splits nicely in two, since its source was *oikos,* house, plus *nemein,* to manage. So *economics* literally means 'household management', which really brings it back to earth,or at least to home and hearth.[12]

In a first articulation of such pneumenomics our doctoral community, from east and west, north and south, came up with the following key tenets:

- Pneumenomics is economic in that its intended outcome is *abundance,* that is *everyone being better off,* rather than being rooted, as conventionally the case, in scarcity. As a discipline, it is concerned with peace and liberty, as well as resource allocation, thus lending itself to those concerned with poverty alleviation and peaceful coexistence.
- It can be considered as eco*nomics* informed by the spiritual, and by life itself (*pneuma).* Such spirituality itself is not defined. Room is provided for those belonging to diverse faith groups, and for those who seek alternative sources of spirituality or meaning and purpose in life, whether associated with a formal religion or otherwise.
- Both rationality and practicality are crucial as enabling characteristics. Together they turn the Pneuma (life and spirit), through academic rigour (men) and practical relevance into a new economics (nomics).
- Pneumenomics is intended to be both universal and particular, as an academic discipline and enterprise practice in its own right. As such we believe that it must be simultaneously conceptually coherent whilst also varying according to specific cultural, and hence spiritual, context.

Interestingly enough, our most recent member of this co-creative group, Mfumiselwa Bhengu, a South African member of parliament and writer on African philosophy, who has joined our southern African Masters Programme, in social and economic transformation, has come up with a derivative term, as expressed in an auspicious e-mail:

> *The author is tempted to coin a new term for this type of economic system as 'Mnothonomics'. Mnotho is a Nguni word meaning economics, therefore, it is mnotho + economics = mnothonomics. In other words, the term mnotho would signify African grounding identity whilst the term economics would signify global integrity: mnothonomics.*

On that 'southern' original note we conclude our societal journey, which has hopefully provided you, the reader, with a first intimation of the major streams of thought serving to build up an Integral Society. We have taken these streams and brought them together

– again – in a kind of dynamic Four World flow, as illustrated in Figure E.2. This final figure of our book provides you with a visual overview of how such an Integral Society may look, and how an Integral Enterprise is lodged within and contributes to such.

Figure E.2   Integral Enterprise in Integral Society

So where does all of this lead?

From Integral Societies to an Integral World

We, the authors of this book, together with our associates around the world, hold a vision. With TRANS4M we have founded an institute in Geneva, which focuses on the research, education and application of integral perspectives on an individual and organizational, communal and societal, as well as ultimately integral, perspective. For organizations ranging from a Virgin Money in the UK, to a Johannesburg City Council in South Africa, or a Royal Society for the Conservation of Nature in Jordan, we offer, through Transformation Management, a means of transforming hitherto segmented private, public or civic enterprises the opportunity to transform themselves into integral, sustainable entities. Such enterprises become Society Builders in their own particular local and global context. Indeed, one of our co-creators as we have seen, Virgin Money, had expressively committed itself to become such a Society Builder. More and more organizations, ranging from a Sekem to a Broad, from Cashbuild to a Virgin Unite, are dedicated to move beyond an economic perspective. We are committed to support them in this aspiration, which we share with them.

Over the past few years, we have grown into an international community of transformation agents. We are dedicated to take the story forward, helping organizations, communities and societies to become more sustainable, by successfully addressing the burning issues today's organizations and societies are facing. We have grouped these burning issues into four main categories, again applying a Four World integral perspective:

1. *Healing the Planet:* Supplanting Communal and Environmental Decay.
2. *Peaceful Co-Evolution:* Overcoming Global Domination and Local Fundamentalism.
3. *Building Open Societies:* Transcending Narrow Parochialism and Rampant Corruption.
4. *Economic Opportunity:* Creating a World without Poverty.

If you like, these four core issues are the 'fourfold vision' we hold. They form the inner motif of our transformational journey. In fact, our following book on Integral Economics is the next step we take in this journey.[13] Closing with William Blake's beautiful 'fourfold poem' we invite you to join us on that journey!

> *Now a fourfold vision I see*
> *And a fourfold vision is given to me*
> *This fourfold in my supreme delight*
> *And threefold in soft Beulah's night*
> *And twofold Always May God us keep*
> *From Single Vision and Newton's Sleep*
>
> *William Blake*

References

1. Branson, R. (2008). *Stripping Business Bare*. London: Virgin Books.
2. Perlas, N. (2000). *Shaping Globalization: Civil Society, Cultural Power and Threefolding*. South Africa: Kima Global Publishers.
3. Steiner, R. (1977). *Towards Social Renewal*. Sussex: Rudolf Steiner Press.
4. Barakat, H. (1993). *The Arab World*. Berkeley: University of California Press.
5. Correa, R. (26. IX. 2007). *Statement by his Excellency Economist Rafael Correa, President of the Republic of Ecuador at the United Nations Assembly in New York*.
6. Hawken, P. (2007). *Blessed Unrest: How the Largest Movement in the World Came into Being*. New York: Penguin Books.
7. Senge, P. et al. (2008). *The Necessary Revolution: How Individuals and Organizations are Working Together to Create a Sustainable World*. New York: Nicholas Brealey.
8. Esteva, G. and Prakash, M. (1999). *Remaking the Soil of Cultures*. London: Zed Books.
9. Sakaiya, T. (1995). *What is Japan?* Tokyo: Kodansha.
10. Polanyi, K. (1971). *Primitive, Archaic and Modern Economies*. Boston: Beacon.
11. Castells, M. and Cardoso, G. (2006). *The Network Society*. New York: Center for Trans-Atlantic Relations.
12. Rima, S. (forthcoming). *Towards Pneumenomics: Spiritual Capital as a Catalyst for Holistic Relational Economics*. Dissertation. Buckingham: Buckingham University.
13. Lessem, R. and Schieffer, A. (2010). *Integral Economics*. Farnham: Gower Publishing.

TRANS4M Geneva

A Four World Laboratory for Social and Economic Transformation

TRANS4M (www.trans-4-m.com), a Geneva based Laboratory for Social and Economic Transformation, has developed an integral approach to enable communities, enterprises and whole economies to address innovatively the most pressing challenges of the societies in which they are located. Jointly founded by Professor Ronnie Lessem and Dr. Alexander Schieffer, the organization has invented fundamentally new approaches to contextualised learning, education and research, so that they lead to transformation and innovation on the ground. TRANS4M, established in Geneva as a non-profit organization, has been particularly active in Southern Africa, the Middle East, Western Europe and North America.

TRANS4M's work is rooted in the belief that integrated and innovative communities, universities and enterprises, that are grounded in and committed to their local contexts and cultures, while being globally conscious, can become inspiring living agents for transforming endangered communities, enterprises and economies into dynamically adaptive ones. Through its integral approach and respective programmes and processes, the Laboratory enables transformation agents and their organizations to make a tangible and transformative impact in their respective societies.

Through its work TRANS4M is responding to the unprecedented challenges the world is facing. The time has come to fundamentally rethink enterprise and economics, and to establish research and educational processes that generate social and economic renewal and transformation. TRANS4M works with leaders from all sectors of society – from business leaders to members of parliament, from community leaders to city counsellors – to generate integrated and innovative outcomes.

The Laboratory is applying its unique approach through a variety of means, spanning the full range from fundamental research to transformative action:

- *Research for Innovation*: published by Gower Publishing in a special 'Transformation and Innovation Series' (part of the Gower Applied Research Programme).
- *Education for Transformation*: Masters & Doctoral Programmes on Social and Economic Transformation.
- *Knowledge Community Hub*: Four World Laboratory in Geneva and Annual Forum to support Transformation Agents.
- *Action Oriented Frontline Engagements*: Facilitating the transformation of organizations and communities.

TRANS4M cooperates with a large number of organizations from all sectors, such as the IBLF International Business Leaders Forum (UK), Virgin Money (UK), Detecon International (Germany) and the Chinyika Community (Zimbabwe). Cooperation partners include a variety of Universities from Africa, Europe and America, such as Buckingham University (UK), Bethel University (USA), the University of St. Gallen (Switzerland) and King's College London (UK).

Together with a range of evolved enterprises and communities, TRANS4M, and its research associates from around the world, aspires to become an Integral University addressing, through its transformational work, peace and poverty, through co-creating a world in balance.

Index

Figures are indicated by **bold** page numbers.